A TIME TO EMBRACE

A TIME TO EMBRACE

Same-Sex Relationships
in Religion, Law, and Politics

SECOND EDITION

William Stacy Johnson

WILLIAM B. EERDMANS PUBLISHING COMPANY
GRAND RAPIDS, MICHIGAN / CAMBRIDGE, U.K.

First edition pubished 2006
Second edition published 2012 by
Wm. B. Eerdmans Publishing Co.
2140 Oak Industrial Drive N.E., Grand Rapids, Michigan 49505 /
P.O. Box 163, Cambridge CB3 9PU U.K.

Printed in the United States of America

18 17 16 15 14 13 12   7 6 5 4 3 2 1

Library of Congress Cataloging-in-Publication Data

Johnson, William Stacy.
A time to embrace: same-sex relationships in religion, law, and politics /
William Stacy Johnson. — 2nd ed.
p.   cm.
Includes bibliographical references (p.   ) and indexes.
ISBN 978-0-8028-6695-0 (pbk.: alk. paper)
1. Same-sex marriage.
2. Homosexuality — Religious aspects — Christianity.
3. Homosexuality — Law and legislation.
4. Homosexuality — Political aspects.
I. Title.

HQ1033.J64   2012
306.84'8 — dc23
                                    2012006942

atimetoembrace.com

www.eerdmans.com

For my wife, Louise

Contents

CONTENTS

Preface to the Second Edition

The Supreme Court has said . . . [m]arriage is the most important relation in life. Now that's being withheld from [same-sex couples]. It is the foundation of society. It is essential to the orderly pursuit of happiness. It's a right of privacy older than the Bill of Rights and older than our political parties. One of the liberties protected by the Due Process Clause. A right of intimacy to the degree of being sacred.

Ted Olson[1]

Dramatic changes are afoot for same-sex couples. Six years ago, when the first edition of *A Time to Embrace* was published, the pro-gay marriage view it took stood in the minority. Now attitudes about gay marriage in the United States have suddenly reached a tipping point. In 2011 for the first time polls indicated a shift toward a solid majority of Americans — 53 percent — who favor allowing gay and lesbian couples to marry. Since only 27 percent were favorable in 1996, and 40 percent in 2004, this represents an astonishing transformation in public attitudes in a very short period of time.[2] Among younger Americans the support is even higher, with a formidable 70 percent approval from people aged eighteen to thirty-four.[3] These demographics suggest there will be even greater majorities supporting gay marriage going forward.

When the book was first published only three American jurisdictions provided some measure of equality for same-sex couples. Back then only one state, Massachusetts, approved of gay marriage, and only two states, Vermont and Connecticut, allowed civil unions. Yet now the number of jurisdictions that either allow or are moving toward gay marriage or civil unions has more than quadrupled. Gay marriage has been approved in seven American jurisdictions (Connecticut, Iowa, Massachusetts, New Hampshire, New York, Vermont, and the District of Columbia). It has been approved in two more, Maryland and Washington, pending possible voter referenda. Civil unions exist in five new states (Delaware, Hawaii, Illinois, New Jersey, and Rhode Island). Nine states have domestic partnership laws which, while falling short of full equality, are likely to offer a stepping stone toward greater equality in the future. If you add all this up, the result is over 20 percent of American states trying to provide some level of marriage equality and over 40 percent permitting some level of legal recognition for gay couples. No matter which side of the debate one is on, these trajectories cannot be ignored.

Why are so many changing their minds on this issue? The best answer became vividly apparent at the 2010 trial in the California case of *Perry v. Brown* (formerly *Perry v. Schwarzenegger*), a challenge brought against so-called Proposition 8. This proposition was the California constitutional amendment that reversed a 2008 court order mandating gay marriage. During the 2010 trial, opponents of same-sex marriage had a golden opportunity to offer empirical evidence for their central claim that same-sex marriage does measurable harm to children and harm to the institution of marriage itself. But when it came time to offer evidence, they had none. The one witness they called to testify on this point admitted on cross examination that same-sex marriage would be beneficial to gay and lesbian couples and to their children. His opposition to gay marriage was based not on empirical research but on his private moral views.[4] In contrast, the legal team supporting same-sex couples called multiple expert witnesses holding professorships at Harvard, Yale, Stanford, Columbia, Cambridge, and UCLA with international reputations in psychology, economics, history, political science, and social epidemiology. They shared peer-reviewed data showing that children raised by same-sex couples are just as likely to be well-adjusted as children raised by heterosexual parents, that same-sex marriage does nothing to harm heterosexual couples or diminish their propensity to procreate, and that denial of marriage to same-sex couples does substantial harm. In short, it is hard data of this sort that is prompting public opinion to change.

This sea change in attitudes is gaining the attention of politicians. On December 22, 2010, President Barack Obama signed a law repealing the so-called "don't ask, don't tell" policy for the American military, under which more than 13,000 gay and lesbian soldiers have been removed from the armed services. A few months later the Obama administration declared it would no longer defend the constitutionality of the Defense of Marriage Act, which defines marriage in federal law as a union between one man and one woman and has the effect of denying Social Security and many other federal benefits to gay and lesbian couples and their families.[5] Although in the past President Obama has said he is for civil unions and opposes gay marriage, he now says that his views on the subject are "evolving."[6]

This increasing openness to gay marriage in America follows a wave of similarly decisive moves internationally as well. When the first edition of this book was published, gay marriage was already recognized in the Netherlands (2001), Belgium (2003), Spain (2005), Canada (2005), and South Africa (2006). It has since been approved in Norway (2009), Sweden (2009), Portugal (2010), Iceland (2010), and Argentina (2010). In Argentina the latest polls show that 70 percent of the people favor this move. Next door to Argentina in Uruguay a same-sex marriage bill has been introduced. In 2010 Mexico began to recognize gay marriages.[7] In Nepal, recognition of same-sex marriage has been judicially mandated and should become part of its new constitution, making it the first Asian nation to recognize marriage equality.[8] Similarly, the list of nations around the world providing civil union or registered partnership arrangements is a long one, including Andorra, Austria, Brazil, Colombia, the Czech Republic, Denmark, Ecuador, Finland, France, Germany, Greenland, Hungary, Ireland, Luxembourg, New Zealand, Slovenia, Switzerland, the United Kingdom, and Uruguay. It is likely that over time many of these nations will move toward same-sex marriage. For example, same-sex marriage legislation is currently being considered in Luxembourg, Finland, and the United Kingdom.

Given this rapid pace of change, and especially the growing strength of legal arguments in favor of same-sex marriage, it is now no longer a mere possibility but a firmly rooted reality. Opponents used to object that marriage is one of the oldest of human institutions. Now the argument has shifted, with supporters of gay marriage insisting that *precisely because* coupling and family bonding are so integral a part of human life, it is unthinkable not to recognize and support gay families. An increasing number of conservatives now accept this shift in thinking. As the conservative Republican attorney Ted Olson argued in the *Perry v. Schwarzenegger* trial, we are unjustly excluding gay couples from "a right of intimacy to the degree of being sacred." So much has the landscape changed that legal discussion has now shifted away from whether gay marriage makes sense and toward how to protect the free exercise rights of those who disagree.[9] In the United States the First Amendment guarantees freedom of religious speech so long as that speech does not cross certain boundaries of harming others. The question is where those boundary lines are rightly drawn and what level of harm is required to trigger them. In some places there are hate speech restrictions, especially in Europe and Canada, that some religious opponents of gay marriage worry will be used against them. In the American context, however, fears about repercussions against religious groups are seriously overblown. A case in point is *Snyder v. Phelps,* where the United States Supreme Court upheld in an 8 to 1 ruling the constitutional right of Westboro Baptist Church of Topeka, Kansas, to picket the funeral of a fallen marine with signs saying such things as "God Hates Fags."[10] Legal outcomes such as this show that religious freedom in the United States is not at risk. Gay marriage laws in some states already contain substantial protections for religious freedom. Ways of addressing the ongoing concerns of religious groups, such as being held responsible for discrimination in the workplace, liability for sexual harassment, creating a hostile work environment, and their fears, such as who gets to teach and what gets taught in public schools, restrictions on religious clubs in public schools and universities, restrictions on receiving federal funds, access to housing, and the like, are presently being addressed. The key here, I think, is that both religious liberty and personal liberty need to be balanced and protected. Throughout this book I discuss ways to accomplish this balance. As constitutional lawyer Douglas Laycock has shrewdly noted, however, "claims to liberty by religious traditionalists would be more credible . . . if they did not devote so much of their energy to restricting the liberty of others."[11]

Changes in Moral and Religious Attitudes

As one might expect, these changes in the legal sphere are matched by shifts in moral and religious attitudes as well. When the first edition of this book was published, most mainline denominations still prohibited the ordination of partnered gay and lesbian people, and the ecclesial discussion of gay marriage was just getting off the ground. In 2005, as the first edition was going to press, the United Church of Christ (UCC), which witnessed the first ordination of a gay man in 1972, became the first major U.S. denomination to affirm equal marriage rights for couples regardless of gender. This meant full inclusion in the institution of marriage — its benefits and its obligations — plus acquiring the societal respect that the "m" word brings with it.

In the UCC, pushing for gay ordination first before working through the question of the sanctity of gay relationships worked out well. In most other mainline churches, however, this sequence has produced turmoil. For over thirty years advocates within mainline churches have been urging the removal of categorical bans against gay ordination. These efforts met early resistance because many in the pews associated being gay with an immoral lifestyle. In other words, advocacy groups in the 1970s and 1980s often pressed their constituents to accept gay *leadership* before first helping them to accept gay *identity* or showing them a way toward a sanctified context for gay *relationships*. When the secular drive for gay marriage gained traction in the 1990s, suddenly a new conversation began in the churches. Greater acceptance of gay identity and the advent of new arguments for the consecration of gay relationships made the possibility of openly gay church leadership seem more morally consistent.

It is for this reason that changes on both the ordination and gay marriage fronts have recently taken root across American mainline denominations. In 2009 the Protestant Episcopal Church in the United States of America voted that local bishops may allow the blessing of same-sex couples.[12] That same year the Evangelical Lutheran Church in America voted to ordain persons in "publicly accountable, lifelong, monogamous same-gender relationships."[13] On May 11, 2011, the Presbyterian Church (U.S.A.) voted to eliminate a provision of its constitution designed to prohibit the ordination of certain sexually active gay and lesbian people. Presbyterian ministers have long been permitted to bless gay relationships, so long as they are not equated with marriage, but a recent Presbyterian task force has pointed out the limitations gay families face when deprived of the "m" word. Aware of all this, United Methodists have decided at their 2012 General Conference to reconsider the declaration from the Book of Discipline that the "practice of homosexuality is incompatible with Christian teaching."

Of course, the growing public and legal support for same-sex couples does not mean the path toward acceptance of marriage equality is moving in a straight line. As with most human endeavors, it has proceeded with two steps forward, one step back. New moral and religious attitudes are being shaped, but old ways of thinking die hard. James Davison Hunter has recently provided an illuminating analysis of how gays, lesbians, and their straight allies have effectively mobilized institutions, networks, and cultural symbols to bring about broad-based change. At the same time, he shows how this change is fiercely resisted by groups that do not want to lose their positions of cultural dominance.[14] The resulting conflict is easy to discern in recent public clashes surrounding gay marriage on the American scene. Two states — California and Maine — adopted gay marriage only to have it invalidated by voter referenda. Similarly, the Colorado legislature tried to enact civil unions in 2011 but failed on a strictly party-line vote. The state of New York passed gay marriage on June 24, 2011, with 58 percent of the citizens in favor but only after months of heated give-and-take. When it finally did pass in New York, it did so because both Democrats and some courageous Republicans decided it should be so. This one legislative act doubled the number of American gays and lesbians who have access to marriage.

All this suggests that gay marriage will continue to make progress but will remain a source of contention. In the first edition of this book I predicted that the number of gay marriage states would increase, though my timetable was far too conservative. What I thought might take ten to twenty years has happened in five to six. In the near future we are likely to see gay marriage advance even further in New England, the mid-Atlantic states, California, and other West Coast states. We have seen gay marriage in Iowa and civil unions in Illinois, and can expect to see continuing change of attitude in the American heartland. But beyond the regions I have mentioned, things will become more complicated. Thirty-eight American states still have either a constitutional amendment, a statute, a court ruling, or some combination aimed at preventing full marriage equality. It is possible that these constitutional amendments could be invalidated eventually by a United States Supreme Court decision. There are good reasons for the Court to do so. Arguably these constitutional prohibitions violate Equal Protection and infringe upon the fundamental right to marry the person of one's choice. The district court in *Perry v. Schwarzenegger* has already so ruled, and on February 7, 2012, the Ninth Circuit Court of Appeals signed *Perry v. Brown*. There is a chance this case will make its way to the Supreme Court.[15] Absent a Supreme Court decision, however, the advent of gay marriage in the rest of the country will proceed on a state-by-state basis. It will take time for these states to undergo change.

This will present a complicated situation for the life of religious communities, and also for gay and lesbian couples. Ministers, rabbis, and other religious leaders are being called upon in places like the Northeast to preside at same-sex weddings, while their official denominational policy may not allow it. Gay and lesbian couples face the dilemma of being legally married in their home state but having their marriage go unrecognized when traveling to another. Imagine, for example, a married gay person whose spouse falls ill in another state where the hospital will not recognize the couple's health care power of attorney. For the time being, then, ministers, gay couples, and religious communities face a patchwork quilt of laws that vary widely from location to location.

How the future of gay relationships fits within this rapidly changing social situation depends not just on secular politics but on moral and religious attitudes that are nurtured in communities of faith and in civic society at large. This book aims to contribute to that conversation.

A Conflict over Sacred Values

The dramatic changes we are witnessing, and the conflicts they provoke, involve disputes over sacred values. The issue is how both religious communities and secular society should honor the deeply felt, public commitments people make to each other. Though the secular and sacred realms operate according to different rules, marriage is an issue regarding which secular and sacred values overlap and impinge upon one another. This is because the decision to give oneself in nuptial commitment to another usually invokes a person's deepest longings, his or her most important notions of what it means to be human. In both secular and sacred contexts, then, nuptial love becomes a cause for celebration and remembrance, communal gathering and societal protection. Whatever else religion may be, and whatever else a secular, democratic government may be, both entail a valuing of the humanity of others. If I truly value your humanity, then I will value your most precious relationships, so long as those relationships are not hurtful to others.[16] What does it mean if I steadfastly refuse to honor your spouse? Your children? Your family? At a basic level, it means that I do not honor you. I am denying something essential about you, your identity, and your right to belong.

This is the reason gay marriage cannot help but impact both religion and politics. This is the reason gay marriage is not going away. And this is why it is important to both religion and society that people of good faith work together to formulate honorable and practical ways to move forward on this issue. To facilitate that goal, *A Time to Embrace* seeks to present an integrated discussion of religion, law, and politics. All three realms are part of the social fabric and none can be ignored as we seek a life-giving way forward. The book speaks from a particular point of view, but it is addressed to people from many points of view.

To that end, a centerpiece of the first edition of this book was a description of seven competing moral and religious viewpoints on same-sex relationships: (1) prohibition, (2) toleration, (3) accommodation, (4) legitimation, (5) celebration, (6) liberation, and (7) consecration. The first three viewpoints — prohibition, toleration, and accommodation — are non-affirming views. As explained in Chapter One, they reject the propriety of same-sex relationships, though accommodationists may be willing to allow domestic partnerships or civil unions. The second three — legitimation, celebration, and liberation — are welcoming and affirming views. As noted in Chapter Two, they reject the stigma that has long attached to gay and lesbian people in modern Western culture and seek full acceptance of their committed relationships both morally and legally. The last view — consecration — tries to combine some of the best of all the views by framing a welcoming, affirming, and *ordering* position. It is introduced in Chapter Two and explained in more detail in Chapter Three. It fully affirms gay identity while also providing a nurturing, supportive, and sacred space for committed gay relationships.

This book's second edition comes at a time when a discernible shift is taking place among the non-affirming toward a position of greater accommodation — a grudging permission of gay relationships but one that still falls short of full acceptance. This is evidenced in greater public approval of domestic partnerships and civil unions, which are seen by the non-affirming as less offensive than gay marriage itself. Shifts are taking place among advocates of the welcoming and affirming viewpoints, as well. For decades those who affirmed gay sexuality articulated positions of legitimation, celebration, and liberation. When the push for gay marriage first arose in the 1970s, some gay advocates objected that marriage was an oppressive heterosexual institution in which gays and lesbians should have no interest. Some still hold that view. But many more have shifted toward seeking consecration of their sacred commitments, mounting a full-court press to gain full access to the institution of marriage.

(These shifts have prompted me to adopt a change of nomenclature. In the first edition I mostly used the term "same-gender." I did this to move the focus away from sex and sex acts and toward people and relationships. However, now that the scope of marriage availability is changing and the term "same-sex marriage" is being widely used, I more often speak in terms of same-sex relationships or same-sex marriage.)

When opponents object that gay marriage will change the institution of heterosexual marriage, they are actually reflecting anxieties about changes that are already taking place. Marriage is shifting from a patriarchal institution with clearly defined gender roles to an egalitarian institution in which the partners themselves negotiate the terms of the civil contract. There are still obligations and benefits associated with the institution but in ways that are more gender-blind than in the past. Now that fixed gender roles are less decisive in what constitutes a marriage, it becomes more natural for marriage to include gay and lesbian couples. As these changes solidify in our society, those who advocate against gay couples and for traditional "family values" will eventually see that the discussion has moved beyond them.[17]

In the book's first edition, the position to which I committed myself was that same-gender relationships should be consecrated within our religious communities, fully validated in law, and welcomed without reservation into the fabric of our democratic society. This position, so I maintain, does not represent a departure from long-standing religious and political principles but rather a deepening of them. The second edition continues to press this case, taking account of the rapidly changing cultural, political, and ecclesial contexts I have just been describing. The most thoroughgoing revision in this edition comes in Chapter Five, where I discuss the state-by-state changes that have occurred on the American political scene since the book was first published. I continue to maintain that debates over civil unions and gay marriage represent far more than a "culture war" or the perpetuation of partisan politics. My claim, then and now, is that in these conflicts the very nature of democracy itself is being tested.

Not only is the integrity of democracy at stake in our current debates, but for Christians the meaning of the gospel is also at stake as well.

This was implicit in the first edition, but I want to make it more explicit here in the second. When I say the meaning of the gospel is at stake in this debate, what do I mean? At the most pragmatic level, the integrity, persuasiveness, and public intelligibility of the church's witness are at stake, since polls indicate young people increasingly equate Christianity with being judgmental and anti-gay.[18] This is an ironic turn of events for a religion whose central figure, Jesus of Nazareth, constantly displayed solidarity with those whom society considered immoral, outcasts, and pariahs. At another level, the meaning of the gospel is at stake because sacred values are being contested. Do we hold a couple's nuptial bond to be sacred or do we not? Will we honor the couple and accept their family or not? Some believe the only people who can answer yes to these questions are "liberals" or "progressives." This is not true. Conservatives who espouse traditional values, who care about strengthening the family, and who wish to encourage moral integrity have good reasons to support committed same-sex couples. Many are becoming convinced that the isolated statements about homoerotic liaisons in the Bible are aimed at culturally specific situations and say nothing explicit about the issue we are considering today, namely, same-sex couples and their families who are seeking to order their lives within a committed, covenantal framework.[19] Many are finding positive biblical reasons, such as the centrality of covenantal love, as a warrant for supporting same-sex couples.

To put it another way, the only reason there is a growing majority approving of gay identity and gay marriage is because religious-minded people, including conservatives, are changing their minds. In a new conclusion I argue that Christians in particular have a responsibility to reexamine their traditional opposition to same-gender sexuality, take seriously their share of responsibility for the discord that has surrounded this issue, and grapple with new arguments for same-sex marriage, which are rooted in tradition and the deep meaning of the gospel.

The first edition of *A Time to Embrace* sought to create a conversation about gay marriage as a new possibility. Now that gay marriage has moved from mere possibility to inescapable social and political reality, the aim of the second edition is to continue the dialogue and chart a path forward. It emphasizes the importance of respectful dialogue, but it especially seeks to honor the people whose lives are impacted by the dialogue. It addresses "the issue" but with an overriding concern for the people behind the issue.

Stories of real people in real situations have influenced the dramatic changes in public policy and public opinion that we have seen in recent years. In increasing numbers, gay and lesbian couples are giving themselves to one another in sacred commitments of love. Contrary to stereotype, gay men form the majority of same-sex couples (by 51 to 49 percent).[20] Whether we are talking about gay or lesbian couples, their relationships have all the major hallmarks of marriage as traditionally understood: faithfulness, self-giving, mutual submission, longevity, the desire to cherish and serve the other without qualification, steadfastness in sickness and in health, the establishment of a household and family, and in many cases the nurturing of children.

This is the reality causing many previous opponents of gay marriage to change their minds. This is the reality some continuing opponents of gay marriage still conveniently ignore and dismiss. This is the reality prompting ground-breaking changes in the way religious-minded people are thinking about same-sex love and the sacred commitments this love inspires.

Preface to the First Edition

It would have been difficult, perhaps impossible, when I first began teaching and lecturing on this issue some fifteen years ago, to write a book of this sort. Back then the building blocks were not in place to pull together a reflection on same-sex relationships based on the highest and best of our religious, legal, and political traditions. Since then everything has changed.

First, an outpouring of scholarship from many different fields has placed this issue in a new light. I am deeply indebted to groundbreaking work from social scientists, historians, lawyers, political theorists, theologians, and biblical scholars, and I have sought to summarize some of their findings in the introduction. One scholar in particular, Professor William N. Eskridge Jr. of Yale Law School, has had a profound influence on my approach. The impact of his definitive works on gay rights and marriage equality is visible on every page of my chapters on law and politics.

Second, it is now much more common for gay and lesbian couples to share their lives and stories openly with others. Many of these couples are raising children and living lives of integrity for all to see. I count such couples among my close friends, and it is with them in mind, and in gratitude for their courageous witness, that I have written this book.

Third, the discussion in the churches has evolved rapidly over the last decade, so much so that it is no longer correct (if it ever was) to say that there are simply two views on the subject, a biblical view and a nonbiblical view. As will become clear in the pages ahead, what the biblical writers confronted in their context and rejected was a one-sided and hedonistic homoeroticism based on who did what to whom. This is very different from the reality we are debating today, namely, the love between two equals joined in covenant fidelity. Recognizing this, the church's more recent reflections have produced a range of views, each of which draws from the deep wells of biblical, theological, and moral traditions. I have learned a great deal from these many different perspectives while also crafting my own constructive approach to the issue.

This book, and especially Chapters One and Two, began with a request by Barbara Wheeler for me to make a presentation in August 2004 before the Theological Task Force on the Peace, Unity, and Purity of the Church of the Presbyterian Church (U.S.A.), of which I was a member. My collaboration with Sharon Youngs on that initial project was especially meaningful, and her friendship remains an inspiration. The members of the Task Force (Mark Achtemeier, Scott D. Anderson, Barbara Everitt Bryant, Milton J. Coalter, Victoria G. Curtiss, Gary Demarest, Frances Taylor Gench, Jack Haberer, Mary Ellen Lawson, Jong Hyeong Lee, John B. [Mike] Loudon, Joan Kelley Merritt, Lonnie J. Oliver, Martha Sadongei, Sarah Grace Sanderson-Doughty, Jean S. [Jenny] Stoner, José Luis Torres-Milán, Barbara G. Wheeler, John Wilkinson, staff facilitator, Gradye Parsons, and our able aide, Bobbie Montgomery) represented the full spectrum of contemporary theological viewpoints, and so I was greatly encouraged by the unanimous and enthusiastic approval they registered to the way I framed the issues. I also have been instructed by their helpful suggestions for improvement. I want to pay a special tribute to Scott Anderson, who has encouraged me in this endeavor more than he knows.

All of my colleagues at Princeton Theological Seminary have been extremely supportive as I have juggled many internal and external responsibilities over the last several years. In particular, I am grateful to those who have assisted me in concrete ways and with whom, from time to time, I have discussed the biblical and theological aspects of same-sex unions, including Brian Blount, Chip Dobbs-Allsopp, Bob Dykstra, Beverly Gaventa, George Hunsinger, Jim Kay, Jacqueline Lapsley, Gordon Mikoski, Daniel Migliore, Jim Moorhead, Dennis Olson, Rick Osmer, Katharine Sakenfeld, Leong Seow, Max Stackhouse, Jack Stewart, Mark Taylor, Iain Torrance, and Ross Wagner. I am also grateful for ongoing conversations with my Princeton colleague, Dave Wall.

I owe a final word of thanks to my wife, Louise, without whose lov-

Gaining Perspective

Our fears are made in our own image. When . . . the feared object is homosexuality, there is a mirror in which we can see reflected the society that rejects it; in the terms used, in the outline of what is being feared, lie the preoccupations and ways of thought of that society. And the greater the force of its rejection, the more naively it reveals itself.

Alan Bray, *Homosexuality in Renaissance England*[1]

In the city of Rome in the year 1578, a small cadre of Portuguese and Spanish men came forward to be married to one another by a Catholic priest in a public ceremony in the Church of St. John at the Latin Gate.[2] It is reported that the priest married them "male-to-male" in the belief that, since marriage consecrates the union between male and female, it must also consecrate unions between two people of the same gender. Whether these men had hit upon a brand-new idea or were harking back to the well-known rite of ritual brotherhood that had flourished in the church in the Middle Ages, we do not know.[3] What we do know is that the men, having thus had their relationships consecrated through the ministry of the church, consummated their unions and began cohabiting. However, when the city authorities discovered what had happened, they arrested the men and summarily imposed on them what was then the penalty of choice for same-gender sexual offenses: they were burned alive at the stake.

This story reminds us that conflicts over the status of same-sex relationships have been with us for a very long time, though they have increased in intensity in recent years. They revolve around not only differences over the propriety of same-sex love itself but also around deep conflicts over the broader explanatory narratives that we use to make sense of our world. Where do same-sex couples fit within these foundational stories of Western culture? Should we think about homoerotic love as the Greeks and Romans did — for whom same-gender sexual pleasure was taken for granted as part of a largely hedonistic view of the world? Or should we adopt the viewpoint that has prevailed in much of Jewish and Christian culture, which considers homoerotic relationships and acts to be a shameful departure from the patterns of marriage and family that God has ordained? Or is there a third alternative that is emerging in our own day, one that combines insights from these two great streams of Western civilization? Is it possible to accept gay and lesbian love while also urging that gay and lesbian people consecrate that love in exclusively committed unions? If so, should society create separate marriage-like "civil union" arrangements, or should the definition of marriage be expanded to include same-sex couples?[4]

I have been thinking about these issues for a long time. On the one hand, as a professional theologian, an ordained minister, and a Christian deeply committed to the gospel, I have watched for over thirty-five years as the issue of same-gender sexuality has been tearing mainline churches apart. Much of the internal debate in the churches has boiled down to a clash of biblical proof-texts, or monolithic appeals to "nature" or "tradition," with little sustained theological or pastoral analysis. On the other hand, as a lawyer and a citizen committed to principles of equality and fairness, I have watched as large swaths of society have become content to treat gay couples and their children with legal and economic indifference. Suppose that your son or daughter, or your brother or sister, or a close friend is gay, commits himself or herself to a life partner, and adopts a child. Suppose further that tragedy strikes and one of the partners dies, leaving the surviving partner and child all alone. If this were a heterosexual couple, the law would step in with literally hundreds of state and federal benefits to aid the family. For the gay couple and their child, however, the response of most states and of the federal government is mostly to leave them to their own devices. Nor is this merely a case of benign neglect. Lately, many states have been taking proactive measures — in the form of statutes and even constitutional amendments — to see to it that gay couples and their families are excluded from the recognition and support that most families simply take for granted.

I have watched all this, and I can watch no longer. I feel the need to contribute to finding a way forward. The Bible says that there is a time for everything (Eccles. 3:1), and I believe the time has come to offer my strongest support to gay and lesbian couples who are seeking to make a life together. To that end, I undertake in these pages to craft a welcoming and affirming posture toward persons in exclusively committed same-sex relationships. My analysis is situated at the crossroads of religion, law, and politics. This is important because anti-gay religious advocates often proceed with little awareness of the legal or political ramifications of their positions. By the same token, pro-gay political advocates often have little understanding of the deep convictions that motivate religious-minded people. Only an interdisciplinary approach has the potential to move us forward successfully.

Taking up this interdisciplinary stance, I devote Part One of this book to "religion" and Part Two to "law and politics." I argue that same-sex unions should be *consecrated* within our religious communities, *validated* within our legal systems, and *welcomed* within the framework of our democratic polity. A welcoming and affirming stance, I believe, is vital to the integrity of our religious communities, imperative for the self-consistency of our legal system, and necessary to the long-term well-being of our democratic culture.

The question to which I direct this book is fairly specific. I do not try to provide an ethics of human sexuality in general. Instead, I ask the following question: Where do gay, lesbian, or other gender-varied persons, whose sexual orientation is firmly established, and who desire to enter into exclusively committed, lifelong same-sex relationships, find their place within the fellowship of our religious communities, within the structures of our legal system, and within the framework of our democratic polity?

Even though the stance I take here is one of advocacy for gay couples, I try to positively engage people from across the spectrum. In Chapters One and Two, I present a range of seven moral and theological ways of looking at same-sex relationships. These include both non-affirming and affirming viewpoints, with perspectives ranging from the categorical prohibition of all such relationships (viewpoint one) to the advocacy of full ecclesiastical consecration for gay couples (viewpoint seven). In an effort to be fair, I discuss the strengths and weaknesses of each viewpoint. Because of my own commitments as a Christian, I consider each of these seven viewpoints in their relationship to the standard Christian way of construing reality, namely, as an unfolding drama of creation, reconciliation, and redemption. At the same time, I discuss the issues in ways that I hope non-Christians will find informative.

For a long time now, opponents of gay relationships have claimed that there is no moral, biblical, or theological warrant for taking a welcoming and affirming position. In order to demonstrate that this is not so, I set forth in Chapter Three a biblical and theological case for the consecration of same-sex unions. I show that the biblical prohibitions were addressed to specifically hedonistic or exploitative forms of sexual conduct, not to those in which mutuality and concern for the other were paramount. These biblical passages are silent about mutually and exclusively committed same-sex love, silent about same-sex couples who are forming families and raising children. I argue, furthermore, that marriage has provided a context for nurturing companionship, commitment, and community. Gay couples are able to embody all three of these ends of marriage, and so there is no reason in principle that their unions should not be honored. If a strong biblical and theological case exists for affirming gay couples, then one of the main reasons for denying them this legal and political affirmation falls away.

Part Two turns to law and politics. Chapter Four delves into recent legal decisions on gay rights. The issues here are basically two: the first is gay identity, which has been conceived primarily in reference to the rights of individuals;[5] yet recent progress in the acceptance of gay identity has opened the door to a new issue, namely, the appropriate level of legal and societal support for gay couples and their families.[6] Regarding both of these issues, the legal arguments are, in turn, basically of two types: *equality* arguments and *liberty* arguments. Equality arguments seek to secure the same legal benefits for gay people that all other people in our society take for granted. Liberty arguments aim to protect the integrity of gay life choices from unwarranted interference by the majority. To put it succinctly, one has a right to be gay or lesbian without undue interference. Most recently, liberty arguments have focused on the right to marriage, the right of a gay or lesbian person to become bound legally to the person he or she loves.

Chapter Five considers all these issues in relationship to the nature of democratic change. I argue that finding a way forward will depend on the renewal of a welcoming democracy, one that encourages free participation on the part of all citizens. The best way to do this is through a form of democratic engagement known as "deliberative" democracy. Deliberative democracy requires that a person be willing to give reasons for his or her views in terms that others can readily understand. It also requires that the deeply held views of all citizens be respected and weighed carefully in the formation of democratic decisions. One of the key points of the chapter is this: how we treat one another and conduct our debates is just as important as the results we eventually reach.

I now devote the remainder of this introductory chapter to putting things in perspective. I will try to provide background to our current debates, a historical survey of different forms of homoeroticism, an introduction to the research on sexual orientation, and an account of how the contemporary quest for marriage equality arose. This introductory material is crucial to the chapters on religion, law, and politics that follow.

Background to Current Debates

Today the quest for social and legal recognition of same-sex relationships has fared much better than it did for the condemned group of "husbands" in sixteenth-century Rome. A new idea when the book first appeared, gay marriage now is permitted in many countries around the globe and in seven American jurisdictions (Connecticut, Iowa, Massachusetts, New Hampshire, Vermont, and the District of Columbia), with more likely to follow. According to a number of polls, a majority of Americans now approves of gay marriage.

To be sure, these developments have provoked strong negative reactions. The new politics of gay recognition has come dramatically into conflict with an older politics of social control. In response to gay and lesbian demands for inclusion in the institution of marriage, others have insisted that changing the definition of who has access to marriage will have bad consequences for society as a whole. Although Europe and Canada have managed the political transition from control to recognition with relatively less social upheaval, in the United States the move toward recognizing same-sex relationships has led to a formidable backlash. This backlash began in the early 1990s, when the state of Hawaii seemed ready to grant gay marriage under court order. It culminated in the 2004 presidential election, when voter referenda that amended the state constitutions to ban gay marriage passed with comfortable majorities in eleven states.[7]

Nevertheless, we need to keep this negative reaction on both the political and ecclesiastical fronts in perspective. The quotation at the head of this chapter from Alan Bray implies that the conflicts we are currently experiencing reveal something important about the anxieties, preoccupations, and fears that drive our culture. So deep-seated are these fears that it is naive to expect them to vanish overnight. But Bray's point is that the intensity of the fears and the way they manifest themselves tell us something important about ourselves. What do we make of a society that whips itself into a frenzy over the prospect of gay marriage but greets the overwhelming evidence of torture by its own country's military leaders with a casual shrug of the shoulders?[8] Or how do we explain the fact that, when it comes to same-gender sexuality, some religious-minded people are quick to interpret biblical prohibitions strictly and literally, yet when the subject is violence or warfare, they find flexibility and numerous alternative interpretations to the Sermon on the Mount's admonition to "turn the other cheek"?

This invites us to cast a critical eye on the past to discern what light it can shed on the issue at hand. Relevant analogies are not hard to find. The first and most obvious is the American experience with slavery and racism. For over 245 years, chattel slavery was imposed on millions of humans who were taken, against their will, from their homeland in Africa.[9] Just as the forces arrayed against gay rights today are dominated by appeals to traditional Christian belief, slavery also was defended by elaborate and self-assured appeals to biblical texts. In fact, more than half of all pro-slavery tracts in the nineteenth century were written and zealously defended by Christian ministers.[10] That our ancestors were so clearly misled in their reading of Scripture does not, of course, mean that all appeals to Scripture are wrong. Indeed, the appeals I will make in this book are thoroughly grounded not only in Scripture but in traditional religious convictions as well. Still, the fact that our predecessors could be so misguided concerning social issues in the past should give us pause. Are we at risk of making similar mistakes today?

Not only have slavery and prejudice against gays and lesbians been supported by religious warrants, but they have followed a similar path of social upheaval. When slavery was finally abolished in 1865; when former slaves were explicitly granted equality under the law for the first time in

1868; and when former slaves were finally assured the right to vote in 1870 — one of the results was a powerful backlash of racial resentment, which was concentrated in the states of the South but was felt throughout the country.[11] Over time, a legal regime of racial segregation arose in the place of slavery, imposing restrictions on African Americans throughout the South. By restricting freedom in the areas of public facilities, education, and social relations, these laws turned African Americans into second-class citizens.[12] In one of its most ignominious moments, the United States Supreme Court upheld these segregation laws in the case of *Plessy v. Ferguson* (1896), thus legitimating the regime of inequality captured in the notorious phrase "separate but equal."[13] It was not until the unanimous decision of *Brown v. Board of Education* in 1954 that the Supreme Court officially overruled *Plessy* and made racial segregation in public education illegal.[14] Although it took years for the Court's various desegregation decisions to take effect, the *Brown* decision had powerful symbolic significance.[15]

We now know, by way of the civil rights struggle, that being treated as separate is, by its very nature, *not* to be treated as equal. This is the reason that Supreme Court Justice Anthony Kennedy, in a pivotal gay-rights case, began by quoting Justice Harlan's venerable dissent in *Plessy*: "Our Constitution . . . neither knows nor tolerates classes among citizens."[16] In other words, it is not permissible to perpetuate a "caste system" in which anyone in this country — gay, lesbian, African American, Asian American, or anyone else — is turned into a second-class citizen. Yet that is precisely what happened to African Americans after the Civil War, and it is still the way people in same-sex relationships are treated under current American law. Even gay couples who live in "gay marriage" or "civil union" states are denied rights and benefits enjoyed by all heterosexual married couples under federal law. Moreover, even if gay couples live in a state that recognizes their union, most of the other states refuse to recognize them or their rights as citizens.

Some have vehemently denied that discrimination on the basis of sexual orientation is analogous to discrimination on the basis of race. One African American minister, Dwight McKissic (pastor of Cornerstone Baptist Church in Arlington, Texas), has gone around the country arguing that "gay rights" and "civil rights" are two different things. McKissic claims that, because gays and lesbians have not suffered as much as African Americans have, it is insulting and offensive to equate their cause with the African American struggle for civil rights. McKissic is correct that the struggle for gay rights has a different dynamic than the struggle against racism. Kwame Anthony Appiah, who is both gay and black, says that being gay is grounded in a narrative of "coming out," whereas being African American is grounded more in a narrative of "opposition."[17] McKissic is also correct in saying that African-Americans as a group have suffered much more than have gays and lesbians as a group; one need only think of the frequent lynching of African Americans in the South.[18]

Nevertheless, it was civil rights leader Martin Luther King who reminded us that "injustice anywhere is a threat to justice everywhere."[19] The evidence of injustice against gays and lesbians is overwhelming. The Nazis shipped homosexual men off to the death camps for extermination during the Holocaust.[20] It is a little known fact that in this country, during the McCarthy era, the effort to root out Communists actually led to the firing of more gays than of Communists.[21] During the 1940s, a California judge gave gay men who had been arrested for having consensual sex a sadistic choice: jail time or castration. A "remedy" for homosexual proclivities that was used at times during this same era was to subject the person to a frontal lobotomy. It would be a mistake to think of this hatred of gender-varied humans as merely a relic of the distant past. In Casper, Wyoming, on October 12, 1998, a twenty-one-year-old gay man named Matthew Shepard was brutally beaten and left to die hanging on a fence.[22] On December 31, 1993, Brandon Teena, a transgender person living as a man, was murdered after it was discovered that Brandon had been born female.[23] Almost all gay men report having been subjected to some form of abuse or intimidation.[24] And just as some African Americans have been routinely subjected to racial profiling by police, so also police in some metropolitan areas would for decades make harassment of gays and lesbians a sort of diversionary sport.[25] Even today, the *false* accusation that a person is gay or lesbian can trigger police reprisal.[26]

On the matter of being barred from marriage, there are even more specific parallels between racial and sexual identity. There was a time in this country when interracial marriages were considered immoral and were strictly forbidden by law in a number of states.[27] Contrary to popular belief, this prohibition against mixed marriages was not confined to the former slave-owning states of the South. Just as there are thirty-eight states today that to some extent prohibit same-sex marriage, so there were forty states then that prohibited interracial marriage — what is sometimes called "miscegenation."[28] Not only was interracial marriage prohibited; in some states fines in the millions (adjusted for today's dollar values) were put on the books lest people dare violate it. In 1912, black boxer Jack Johnson married a white woman, and congressmen from the South immediately began proposing a constitutional ban on interracial marriage. Does this sound familiar? As with the stricture against same-gender relationships today, these politicians claimed that, if interracial couples were allowed to be together under the umbrella of marriage, the very fabric of society would dissolve. Even relationships that *approximated* marriage were prohibited.[29]

To its credit, the state of California was the first to invalidate its anti-miscegenation laws in 1948, but it then took another nineteen years before the United States Supreme Court reached the same decision in the landmark 1967 opinion *Loving v. Virginia*.[30] In 1959 the state of Virginia had imposed a one-year prison sentence on Richard Loving, a white man, for marrying Mildred Jeter, a black woman, in a ceremony in the District of Columbia (the sentence was suspended on the condition that the couple leave the state and not return). It took eight years of litigation for this case to finally reach the Supreme Court.[31] In a unanimous opinion, the Court invalidated the law on two grounds: first, that the law was racially motivated and thus violated the couple's right of equal protection; second, that the law violated due process of law by depriving them of their fundamental right to marry.[32]

Revisiting this history of prejudice against interracial couples provides an illuminating background for approaching the claims now being made against same-sex couples. If there is a fundamental constitutional right to marry the person of one's choice, as the Supreme Court held in *Loving v. Virginia*, then by what logic — legal or otherwise — do we deprive gays and lesbians of that right today? Pastor Dwight McKissic to the contrary notwithstanding, civil rights are the rights enjoyed by all citizens. They are not the rights of some and not others. To make the suggestion that some people's rights are more important than others is to misunderstand the very nature of human rights.

Judging by the willingness of majorities to vote to eliminate rights for gays and lesbians today, it appears that we have lost touch with what a "right" actually is. On the one hand, in a negative definition of rights, a right sets a boundary beyond which others may not go: a right constrains what a government, an individual, or a group of individuals can do to another individual. The very notion of a "right" is that it places limits on the arbitrary power of the majority. One helpful way to think of rights, in this negative sense, is that they constitute "trumps" — or limits on the power of the majority.[33] If you have a right of free speech, you may exercise that right even if your speech happens to be offensive to the majority. On the other hand, there is also a positive understanding of rights, and that is where a right is a badge of belonging: it entitles one to full participation in the privileges of the community. If you are a citizen, you have a right to participate through voting, to freely associate with others, and to enjoy the benefits that all other citizens enjoy. In both of these senses, negative and positive, rights correlate with duties.[34] If one person has a right, then others have a correlative duty to respect that right.

If Americans have been blind to the rights of racial minorities, we have also been blind in the past to the rights and legal status of women. Until the Nineteenth Amendment was enacted in 1920, women in the United States were denied the right to vote. In addition, under so-called coverture laws, the legal title to a woman's property was vested solely in her husband, which also meant that she lost all power to sign contracts or conduct any business in her own name. Moreover, there was a time when a woman could be beaten by her husband or forced by him to have sexual intercourse against her will — and she had no recourse in law. All of these restrictions were justified in the name of the sanctity of marriage: it was thought unnecessary for a woman to vote because her husband already voted for her; she needed no right to transact business because her husband knew better than she did. In fact, the man's authority in the marriage relationship was deemed by both civil and ecclesiastical authorities to be sacrosanct by order of the divine Creator. Since women were claimed to be inferior as a matter of "natural law," they were excluded from colleges and universities, from various social pursuits, and from most of the professions, including the practice of law.[35]

If previous generations could be so sure that they were correct in denying rights to racial minorities and women, when they were clearly so mistaken, doesn't it stand to reason that the current effort to deny rights to gays, lesbians, and other gender-varied persons could be similarly mistaken? Just as many people in the past told African Americans and women not to be "uppity" but to remain in their place, many in society now want gay and lesbian people to remain hidden. Indeed, what inflames the passions of anti-gay sentiment most is precisely gay people's act of coming out, of refusing to adhere to the secrecy of the closet. In her ground-breaking book *Epistemology of the Closet* (1990), Eve Kosofsky Sedgwick argues that in our culture gay sexuality has precisely been constituted *as* secrecy.[36] It is for this very reason that gay sexuality is often spoken of as the "love that dare not speak its name."[37]

Nevertheless, people's perspectives on gay and lesbian life are changing dramatically. For one thing, more and more people have friends who are openly gay or lesbian, prompting them to question the prejudicial stereotypes that abound concerning gay life. Moreover, movies such as *Philadelphia, The Bird Cage,* and *Brokeback Mountain,* and television shows such as *Will and Grace* and *Queer Eye for the Straight Guy,* have raised popular consciousness concerning gay and lesbian issues, as well as helping to mitigate the social stigma faced by people who are gay. At another level, historical, sociological, and anthropological studies have made society as a whole increasingly aware that same-sex relationships have meant very different things — and have been regarded in many different ways — in divergent times, places, and social contexts.[38] A Roman soldier exploiting his boy-slave sexually is not the same thing as the equal-status and mutually committed love of a gay or lesbian couple who together are raising a child. To treat the two cases as morally equivalent is simply absurd. Yet this is what many anti-gay advocates would ask us to do: they argue that same-sex eroticism is always wrong in every case, no matter what the context, no matter what the circumstances. In order to evaluate this claim, we will find it useful to consider the many different cultural contexts in which same-sex eroticism occurs. While it is beyond the scope of this book to describe this diversity in detail, a brief synopsis of some of the relevant historical data may be illuminating, starting with the Christian West.

Same-Sex Relationships in Historical Perspective

As is well known, Western Christianity has a forceful history of rejecting same-gender sexuality. Yet this rejection has not always been as clear, nor as uniform, as anti-gay advocates want to believe. The oft-heard claim made against same-sex relationships goes something like this: to allow a legitimate place for gay couples is to fly in the face of two thousand years of Christian history. This "two-thousand-years-of-history" argument, though widely touted, fails because it is based on a revisionist notion of history. There is a difference between what a community explicitly rejects in theory and what it implicitly finds it must accommodate in practice. For example, the Roman Catholic Church rejects the use of artificial birth control. One might make a "two-thousand-years-of-history" claim about this issue, too, but the church's official teaching is widely repudiated in the lived experience of otherwise faithful and loyal Catholics. Many Christians, in fact, are convinced that in a world plagued by overpopulation and poverty, and especially in a world of sexually transmitted diseases such as HIV/AIDS, the traditional teaching against birth control is itself immoral.

Similarly, the rank-and-file members of the church have not always found the theologians' traditional rejection of same-gender sexuality to fit the facts and circumstances of individual cases. The late-medieval experience with sodomy in Florence, Italy, provides an illuminating case. In Florence, a special judicial commission known as the "Office of the Night" was established in 1432 to prosecute sodomy cases. The term "sodomy" was not coined until around the year 1050. Contrary to popular belief, the term traditionally referred to a range of sexual activity — both same-sex and opposite-sex activity.[39] But from time to time same-gender offenses became the special preoccupation of some within the church. During a seventy-year period after the creation of the Office of the Night, accusations of sodomy were made against seventeen thousand persons, of whom about three thousand were convicted.[40] In the city of Florence the pendulum had swung back and forth for several centuries between benign tolerance of same-sex relationships and fierce persecution. The persecution reached a crescendo in the preaching of the Dominican friar Girolamo Savonarola, whose motto during his years of influence (1494-1498) was that Florentine "sodomites" should be either stoned or burned. So violent was his persecution of same-gender sexuality that, when his own political fortunes eventually went sour, Savonarola himself was hanged and burned, accompanied by shouts of wild approval from the citizenry. It was a fitting comeuppance, so they believed, for a man who had committed so many of their fellow Florentines to the flames.

In other words, our two thousand years of Christian history have been more mixed than monolithic when it comes to church and state views of same-sex love. To take another example, the literary scholar and historian Lillian Faderman has shown that committed romantic friendships between women were socially accepted for long periods of time in both Europe and the United States.[41] American newspapers and magazines in the nineteenth century could publish stories of romantic love between women with no hint at all that any eyebrows would be raised. In Europe one of the most famous examples was the "elopement" in 1778 and the subsequent cohabitation of two Irish women, Sarah Ponsonby and Eleanor Butler, who went on to enjoy a fifty-three-year relationship in Llangollen Vale in Wales. Their love was accepted by such notables of the day as the Duke of Wellington, William Wordsworth, Robert Southey, Josiah Wedgewood, Hester Thrale Piozzi, Sir Walter Scott, and even the famous conservative politician Edmund Burke.[42] There was seldom any public mention of a sexual component to relationships such as these, but in some cases we have clear evidence that such a component was present.[43]

Although it seems that women-who-love-women have been less threatening to the heterosexual male ego than have men-who-love-men, there were times in the Christian West when even love between men found public acceptance. The most cogent exploration of this phenomenon can be found in the remarkable book *The Friend* by Alan Bray, scholar of the late Renaissance.[44] What are we to make of the fact, asks Bray, that for several centuries Europeans publicly recognized exclusive bonds of sworn friendship between men? And how do we interpret the fact that sometimes these unions were ritually consecrated within the blessing of the Christian church? Scholars have long known of these unions, but there has been heated disagreement over how to understand them. On the one hand, the historian John Boswell created a sensation when he argued in *Same-Sex Unions in Premodern Europe* (1994) that these unions were sexual in character and constituted something akin to gay marriage.[45] Other scholars have strongly contested this claim: they have pointed out that there was nothing intrinsically sexual about the covenants, that they were sometimes used merely to cement social and political bonds, and that enacting a ritual of "wed brotherhood" did not prevent a man from marrying a woman as well.[46]

Taking a very different approach, Bray has argued that both views — the "of course they were having sex" and the "no, they were not having sex" views — are misguided. Both are overly fixated on genital sex in a way that skews the most important thing about these relationships — that these sworn unions between men were a form of voluntary kinship. The better question is: Why would men enter into such unions? The evidence suggests that the reason was not merely to cement ties of wealth and power but more often to ratify an uncommon love for another person of the same gender. A man chose to enter into a union with this particular man and no other. Did these voluntary kinship bonds include sexual intercourse? Sometimes they did and sometimes they did not. But the main consideration, according to Bray, is that these were committed, spiritual friendships of a kind that the modern West no longer values or comprehends.

Some of the most fascinating pieces of evidence that Bray explores are the various tomb monuments of covenanted male friends who, at their own direction, were buried side by side with the sanction of the church. For example, in 1391 two English knights, Sir William Neville and Sir John Clanvowe, were buried next to each other in a tomb in Turkey, where they had died on a military campaign. The tomb's inscription reads: "An English couple." Moreover, the heraldry on their monument is in the configuration of a married couple: the Neville and Clanvowe coats of arms have been combined into one. A notation in the records of Westminster Abbey further indicates that the men were regarded as a couple by the Abbey monks, who wrote that Clanvowe had been killed in battle, and that Neville, who consequently fell into a state of inconsolable grief, refused to take food, and died days later of sadness.

Bray examines many other such male-to-male betrothals, noting that they were treated not as unique or even unusual in their day, but rather as "usual and familiar." Examining the long tradition of songs and literature that allude to sworn brotherhood, Bray argues that, from the eleventh to the seventeenth centuries, traditional European society made a place for this kind of same-sex loyalty and love that our own society has lost. Bray concludes his study with an account of a more recent example of same-sex devotion. Shortly before his death in 1890, Cardinal John Henry Newman directed that his body be buried with that of a friend, Father Ambrose St. John.[47] In his diary Newman said this of Ambrose St. John: "From the first he loved me with an intensity of love, which was unaccountable." Bray's point is not that Newman and St. John were sexually active lovers. Instead, their love was about something more transcendent than sex: "Their love was not the less intense for being spiritual. Perhaps it was the more so."[48]

Whatever one may make of such historical unions, their existence raises further challenges to the claim that Western civilization in general and Western Christendom in particular have been uniformly negative in their treatment of same-sex love. The thesis Bray pursues in *The Friend* dovetails with an earlier argument he made in his classic work on same-sex love, *Homosexuality in Renaissance England*.[49] In that book he traces the development of British attitudes toward homoeroticism from the seventeenth to the early eighteenth centuries, showing that a shift took place from same-sex relationships as amorphous, episodic, and ill-defined to the emergence of a well-defined homoerotic subculture and a new labeling of people who participated in that subculture with the ugly name "sodomites." Indeed, prior to the eighteenth century, the men who wrote about or cultivated same-sex desire, argues Bray, did not think to equate that desire with the debauchery that was called "sodomy." In other words, there was a disconnect between rhetorical condemnations of same-sex acts and the diffuse forms of accepted homoerotic desire that flew beneath the radar of those condemnations. By the beginning of the eighteenth century, however, the merely symbolic condemnations that had prevailed earlier had hardened into arrests, public humiliations, and even executions.

What accounts for the difference between a society that accepts same-sex erotic attachments and one that condemns them? Bray argues that the persecution of same-sex affection tells us much more about the anxieties of the heresy hunters than about the perceived sins of those they hunted. Early-modern England was undergoing profound cultural changes, and it was all too easy to make same-sex desire the scapegoat for the perceived ills of that society. The same is true today. Why are certain people in American churches more upset about gays than they are about unjust war or torture? What does it tell us about our own preoccupations that this issue and not others can motivate busloads of people to mount protests and spring into political action?

It is instructive to compare this Western fixation on homoeroticism with the relative nonchalance of other cultures. In Chinese culture, especially during the two and a half millennia of the "Middle Kingdom" (500 BCE to 1849), same-sex relationships were looked upon benignly.[50] We have unabashed accounts of Chinese emperors who engaged in same-gender sexuality. The same insouciance was true of the neo-Confucian society of Tokugawa Japan (1603-1868).[51] In the Arabic world, same-gender sex acts are officially forbidden by the Qur'an, just as they are in parts of Hebrew and Christian Scripture. But as long as discretion is maintained, a certain tolerance of same-gender behavior has usually prevailed in Arabic culture.[52] In Buddhism, while the suppression of passion is one of its guiding themes, same-gender sexuality has been commonplace among Buddhist monks in Tibet, Sri Lanka, Japan, and elsewhere.[53] A similar acceptance has prevailed in Taoism, at least with regard to male homoeroticism. Although Hindu society, especially under the influence of the Victorian ideals of Great Britain, did not want to make homoerotic practice speakable, the Indian *Kāma Sūtra* contains detailed instructions on such practice.[54] Moreover, the mythic foundations of Hinduism transcend the binary understanding of gender as male and female, with the Sanskrit language including words for persons who constitute a "third sex."[55] Similarly, the Jain religion of India conceived of males who were psychologically female and females who were psychologically male.[56] Though same-sex eroticism is not encouraged in either Hinduism or Jainism, neither is it classified as a "sin"; and Hindu stories include many figures who combine characteristics of both genders.[57] In virtually all of the Native American cultures on the continent of North America in the 1700s, native peoples knew of a third gender that combined the spiritual gifts of men and women. These shamanic individuals, whom external observers called the "berdache," were highly honored by the tribe, and their same-sex marriages were not considered unusual.[58] There is also abundant evidence of same-sex eroticism throughout the continent of Africa, including some instances of same-sex marriages.[59]

These historical instances of same-sex eroticism can be further classified according to three types: age-differentiated, status-defined, and egalitarian.[60] The kind of relationship I am concerned with in this book is of the third type: committed, monogamous, and egalitarian unions. Yet a brief word about the other two types is in order.

First, in certain cultural contexts, age-differentiated, intergenerational kinds of same-sex practice are associated with rites of passage from adolescence to adulthood. Such rites of passage differ significantly from one culture to another. For example, in Melanesian cultures, all male bachelors engage in sexual activity with young boys. This is predicated on the belief that such activity is the only way for virility to be passed on from one generation to another; it is thought to serve as a preparation for heterosexual marriage.[61] This ritualized same-sex practice is similar to but also differs decisively from Greek homoeroticism. In Greek culture, same-gender sexuality occurred in athletic, military, and academic contexts. As in Melanesian culture, it was part of a society-wide form of ritual male bonding; in the Greek case, however, the rationale was not to pass on virility per se but to turn young men into educated citizens.[62] As James Davidson has recently shown, Greek pederasty was a practice cultivated among elite families.[63] This practice of beardless young men providing sexual favors to their mentors and teachers, which is known as *pederasty,* was viewed approvingly as a natural part of a young man's education. In that sense it differed sharply from what we call *pedophilia*, which is the intentional exploitation of children. Nor were these men "homosexuals" in our contemporary sense, for almost all of them would go on to have wives and children of their own.

Second, status-defined relationships are those in which one partner performs an active sexual role and the other a passive (usually stigmatized) role. Greek pederasty in Athens was both age-differentiated and status-defined: the older male *erastēs* (lover) was supposed to be the model of virtue for the younger *eromenos* (beloved), who in turn was to be the passive recipient of his mentor's affections. The *eromenos* was not to become aroused or to experience pleasure, but instead provided pleasure through intercrural sexual contact, which was a form of masturbation between the thighs. The *eromenos*, being a free though not yet mature citizen, was not subjected to anal sex, for this would have upset established gender roles and, in effect, would have emasculated him.[64]

The status-defined relationship is especially important for interpreting pronouncements about homoeroticism in the New Testament, all of which arose within the sexual ethos of domination and submission that pervaded the Roman Empire.

Roman Sexual Ethos of Dominance and Submission: Its Relevance to the New Testament

The Romans used sexuality in general, and homoerotic sexuality in particular, as an instrument of state-sponsored terror. Roman rule was synonymous with sexual humiliation, rape, and death. When the Romans conquered a city, it was standard practice to rape the women, to sexually humiliate the defeated soldiers, and to consign significant portions of the population to slavery. The Jews living in Palestine in Jesus' day were no strangers to these oppressive practices. For example, in 4 BCE, around the time that Jesus was born, a Jewish uprising against Roman power led the Romans to sack and raze the city of Sepphoris (Tzippori), which lay just a few short miles from Jesus' own village of Nazareth. Similarly, when Jewish revolt broke out again in 66 CE — during the very years when the earliest writings of the New Testament were being formulated — the Romans destroyed the city of Magdala (Migdal), slaughtering many of the city's inhabitants and taking many more away into slavery. Sexual humiliation was part of an active Roman campaign of psychological terror. It was no accident that Roman iconography portrayed defeated peoples as women being sexually subdued. So widespread were these violent practices that if a woman hailed from a conquered city, it was presumed that she had been raped. Some have even wondered whether the situation of widespread rape of Jewish women during this time period prompted the Rabbinic rule that regardless of the identity of the father, the child of a Jewish mother is considered to be a Jew.

In addition to acute and violent acts of sexual humiliation, the Roman ideology of social dominance and submission was woven into notions of sexually permissible behavior for free male citizens. In the sexual ideology of the Romans, male sex acts — whether heterosexual or homosexual — were performed by social superiors upon social inferiors. In keeping with this ideology of dominance, all male Roman citizens were expected to gratify their urges through both homosexual and heterosexual encounters. The famous Roman poet Catullus considered it normal for a freeborn male to have sexual relations with both males and females. At the same time, Catullus looked down on any citizen who allowed himself to be sexually penetrated by another man. This was so, because the male Roman citizen was always expected to be the "doer" of the sexual act. For him to become the passive partner of another male was considered shameful. On the other hand, he was both permitted and expected to gratify his sexual urges with social inferiors. In short, when it came to sex, the primary concern was about who did what to whom. Egalitarian notions of sexuality were simply not to be found — not even in heterosexual marriage.

Extreme sexual aggressiveness and obscenity was even the hallmark of Roman humor.[65] Yet for the victims of Roman aggression, this was no laughing matter. Imagine if atrocities of the sort committed in Sepphoris had been committed in an American city today. Would not all our news stories, literature, poetry, and moral reflection be permeated with the memory of such things? We need only recall how the events of September 11, 2001, impacted American consciousness to see how events of violence can shape the worldview of a people. In the same way, it is impossible to interpret New Testament comments about gentile sexuality apart from the context of imperial domination that made Rome what it was — including its gender expectations for both males and females, its enforcement of class boundaries and citizenship, and its understanding of honor and ethics.

The New Testament comments about homoerotic behavior are few, but they fit precisely within the context of Roman imperial domination I have just described. The noted classics scholar, Marilyn B. Skinner, observes that under Roman law there were only two legitimate objects for homoerotic release available to the Roman citizen in New Testament times: male prostitutes and male slaves.[66] This we know not only from literary evidence but from artifacts such as the so-called Warren Cup, which depicts an elite Roman having sex with a slave boy on one side and another having sex with a male prostitute (or older slave) on the other.[67] So then it is not surprising when we turn to the New Testament that these are the two categories — *male prostitutes* and *slaves* — that we find mentioned in the vice lists that allude to homoeroticism. In 1 Corinthians 6:9-10, there is a specific mention of *male prostitutes,* while in 1 Timothy 1:10 *men-who-have-sex-with-men* are mentioned in the same breath with the *slave traders,* who carried on a lively commerce in boys being sold into sexual bondage. Both of these passages are considered in more detail later in Chapter Three.

Some have taken the apostle Paul's comments in Romans 1:26-27 as a universal denunciation of homoeroticism in all times and all places. Yet a more careful reading shows that Paul's letter to the Romans clearly is aimed at the homoerotic behavior of the Greco-Roman world of his day. His discussion is not focused on homoerotically inclined individuals, as would be the case if his concern were with what we call "sexual orientation." Instead, he speaks of heterosexual people, those who have given up "natural intercourse" and who are violating their God-given nature (what we would call "orientation") to engage in sex acts with people of the same gender.

Some have claimed that references to gentile homoeroticism in Paul include not just these exploitative, one-sided relationships of dominance and submission but even those that are loving and committed. They point to all the well-known ancient literature that extols love between men, which educated people like Paul must surely have known. What this argument ignores is that the bulk of this literature is speaking of love that by definition is *not* consummated sexually. After all, this is what "Platonic love" is all about; men who may have had pederastic sexual relationships in the past grow up to continue a love that transcends sexuality. We need look no further than the quintessential Greek example of bonded male lovers: Achilles and Patroclus in Homer's *Iliad*. Despite their bond, the two are never explicitly portrayed by Homer as engaging in sex with one another.

19

When they are depicted as having sex, it is with women. People who treat biblical texts in this way ignore what classicists take for granted, namely that there is a vast cultural difference between the same-gender sexuality of ancient Greece and Rome and the loving covenantal bonds of gay and lesbian committed couples today.

The specific things Paul says about homoerotic practices, especially his claim that such practices are "against nature" *(para phusin)*, are mostly borrowed from the teachings of Roman Stoicism — in particular Stoic criticism of the promiscuous exercise of sexual passion. The picture he paints is one of Roman sexuality run amok. He is not characterizing specific individuals but the gentiles as a whole. As has often been pointed out, Paul is employing a familiar rhetorical convention here, using a sexual slur to elicit consent from his audience, many of whom would have agreed that sexual profligacy was rife within the ancient Roman world. While he lifts up homoerotic behavior as an example of how the gentiles have departed from the ways of God, he does not elevate it above other gentile vices, which he enumerates in detail (1:29-32). He makes clear in the very next chapter that the sins of the Jews are just as bad and just as in need of God's grace (2:1-29) as those of the gentiles. According to the esteemed classics scholar Amy Richlin, "there is no [literary] trace of a real and established homosexual relationship between men of the same age."[68] All references to such relationships occur as jokes and not as a serious possibility. Paul's comments on homoeroticism, then, are on a par with his culture-bound assumptions about male dominance and female submission. He was no more imagining our modern, egalitarian institution of gay marriage in his letter to the Romans than he could have imagined a world in which wives did not obey their husbands or slaves their masters. These culture-bound assumptions should give us pause lest we think we can develop a viable biblical ethics for the modern world simply by repeating a chain of biblical proof-texts. I shall return to Romans at a number of points in the chapters ahead.

There is another aspect of the interplay between the New Testament and imperial Rome that few New Testament commentators have mentioned. The New Testament admonishes slaves to obey their masters (Eph. 6:5; Col. 3:22). Paul specifically advises them not to seek their freedom but to "remain as they are" (1 Cor. 7:6). Yet under Roman law, slaves were expected to grant sexual favors on demand — whether to the master or to someone else at the master's bidding. This applied to both male and female slaves. In short, a Roman slave was to submit to the master's sexual whims without question. Refusal was an act of rebellion punishable by death. Therefore, slaves were not able to refuse a master's homoerotic advances, and nothing in the New Testament advises otherwise. To be sure, early Christians no doubt would have expected Christian masters not to exploit their slaves. But the vast majority of slave-owners were not Christians, and exploitation after all was at the very root of the Roman social system. How then to explain the New Testament's silence about slaves as passive recipients of homoerotic sexual advances? Likely the New Testament was silent about this for the very same reason it refrained from directly challenging slavery as an institution: the early Christian community knew that homoerotic activity was occurring, that it occurred with some regularity, and that it was simply accepted as inevitable. It might even be that many Christians accepted the Roman assumption that such acts were ethically neutral. In any event, there was no blame assessed against the Christian who simply passively did his or her master's bidding.

From Homosexuality to Homosexualities

The point of this brief historical tour has been to underscore the fact that there is not a single, monolithic homosexuality throughout history. Given all this diversity, it becomes clear that the continued use of words such as "homosexual" and "homosexuality" can only mislead us. These words lull us into assuming that there is a unique kind of person, a "homosexual," and a peculiar kind of condition, "homosexuality," that have been the same in ancient times, in contemporary times, and in all times.[69] It is certainly true that there have been people with homoerotic desires in all times and places, and in all cultures, races, and religions. Nevertheless, the way such same-sex desire works itself out practically and culturally has differed dramatically through the centuries. Therefore, there is no such thing as the singular abstraction we call "homosexuality"; instead, there are many homosexualities, and these differ profoundly according to time, place, social condition, and culture.[70] For this reason, I shall refrain from using the word "homosexual" to refer to a specific kind of person or condition.

The continuities and discontinuities among kinds of same-sex desire raise the question of whether we can pinpoint an "essence" of such desire that is the same in all times and places, or whether such desire and its outworkings are completely dependent on context and thus are socially constructed. This is usually framed as the "essentialism versus constructivism" debate. This debate focuses on the meaning of what today we call "sexual orientation," a term that has gained traction since the 1970s and refers to the more or less stable and enduring focus of a person's erotic desires. As is well known, individuals who are attracted primarily to persons of the opposite gender are said to be "heterosexual" in orientation; individuals who are sexually attracted primarily to persons of the same gender — that is, gays and lesbians — are said to be "homosexual" in orientation. Sexual "orientation" as a category refers to something more abiding and more substantial than mere sexual "preference" or "choice." Sexual orientation is not a straightforward choice, for it arises from deep psychosocial and perhaps biological forces that are not under a person's control. One does not simply choose one's sexual orientation — that much is clear. Instead, it is something one experiences as a "given," and often from a very early age. Understanding the scientific research into sexual orientation goes hand in hand with formulating an intelligent religious, legal, and political approach to same-sex unions.

Research into Sexual Orientation

The empirical foundation for the concept of "sexual orientation" was laid by the research of Alfred C. Kinsey in the 1940s and 1950s, though this usage is somewhat ironic, since Kinsey did not use the term itself. Kinsey resolutely refused to divide the world between heterosexual and homosexual; in fact, Kinsey himself focused on behavior rather than orientation. As Francis Mondimore puts it, "For Kinsey, homosexuality was something one did, not something one was."[71] Nevertheless, Kinsey's work posed an inescapable challenge to the view that the "natural" sexual orientation of all human beings is heterosexual and that same-gender sexuality constitutes a deviation from a fixed norm. Instead, Kinsey's findings showed that sexual behavior exists on a continuum: now known as the Kinsey Scale, this continuum ranges from "0" (exclusively heterosexual) to "6" (exclusively homosexual), with gradations in between.[72] Kinsey and his associates conducted interviews of some 20,000 persons and published the results in two volumes, one on male sexuality in 1948 and the other on female sexuality in 1953.[73]

Some have objected that Kinsey's research was more observational than selective: that is, Kinsey interviewed anyone who would talk to him rather than selecting his subjects based on systematic criteria. Still, what Kinsey observed has been confirmed, refined, and supplemented by more recent research. Cumulatively, all this research has demonstrated that, for a certain small percentage of people, a same-gender sexual orientation is experienced as a given rather than a straightforward choice. In other words, the attraction that gay men and lesbians experience toward persons of the same gender is simply the way their love and sexuality are expressed. Such attraction is as normal and as much a part of a gay person's constitution or makeup as heterosexual desire is for others. Therefore, that desire cannot be easily discarded or eliminated as though it were somehow only an incidental part of a person's identity. To be sure, there are all kinds of things people may feel a desire to do that are immoral — the desire to steal, to kill, or to take advantage of others. Yet decades of research, including not only the work of Kinsey but the ground-breaking studies of Evelyn Hooker in the 1950s, have made it clear that, when gay and lesbian people live out their sexual orientation in responsible ways, the result for them is life-giving and healthy.

In order to debunk the idea that being gay is a "pathology," Evelyn Hooker administered a series of psychological tests to a group of gay and straight men. She then asked a group of eminent psychologists to interpret the tests without telling them which men were gay and which straight. Although the psychologists were convinced ahead of time that they would be able to detect the "pathology" easily in the gay subjects, they were completely unable to distinguish gay from straight. In other words, the gay men appeared to the psychologists to be just as "normal" as the straight men.[74] And this research has been confirmed by other studies since then.[75] It is for this reason, among others, that the American Psychiatric Association decided in 1973 to remove homoerotic desire from its list of "mental disorders," no longer defining that desire as mental illness or moral depravity.[76] The following year (1974) the American Bar Association declared that adult, private, consensual same-gender sexual conduct should no longer be criminalized.[77]

Based on empirical findings, a consensus has emerged among psychiatrists and psychologists that same-gender sexual orientation is a normal variant of human sexuality. This consensus lies at the heart of the "welcoming and affirming" viewpoints I shall be describing in Chapter

Three. It is also a consensus, as I shall explain in more detail below, that same-gender sexual orientation is a variant that occurs with a certain statistical frequency in the human population. It is not to be stigmatized, and no empirical studies link same-gender sexual orientation to family dysfunction or trauma. Practitioners should adopt a client-centered approach that encourages self-acceptance and positive adaptation to one's sexuality. For most people — gay and straight — sexual orientation can be clear and well-defined. However, for a small number of people sexual orientation is variable and even ambiguous. For them, the way sexual desire and sexual identity interact may not be clear-cut. Some may identify as bisexual, meaning they may at times feel sexual attraction to men and women. Some may feel a sexual desire, say, for men but an emotional desire for women. The sexual orientation of some may evolve over time. Despite these uncertainties, however, there is also a strong consensus, based on empirical evidence, that gay and lesbian couples are just as capable of forming healthy, loving relationships as are heterosexual couples.

We now know that, especially for gay men in our culture, the process of same-gender sexual identity formation follows a fairly typical pattern.[78] Perhaps as early as age six, the boy begins to have a sense deep inside that he is sexually different from other boys. With the onset of puberty, somewhere between the ages of twelve and fourteen, the boy may experience his first "crush" on another male. Some lesbians follow a similar pattern of sexual identity while young. But it is not unusual for a lesbian to have established her reproductive identity before her lesbian identity becomes clear: that is, she may get married and have children and only later come to clarity about her sexual orientation.

For both gay men and lesbians, the first experiences of same-sex desire can bring on feelings that are exhilarating. At the same time, those feelings can be humiliating, because society sends all sorts of signals that it does not approve of same-sex desire. The result is what psychologists refer to as "internalized homophobia," the aversion and internal conflict that come from having imbibed society's anti-gay biases. In refusing to acknowledge his or her same-gender sexual desires, the person may experience identity confusion, including feelings of "denial" and even depression. Over the years, some may try to erase all erotic images from their mind by pouring themselves into their studies or by keeping an emotional distance from people. Such gestures are known as "identity foreclosure," the refusal to acknowledge the truth of one's sexual orientation.

Over time, the challenge for a gay person becomes one of acknowledging one's own identity. This is why it is often said that, if one is gay, the most difficult person to "come out to" is oneself. The dynamics involved in this process are complex. I noted above that having a same-gender sexual orientation is not a choice; nonetheless, what one does with one's gay identity, at least at some level, *is* a choice. Every person who experiences a same-gender sexual orientation has to decide whether to live according to that orientation. Some may choose to keep their orientation hidden. But for others, as psychiatrist Richard A. Isay observes, the decision to live an authentic gay identity requires that they "come out" — first to themselves and then to others.[79]

How many people are there who experience same-gender sexual desire or engage in same-gender sexual behavior? This is a matter of some considerable dispute, and we are likely never to know for sure. Anti-gay polemicists want to insist that the number is very low, in part because they want to maintain that being gay or lesbian is a "perversion" from the pure norm of heterosexuality. The more gays there are in the population (or are purported to be), the harder it is for anti-gay advocates to make the "perversion" label stick.[80] Gay advocates, on the other hand, tend to exaggerate the number: they often cite the popular understanding, derived from a misreading of the 1948 Kinsey studies of male sexuality, that puts the proportion of gays in the population as high as 10 percent. What Kinsey actually reported was that 10 percent of the population *he was studying* had been exclusively homosexual in a given three-year period between the ages of sixteen and fifty-five. Even more astonishing, Kinsey found that 37 percent of the men he studied could claim at least one homoerotic experience in their lifetimes. It is now clear that problems with the nonscientific way Kinsey chose his subjects may have exaggerated the results. The idea that 10 percent of the American population identifies with the politically loaded word "gay" has not held up in more recent research.

Nevertheless, Kinsey's 10 percent figure remains credible as a measure of the frequency of homoerotic desire in the general population. In a comprehensive and widely cited study of 3,500 subjects (completed in 1992), researchers distinguished three ways in which homoeroticism may be classified: (1) having same-gender sexual *desire;* (2) engaging in same-gender sexual *behavior;* and (3) claiming a gay or lesbian *identity.*[81] In other words, some people may experience homoerotic sexual desire — and many apparently do — but never engage in homoerotic behavior. Further, some may act out homoerotic desire but refuse to be self-identified as gay or lesbian. For example, a number of African-American men engage in same-sex practices secretly, or "on the down low," even though they do not consider themselves to be gay.[82] Similarly, there is in contemporary Greece the *parea* (or "company of friends"), a group of women who secretly engage in same-sex love affairs but who are also wives and mothers and do not consider themselves to be lesbians.[83] Third, there are those who experience homoerotic desire, engage in same-sex behavior, and publicly declare their gay or lesbian identity (i.e., "come out of the closet").

Thus, when we play the gay numbers game, we must try to remain clear about whether we are speaking of identity, behavior, or desire, for the statistics vary with each category. According to the demographic data used in the 1992 study, there are at least 4.3 million Americans who identify themselves as exclusively gay or lesbian, though other estimates place the number much higher.[84] Framed in terms of percentages, the 1992 numbers break down as follows: 2.8 percent of men and 1.4 percent of women reported that they self-identified as either exclusively homosexual or bisexual.[85] Ten years later, in an even more comprehensive 2002 study, the figures were slightly different. Of the men in the study, 90.2 percent identified themselves as heterosexual, 2.3 percent identified themselves as homosexual in orientation, 1.8 as bisexual, and 3.9 percent as "something else" (1.8 percent did not respond). Of women, in addition to the 90.3 percent who self-identified as heterosexual, 1.3 percent identified as lesbian, 2.8 percent as bisexual, and 3.8 as "something else" (1.8 percent did not respond). Thus, to say that only 2 or 3 percent of the population is gay is both true and not true. The relevant — and often overlooked — fact is that just under 10 percent of Americans see their sexual identity as something *other* than heterosexual. If it is *not* true that 10 percent of the population identifies as "gay," it *is* true that almost 10 percent of the population declines to identify as heterosexual. In short, Kinsey's number may not be as far off base as it is sometimes claimed to be.

When one examines "behavior" rather than "identity," the numbers are different still. As many as 7.1 percent of men in the 1992 study and 3.8 percent of women claimed at least one instance of same-gender sexual contact at some point in their lives, and 2.7 percent of men and 1.3 percent of women claimed that they engaged in some form of same-gender sexual contact in the previous twelve-month period. But the even more comprehensive 2002 study tells a somewhat different story. While reporting that 6 percent of men had experienced some form of sexual encounter with another man (a finding in keeping with the 1992 study), this study's statistic for women jumped significantly: some 11.2 percent of women reported having a sexual experience with another woman at some point in their lives. Moreover, in contrast to the 1.3 percent of women who reported having sexual relations with another woman in the last twelve months in 1992, fully 4 percent of women reported in that category in 2002.

If we look beyond sexual identity and sexual behavior to the presence of sexual desire, the numbers are different still. The 2002 study of adult men found approximately 6.9 percent of them saying that they currently experienced some attraction to other men, with a further 1.7 percent claiming to be bisexual.[86] This raises the question of how much same-sex desire is a component of the sexual experience of those who identify as bisexual. A recent study conducted by a group of psychologists used a sensoring technique designed to measure male arousal responses directly and empirically.[87] They applied these measurements as men watched movies of same-gender and opposite-gender sex acts. The unsurprising result was that gay men were aroused by gay sex and straight men by straight sex. But what was surprising was that three-fourths of the men who identified themselves as bisexual — meaning that they claimed to be attracted to persons of either gender — actually had sexual arousal patterns that were identical to those of gay men. In other words, despite claiming to be bisexual, they were physically aroused by men but *not* by women.[88] Some have interpreted this to mean that there are more people who experience predominantly homoerotic desire than we may think — or than has been thought in the past.

In order to put this in perspective, consider the following: if we combine the 6.9 percent of men who say they experience some measure of desire for other men with the 1.7 percent who say they desire both men and women, then it appears that approximately 8.6 percent of American men experience some degree of sexual attraction to other men.[89] Among women, the numbers are even higher: approximately 13.6 percent of American women say that they have some degree of attraction to other women.[90]

In summary, when it comes to arguing numbers, there are misleading statements made on both sides of the debate. On the one hand, the idea that 10 percent of the population is "gay" is an urban legend: we now know that not that many people in the population at large are willing to identify themselves as gay or lesbian. On the other hand, the 10 percent figure is not completely off base: it is a fact that almost 10 percent of the population self-identify as something other than heterosexual; and it is also a fact that *over* 10 percent of the population (8.6 percent of men, 13.6 percent of women) claim some degree of sexual attraction to members of the same sex. And it is a fact that well over 8 percent of the population (6 percent of men, 11.2 of women) have at some time engaged in same-gender sexual behavior.

One of the most controversial issues is that of "sexual orientation change efforts" (SOCE). These are therapeutic interventions, mostly by groups adhering to conservative religious viewpoints, to change a person's sexual orientation. The overwhelming consensus among therapists and empirical researchers is that such efforts are unlikely to produce enduring change and can sometimes result in harm. In 2009 a task force of the American Psychiatric Association (APA) reiterated this consensus but provided more nuanced advice on treating clients who are distressed over their sexual orientation and may wish such therapy.[91] Therapists were directed not to misrepresent to clients that change was possible or necessary, but they were also instructed to provide responses that respect the values of the client. The task force opinion was based on a study of all the empirical data from 1960 to 2007 — all of which confirmed that SOCE has little chance of success in the majority of cases. A small number of people undergoing SOCE do report a decrease in homosexual desire and an increase in heterosexual attraction, but most do not.[92] Where SOCE has its highest success is at the level of sexual identity rather than sexual desire. Evidence suggests that persons who report change are choosing their religious identity over their sexual identity. In such cases, the APA recommends that therapists be guided by the client's wishes and provide "acceptance, support, and recognition of important values and concerns."

Research into the Origins of Same-Sex Desire

Once it became clear that same-sex erotic desire occurs with a certain statistical frequency in human populations, many became curious in the 1980s and 1990s whether sexual orientation has a biological origin. One type of research focused on *endocrinology*. We know that the presence or absence of certain prenatal hormones can affect the developmental process of gender differentiation. At about six to eight weeks of development, the presence of testosterone and other hormones in human male embryos

causes the male reproductive organs to form. A condition called "andro-
gen insensitivity syndrome" prevents the right combination of hormones
from working during this critical period. Though the embryo is genetically
male, it will develop sex organs that are female. Not only does "he" become
anatomically female, but such individuals almost always are sexually attracted to men, notwithstanding the presence of the Y (male) chromosome. Similarly, there is a condition in females called "congenital adrenal
hyperplasia," or CAH, in which an enlarged adrenal gland causes the production of abnormal levels of testosterone. In female embryos this can
cause genitalia that appear to be male. In one study such females were
shown to have a higher instance of being "tomboys" and a somewhat
greater chance than the overall female population of becoming lesbians.
Although none of this is conclusive, it at least suggests that prenatal hor-
monal levels can affect, if not determine, a person's sexuality.[93]

Another type of research focused on *neurobiology:* it zeroed in on the
sexual differentiation of the brain. There is evidence suggesting that the
brain is sexually dimorphic, that is, certain features of the brain differ
physically in men and women. Some of these differences pertain to the organization of various functions on one side of the brain or the other — the
so-called right brain–left brain differentiation — or what is more technically called cerebral lateralization. These physical features may correspond
to gender differences such as greater visual-spatial abilities in men or
greater verbal abilities in women. Mind you, these are relative differences
reflective in large populations; they do not translate into absolute differences between individual men and women. That is, any individual man
may have superior linguistic abilities, or any individual woman may have
superior abilities in spatial matters or in math or science, or what have you.
Why might this be important? Because a number of studies have found
tentative evidence of brain differentiation related to sexual orientation.
The one that has received the most media coverage is the 1991 finding of
neurobiologist Simon LeVay that a region of the anterior hypothalamus
(which is ordinarily larger in men than in women) appeared to be smaller
in gay men.[94] Subsequent studies have not duplicated LeVay's results, but
research in this area continues.

Yet another type of research arose out of *genetics.* Several studies of
gay people with twin siblings, including a well-known study published in
1991 by J. Michael Bailey (Northwestern University) and Richard Pillard
(Boston University School of Medicine), have indicated that heredity may

play a part in sexual orientation. The Bailey and Pillard study showed that in 52 percent of identical (monozygotic) male twins, where one of the twins was gay, both were gay; the rate was 24 percent for fraternal (dizygotic) twins. These rates are much higher than would be expected if heredity were not a factor. In a later study, similar concordances were found among female twins: both twins were lesbians in 48 percent of the cases of identical twins, 16 percent in the fraternal twins. Obviously, these data cut in more than one direction. Although they strongly suggest a hereditary component in sexual orientation, they also make it clear that, whatever part heredity plays, it does not operate in a strictly deterministic way — so far as we now know. After all, many gays in these studies had twins who were not themselves gay.

These twin studies match up with the well-publicized genetic research of gay brothers by Dean Hamer and his associates at the National Institutes of Health. Investigating pairs of gay brothers, Hamer found in two separate trials that a majority of these brothers shared certain markers in an area designated Xq28 of the X chromosome.[95] Brothers who were not gay did not share this marker. The news media immediately hailed these findings as the discovery of a "gay gene," but there were questions raised about the research. One of the major problems was that other researchers could not verify the same results. Another problem was that speaking of a so-called "gay gene" was misleading because the research looked only at gay brothers and not at gays in general.[96] A more recent study by Sven Bocklandt at UCLA found a skewing in the X chromosome in mothers of gay men.[97] In the cells of every woman there is a random shutting down of one of the X chromosomes. However, Bocklandt found that a shut-down of one of the chromosomes rather than the other was far more likely in women with one or more gay sons. Whereas only 4 percent of mothers without a gay son showed this skewing, 14 percent of mothers with one gay son and 23 percent of mothers with two or more gay sons exhibited this skewing. This in itself proves nothing conclusive, but it does open an avenue for further research.

All of this research hints that biological factors may play some role in the formation of sexual orientation; precisely what role they play is still not clear. In no way do we have evidence that such factors play the *only* role in the emergence of sexual orientation. Human behavior, to say the least, is extraordinarily complex. A person may appear to have an innate aptitude for sports, or music, or academics, or whatever; but whether or to what extent a person cultivates those aptitudes varies in marked ways from one individual to the next. Whether one person persists in perfecting his or her golf swing, or another in playing J. S. Bach on the cello, or another in mastering the finer points of quantum physics depends on a host of factors, both internal to the person and external. The same is likely true regarding a person's sexual orientation. There is probably a complex "biology of sexual orientation," but there are also developmental and psychological processes in early childhood, as well as culturally bound determinants throughout life, that contribute to the way each individual experiences sexual orientation. Some have compared the emergence of sexual orientation to the speaking of one's native language. Just as all human beings have the innate capacity to learn a language, so it seems that some human beings may have an innate predisposition toward same-sex orientation. At the same time, just as it is only through interaction with one's culture and environment that one acquires language skills, so there are likely other indeterminate factors that influence the emergence of a gay or lesbian identity.[98]

Therefore, the question of "essentialism versus constructivism" presents us with a false dichotomy. There may be some component of sex or sexual orientation that is the same in all places and times, but the historical evidence of diversity makes clear that how sexual orientation works itself out in any given time and place is, at least in part, socially constructed. Figuring out which part is innate and which is constructed is itself controversial.[99] Some contend that sexual orientation as such (i.e., the gender to which one is sexually attracted) is biologically or psychosocially fixed, but that the meanings we assign to sexual behavior and perhaps even the kind of sexual behavior itself are socially constructed. Others contend that both sexual orientation and one's overall sense of sexual identity are socially constructed, with only the simple physical capacity for sex being biologically fixed. Some even go so far as to see the very bodily sensations of sex itself as formed by the society in which one lives.[100]

There is no doubt that this inquiry into causation will continue. Whatever may be its cause, we know that most people do not experience their sexual orientation as a choice. This has led many to argue that society in general — and religious society in particular — is wrong when it blames people for something that is beyond their control. This is the "born-that-way" argument: if gays and lesbians are "born that way," then society must extend them a certain degree of tolerance. Ironically, the born-that-way argument has provoked opposition from both anti-gay and pro-gay perspectives alike. Advocates on both sides insist that, at least in some measure, being gay *is* a choice. On the anti-gay-rights side, some bend over backward to refute even the least scintilla of scientific evidence that being gay is determined or heavily influenced by natural factors, such as prenatal hormones, genetics, or the like. Why? Because their anti-gay case depends on assigning moral blame, and moral blame is inappropriate if being gay is not a choice. On the other side, some pro-gay advocates are also wary of born-that-way arguments. For one thing, they worry that such arguments portray gays and lesbians as pathetic victims who are driven by forces that are beyond their control instead of free agents who are entitled to be respected in their own right.[101] Others hold that born-that-way arguments lead to a legal and religious tolerance that is merely superficial and patronizing.[102] While some may feel that tolerance is a good thing, the reality is that tolerance is not enough. Tolerance may lead to an acceptance of same-gender sexual orientation but not to an affirmation of same-gender love itself. To that extent, many feel that born-that-way arguments are actually dangerous in that they fail to promote either sexual freedom or the true acceptance of gay life.

Nevertheless, whether nature or nurture, compulsion or choice, play a greater role in sexual identity formation, a consensus has emerged that it no longer makes sense to blame someone for being gay. It is in the context of this broad shift in perspective that the argument for marriage equality needs to be understood.

The Quest for Marriage Equality

The definition of marriage in the United States is, and always has been, set by the civil powers of the individual states. This is a key fact to remember in accessing the debate about validating same-sex relationships and one that many religious-minded advocates forget. Marriage is a civil institution, and it is governed by secular legal principles that apply to all citizens regardless of their particular moral or religious beliefs. "If the separation of church and state means anything," constitutional scholar Evan Gerstmann argues, "it surely means that the state cannot prefer the views of, say, Catholics and Baptists over those of Unitarians and Reform Jews because the former outnumber the latter."[103]

Marriage confers a legal status and a place in society, including access to a well-defined structure of benefits and obligations. This structure is defined by the political authority and not by married couples themselves. When two people pledge themselves to each other in marriage, they become subject to this structure, including its many state and federal benefits. As of December 31, 2003, government researchers in Washington, D.C., identified 1,138 statutory benefits conferred upon married couples by the federal government alone. These federal benefits include such things as Social Security, Medicare, and various provisions for veterans; programs regarding fair housing and public welfare; numerous advantages in estate and gift taxation; regulations concerning retirement plan assets; rules concerning immigration and naturalization; and so forth.[104] This is an impressive number of federal benefits, especially considering that marriage has historically been a matter of state, not federal, law.

In addition to these federal benefits, each of the states gives married couples protections regarding the disposition of property in the event that one spouse dies without a will; regarding spousal immunity from testifying in court; and regarding protection from creditors in the event of financial hardship. If two people are married and seek a divorce, there are rules and precedents concerning child custody, child support, and fair disposition of assets. But if two parties live together without being married, they are more or less on their own if their relationship dissolves. There are few if any benefits that apply. Thus, in addition to its symbolic benefits, being married affords a couple significant practical advantages.

How does the civil authority define marriage? Marriage is the joining together of two lives in a loving commitment that is intended to be lifelong.[105] This commitment carries with it mutual obligations of fidelity and support that are recognized and upheld by the laws of civil society. Marriage establishes a new legal status between the parties, including new obligations as well as all the benefits just discussed. It also bestows a certain symbolic capital: even though couples with a marriage license may not be morally superior to couples without this piece of paper, society tends to invest more legitimacy in the family of the couple with the license. It is no wonder, then, that gays and lesbians have struggled to have their unions blessed by society.

A common objection raised against marriage equality for same-sex couples is that marriage should be for procreation. Surely procreation is a part of marriage, but it is by no means the main part. By and large, people in our culture do not marry just to acquire children. They marry because they want to spend their life with this particular person and no other. It is difficult to take the procreation objection seriously when we allow couples past childbearing age to marry without blinking an eye. Not only that, the whole issue of procreation has been changed fundamentally with the widespread societal acceptance of artificial means of birth control. It is impossible to overestimate the impact birth control has had on society's view of sexuality over the last half century and more. For all the talk about marriage and procreation, in most places there is no legal requirement that a couple engage in sexual intercourse for the marriage to be valid. Nor is the inability to have children among the usual grounds for divorce. The traditional grounds for divorce have more to do with the ability or inability of the couple to make a life together.[106]

The gay struggle for marriage and family equality began in the 1970s. In 1971, John F. Singer and Paul C. Barwick sought a license to marry in Seattle, Washington. Their request was denied, and the men sued the state. In *Singer v. Hara* (1974), the Washington Court of Appeals brushed aside the two men's claim that the denial of a license constituted sex discrimination under Washington's "equal rights amendment."[107] According to the court, the license was denied not because of sex discrimination but because of the very definition of marriage as between a man and a woman.[108] In the meantime, Singer had been dismissed from his job at the Equal Employment Opportunity Commission (EEOC) solely because he was gay, which was ironic because the EEOC is the agency of the federal government charged with enforcing antidiscrimination laws. Although Singer and Barwick would lose the gay marriage case, Singer himself would eventually win the discrimination lawsuit.[109] And this pattern persisted throughout the 1970s: gay people made advances in the areas of individual discrimination but lost their early efforts to break down relationship discrimination.

Thus, when Cela Rorex, the county clerk of Boulder, Colorado, began issuing marriage licenses to same-sex couples in 1975, she was quickly overruled by the Colorado attorney general.[110] Similarly, lawsuits in the 1970s demanding marriage equality in Minnesota and Kentucky went nowhere, as did requests for marriage licenses in Florida, Connecticut, Illinois, New York, and Wisconsin. A bill was even introduced in the Wisconsin legislature to expand the definition of marriage to include gay and lesbian couples — but to no avail.[111]

However, since the time of those early defeats during the last decades of the twentieth century, a number of new factors have combined to revitalize the quest for marriage and family equality in the twenty-first century. Two factors in particular are underscored by University of Chicago historian George Chauncey. First, the crisis of HIV/AIDS in the 1980s and 1990s impressed on gay and lesbian partners the vulnerability of their relationships without the legal protections afforded by marriage. Before that time, the gay rights movement had focused on eliminating discrimination generally without focusing particularly on marriage. Many gays thought of marriage as a heterosexual institution in which they had nothing in particular at stake.

All that changed with HIV/AIDS. Suddenly, gay men who were nurturing extremely ill partners found themselves being barred from participating in medical decisions, barred from receiving medical or bereavement leave, barred from the financial benefits of marriage, and barred from other legal benefits enjoyed by married couples. For example, in some places a surviving spouse can continue in a rent-controlled apartment, but if the surviving partner's name is not on the lease, the same advantage does not apply to gay and lesbian couples. While it is true that some marital benefits can be created by contract or through complex legal documents, the financial costs of doing so can be very high. Also, if the family of a deceased partner does not agree to honor the contract, the cost of enforcing the contract through litigation can be prohibitive.

A second thing that has caused more gays and lesbians to seek marriage is that many of them — more than half a million in the United States as of the 2000 Census — are now rearing children. And like all parents, they want what is best for their children, including protection in the event of catastrophe. Consider the case of a stay-at-home mother whose working husband dies, leaving her and her infant child to fend for themselves. In such circumstances, a heterosexual surviving spouse immediately falls into the safety net of a matrix of state and federal benefits, including inheritance provisions and survivorship benefits under Social Security. The situation is very different if the same stay-at-home mother is partnered with another woman, who dies suddenly. In the latter case, none of this protection will be there — either for the woman or for her child.

Some believe that gays and lesbians should be legally prevented from raising children.[112] Yet there is plenty of evidence that gay men and lesbian women make good parents and that sexual orientation by itself tells us little about what kind of parent a person will be.[113] Some worry that the children raised by gays or lesbians are at greater "risk" of becoming gay or lesbian themselves. Yet there is no credible evidence that the sexual orientation of a child's caregiver affects the sexual orientation of the child. Numerous studies suggest, in fact, that children being nurtured by gay or lesbian parents turn out the same as those growing up in traditional heterosexual households. If anything, they may turn out better: they may have a more open and accepting posture toward those who differ from themselves.[114] One study, which tracks children over a fifteen-year period, does suggest that girls raised by lesbian women have a greater openness to homoerotic experience than the population at large; but these girls showed no evidence of a greater likelihood to self-identify as lesbians themselves.[115] In one study, more than 90 percent of the boys raised by gay men self-identified not as homosexual but as heterosexual, which is almost exactly the number one would expect in the general population, based on the 2002 study discussed above.[116] Moreover, children of gay and lesbian parents do not seem to have any greater struggles regarding gender identity, gender roles, or sexual orientation than do children of heterosexual parents. There is some evidence indicating that the social stigma imposed on gay families in our culture creates greater levels of anxiety for children of those families, but this is only a compelling reason for removing the stigma.

Notwithstanding these facts, some courts have removed children from their *biological* parents when they have learned that the parent was gay or lesbian.[117] In addition, some states prohibit gays and lesbians from adopting outright, while others place tighter restrictions on such adoptions than on those of heterosexual persons.[118] The state of Florida has become infamous in this regard. Consider the case of the long-term, committed gay couple Stephen K. Lofton and Roger Croteau, who, functioning as foster parents, began taking in and caring for unwanted HIV-positive babies. As a measure of Stephen Lofton's commitment to these children, he gave up his job as a registered pediatric nurse in order to devote himself to this task full-time. In 1994, one of the children, a boy named "Bert," became available for adoption, and Lofton petitioned to adopt him under Florida law. However, Florida law prohibits anyone who is a "homosexual" from adopting a child. When Lofton's petition was denied, he joined other gay plaintiffs in challenging the Florida law as a violation of equal protection under the law and an infringement of liberty under the Due Process Clause.[119] Both the federal district court and the circuit court of appeals denied the claim of the gay plaintiffs and upheld the Florida law. The courts reasoned that the state of Florida has a legitimate interest in promoting the best interests of the child, including seeing to it that each child has both a father and a mother. In this particular case, of course, Stephen Lofton and his partner, Roger Croteau, were the only parents young Bert had ever known.[120] Why was it not in Bert's best interests to have the care that these men — and no one else — had given him continued and legitimated? It is difficult to avoid the conclusion that this law discriminated against Stephen Lofton and Roger Croteau simply because they are gay.

In 2010, one state district court of appeals in Florida agreed, striking down the Florida adoption prohibition as unconstitutional.[121] A court ruled similarly in a 2011 Arkansas case. Through a 2008 Arkansas voter initiative, the state enacted the Arkansas Adoption and Foster Care Act of 2008, or Act 1. This law made it unlawful for any unmarried person who was cohabiting with another person outside of marriage to adopt a child. The law applied to both same-sex and opposite-sex couples. It affected hundreds of children who needed a permanent family but were unable to find one. On April 7, 2011, a unanimous Arkansas Supreme Court ruled the law unconstitutional as a violation of the privacy rights of same-sex and cohabiting couples. The court reasoned that under Act 1 a person wanting to adopt a child was unfairly forced to give up the relationship with his or her significant other.[122]

The quest for gay marriage, then, is not only about civil rights for gays and lesbians but also about legal and social recognition for their families. After the string of defeats in the 1970s and 1980s, a breakthrough suddenly occurred in the early 1990s: in Hawaii, Ninia Baehr and Genora Dancel, a lesbian couple, filed a lawsuit, along with two other same-sex couples, demanding the issuance of marriage licenses and claiming that the state of Hawaii had unconstitutionally denied them the rights afforded by the state to all opposite-sex couples. On May 5, 1993, the Supreme Court of Hawaii agreed with them and handed down the decision in *Baehr v. Lewin*, which held that the marriage law in Hawaii, because of its exclusion of gay and lesbian couples, was presumed to be unconstitutional.[123]

Both the rationale and the result of this case are instructive, and we need to consider them carefully. With the conservative shift in the judiciary in recent years, courts have been reluctant to recognize rights that are not deeply rooted in the traditions of the nation. These same courts have been extremely reluctant to grant rights to gays and lesbians. Therefore, the Hawaii court admitted:

[W]e do not believe that a right to same sex marriage is so rooted in the traditions and collective conscience of our people that failure to recognize it would violate the fundamental principles of liberty and justice which lie at the base of all our civil and political institutions.[124]

Rather than making a case for gay marriage on the more controversial basis of sexual-orientation discrimination, the court based its reasoning on narrower and more socially acceptable grounds, that is, sex discrimination.[125] The argument was framed this way: if Ninia Baehr were a man, she could marry the woman she loves; but because she is a woman, she is denied this privilege.[126]

As a remedy, the court sent the case back to the trial court to determine (a) whether there was a "compelling state interest" for this exclusion, and (b) whether the exclusion was narrowly enough drawn so as not to infringe unduly on the constitutional rights of gay and lesbian couples. The evidence presented at the trial was instructive. Even the state's expert witness, who argued against same-sex marriage, admitted that gays and lesbians were good citizens and good parents. On hearing evidence, the trial court in 1996 held that the state of Hawaii had no compelling interest for refusing to extend the meaning of marriage to gays and lesbians. In this way, the Hawaii court was the first to open the door to gay marriage.

But the *Baehr* case produced an immediate and vociferous anti-gay backlash, one that is being felt to this day. First of all, more than thirty states enacted provisions preventing same-sex marriages from being recognized in their courts.[127] The Hawaii case also prompted the U.S. Congress in 1996 to enact the so-called Defense of Marriage Act (DOMA), which defined marriage as a "union of one man and one woman" for purposes of federal law; it also sought to relieve the various states of their obligation to recognize same-sex marriages from other jurisdictions.[128] By April 1, 2001, thirty-five states had followed suit by enacting their own versions of DOMA.

A second form of backlash occurred in the state of Hawaii itself, and it came in a form that would be repeated again and again in other states. A popular referendum was called in 1998 to amend the state constitution to reserve marriage for opposite-sex couples; that referendum passed and in effect nullified the decision in *Baehr*, making it possible for the legislature to ban same-sex marriage.[129] In the meantime, through a political compromise, the Hawaii legislature created a "reciprocal beneficiaries" provision as an alternative to marriage. But this reciprocal beneficiaries legislation fell far short of the equality gays and lesbians were seeking: it gave same-sex partners only about 50 of the 250 benefits under Hawaii law accorded to married couples. The benefits included some property rights, limited health benefits (which were subsequently removed), and the right to sue for wrongful death or injury to one's partner.[130] It did not include any tax benefits or parental rights or rights of adoption. Perhaps even more significant than the way it shortchanged gays and lesbians regarding benefits was the way the law placed no permanently binding obligations on the partners. In 2011 Hawaii passed a civil-unions law that more closely approximates marriage and went into effect January 1, 2012.

What to do about same-sex relationships has become one of the most contentious cultural issues of our time. On the one hand, the trend in Europe and Canada has been toward greater and greater recognition of gay unions. The process has been a gradual one that began in 1987, when, after years of study, Sweden adopted a law that provided many of the benefits of marriage to cohabiting couples, whether of the same sex or opposite sexes. Then, in 1989, Denmark enacted a registered partnership arrangement, which matched almost all the obligations and benefits of traditional marriage; and similar laws eventually were passed in all the Scandinavian countries. Denmark also decided in 1999 to allow gays to adopt children. France and Germany created their own partnership laws in 1998 and 2000 respectively. Then, in 2001, The Netherlands became the first nation to adopt gay marriage. In 1996 the Dutch parliament had established a committee to investigate the possibility of expanding marriage to cover same-sex couples. By a 5-3 vote the committee recommended going forward with the idea, noting that many gays and lesbians were in committed relationships and some were raising children already.[131] The parliament voted to approve it by a substantial majority. Belgium followed suit in 2003, then Canada and Spain in 2005. Elsewhere in Europe gay marriage is legal in Norway (2009), Sweden (2009), Portugal (2010), and Iceland (2010); it is being considered in Luxembourg, Finland, and the United Kingdom. The idea of gay marriage has become so commonplace that in early 2006, when rock star Elton John joined himself with his partner of eleven years, David Furnish, under Great Britain's Civil Partnership Bill — a law that falls short of marriage — ordinary people were speaking quite easily of the couple's "wedding."

On the other side of the coin is the more volatile political situation in the United States, which is in stark contrast to the relative ease with which Europe and Canada have recognized gay unions. Martha Nussbaum has wryly noted: "American society . . . appears willing to tolerate, somewhat grudgingly, the existence of lesbians and gay men — provided it does not have to put up with their happiness, that is . . . their enjoyment of full equality in all the major areas of life that are affected by law and public policy."[132] Nevertheless, there has been decisive progress on gay rights in the United States in recent years. First, there have been two pro-gay-rights decisions by the United States Supreme Court. In *Romer v. Evans* (1996) the Court declared it unconstitutional to target gay and lesbian people for discrimination merely because of their identity.[133] And in *Lawrence v. Texas* (2003) the Court struck down the so-called "sodomy law" in the state of Texas and twelve other states on the grounds that gay people have a liberty interest that protects them from unwanted government interference in their lifestyle. In cultural debates since the 1970s, the term "sodomy" has become synonymous with homoerotic sexuality.[134] But, as I have indicated above, this usage reflects an ignorance of history. For more than a thousand years, the term "sodomy" applied to *any* sexual activity that departed from heterosexual vaginal intercourse — whether heterosexual or homosexual. Thus, oral sex between a man and a woman — even between husband and wife — was condemned and outlawed as sodomy.

We need to underscore this fact because empirical studies tell us that well over three-quarters of adult Americans between the ages of 25 and 44 have engaged in heterosexual activities traditionally defined as sodomy.[135] Therefore, if political and religious leaders want to impose penalties, whether criminal or ecclesiastical, based on traditional teachings about sodomy, then they will have to apply them against most of the people they know and not just against gays and lesbians. The Supreme Court no doubt took note of this double standard.

Second, two landmark state court decisions on gay marriage have had a decisive impact on the debate. In Vermont, *Baker v. State* (1999) led the way to a marriage substitute that was created for gays and lesbians — the so-called civil union.[136] In Massachusetts, *Goodridge v. Department of Public Health* (2003) went a step further, paving the way for that state to be the first in the country to make gay marriage a reality.[137] I discuss these decisions in detail in Chapter Four. As a result of further judicial and legislative decisions, gay marriage is now legal in Connecticut, Iowa, Massachusetts, New Hampshire, New York, Vermont, and the District of Columbia.

Civil unions are recognized in Delaware, Hawaii, Illinois, New Jersey, and Rhode Island.

In Chapter Five I discuss the political implications of the marriage equality debate, including the roles of courts and legislatures as well as the impact of state constitutional amendments prohibiting gay marriage. Especially noteworthy is a shift in judicial opinion that began in 2008 and continued into 2009 when courts in California, Connecticut, and Iowa began to acknowledge more readily that same-sex couples have a right to marry and that persons with a same-gender sexual orientation constitute a class suffering from discrimination that requires greater court protection. But first, before turning to these political and legal issues, Chapters One, Two, and Three provide an overview of the moral and religious dimensions of the debate and proposed solutions to it. This discussion is crucial because arguments from the Bible, theology, and religious tradition have provided the fiercest fuel for the anti-gay movement. It is only by first successfully confronting the moral and religious questions that we may discover a way forward on this issue.

PART ONE

RELIGION

CHAPTER ONE

The Non-Affirming Church

The difficulty with the biblical references to homosexuality is that they are so incidental that they give us little help in situating them doctrinally. . . . We need . . . a broader doctrinal base than those texts on their own afford, yet not forgetting that they, too, demand an account.

Oliver O'Donovan[1]

For decades now, disputes over same-sex relationships have been waged as a clash between two completely antithetical viewpoints. This has certainly been the case in the Christian churches. One side passionately calls for an affirmation of gay identity and life; the other argues with equal vigor that the church and society must maintain their traditional non-affirming stances. Often the debate has been fueled by advocacy groups whose fund-raising efforts depend on defining the conflict in apocalyptic, either-or terms. These dynamics have prevailed in both the civil and religious arenas. Within civil polity, the debate focused on toleration, antidiscrimination, and the achievement of civil rights by gay people during the 1970s and 1980s. From the 1990s until today, the debate has shifted to gay marriage and civil unions. The controversy within the churches has focused almost exclusively on ordination to church office and has only recently begun to explore the ethical contours of gay relationships. This has put religious communities in the anomalous position of asking their members to accept gay *leadership* without first giving them the time or the biblical, theological, and practical resources to assimilate gay *identity*. One author has compared the resulting impasse to a pair of wrestlers who have fought each other to a draw, each remaining locked in the other's grip, with neither one able to achieve a decisive win and neither one willing to quit the contest.[2]

If we are going to move beyond this impasse, we need a new way of understanding what is in dispute. Framing the debate as a clash between two antithetical viewpoints — one pro-gay, the other anti-gay — only perpetuates what has become an impenetrable roadblock. In order to help us move beyond this impasse, I will discuss in this chapter and the next a spectrum of seven theological ways of looking at same-sex relationships.[3] These include both non-affirming and affirming viewpoints, with perspectives ranging from the categorical prohibition of all such relationships to the advocacy of their full ecclesiastical consecration. The spectrum runs as follows:

(1) *Prohibition:* does not approve of and would bar same-sex unions.
(2) *Toleration:* does not approve of, but would not prosecute or reject gay and lesbian people.
(3) *Accommodation:* does not approve ordinarily, but would allow for exceptions on a "lesser-of-the-evils" rationale.
(4) *Legitimation:* wants to include gays and lesbians in the community, and wants to prevent them from being singled out and condemned unfairly.
(5) *Celebration:* believes same-sex unions should no longer be scorned but affirmed as good.
(6) *Liberation:* perceives societal attitudes concerning gays and lesbians as being caught up in wider injustices, which need to be remedied.
(7) *Consecration:* argues for the full religious blessing of same-sex unions.

This sevenfold typology could be applied to many other issues. Imagine that we were not talking about sexuality but about something like the consumption of alcohol. Some religions, such as Islam, *prohibit* the drinking of alcoholic beverages (in fact, it was also prohibited for a period of time in the United States). Later it came to be *tolerated* by religious groups and then *legitimated* under law. One can also think of our present approach to drinking alcohol as one of regulating or *accommodating* it under carefully defined circumstances, such as only when sold with a valid license, only when consumed by persons above a certain age, or only when served in places where zoning laws allow. We know that the *celebration* of alcohol for its own sake may occur as a reaction to prohibition — all the more so when prohibition has been ruthlessly enforced. Those focused on *liberating* people from the social consequences of injustice might observe that the use of alcohol, though ostensibly an exercise of individual freedom, is often connected to conditions of poverty and oppression that society has neglected. Even the *consecration* of drinking is well-known to us in ritual contexts such as the Sabbath for Jews or the Lord's Supper for Christians.

I have two aims in presenting this typology. First, my goal is to promote mutual understanding. There is more nuance and contour in people's approaches to this topic than the typical either-or dichotomy allows. Even people who disagree with my conclusions can perhaps be informed by my analysis. Second, I treat all seven positions in some detail because I believe that each of the positions has something of value to teach us. Because I approach this topic as a Christian theologian, I shall consider each of the seven viewpoints here in its relationship to the Christian way of telling the story of God's relationship to the world. It is the unfolding of a three-part story of creation, reconciliation, and redemption. From a Christian point of view, it makes sense to investigate how each of these seven viewpoints understands the place of gay and lesbian people within this drama. Those in other traditions naturally will think of this differently. But even those who espouse a nonreligious perspective or who reject Christianity would do well to pay attention here, for much of the current controversy is fueled by Christian presuppositions. Even thoroughly secular people need to know something about this framework.

First of all, by "creation" I mean the belief that God brought us and the world into being. One of the main issues in the dispute is discerning where homoerotic desire or sexual orientation fits within the scheme of creation. Is same-sex orientation a violation of creation, as some Christians insist? Or is it a fairly consistent feature of the natural world? Permeating discussions such as this are notions — both implicit and explicit — about the nature of bodily existence. Contained in all these reflections, too, are assumptions about the character of sin and wrongdoing, the attitudes and actions by which human beings turn aside from God's purposes.

Second, the term "reconciliation" is one of many biblical words that speak about what God does to save human beings from wrongdoing and sin.[4] Reconciliation presupposes that human beings have sinned and are in need of the restoration of a right relationship with God and with one another. The act of reconciliation is at the gracious initiative of God, but it also calls forth a human response. This response includes faith, repentance, and a life of holiness. One of the pivotal biblical passages concerning reconciliation makes an unmistakable connection between God's action and our own:

> All this is from God, who reconciled us to himself through Christ, and has given us the ministry of reconciliation; that is, in Christ God was reconciling the world to himself, not counting their trespasses against them, and entrusting the message of reconciliation to us. (2 Cor. 5:18-19)

A key question in any Christian discussion of gay and lesbian life is how reconciliation in Christ becomes real in lived experience. Some speak of the need for gays and lesbians to repent of their lifestyle; on the other side, others remind the broader church that it, too, needs to repent of sins of hatred and exclusion directed toward gay and lesbian people. Still others insist that we should all be reconciled to the goodness of gay life and love. Through it all, we must understand that reconciliation includes both a vertical and a horizontal dimension: we are to be reconciled both to God and to one another. This suggests that, even when we disagree about a subject as controversial as sexuality, we should still look for a way to live together in harmony.

Third is redemption. It is sometimes difficult to see the difference between reconciliation and redemption. *Reconciliation* has to do with the restoration of a broken relationship. *Redemption* has to do with living out the wholeness that has been re-established. *Reconciliation* is something Christians believe was accomplished in the past by the gracious act of God in Jesus Christ, and which is still working itself out today. By contrast, *redemption* in the New Testament is almost always a future-oriented reality.[5] We have been reconciled to God and are being reconciled to one another; and now we are moving forward toward redemption in the power of the Spirit. As with reconciliation, the power of redemption is already being experienced; but the fullness of our redemption lies always in front of us, awaiting the final consummation of all things. Therefore, when we speak of redemption, we are asking about how to live into the fullness that God desires for each one of us. To speak of redemption is to speak of the ethical life we must live by grace in order to become what God would have us be.

To sum it up, the words "creation," "reconciliation," and "redemption" give us a shorthand for speaking about the grand narrative in which God is at work to bring humanity to salvation and wholeness. I understand these three movements as individual moments in a unified drama, which proclaims the work of the Triune God, who is for us and with us in Jesus Christ and who invites us by the Spirit's power to be for and with one another.[6] The creation-reconciliation-redemption framework states a certain logic that is at work in all seven of the theological viewpoints considered here. This does not mean that every advocate of one of the seven positions refers to creation, reconciliation, or redemption explicitly. However, a Christian treatment of this subject must take into account God's actions in creation, reconciliation, and redemption at least implicitly.

Finally, I make no claim that these seven viewpoints exhaust all the possibilities. Indeed, the reader may find that his or her own views do not line up neatly with any one position sketched here — or that he or she may resonate with aspects of more than one viewpoint. Nonetheless, by attending to each of the viewpoints in its own integrity, the reader will be able, I hope, to push beyond surface labels and reach a new understanding of the issues.

THREE NON-AFFIRMING VIEWPOINTS

For centuries there have been Christians who claim that all homoerotic behavior of any kind is an absolute violation of the will of God, making it wrong to affirm such conduct in any way.[7] These non-affirming viewpoints lie on a spectrum from prohibition to toleration to accommodation.

I. Prohibition

Now if you are unwilling to serve the LORD, choose this day whom you will serve, whether the gods your ancestors served in the region beyond the River or the gods of the Amorites in whose land you are living; but as for me and my household, we will serve the LORD.

(Josh. 24:15)

49

Discerning the Ways of God

Many argue that homoerotic desire is a perversion and that homoerotic behavior should be prohibited. This viewpoint is based on a vision of God as a lawgiver who gives human beings absolute commandments that must be obeyed. Within society at large, the prohibitionist concern about gays is part of a larger anxiety about upholding traditional morality. This includes worries about sexual promiscuity (especially among teenagers), the decline in marriage rates, the rise in divorce rates, the dramatic increase in out-of-wedlock childbirths, and the legalization of abortion. Those advocating prohibition of all homoerotic conduct feel that support of gays and lesbians lends an inappropriate symbolic support to the decline of marriage. Some express concern that there is a "homosexual agenda" to undermine the family. In keeping with this, many believe that certain leadership positions should not be occupied by gay people, as recent controversies over gays in teaching positions, in the military, and in the Boy Scouts attest.[8]

For advocates of prohibition, living a righteous life requires steadfast adherence to God's ways — in church, in society, and in the life of the individual.

The Case for Prohibition

This first non-affirming viewpoint is supported by four interconnecting layers of argument.

1. Arguments from Scripture   The first argument is based on the Bible. It is largely a negative argument, and it is drawn from several biblical prohibitions uttered against certain same-gender sex acts. There are not many such biblical passages, but prohibitionists insist that their meaning is clear and uniformly negative. I shall discuss most of these biblical texts in much more detail in Chapter Three, but here I will provide a brief treatment of how these biblical texts are appropriated by advocates of prohibition.

One set of these biblical texts has had a lasting impact on the history of Jewish and Christian attitudes toward homoeroticism. These texts speak against same-sex rape and cultic prostitution.[9] The most famous passage in this category is the cataclysmic destruction of the non-Jewish biblical cities of Sodom and Gomorrah (Gen. 19). In the story of Sodom, God hears an outcry from the city and sends angelic messengers to investigate what is wrong (Gen. 18:20-21). When the messengers arrive, the male inhabitants of the city have surrounded the angelic beings and are attempting to rape them (Gen. 19:4-5). Abraham's nephew Lot, who is playing host to the divine messengers, offers the men his virgin daughters to satisfy their lust. But the power of God blinds the men of Sodom before they are able to do harm to Lot's daughters or the angelic beings (Gen. 19:11).

In a parallel story (Judg. 19), a Jewish priest is on a journey with his concubine, and they find shelter for the evening in the Jewish territory of Gibeah. The priest has just finished dinner with his host when local "perverted men" surround the house with the intent of raping him. To appease these marauders, the host offers them his virgin daughter. They refuse his offer, so the priest offers them his concubine, whom they take instead. The text says: "They wantonly raped her, and abused her all through the night until the morning" (Judg. 19:25). The next day the priest discovers his concubine dead on the doorstep.

Prohibitionists argue that both the Sodom and Gibeah stories condemn the homoerotic behavior they describe. This is most certainly true. However, one must ask whether the proposed behavior in question is morally reprehensible because of its same-sex character or because it is violently abusive. I shall say more about this in the reflection section below.

Two other sets of biblical passages figure into the non-affirming case: the legal pronouncements in the book of Leviticus directed against certain sex acts performed by one man on another (Lev. 18:22; 20:13) and three references by (or attributed to) the apostle Paul concerning same-sex acts within the world of Roman antiquity (Rom. 1:18-32; 1 Cor. 6:9-10; 1 Tim. 1:9-10). The two texts from Leviticus prohibit one male from sexually penetrating another male, and they impose the death penalty for doing so. That is, within a society with strict male and female gender roles, they prohibit one male from doing certain things *to* another male. Put bluntly, the prohibition is against a male being penetrated as if he were a female.

The Pauline texts are directed primarily against the hedonistic sexual practices of the Roman world and trade on certain cultural assumptions about proper male roles. 1 Corinthians 6:9-10 and 1 Timothy 1:9-10 mention forms of homoeroticism that are thought to be a departure from a life of holiness. What is open to debate are the *reasons* that these specific behaviors are labeled vices. Similarly, in Romans 1:18-32, Paul invokes the hedonistic same-sex eroticism of the Greco-Roman world as an example of the idolatry of non-Jews. He forcefully declares that such hedonistic activity is both shameful and degrading and thus has no place in the life of Christian people.

2. Marriage as an Order of Creation   The second argument for prohibition is institutional in character. It links the negative argument from Scripture with a positive argument based on the institution of marriage as a divinely ordained and unchangeable "order of creation." The argument is that marriage between a man and a woman is the only appropriate context for sexual relations. Therefore, one must prohibit all sexual acts, including same-gender sexual acts, that occur outside its bounds. This is such an important argument that I devote the entire third chapter of this book to it.

3. Arguments from Nature   Either explicitly or implicitly, almost all advocates of non-affirming positions draw on a third resource: an appeal to the natural law tradition. This tradition had its roots in ancient Greek and Roman Stoic philosophy and was incorporated into the later Christian theology of St. Thomas Aquinas and others.[10] The basic natural law argument is that marriage creates an organic communion between a man and a woman, a so-called "one-flesh union" (cf. Gen. 2:24) that is by definition meant to be committed, exclusive, and indissoluble.[11] When experienced within marriage, sexual intercourse is said to be an intrinsic good. Intrinsic goods are those that are valuable in themselves, in contrast to instrumental goods, which are pursued for the sake of something else. According to this way of thinking, masturbation, sex outside of marriage, and gay sexuality are merely instrumental because they serve only to advance the private pleasure of those engaging in them. Sex between a man and a woman within marriage, by contrast, promotes an organic fellowship that is intrinsically open to bringing new life into the world, as well as contributing to the goods of love and companionship between spouses. In short, the purpose of marriage in the natural law tradition is procreation.

4. Arguments from Tradition   Fourth, the prohibition perspective also appeals to several thousand years of Jewish and Christian moral teaching against same-gender sexuality. This tradition, on the whole, has condemned homoeroticism in the strongest terms. Indeed, some insist that, compared to the rest of the world, Jews and Christians have been unique in their consistent denunciation of homoeroticism. In one sense, this entire book is aimed at contesting that claim.

A. Creation

Each of the seven positions tends to place more emphasis on one doctrine than on another. For the prohibitionist the focus is primarily on creation. Prohibitionists believe that it is God's intention for everyone to be heterosexual. Consequently, same-gender sexual expression is not a part of the goodness of creation, nor is it a gift of God. Instead, it is a perversion.

Prohibitionists view homoerotic desire as a deliberate choice for which persons must be held morally accountable. Such acts violate nature and undermine the complementarity of male and female visible in the created world. This kind of thinking leads many prohibitionists to be unsure about the legitimacy of the contemporary category "sexual orientation," since by definition a sexual orientation is a given and thus something beyond one's own choosing. Prohibitionists agree that all human beings are created in the image of God; but committing acts of sin, especially homoerotic behaviors, tarnishes that image. St. Thomas Aquinas, for example, held that one man having sex with another is more morally reprehensible than a man engaging in a violent act of rape against a woman.[12] At least an act of rape was a "natural" act, he reasoned, whereas a homoerotic act is not only sinful in itself but is also one of the worst sins a person can commit. In keeping with St. Thomas's position, the Roman Catholic hierarchy in recent years has taken a hard prohibitionist line: it has declared that homoerotic conduct "is intrinsically evil, and therefore must be considered objectively disordered."[13]

B. Reconciliation in Christ

Once we know where same-sex desire and behavior fit within the order of creation, prohibitionists argue, we also know where they fit within reconciliation and redemption. To be fallen and in need of reconciliation means that we must be "justified," or made right with God — and forgiven through the grace of our Lord Jesus Christ. To be justified by grace, however, does not give us an excuse to continue sinning. We still need to grow in grace, which the tradition calls "sanctification," or being made holy. One of the first steps in sanctification is repentance, that is, turning away from sin. Because they believe that biblical teachings on this subject are without ambiguity, prohibitionists maintain that gays and lesbians must repent not only of homosexual deeds but even of homosexual desire, for both the deed and the desire contradict God's intention for creation.

In order for gays and lesbians to achieve this repentance, many prohibitionists recommend "reparative therapy." This is a form of counseling designed to help gays and lesbians give up their homosexual desire and either remain chaste or enter into marriage with a member of the opposite sex. Proponents of such therapy acknowledge that the success rate is not high; still, they argue that gays and lesbians have a moral obligation at least to try reparative therapy.

C. Redemption in the Spirit

Redemption points toward God's intended future for individuals, communities, and ultimately the whole of creation. Christians affirm this redemptive vision whenever they repeat the words of the Lord's Prayer, "Thy will be done *on earth* as it is in heaven." The question becomes this: How do we live so that God's will is done, so that we can be set free by the Spirit from our human bondage to sin? Given that same-gender sexuality is considered by prohibitionists to be "perverse" in every case, living a life of redemption requires that gays and lesbians return to their "true" God-given heterosexual nature or else remain celibate.

Reflection

The primary strength of the prohibition position is its tight internal consistency. Conclusions follow effortlessly from the major premise, which is that certain forms of homoerotic behavior have been clearly prohibited by Scripture, tradition, and morality. This viewpoint also has the merit of advocating definite and firm standards by which persons can live their lives. Nevertheless, when we examine this position carefully, we will see that the prohibitionist arguments rest on a flimsy foundation. Or, to put it another way, its logical conclusions are only as good as its premises — and its premises are wrong. I shall say more about the biblical witness in the next chapter, but a few comments are in order here as well.

From what I have already said, it should be clear that the biblical passages invoked by prohibitionists have nothing explicit to say about the relationships of mutually and exclusively committed same-sex couples. In both the Sodom and Gibeah stories there is something *other than* the same-sex character of the conduct that makes it bad. Rape is wrong simply because it is rape, irrespective of the gender of the victim. In fact, in each of these stories, both men and women are made the targets of male sexual abuse. The shocking thing is that anti-gay advocates are eager to quote the Sodom and Gibeah passages as authoritative for excluding all same-sex eroticism while acquiescing in one of the central assumptions made by the men in these stories, namely, that raping a woman is somehow more acceptable than raping a man. The silence of many prohibitionists concerning the subordination of women in the Bible should make us think twice about the moral clarity of their position.

The Sodom and Gibeah stories underscore that violent, exploitative behavior is wrong, but they tell us nothing about gay and lesbian life today. This conclusion is confirmed by other passages in the Bible itself. The clearest statement comes from Ezekiel 16:49, where the sin of Sodom is said to be lack of concern for the poor: "This was the guilt of your sister Sodom: she and her daughters had pride, excess of food, and prosperous ease, but did not aid the poor and needy."[14] In short, these biblical passages condemn homoerotic rape and violence, not same-sex love. They declare rules that most likely existed for the purpose of preserving a certain understanding of male dignity. They do not provide a foundation for a universal law that applies in all times and contexts.

The same is true of the Pauline vice lists and the opening chapter of Romans. As explained in the Introduction, Paul wrote at a time when male prostitution was widespread and when homoerotic sex acts were frequently performed by social superiors upon their social inferiors of all kinds. There was a sexual double standard in which a freeborn male was allowed to gratify his own sexual urges with a woman, a male slave, or another social inferior. Such activity was not only permitted, it was even expected — as a part of manly behavior. At the same time, for a freeborn male to allow himself to be sexually penetrated by another male was considered shameful, even criminal.[15] This is the primary context and thus the main target of Paul's comments. One especially pernicious feature of Roman sexual practice was the lively trade in young boys who had been captured by the military as prisoners of war. Soldiers sold these boys to slave traders, who castrated them and quickly sold them as sex slaves. This is almost certainly the context that is behind the denunciation in 1 Timothy 1:10 of "fornicators, men who have sex with men, and slave traders." This was such a rampant problem that Roman emperors, on three separate occasions, promulgated laws aimed at banning slave boy castration.[16] It is thus no wonder that Paul followed the opinion of Philo, Josephus, and other Jews of his day in rejecting such exceedingly cruel and wanton behavior.

To sum up, there are biblical texts that prohibit some kinds of homoerotic conduct, but the question is how we should interpret these prohibitions. Should they be interpreted broadly, so that all gay and lesbian relationships are rendered morally illegitimate? Or should the scope of these prohibitions be restricted to their own social contexts, thus opening the door to the possibility that at least some gay and lesbian relationships can be viewed favorably? In the next chapter I shall return to these biblical texts, arguing that they say nothing about exclusively committed unions between equals. Even John R. W. Stott, the conservative British evangelical preacher, has acknowledged my main point: that the biblical prohibitions by themselves say nothing about such partnerships.[17]

It is because they realize these biblical pronouncements are inconclusive (i.e., time- and context-restricted) that Stott and others have had to shift their arguments from the so-called prohibition passages to the more general contention that marriage is an order of creation. However, the argument that there is a fixed and timeless order of creation also rests on a weak foundation. Historically speaking, the organization of marriage and family life has varied significantly over time. For centuries, marriage was more about shoring up kinship ties than it was about achieving personal fulfillment. Ancient kinship systems were configured as extended families rather than the modern male-female "nuclear" family, which gained prominence in our civilization under the influence of the Protestant Reformation.[18] Even where the nuclear family has been the norm, women have been mostly treated as social inferiors, though even this has varied from age to age.[19] For that matter, the Christian tradition itself has not always held up marriage and family life as the highest norm. On the contrary, up until the Reformation, celibacy was recommended for the most devout, and it is still required for priests in the Roman Catholic Church and for bishops in Eastern Orthodoxy. From a philosophical point of view, the "orders of creation" thinking has also been linked with the notion of a single divinely sanctioned form of government, of social stratification, and of political economy. And yet, we all know that structures of government and the economy have changed dramatically through the ages. To posit a single "order" that is supposed to hold true for all time, therefore, is at best a quixotic dream. Indeed, sometimes the advocacy of a single "order" has turned into a nightmare.

The natural law argument is also flawed. It claims that the purpose of marriage is procreation, yet this is contradicted by the fact that we allow people to marry who are completely incapable of having children, for example, couples who are beyond child-bearing years.[20] Why is their infertility treated differently than the inability of same-sex couples to procreate? Similar problems attend arguments that there is something about heterosexual sex acts — or about male and female genitalia in union with one another — that make them especially suitable to symbolize God's grace toward human beings.[21] This focus on body parts for the sake of body parts implies that every heterosexual union of those parts is uniquely able to symbolize God's grace in a way that same-sex unions are not. We need only think of the examples of heterosexual rape and incest to see that this is a false argument.[22]

The truth is that the natural law position, at least in some of its forms, downplays and devalues the personal dimension of physical love and has no way to account for the giving and receiving of pleasure, even though most people would mark such reciprocity as a chief feature of their committed sexual love. For the natural law theorists, pleasure without procreation is meaningless. However, if the nonprocreative giving and receiving of pleasure is meaningless, what are we to make of female orgasm in sexual intercourse? From the standpoint of traditional natural law theory, as soon as male ejaculation has occurred, sexual functionality has been successfully completed. Efforts to bring a woman to orgasm are deemed meaningless or beside the point. In some ancient societies, in fact, efforts to please a woman sexually were actually considered to be "unmanly." Presently there seems to be a cultural shift toward glorifying physical pleasure, but here a double standard exists: the giving and receiving of pleasure within marriage is now said to be part of God's "beautiful plan" for sexuality; this is in contrast to the "meaninglessness" of what happens between people committed to one another who are gay.

Finally, the argument from "thousands of years of Jewish and Christian history" also fails to tell the whole story. As I have noted in the introduction, Jewish and Christian traditions have been less monolithically opposed to homoeroticism than is usually admitted. In addition, the "two thousand years of tradition" argument actually points us in another direction. For two thousand years and more, biblical religion has promoted exclusively committed, covenantal relationships. Why should the church not extend its endorsement to the faithful integrity of gay and lesbian couples?

This only underscores that rarely do prohibitionists acknowledge biblical or historical facts that would call into question their premises or conclusions. There are, for example, alternative readings of Scripture, tradition, and morality that some prohibitionists either ignore or belittle. Everything rests on deductive reasoning derived from definitions they have put forward in advance. They pay little attention to empirical or scientific study, except where it supports the prohibitionist agenda. For example, they emphasize stories of gay male promiscuity but usually ignore counterbalancing evidence of gay or lesbian faithfulness.

Remarkably, prohibitionist arguments contradict themselves by alternating between a rhetoric of disgust and a rhetoric of trivialization. On the one hand, prohibitionists treat gay life as abhorrent, often tarring gays and lesbians with the same brush that they use for child molesters and other sex offenders. Usually they link this with a "slippery slope" argument, claiming that if society adopts a favorable view of gays and lesbians, it will inevitably lead to the legitimation of polygamy and incest. This is quite interesting. If gay sex is so disgusting, then the question arises, why are prohibitionists constantly drawing so much attention to it?[23] On the other hand, there is also a rhetoric of trivialization. According to the natural law argument, because same-gender sexuality is nonprocreative, it is therefore trivial and meaningless. Again, one has to wonder: if gay sex is so trivial and meaningless, why is so much energy being expended to denounce it?

These and other dissatisfactions with the prohibitionist position have led some in the church to seek a different way of thinking about these issues. Some conservatives themselves have argued that supporting gays and lesbians who are ordering their lives in committed, covenantal ways is the true conservative position.[24] This is especially true now that well over half a million gay and lesbian families are also raising children. To say that every child "deserves" a mother and a father is a commendable ideal, but the children who are being raised by two mothers or two fathers also deserve societal support, not condemnation.

II. Toleration

The scribes and the Pharisees brought a woman who had been caught in adultery; and making her stand before all of them, they said to him, "Teacher, this woman was caught in the very act of committing adultery. . . ."

When they kept on questioning him, he straightened up and said to them, "Let anyone among you who is without sin be the first to throw a stone at her. . . ."

When they heard it, they went away, one by one, beginning with the elders; and Jesus was left alone with the woman standing before him. Jesus straightened up and said to her, "Woman, where are they? Has no one condemned you?" She said, "No one, sir." And Jesus said, "Neither do I condemn you. Go your way, and from now on do not sin again."

(John 8:3-4, 7, 9-11)

Discerning the Ways of God

Most mainline religious communities in the 1970s underwent a major shift in their view of same-gender sexuality, significantly altering the prohibition position they had inherited. This shift was based on research that challenged the perennial assumption that the "natural" sexual orientation of all human beings is heterosexual.

As I have noted in the introduction, sexual orientation is a psychological term that refers to the predominant focus of a person's erotic desires. Research beginning in the 1940s and 1950s challenged the prior assumption that sexual orientation in all persons is naturally heterosexual. It demonstrated, at least to the satisfaction of many, that for a small minority of people, a same-gender sexual orientation is experienced as a stable and enduring feature of their lives. That is to say, their attraction to persons of the same gender is as powerful and feels as "normal" as the attraction of others to persons of the opposite gender. In short, sexual orientation is experienced as a given rather than a simple choice.

Moving away from the strict prohibition position, most mainline churches adopted a policy of qualified toleration of gays and lesbians. As one person has summed it up, this policy was "welcoming but non-affirming": it welcomed gays as people but did not affirm their lifestyle.[25] To make clear their disapproval of same-gender sexuality, many religious communities adopted so-called "fidelity and chastity" standards, enjoining fidelity within the covenant of marriage between a man and a woman or chastity in singleness.[26] This posture sees God as one who has standards that must be upheld, but who is also forbearing. God's invitation of grace goes out to all to be included in the fellowship of the community, but because of God's abiding commandment, only certain people are qualified to lead that community. One way to think of this is as a kind of political compromise. Even though mainline religious communities moved toward toleration of gay members, they appeased the prohibitionists by keeping in place a prohibition against allowing openly gay people in church office.

The Case for Toleration

The new professional declarations concerning sexual orientation led many to conclude that being gay or lesbian is not a sin but a condition of life. If gays and lesbians do not experience their sexual orientation as a straightforward choice, then what sense does it make to join the prohibitionists in condemning them? The phenomenon of "coming out of the closet" was just beginning in earnest in the 1970s. The church has always ordained people with homoerotic desire; what was new in the 1970s was that some of these people were making their sexual orientation known.

In one sense, the question concerning gay ordination was a logical outgrowth of new understandings about human sexuality; in another sense, there were many who were not yet ready for the question. Many people could not name a person who was openly gay or lesbian. A poignant example was Justice Lewis F. Powell, Jr., a Virginia churchman who served on the United States Supreme Court from 1972 to 1987. Looking back with regret on a vote he had cast against gay rights, Justice Powell mused that in all his seventy-eight years he had never met a gay person.[27] Years later we know just how astonishing this statement was: it turns out that in the 1980s, Justice Powell had worked on a day-in and day-out basis with at least six law clerks who were gay.[28]

In light of anecdotes like this, it is now clear that, in asking for gay ordination in the 1970s, advocates were seeking the politically impossible. As I noted earlier, by beginning with the question of ordination, pro-gay advocates were asking for churchwide recognition of gay *leadership* before most people in the church had yet come to recognize gay *identity*. They were asking leaders of the "establishment" in church and society to recognize a group that, according to the establishment's own rules, did not exist. Or, at the very least, their existence was expected to remain out of sight, their identity buried in the closet. To put it another way, advocates of gay ordination were asking for the implicit endorsement of gay relationships before any religious context for the blessing of those relationships had been forged. It is no wonder that traditionalists interpreted this move as the advocacy of licentiousness. From this perspective, the churches may have had their questions exactly backward. As I shall explain in Chapter Four, civil rights for gay *individuals* (the presenting question of the 1970s) logically had to precede the question of civil rights for gay *relationships* (the presenting question today). Yet things sometimes work differently in the church. Because of the priority the church places on the exemplary character of ordained leadership, the morality and hence legitimacy of gay relationships logically precedes the question of the integrity of gay leadership. In other words, if the church were to create an appropriate context and standards for same-sex relationships, then the question of gay leadership would quickly fall into place.

The response of mainline religion was to welcome open and active gays and lesbians into church membership but to prevent them from becoming church leaders. This response was both innovative and traditional at the same time. It was innovative in pushing religious bodies beyond blanket condemnations and toward a more welcoming stance with respect to gay and lesbian persons as members of the community. At the same time, the policy was traditional in that it kept in place a modified form of prohibition, only now focused more narrowly on the issue of ordination: people in open gay or lesbian relationships were not to be ordained.

Reading Romans

In setting forth the prohibitionist position, I briefly examined the argument prohibitionists make from various passages of Scripture. Rather than rehearsing how each of the other six positions treat every relevant passage of Scripture, I shall instead focus illustratively on how the remaining positions treat just one text, namely, the apostle Paul's reflections on Greco-

Roman homoeroticism in Romans 1:18-32. This approach makes sense because many Christians consider Romans to be the pivotal text on this topic.

The key verses in Romans occur in a section where the apostle is describing humanity's descent into idolatry. Human beings have enough knowledge of God from the created order to know right from wrong, but because they have given up worshiping the Creator, God has given them over to the ungodly desires of their hearts. Says Paul:

> For this reason God gave them up to degrading passions. Their women exchanged natural intercourse (*phusikēn chrēsin*) for unnatural (*para phusin*), and in the same way also the men, giving up natural intercourse (*phusikēn chrēsin*) with women, were consumed with passion for one another. Men committed shameless acts with men and received in their own persons the due penalty for their error. (Rom. 1:26-27)

The picture here is one of a world run amok. Both the desires and the behaviors in question are said to be degrading and shameless. Therefore, such desire and conduct should be prohibited in the religious community and in society at large. It is useful to compare the tolerationist approach to this text with the prohibitionist approach. Advocates of prohibition tend to take what we might call a strict textualist approach to the Bible. They seek to discern the literal meaning of individual Bible verses and apply that meaning without compromise to the contemporary situation. In this approach, what the text says on its face is more important than how the text spoke to its own social or political context. The tolerationist position moves beyond the interpretation of isolated verses to look at how these verses function within the broader biblical passage. Instead of declaring that "these individual verses say X," the tolerationist approach is more one of "this passage as a whole says X."

The new tolerationist position toward gays that arose in the late 1970s noted that Paul is not speaking of specific homoerotically inclined individuals in this Romans text, but is speaking of gentile people in general. The overriding point of what he says in this first chapter of Romans is that both Jews and gentiles must live, not by the particulars of the Jewish Torah, but by faith in God's righteousness (1:17). Verses 16 and 17 begin a long string of subordinate clauses, each point flowing from what has preceded it.[29] The righteous must live by faith in order to escape the judgment of God, a judgment that justly falls on all, because all in various ways suppress the truth of God (1:18). This suppression of truth occurs even though God has made truth plain (1:19). Though in one sense divine truth is invisible, it has been made plain in creation, leaving people without excuse (1:20). Because humans have not honored what has been made known of God, the consequence is that their minds are clouded (1:21). This has become so much the situation that, even though people may claim wisdom, they have actually become fools (1:22). And their foolishness is manifest in that they have exchanged worship of the Creator for worship of things creaturely (1:23). This chain of reasoning leads Paul to the following conclusion:

> Therefore God gave them up in the lusts of their hearts to impurity, to the degrading of their bodies among themselves, because they exchanged the truth about God for a lie and worshiped and served the creature rather than the Creator, who is blessed forever! Amen. (1:24-25)

It is thus not so much that isolated individuals have chosen to be sexually profligate. Rather, this sexual chaos is the general result of living in a fallen world. Because Paul speaks negatively about certain homoerotic behavior here, such behavior cannot be approved. But because advocates of toleration believe that sexual orientation is not a choice, they try to accept gay people even while being disapproving of gay conduct.

A. Creation

The tolerationist position teaches that being gay or lesbian is not God's wish for humanity. However, because sexual orientation is not experienced as a straightforward choice, advocates of tolerance insist that same-gender sexuality should no longer be viewed as a "perversion" to be condemned but as something more akin to a "tragic condition" that needs to be understood. It is "tragic" not in the theatrical sense of a fatal personality flaw that leads to a person's downfall; rather, it is "tragic" in the sense that something unfortunate has befallen gay or lesbian people that is not of their own choosing or doing.

Because this is so, having a same-gender sexual orientation is a confusing and complex matter. One is not responsible for the condition, yet one is responsible for what one does with the condition. The condition is

63

not something to be condemned, but neither is acting out the condition something the church can say that God approves. This new teaching about sexual orientation also carried with it a recognition of a new phenomenon called *homophobia*. "Homophobia" is a word describing the irrational contempt for, hatred of, or fear of gay and lesbian people. According to typical mainline church statements, gay and lesbian persons are to be valued for who they are as fellow human beings made in the image of God, and not looked down on, hated, or feared.

B. Reconciliation in Christ

The key stance of the toleration position is *acknowledging* "homosexual orientation" while *rejecting* "homosexual practice." This has allowed a move from a condemnation to a noncondemnation of gay and lesbian people, while it has retained a scaled-down version of prohibition. In other words, perhaps a gay or lesbian person cannot help having a same-gender sexual orientation, but he or she can help acting on it — and thus should repent of any conduct deemed to be sinful. So how does the distinction between orientation and practice work itself out in the world of lived experience? Whereas the key doctrine is creation for prohibitionists (same-sex orientation is a perversion of the created order), the weight shifts to the doctrine of reconciliation for tolerationists (how we respond to the grace of God in Christ).

Recall that the prohibitionist position speaks in strong terms of the necessity for gays and lesbians to repent of homoerotic desire and conduct. The tolerationists see things differently: in keeping with the theology of Karl Barth and other theological movements from the mid-twentieth century, tolerationists see reconciliation as an event that involves the entire community and not just the isolated individual. A "double repentance" is required in order for all people to be reconciled in Christ. Straight people must repent of homophobia and of acting hatefully toward gay people; and gay people, even though they cannot help their gay *identity*, must repent of their gay *behavior*.

This double repentance is easy to identify in theory, but what it means for rank-and-file members of a religious community is not entirely clear. In the case of exclusively committed gay or lesbian couples, what support they can expect to receive from a tolerationist church is a murky business. On the one hand, by rejecting all same-sex practice, tolerationists seem to make no place at all for the enactment of such relationships; on the other hand, by affirming sexual orientation and freely inviting gays and lesbians into the fellowship of the church, they open the door for individual congregations to support gays and lesbians in ways they consider appropriate. The upshot is that some congregations welcome not only single gay individuals but gay couples in their midst, while other congregations welcome individuals but are ambivalent about gay relationships. This is the tension within which many religious communities are presently living.

C. Redemption in the Spirit

This leads us to the question of redemption. When one thinks through the reasoning of the tolerationist position all the way to the end, it is not apparent what a redeemed sexuality would look like for gay and lesbian people. Under this regime of a halfhearted toleration, is it possible for a gay or lesbian person to find any redemption or solace? The tolerationist teaching appears to be that gays and lesbians should not feel guilty about their sexual orientation, and yet they should refuse to act on it. They are best advised to accept their sexual orientation as a tragic burden and live life in a sort of Stoic abstinence.

Reflection

The strength of the tolerationist position is that it attempts simultaneously to hold a commitment to certain traditional biblical understandings about sexuality along with a recognition of new understandings about sexual orientation. Another advantage is that it tries to avoid the blanket condemnations that have often characterized prohibitionist rhetoric. The weaknesses of this approach will become apparent throughout the discussion of the remaining positions. But one major weakness is its inherent instability, as we can witness in the protracted conflict it has engendered in the churches for more than a quarter of a century. This instability comes from the sharp distinction it draws between orientation and practice, identity and behavior. Many people consider tolerationists inconsistent in accepting a person's sexual orientation but condemning the behavior to which that orientation

Table 1. Comparison of Viewpoints One and Two

Non-affirming Viewpoints

	Creation	*Reconciliation*	*Redemption*
Prohibition	Same-sex desire and be-havior = *perversion*	Repent of gay *identity;* the church prohibits gay desire and behavior	Return to true heterosexual nature
Toleration	Same-gender sexual orientation = *a tragic burden*	Repent of gay *choices;* welcoming of persons, non-affirming of deeds	Stoic acceptance of one's tragic fate through abstinence

naturally leads. If the church does not choose to condemn people for their gay identity, why condemn them for their gay behavior, provided that behavior is ordered in an ethically responsible way?

The net result is that gay and lesbian people are told that they are respected in their identities but not affirmed in them. They are told not to be ashamed of their desires but also not to act on them. They are welcomed as individual church members but not as committed couples. They are told to be visible in worship, but that in personal matters they should hide.

Similar anomalies are at work regarding whether gays can be ordained leaders. The tolerationist policy provides that sexual orientation is no bar to ordination, but then it adds the caveat that a gay individual's "self-affirming," "self-acknowledged," or "unrepentant" sexual conduct will bar ordination. For example, under the polity of the Presbyterian Church (U.S.A.) prior to 2011 the operative question was whether a person "refuses to repent" of a practice the church's confessions "call sin." Besides lacking any precision (in what does self-acknowledgment or refusal to repent consist?), this policy has led to hypocrisy in the churches that constantly scrutinize the supposed sins of gay people while simply ignoring other kinds of sin. In order to be disqualified, does a person first need to be asked to repent and then "refuse"? Or if the person engages in a persistent course of behavior, does that fact in itself constitute a "refusal to repent"? And how are these distinctions to be applied to persons in the church who run afoul of other forms of behavior that the confessions "call sin," such as greed, pride, arrogance, and so forth? What are the implications if the church ignores nonsexual departures from moral standards but continues to target people who are gay or lesbian?

Some have interpreted the net result of the tolerationist approach as something akin to the "don't ask, don't tell" policy that used to prevail in the U.S. military.[30] If gays and lesbians play by the rules and are circumspect about who they are, then certainly they may be ordained; however, if they insist on being both "self-affirming" and "practicing," then ordination is prohibited. One problem with this policy is that, if a gay or lesbian person gets "outed" through no choice of his or her own, then the toleration approach fails miserably. A person whose life is exposed in this way — and many have been — may be barred from ordination, even though he or she made no issue of his or her sexuality. To that extent, the toleration position places a much greater burden on gay and lesbian people than it does on others: they cannot be transparent about their lives.

Imagine a young gay man who is actively committed to the local ministry of his church and quietly committed to a lifelong partner. If this person is asked to become a deacon or elder in the local congregation, the practical result of the various tolerationist positions in mainline churches is this: no matter which way he turns, he must sacrifice his identity, his integrity, or his calling — and probably, at some deep level, all three. Advocates of this particular ecclesiastical policy tell gays and lesbians that the requirement that they remain celibate puts them in a position no different from that of a heterosexual person who, for whatever reason, is without a marriage partner. Yet this way of thinking is predicated on a hidden double standard. Even if a heterosexual person is presently without a mate, he or she still may nurture the hope of a union the church will gladly bless. This is not true for a gay or lesbian person under this church policy: he or she is told to renounce any such hope.

Tensions such as these create ambivalence concerning gay identity and gay life. And these kinds of tensions have led to various modifications and further critiques of the church's current position as represented in the viewpoints that follow.

III. Accommodation

Then Peter came and said to him, "Lord, if another member of the church sins against me, how often should I forgive? As many as seven times?" Jesus said to him, "Not seven times, but I tell you seventy-seven times."

(Matt. 18:21-22)

Discerning the Ways of God

The accommodationist position seeks to make a gracious exception for gay and lesbian people based on principles of compassion and the biblical view that all have sinned and fallen short of the glory of God (Rom. 3:23). This position was first put forward years ago by the German Lutheran theologian Helmut Thielicke in *The Ethics of Sex* (1964).[31] Thielicke describes same-sex eroticism as presenting a "borderline" ethical case, one in which the answer is neither straightforward nor obvious. According to Thielicke, the person who is constitutionally gay or lesbian exhibits a disordering of God's intention in creation. As such, he or she should be open to a "re-ordering" if possible. Barring that, the gay or lesbian person should live out his or her sexual orientation in an ethically responsible way. According to Thielicke, the church is empowered to extend pastoral acceptance to faithful gay or lesbian partnerships.

This accommodationist approach is based on a view of God as a gracious Redeemer who loves us and wants to see us flourish despite our many weaknesses. The idea of accommodation has a venerable pedigree in Christian theology. For example, the great Reformation theologian John Calvin emphasized God's benevolence, mercy, and understanding of our limited human capacities. The definition of religious faith, for Calvin, is to trust in God's accommodating mercy toward human beings. The central affirmation of the accommodation position is that we should show to other people the same mercy God shows to us.

The Case for Accommodation

Advocates of accommodation agree with the official "welcoming but non-affirming" teaching of the mainline churches, but they also hold that the church needs to extend grace to persons who are doing their best to live their sexual lives with integrity. Evangelical theologian Paul K. Jewett argues that, in a fallen world, the church may need to accept people and situations that it can neither celebrate nor bless.[32] Though such relationships are disobedient in form, they may nevertheless be obedient in substance. That is, there may be many virtuous aspects of such relationships even though they depart from the perfect will of God. Even those who have only limited experience with gay and lesbian people are aware that the real issues of life are complex and not easily handled with pat answers or superficial nostrums.

Many in the church know gay and lesbian people who are in lifelong relationships that are faithful, exclusive, and committed. Accordingly, they seek to discern a biblical and theological approach that takes account of this fact. They have seen gay and lesbian couples form families, rear children, care for aged parents, and watch with wonder as their children bring grandchildren into the world. They have witnessed gay and lesbian partners caring selflessly for each other through times of illness or trial, exhibiting the very same "till death do us part" kind of love that is the ideal of Christian marriage. Is it really responsible of the church to treat the families of gay and lesbian people as though they were somehow less righteous or holy than other families? The mainline churches have said, in effect, that a gay or lesbian sexual orientation is morally neutral. Does that mean that there is no morally acceptable expression of a gay or lesbian sexual orientation?

The formation of sexual identity in all persons — gay or straight — is a mystery fraught with potential for good and for ill. To reduce the relationship of any gay or lesbian couple to the sexual intimacy they may (or may not) be sharing is just as offensive and wrong-headed as declaring that heterosexual marriage is all about sex and nothing else. Take, for example, the advice given to gay and lesbian people by prohibitionists to try to "go straight." Is it really responsible to encourage gay and lesbian people to enter into marriages with members of the opposite sex when so often those marriages end in tragedy? It is true that some people have made such marriages work; and it is true that some of these marriages have ended with the former spouses remaining amicable. Yet how does one compensate for the ruined dreams of a woman who has given her life in good faith to her husband, only to find herself devastated and alone when he finally explains to her that he is gay, that he has known he was gay from his earliest days, and that he cannot force himself to live a charade any longer? What is the church's word to her? And at what point does the practical, human unworkability of a church teaching call the validity of that teaching into question?

The Bible itself praises the leadership and gifts of people who clearly departed from various moral commandments. Moses was a murderer, David an adulterer and murderer, and Paul a persecutor of Christ's church. The genealogy of Jesus himself is replete with persons of questionable sexual purity. This observation does not imply that we should therefore approve of murder, adultery, persecution, or any other sinful behavior. What it suggests is that, when the church says that a person is a "sinner," it is not the only — and certainly not the final — thing the church has to say about that person. All humans are sinners. The question is how to situate the lives of all sinners, whether gay or straight, within the arc of the unfolding drama of salvation.

Reading Romans

Given the fact that the New Testament does not anticipate the category of sexual orientation, accommodationists maintain that the church has the freedom in Christ to formulate pastoral advice to Christians who are living out a gay or lesbian existence in good faith. Richard Hays, a noted evangelical biblical scholar, points out that neither Romans nor any other New Testament passage articulates a clear "rule" about how to handle homoerotic conduct.[33] Rather, Hays observes, Paul provides in Romans a "diagnosis" of the human condition, in particular a description of how human beings have fallen into a condition of idolatry, namely, by worshiping the creature instead of the Creator (Rom. 1:25). Paul then points to the homoerotic practices of the Greco-Roman world as a vivid example of refusing to acknowledge God and the ways of God. In Hays's interpretation, it is a misreading of the passage to see homoerotic conduct as something that particularly provokes God's wrath; instead, it is the result of God's leaving human beings to their own devices.[34] Hays is very clear in his judgment that the Bible is uniformly negative in its assessment of homoerotic conduct: he calls it a "tragic distortion of the created order." Nonetheless, he concludes that "such a judgment leaves open many questions about how best to deal with the problem pastorally."[35] It is one thing to acknowledge a biblical injunction; it is another thing to live with it. If Jesus could be forgiving toward the woman caught in adultery, say accommodationists, there is room to be gracious toward people who are gays and lesbians.

A. Creation

Accommodationists usually agree with advocates of prohibition and toleration that a same-gender sexual orientation is a "tragic distortion of the created order." Yet all of life is marked by moral ambiguity, and the best any one of us can do, whether we are gay or straight, is to approximate goodness. Also, woven into the pastoral reflections of accommodationism is the recognition that a theology that focuses too much on creation is inadequate. Creation longs for and needs reconciliation and redemption; therefore, accommodationists argue that same-sex erotic relationships call for fresh thinking. They may require us to think beyond Scripture, as theologian George Hunsinger puts it, while still thinking with — not against — Scripture. Citing the ambiguities of human life, Hunsinger notes that having a same-gender sexual orientation is not a straightforward choice; that "reorientation" is a realistic option for only a few; and that while "chastity" may be demanded of all people, lifelong "celibacy" is a special gift of grace not given to everyone.[36] Therefore, even though same-sex eroticism cannot be declared normative, it is within the range of permissible exceptions.[37]

B. Reconciliation in Christ

Many accommodationists agree with the policy that the church should be welcoming but officially non-affirming. Still, they are ready to make exceptions in practice, often in the case of committed partnerships between gays and lesbians they happen to know. They are likely to point out that one biblical definition of sin, *hamartia,* is "missing the mark." We all miss the mark and are in need of grace. Gay and lesbian relationships may be imperfect, but so are relationships between married couples. In fact, though gay and lesbian relationships may be disobedient to the letter of Scripture in form, they may be obedient to the substance of Scripture when they involve lifelong, exclusive, and committed love.

Some have made the case for accommodation using a "lesser-of-the-evils" way of thinking. The church in the past has found it necessary, so the argument goes, to invest moral worth in relationships and deeds that do not, in themselves, reflect the perfect will of God. We know, for example, that the devastation of war is not God's will, yet sometimes war is the lesser of the evils. We know that the Sermon on the Mount speaks ill of divorce and remarriage, yet the church has permitted married people in distress to divorce and later remarry. If calculating the "lesser of the evils" has proven necessary in so many arenas of human life, then it does not make sense suddenly to apply an either-or, "take-it-or-leave-it" approach in evaluating the lives and loves of committed same-sex couples.

Accommodationists are also critical of interpreters who would read certain biblical admonitions literally and draw from them a mandate to strongly discipline or excommunicate gay and lesbian people. In a culture such as ours, in which marriage is being increasingly postponed until long after people reach sexual maturity, Hunsinger reminds us that the church has come to tolerate certain heterosexual "living together" arrangements. These arrangements are no more normative than same-sex partnerships are; but, he argues, neither are they outside the range of gracious accommodation.[38]

C. Redemption in the Spirit

If creation is central for prohibitionists and reconciliation for tolerationists, then redemption is the key doctrine for accommodationists. They seek not only the redemption of gay people but the redemption of the church's own integrity. As Paul Jewett comments, "Something has to be wrong with teaching that evokes absolute hatred, loathing, and disdain for homosexual people."[39] Some accommodationists may say that, in an ideal world, gays and lesbians would abstain from sexual relations altogether. Yet, being acutely aware of sin, many church people are also realists. Human beings were created to live in community. The desire to give and receive love is common to us all. Therefore, a committed partnership is better than promiscuity and may be the best moral choice for non-celibate gay and lesbian people. Seeing it as the lesser of the evils, then, many of today's Christians support sexually active gay men and lesbians who are faithful to a monogamous partner. In addition, the accommodationist position allows for responsible gradations in judgment. Most ordination standards include, either implicitly or explicitly, a requirement or vow of obedience to Scripture. Yet no one can live up to this standard fully.

Central to the accommodationist position is the conviction that God's grace extends no less freely or lovingly to gays and lesbians than it does to any other group of God's children. One of the basic teachings of the gospel is that each one of us has been adopted into God's family, not through any merit of our own, but solely through divine grace (Rom. 8:1-17). This is an adoption in which all of God's children are loved equally and extravagantly.

Reflection

The accommodationist position seeks to live within the traditional standards for sexuality but to interpret them with pastoral grace and sensitivity. It takes heterosexual marriage to be normative, but it allows for a range of pastoral exceptions. At their best, of course, all of the positions can be held with compassion and pastoral concern. The distinction is that the accommodationist position places the pastoral concern front and center, seeking to "accommodate" but not to "affirm" same-sex relationships. As such, this position arises as an internal modification and critique of the "welcoming but non-affirming" posture of the tolerationists. It offers a critique of but not a break with the other non-affirming views. The similarities and differences are summarized in Table 2.

One tension is that advocates of accommodation seem to want to have things both ways: they refuse to affirm same-sex relationships officially, but they make exceptions for them in private. They neither condemn gay relationships outright, as the prohibitionists do, nor can they bring themselves to bless them openly. For this reason, accommodationists may receive criticism from non-affirming and affirming positions alike. On the one hand, strict prohibitionists will object that accommodation leads to unacceptable compromises of biblical admonitions. On the other hand, gays and lesbians themselves may consider it condescending to have their commitments characterized as the "lesser of the evils." They may also wonder why accommodationists are willing to affirm only the exclusivity and commitment of gay and lesbian relationships but not to officially affirm or bless the relationships themselves.

Summary

Some people assert that all same-gender sexual behavior is immoral, and therefore they believe it is wrong to "affirm" such conduct in any way. These beliefs are based on (1) a judgment that the Bible is clear about prohibiting same-gender sexual behavior; (2) an argument that the church's theology of marriage requires that Christians limit sexual expression to marriage between a man and a woman; (3) arguments from "natural law," according to which sexual relationships between a man and a woman are natural and those between persons of the same gender are against nature;

Table 2. Comparison of Viewpoints One, Two, and Three

Non-affirming Viewpoints

	Creation	Reconciliation	Redemption
Prohibition	Same-sex desire and be-havior = *perversion*	Repent of gay *identity;* the church prohibits gay desire and behavior	Return to true heterosexual nature
Toleration	Same-gender sexual ori-entation = *a tragic burden*	Repent of gay *choices;* welcoming of persons, non-affirming of deeds	Stoic acceptance of one's tragic fate through absti-nence
Accommodation	Same-sex desire = tragic burden, but open to traces of grace	*Focus: gay and lesbian relationships.* While these are disobedient in form, they may be obedient in substance, if monoga-mous.	Exclusive, same-sex partner-ships are better than promis-cuity, i.e., they are the lesser of the evils.

and (4) centuries of Jewish and Christian moral teaching that condemns same-gender sexuality.

Prohibitionists, those who would absolutely ban same-sex unions, focus primarily on the order of creation. Thus, a particular understanding of the place of same-sex relationships in creation determines what prohibitionists say about reconciliation and redemption. In the 1970s, most mainline religious communities underwent a major shift in their view of same-gender sexuality, adopting an attitude of toleration but non-acceptance. This posture was innovative in that it pushed religious communities beyond blanket condemnations of gay people; but it retained a certain measure of prohibitionist sentiment, just that it was now directed at those who would seek leadership positions in the church.

The prohibitionist and tolerationist positions have in common the desire to uphold certain moral standards. A third position, accommodationism, seeks to carve out a quiet space to support gay and lesbian couples who desire to enter into such committed unions. Based on a "lesser-of-the-evils" argument, accommodation offers something less than full acceptance but something more than defining gays and lesbians as moral and religious pariahs. A strength of the accommodation position is its acknowledgment that, in living out our moral aspirations, we are all equally in need of the mercy and grace of God. The accommodationist perspective demonstrates this grace by reaching out in compassion to gays and lesbians as fellow children of God. Many people who in principle agree with the first two positions — prohibition or toleration — find themselves operating as accommodationists in practice when they are faced with gay people in real-life circumstances.

This means that the accommodationist position has great strategic importance in the struggle to gain affirmation for same-sex couples. Because accommodation offers something less than full acceptance, I believe that it is inadequate and wrong. Yet an accommodating posture has the merit of drawing religious communities one step further from the condemnation that has so often characterized Christian teaching on this subject, and one step closer to the welcoming and affirming stance to which, I believe, we should aspire.

As a practical matter, I believe that it takes two things for religious-minded people to move from being non-affirming to affirming. The first is actual firsthand experience with gay and lesbian people who are living lives of integrity. This first thing is the most important thing: it cannot be provided by books; it requires real-life experience. The second thing will be biblical and theological arguments that demonstrate the error of past moral teaching and provide persuasive reasons to begin thinking about this issue in a different way. It is to provide such arguments and reasons that I devote the next two chapters.

CHAPTER TWO

Toward a Welcoming, Affirming Church

The life of the Christian community has as its rationale . . . the task of teaching us to so order our relations that human beings may see themselves as desired, as the occasion of joy.

Rowan Williams

The official position of many religious communities, as I have noted in Chapter One, is to be welcoming of gay men and lesbians as individuals but to be non-affirming of gay and lesbian relationships. It is gay relationships, and especially gay relationships that dare to step out of the closet, that pose the stumbling block. Yet this "welcoming-but-non-affirming" policy is both self-contradictory and cruel. It is contradictory because it draws a distinction in theory that does not work in fact: to say to a person, "I accept your sexual orientation, but I condemn you for acting upon it," makes no sense either logically or practically. This religious teaching is also exceedingly cruel: its effect is to heap judgment and shame on gay and lesbian people while at the same time withholding from them — and from their families — the love and support that heterosexual people take for granted. In short, to be non-affirming is itself to be unwelcoming.

This does not mean that the three non-affirming positions presented in Chapter One are in every way false. First, the concern for upholding moral standards, as championed by the prohibitionist position, is in itself not a bad thing. But the standard that prohibitionists champion is, in fact, a double standard. What we need is a consistent standard that applies to gay and straight alike. The second viewpoint, toleration, seeks simultaneously to uphold standards while also rethinking standards in a way that moves beyond the harshness of prohibitionism. The problem is that mere toleration of gays and lesbians is not enough: it falls short of the mutual communion and fellowship that our religious beliefs themselves call us to embrace. The third viewpoint, the idea that we should accommodate one another in our differences, is a promising start toward a new way of living together with this issue. The point of this chapter, however, is to show that there are good biblical and theological reasons for going one step further.

The four positions explored in this chapter offer various ways of moving the church toward a welcoming and affirming stance toward exclusively committed same-sex couples. Being both welcoming and affirming of gays and lesbians is not a contradiction of the gospel but is a logical extension of everything the gospel teaches. More specifically, the gospel teaches that God has reached out in grace to embrace the human condition in Jesus Christ through the power of the Spirit. In other words, the doctrine of the Incarnation contains at its heart the divine welcoming of the other; and embodying that same welcome is at the heart of our obedient response to God's grace. The God who is for us and with us in Jesus Christ invites us, by the work of the Spirit, to be for and with one another. In order to be consistent with everything we know about the gospel and everything we know about the lived experience of gay and lesbian people, the church needs to craft a new teaching that can guide the people of God into a new day.

Viewpoint IV. Legitimation

There is therefore now no condemnation for those who are in Christ Jesus.

(Rom. 8:1)

Discerning the Ways of God

This position offers a stinging critique of the non-affirming stances, arguing that fundamental justice and fairness call into question the way both church and society treat gay men, lesbians, and other gender-varied persons as second-class citizens. To single out one group of people for special scrutiny, a scrutiny that is based on their sexual identity alone, is unfair. Moreover, there are good theological reasons for legitimating same-sex relationships and providing ethical guidance for living gay life with happiness and integrity. Advocates of legitimation argue that the policy adopted by most mainline churches of welcoming gays and lesbians as members but denying them access to ordained leadership — in essence treating them as second-class citizens — is unjust, denies the grace and love of God, and rests on a fragile biblical basis.[1]

To support these arguments, advocates of gay and lesbian legitimation point to the way the Bible portrays God as a God of righteousness and justice who embraces all people of every kind, especially those whom the world excludes. The founding narrative in Scripture is of God's activity to bring release to the captives (the Exodus) and deliverance to the despised and rejected (the Resurrection). Advocates of gay legitimation see the drama of creation, reconciliation, and redemption as a story of ever-widening grace. Given that God has reached out to all of us in grace, by what authority do we withhold that grace and acceptance from others?

In addition to pointing to the intrinsic character of God, advocates of gay and lesbian legitimation point to the witness of the Hebrew prophets, who chastised God's people when they failed to do justice. They point to Jesus' practice of sharing table fellowship with those whom Jesus' contemporaries considered outcasts and sinners. In that culture, Jesus' eating with those social outcasts was a sign of his acceptance of them. Furthermore, Jesus chose leaders who were deeply flawed by the world's standards but who nevertheless nurtured a passion for God's reign.

The Case for Legitimationism

Arguments for legitimationism appeal to justice, and these arguments take both political and religious forms. Within the political arena, many in our society have argued that discriminating against gay and lesbian people and excluding them from the benefits of the civil polity is a denial of the deepest principles of democracy. (I shall examine these arguments in detail in Chapters Four and Five.) A similar form of discrimination is also at work within the church. At the present time, gays and lesbians may be allowed to worship and/or become members of a church, but ordination to church office is often forbidden. A justice argument can be made that gay and lesbian church members should have the same opportunities for service as any other members. It is certainly true that no one "deserves" to be ordained to church office; it is a calling and a privilege, not a right. But, according to standard Christian teaching, those who present themselves for ordination are no more inherently worthy than members who are not ordained. As Paul points out in Romans, "There is no one who is righteous, not even one; there is no one who has understanding, there is no one who seeks God" (Rom. 3:10-11). He goes on to declare that, "since all have sinned and fall short of the glory of God," all must be "justified by [God's] grace as a gift" (Rom. 3:23-24). The implication is that no one has become a part of the church, nor has anyone been made an officer of the church, because of his or her intrinsic merit. This justice argument insists that, since all are equally sinners and — at least within the life of the church — all are equally saved by grace, then all should be equally eligible to serve.

Another argument within the church is that gay and lesbian equality is a consequence of Christian baptism. In baptism one acquires an identity in Christ that is not dependent on one's gender or gender orientation. Church policies of excluding gays and lesbians from leadership constitute a denial of the Christian identity that rightfully belongs to them by virtue of their inclusion in the covenant of grace at baptism. Such policies create first-class and second-class citizenship status in the church, which is a fundamental denial of the equality and justice to which all are entitled in Christ. In addition, the legitimationist position decries the way that simply *being* gay triggers a higher level of scrutiny in the church, no matter how much integrity may characterize a gay or lesbian person's way of life. This kind of scrutiny can evoke "witch-hunts," in which gay and lesbian people are viciously forced out of the closet (or "outed") and exposed through no self-avowal of their own. Many individuals who have been outed in this way have lost their ordination and have thus been denied their calling. And this goes on, say legitimation advocates, even while the church winks at heterosexual conduct that clearly falls short of the "fidelity and chastity" standards imposed to exclude gays.

It would seem that being anti-gay is somehow a socially accepted prejudice. This is so evident that theologians, including even some who have a non-affirming posture, have objected to the way the church zeroes in on the perceived sins of gay and lesbian people while shrugging its shoulders at so many other issues. One such scholar is Richard Hays, who sees no reason to erect a ban against gays while the church ignores other larger issues.[2] Hays insists that taking a stand against war and violence, for example, should be a higher priority for the church than enforcing certain rules about sexuality. After all, there are hundreds of sinful practices named in Scripture and in the traditions of the church. When was the last time that gluttony, for example, became a subject of special ecclesiastical scrutiny and inquiry?[3] Or what about "envying the prosperity of others"?[4] The Christian tradition has considered "twisting anyone's words" a sin, and this practice is amply evidenced in most church debates.[5]

Along this same line of argument, many advocates of the legitimation position want to take the same moral spotlight that has been directed at gays and lesbians and turn it back on the church itself. For a long time the church has been asking gays and lesbians to justify themselves before the bar of a high moral standard. Yet the church itself needs to account for its own acts of complicity in anti-gay attitudes. Churches spoke in favor of *civil* rights for gay people in the 1970s, but since then the churches on the whole have done little to make that — as well as ecclesiastical rights — a reality.

In short, advocates of legitimation emphasize that gay and lesbian people are our sons and our daughters, our brothers and our sisters, our coworkers and our friends — and our brothers and sisters in the church. They are children of God like everyone else, and both church and society have seriously let these children of God down, often with devastating consequences to them.

Reading Romans

As I have noted earlier, Paul refers to the hedonistic homoeroticism of the Roman world as an example of what happens when human beings do not give honor to God. Paul is not singling out the specific behaviors of specific individuals; rather, he is repeating a crude sexual slur that was commonly used in his culture to denigrate an opponent. He is engaged in a rhetorical ploy. To put it another way, the whole argument from Romans 1:8 to 3:20 is a highly polemical piece of writing that, ironically, follows pagan conventions. It is noteworthy that Paul mentions Christ only once (Rom. 2:16) in this whole passage, underscoring that here he is repeating a caricature with which many in the Roman Empire — both Jews and non-Jews — would have been familiar. His theological point is that failing to honor God has led many people into immorality and sexual chaos.

In addition, legitimationists argue, it will not do to quit reading Romans after the first chapter. If we continue reading, we discover that there is no condemnation from God for those who are in Christ (Rom. 8:1). Instead, Paul says that we are justified by grace through faith. This declaration has many implications; one of them is that the new life in Christ requires us to refrain from viewing one another in an overly harsh light:

> Why do you pass judgment on your brother or sister? Or you, why do you despise your brother or sister? For we will all stand before the judgment seat of God. . . . Let us therefore no longer pass judgment on one another, but resolve instead never to put a stumbling block or hindrance in the way of another. (Rom. 14:10, 13)

When Paul speaks of how to live an ethical life, he does not deal in rules and regulations but in placing one's whole being in the service of God. He understands specific commandments, including those regarding sexuality, to be summed up in the commandment to "love your neighbor as yourself" (Rom. 13:9). Knowing that who we are is a gift from God, we are called to live our lives through God and to God (Rom. 11:34-36). This means giving our bodies to God as a living sacrifice and living a life that constantly seeks to discern God's will (Rom. 12:1-2). There is no reason in principle that gay couples who are committed to God and exclusively committed to each other are incapable of seeking God's grace to live in an acceptable manner.

A. Creation

Legitimation advocates do not believe that being gay is a perversion, as the prohibitionists do, and they are not fixated on whether being gay is "unnatural." Some of them may share the assessment of various church statements that being gay or lesbian is an unfortunate tragedy. It may be something, frankly, that many of them would not wish for their own children. And yet, neither would they want their children — or any of God's children — to be subjected to the church's hypocrisy in handling this issue. To whatever extent being gay or lesbian is involved in sinfulness, a gay or lesbian is no more a sinner than anyone else.

B. Reconciliation in Christ

The key doctrine from the legitimationist standpoint is not creation but reconciliation. We saw in the preceding chapter that current church teaching, with its call for a double repentance, also emphasizes reconciliation. Yet legitimationists feel that the non-affirming positions do not carry reconciliation far enough. Legitimationists reject the logic (to them the illogic) of inviting people into church membership while excluding them from one of the benefits of membership, namely, church leadership. If one has the gifts for leadership, then one ought to be eligible for a leadership position. In particular, legitimationists object to treating the self-affirmation of gays and lesbians as somehow reprehensible. Being gay or lesbian is complex, and none of us is in a position to say what all gay people are like, any more than we can say what all racially or ethnically diverse people are like. We should deal with gay and lesbian people responsibly and respectfully as individuals created in the image of God.

C. Redemption in the Spirit

Legitimation advocates maintain that, in order to deal redemptively with gay and lesbian people, the church must offer them a greater hope than the stoical acquiescence to fate articulated by many of the older church position papers on this topic. God wants more for people than a lonely life of unhappiness. Moreover, the model of what redeemed life looks like should not be taken from "Ozzie and Harriet" or other stereotyped versions of the good life. Instead, redemption flows from the ministry and mission of Jesus Christ. To those who say that gays and lesbians are special kinds of "sinners" who are not fit for church leadership, legitimation advocates point out that many gay people have served in leadership positions through the ages. What is different now is that gays are making their sexual orientation known, that is, they are coming out of the closet. Even if there is some sin involved in gay relationships, all people are sinners by definition. Christ invited sinners of every kind to have table fellowship with him, and he chose leaders for the Christian movement who were hardly conventional. So many of the church's words and so many of its actions concerning gays and lesbians are profoundly contradictory to what the gospel proclaims. Legitimation advocates say that the church must quit speaking *to* or *at* gays and lesbians and begin walking in solidarity *with* them. And we should all yearn for that new form of community Jesus himself promised us, namely, a redeemed community in which our differences need no longer make a difference.

Reflection

It is difficult to dispute the claim that gays and lesbians have been singled out for special scorn in the church. Yet one problem the legitimationist position faces is how to translate its convictions about this exclusion into change within the church. Often legitimationists borrow their vocabulary from secular understandings of justice, and in doing so they fail to communicate effectively with rank-and-file church members. Even if some people are being unfairly excluded from church office, most church members do not think of ordination as a "right" that can be demanded in the cause of justice. Instead, it is a privilege that must be conferred for the benefit of the church. Genuine church leadership, many Protestants feel, should be servant leadership and not a leadership that draws attention to itself or is politicized.

Legitimation advocates readily grant this point; but they quickly counter that the privilege of ordination should be extended to all who have the gifts, regardless of race, ethnicity, gender, or gender orientation. They also point out that gay and lesbian Christians have already been ordained as servant leaders for years. Indeed, many have remained faithful to the church, even though they have experienced painful rejection at the church's hands.

A problem with the legitimationist appeal to justice is that, from time to time, it is off-putting to gays and lesbians themselves. It is not uncommon, for example, for some legitimation advocates to resort to the rhetoric of contemporary identity politics, adopting the language of "oppressors" and "oppressed," the language of "us against them." Andrew Sullivan, a gay Catholic, a blogger, and a former editor of *The New Republic,* has argued that gay people should not be portrayed as mere victims without choices, even with the burdens they sometimes face; nor are they

Table 3. Comparison of Viewpoints Three and Four

Non-affirming Viewpoint

	Creation	Reconciliation	Redemption
Accommodation	Same-sex desire = tragic burden, but open to traces of grace	*Focus: gay and lesbian relationships.* While these are disobedient in form, they may be obedient in substance, if monogamous.	Exclusive, same-sex partnerships are better than promiscuity, i.e., they are the lesser of the evils.

Critique of Non-affirming Viewpoint

	Creation	Reconciliation	Redemption
Legitimation	Same-sex desire = like all other sinful conditions	*Focus: ordination.* Repent of singling out gay sins and ignoring other sins.	Create a just world in which difference no longer makes a difference.

without powers of self-determination.[6] This places legitimation advocates in an awkward position as they seek to frame their message: on the one hand, gays and lesbians still suffer unfair abuse, sometimes of an outrageous sort; on the other hand, it is not accurate to portray them solely as victims. A better approach might be to connect the legal concept of *justice* to the theological concept of *justification*. According to the doctrine of justification by grace, all are in need of grace; all must rely on the justice and mercy of God for grace; and God's penchant for compassion and justice demands that all are entitled to equity and fair treatment.

V. Celebration

God saw everything that he had made, and indeed, it was very good.

(Gen. 1:31)

Discerning the Ways of God

The celebrationist position calls for the celebration of gay and lesbian relationships on the basis of a vision of God the Creator's delighting in the joys of the creature. A key biblical conviction for celebrationists is God's declaration that all things have been created to be "good" (Gen. 1:4, 10, 12, 18, 21, 25, 31). This includes the goodness of our embodied, sexual existence. Therefore, the question is whether gay and lesbian sexuality participates in this created goodness.

The Case for Celebration

The key assumption of celebrationists is that sexual orientation is not a choice but a given: it is part of a person's essential makeup. If this is true, it makes no sense to judge same-sex desires per se as somehow being perverted. As evidence for their position, celebrationists point out that same-sex coupling is a straightforward fact of natural life amply documented in scientific literature. Biologist Bruce Bagemihl, in a book entitled *Biological Exuberance: Animal Homosexuality and Natural Diversity*, presents evidence that some 471 animal species exhibit various forms of same-gender sexual activity, including in some cases mating for life.[7] Same-sex mating is evidenced in primate species closely connected to us, such as apes and chimpanzees, as well as in dolphins and other mammals, not to mention myriad species of birds. If same-gender mating patterns are so abundantly manifest in the animal world, celebrationists insist, then arguments that gay and lesbian life "violates nature" lose their credibility.

The celebrationist position offers the most direct counterpoint to prohibition. In some ways, in fact, it is prohibitionism's polar opposite, though at its best this position strives to be something more than merely a rebuttal. Whereas prohibitionists see nothing at all to "celebrate" in being gay, advocates of celebration argue that God wants gays and lesbians to celebrate the love they have found in their committed relationships — just as married heterosexual couples do. Most married couples would consider it degrading to have their relationships reduced to nothing more than a series of sex acts. And the same is true of gay and lesbian couples, many of whom resent the prohibitionists' fixation on genitalia, procreation, and kinds of sex acts. A powerful statement of the celebration position is provided by James Alison, a gay Roman Catholic priest. Recounting the suicidal feelings he struggled with as a gay adolescent, Alison tells of how the Catholic faith helped him discover what it means "to be rejoiced in as being gay."[8] Alison discovered not only the love of God but the profound fact that God actually "likes us."[9] God enjoys us and wants to have fellowship with us.

The celebrationists' affirmation of gay life goes beyond mere accommodation. They argue that committed gay and lesbian relationships should not be viewed simply as the lesser of the evils but as a positive good. Celebrationists also move one step beyond legitimationism because the latter argument can sometimes leave gay and lesbian people feeling that they are being patronized. It is not that church and society need to legitimate gay life, celebrationists argue; God has already legitimated gay and lesbian persons as part of the goodness of God's creation. Celebrationists insist that it is time for gays and lesbians to become comfortable with their own sexuality, to take control of their own destinies, and to quit making apologies for who they are. A hallmark of the celebrationist position is the admonition that gay and lesbian people need to put aside the self-loathing that society has taught them to feel.

For many gay men and lesbians the desire for a partner of the same gender is an enduring feature of their identity. And, as is the case with heterosexual marriage, what most homosexual people desire is not just the sex act but a deep and lasting relationship with another person. If that's true, then the church's telling a person with an exclusively same-sex orientation that he or she should be celibate or become heterosexual, as noted earlier, is both misguided and cruel — a denial of their basic humanity. According to celebrationist thinking, gay and lesbian people must thus learn not only to accept their sexual orientation but to embrace and affirm it.

In living into this affirmation, some lesbians have found that their experience differs from that of gay men. Lesbians not only have had to overcome the church's prejudice against gay people in general, but they must also contend with historic efforts in both church and society to keep women and women's sexuality under control. As one theologian has observed, every openly lesbian woman has had to affirm her own sexuality as being independent of men.[10] She has also had to say no, almost by definition, to traditional gender roles. In addition, it is not unusual for a lesbian to discover her sexual identity later in life, sometimes after having children of her own. In other words, lesbian sexuality can be seen as constituting a double threat to the traditional male leadership of the church, and for that reason the power dynamics play themselves out in unique ways.

Reading Romans

When gay and lesbian advocates of celebration read Romans, they feel the shock of nonrecognition, and their response is that Paul must be talking about someone else. When gay and lesbian people give themselves to one another in mutually committed love, they do not feel that they are following "the lusts of their hearts" or that they are engaging in "impurity" or the "degrading of their bodies." Insofar as they are committing their relationships to God, they definitely do not believe that they have "exchanged the truth about God for a lie and worshiped and served the creature rather than the Creator" (Rom. 1:25).

Celebrationists urge us to consider Paul's appeal to "nature" in its context. First of all, there is no word for "nature" in Hebrew, which means that Paul is not drawing directly on the Old Testament as his background source. Paul is a product of his time, and his thinking reflects the view that something is unnatural if it is unconventional or out of the ordinary: he applies the term "unnatural" to a range of behavior, from extreme acts of courage to such things as the perceived unnaturalness of eating meat.[11] Thus, when he speaks of sexuality in his letter to the Romans, Paul looks askance at people who "degrade" *(atimazō)* their bodies and do things that are "unnatural" *(para phusin)*.[12] But elsewhere in the New Testament, Paul uses the very same language to criticize men who wear long hair: "Does not nature *(phusis)* itself teach you that if a man wears long hair, it is degrading *(atimia)* to him?"[13] He considers the same to be true of women's hair fashions: "It is disgraceful *(aischron)* for a woman to have her hair cut off or to be shaved; she should wear a veil" (1 Cor. 11:6).[14]

If a cultural convention such as the length of one's hair is unnatural and degrading, this should signal to the New Testament interpreter that Paul is reflecting his own culture here and not the gospel; it should give pause to those who think that Paul, here in Romans, is speaking a word for all time. He cites the example of hedonistic homoeroticism from his culture to make a point that applies in all cultures, namely, that we should honor God. Thus, if gays and lesbians in our culture are seeking to honor God and one another in their relationships, the example is no longer applicable.

A. Creation

Creation is the key doctrine for this position. For celebrationists, the Christian tradition's long-standing denigration of pleasure needs to be reconsidered. Sexuality is not something to be ashamed of, and neither is one's sexual orientation. Throughout our lives we human beings need the physical, emotional, and spiritual embrace of other people. The celebrationist claim is that same-gender sexual orientation is neither a perversion (the prohibitionist viewpoint) nor a tragedy (the tolerationist and accommodationist viewpoints) but an integral feature of a person's identity. If this is true, it opens the door to recognizing that the desire to find a loving partner is something deeply and abidingly human.

In thinking about the reality of sexual orientation, most celebrationists are essentialists. They believe that people experience sexual orientation as a given rather than something they choose. After all, they point out, why would someone choose to be gay and thus become the recipient of so much anti-gay scorn? There are people with same-gender desire in all cultures, suggesting that such desire comes from somewhere other than custom, environment, or conditioning. Whether this is the case because of biology or because of a combination of other factors is not clear. But for essentialists, being gay or lesbian is not a simple choice but a natural fact of life, and hence it is part of the goodness of creation.

B. Reconciliation in Christ

While prohibitionists call upon gays and lesbians to repent of same-sex desire as well as sexual activity, celebrationists encourage gays and lesbians not to listen to these condemnations. They believe that all people have a right to give and receive love. Furthermore, all people have the responsibility to express their sexuality in a way that has integrity and does not do harm to others. In other words, the sin that gay people must repent of — as opposed to what the prohibitionists would declare — is the powerful self-loathing that society has taught them to feel about themselves. Psychiatrists have called this self-loathing "internalized homophobia," meaning that the fears and renunciations of society have become inscribed on the psyches of gays and lesbians themselves.

Hence reconciliation, for gays and lesbians, means coming to grips with the true goodness of their sexuality and especially the goodness of their same-sex orientation. The experience of "coming out" to themselves and to others is a way of saying yes to the God-givenness of the diversity of creation and the God-givenness of one's sexual orientation itself. Christian celebrationists, though they underscore sexuality as God's good gift, also acknowledge the need to confess when this good gift is abused and to take responsibility for the healing and restoration of broken relationships.

While the prohibitionist position locates sin in the "perverted" deeds of gays and lesbians, the celebrationists locate the sin in the way society persecutes, labels, and rejects gay and lesbian people. This rejection is all the worse for being based on what celebrationists are convinced is a misunderstanding of the biblical and scientific evidence.

C. Redemption in the Spirit

According to celebrationists, to be redeemed is to enter into the joy of celebrating one's God-given gay or lesbian identity and to be delivered from the unjust condemnation of an anti-gay society. In calling anti-gay condemnations "unjust," some celebrationists have taken pains not to turn the condemnation back on their accusers. In his book *Faith Beyond Resentment*, James Alison provides an account of how grace enabled him not to resent the mistreatment he endured at the hands of the church.[15] Many Christian celebrationists have been bold to claim that the fidelity gay and lesbian people show to the church, even in the midst of persecution, constitutes a transformative witness to the gospel.

Ethical guidance for celebrationists focuses on the nurturing of sexual relationships that are responsible, noncoercive, and nonabusive. Like the pastoral accommodationist approach, celebrationists are realistic in acknowledging that, even if gay marriage were an option, some gay and lesbian people would live together outside the bonds of marriage. Celebrationists insist that many couples who live together without being married — both gay and straight — have formed these relationships in Christian integrity. Examples they bring up include not only committed same-sex couples but elderly opposite-sex couples for whom marriage would work an economic hardship. Celebrationists also point out that living within the covenant of marriage does not in itself guarantee that a relationship is just or fair.[16] Celebrationists usually believe that there should be a single ethical standard that applies to all people.

Reflection

One of the strengths of the celebrationist viewpoint is that it holds up the core biblical belief that creation is good, providing a balance to the tendency of some prohibitionists to turn sexuality into something "dirty." In Christian terms, this is just one illustration of how the "no" uttered by the law can become separated from the "yes" declared by the gospel. The celebrationist position insists that the pendulum must swing back toward God's overriding, gracious "yes." Divine judgment is a part of the gospel, to be sure, but God's judgment is not the same thing as God's ultimate condemnation. Parents may issue a judgment that their children's behavior has gone astray; but a good parent does not let judgment and discipline come across as condemnation. Similarly, God's judgment reveals human deficiencies, but despite being under the judgment of God, God's "yes" resounds: "There is . . . now no condemnation for those who are in Christ Jesus" (Rom. 8:1).

Like the prohibitionists, celebrationists focus more on creation than on redemption. Prohibitionists take what they regard as the "fact" of gender complementarity in creation and make that normative for what it means to live a redeemed life. Similarly, celebrationists take what they believe to be a particular "fact" of creation — that is, sexual orientation — and make that normative for a redemptive Christian ethics. In other words, because one's sexual orientation is God-given, one must be entitled to celebrate it.

Critics may legitimately wonder whether celebrationists have clear ethical standards for same-gender sexuality. It is one thing to argue that gay and lesbian relationships can exhibit ethical standards that are the functional equivalent of "fidelity and chastity"; it is quite another thing to reject those standards outright. For instance, not all celebrationists have included monogamy among the ethical norms for sexuality.[17] They have sometimes answered this charge by pointing out that gay men and lesbians have had no choice but to love one another without the external constraints of monogamy; besides, their thinking goes, monogamy is not the only standard by which sexual relationships can function. Would it not be better to craft a single standard for all, some ask, one that is honest rather than hypocritical? This posture sometimes leads advocates of the other viewpoints to wonder, rightly or wrongly, whether the very language of "celebration" tends to glorify sexuality inappropriately. Why should the church modify its standards to conform to those of a culture that operates by a different set of values? If the church were to accommodate — or perhaps even affirm — same-sex relationships, why should it give its blessing to unions that are anything less than exclusive, monogamous, and intended to be for life? If there is to be a single standard for all, then shouldn't that standard be monogamy?

VI. Liberation

"The Spirit of the Lord is upon me, because he has anointed me to bring good news to the poor. He has sent me to proclaim release to the captives and recovery of sight to the blind, to let the oppressed go free, to proclaim the year of the Lord's favor."

(Luke 4:18-19)

Discerning the Ways of God

The liberationist position makes a pointed critique of all the other positions because of its unique vantage point. The liberation approach to theology is rooted in political engagement — and especially engagement on behalf of the disenfranchised. Liberationists are especially keen to critique abstract religious concepts that float free of lived experience. The published origins of the movement trace back to a 1972 text, *A Theology of Liberation,* by a Peruvian Roman Catholic theologian, Gustavo Gutiérrez.[18] Its deeper origins are in the radical Latin American social movements of the 1950s and 1960s, including the creation of ecclesiastical base communities that worked toward a critical transformation of society.[19]

Liberation theology is especially focused on the situation of struggle in which so many of this planet's humans find themselves living, especially in the so-called Third World. Some of the issues raised by the other positions we have discussed are controversies over the meaning of the good life, and as such these issues are important. However, liberationists point out that, for many people in the world, the pressing issue is one not merely of meaning but of survival. Liberation theology takes up a stance from the social and political margins: it argues that the God of biblical religion judges the proud and exalted in order to carry out what Gutíerrez has called a "preferential option for the poor." This does not mean that God cares only for the poor; rather, liberationists argue that God's concerns are best understood through the eyes of the suffering, the outcast, and the oppressed.

The Case for Liberation

Liberation theology insists that theological work must be contextual, rooted in the real struggles of oppressed peoples. Many varieties of liberation theology have emerged out of these struggles, including feminist, womanist, and mujerista theologies; black theologies in the United States; anti-apartheid theologies in South Africa; and various Asian liberation theologies, including Minjung theologies in Korea. It is not surprising, then, that a liberationist movement has been emerging that focuses on the oppression of gay, lesbian, bisexual, and transgender persons.[20] This GLBT liberationist movement is marked by significant diversity, which is not easy to capture in a brief summary.

One of its chief claims is that gender is highly complex and varies from culture to culture, and that it is about much more than sexual orientation. Like everything else, sexuality is a product of power relationships that pervade the religious, educational, medical, and other spheres in which we live our lives. According to the French theorist Michel Foucault, it is not merely that power regulates the way we think about our bodies; but power actually inscribes itself on our bodies and gives them their gendered features in ways that are quite culturally specific and controlling.[21] The way a man carries himself, the way a woman walks, or the way we regard one another's bodies — all are culturally inscribed. One reason that same-sex desire looks different in different times and places is that hidden social forces cause it to emerge in unique ways in various contexts.

As one might expect, liberation theology shares many of the concerns of the legitimationist position I have investigated above. Both positions are committed to seeing biblical justice realized; both understand that justice requires a special effort to care for persons who have been disenfranchised; both long for a world in which human differences need not make a difference, nor divide people needlessly. Nevertheless, the two positions are not the same. Liberationists are concerned that some liberal versions of justice are satisfied with mere "progress" rather than striving for more fundamental and systemic change. In particular, many liberation theologians have found inspiration in Marxist class analysis, and they sympathize with its critique of the capitalist economic system.[22] Even though Marxism is no longer as potent a political force today (following the collapse of the Soviet Union in 1990) as it was last century, it would be a mistake to think that the concept of economic class has ceased to play a role in contemporary social analysis.[23] This is especially true regarding issues of marriage and family: some scholars argue that the family has been reduced to an engine of consumption, and that it works to exploit all its members — particularly women.[24]

The liberationist stance also shares certain concerns with the celebrationist position. Among these is its desire to remove the stigma from GLBT people that has been imposed on them by the non-affirming positions.[25] However, liberationism also differs from celebrationism in significant ways. First, whereas celebrationists tend to be essentialists in their views of same-gender sexual desire, liberationists for the most part are social constructionists: they emphasize that, no matter what the biological basis of sexuality might be, same-gender sexual orientation is culturally conditioned and needs to be interpreted as such.[26] Greek pederasty, for example, differs from female romantic friendship in the nineteenth century. The occasional but deep same-sex friendships of an Eleanor Roosevelt or an Abraham Lincoln are very different from same-sex acts performed as a rite of passage to adulthood among the tribes of New Guinea.[27] This has led liberationists to emphasize the complexity of gender formation. Whereas celebrationists are more concerned with validating a particular gender identity, liberationists are more concerned with protecting a range of gendered differences. If the slogan of celebrationism is "Gay is good," one of the slogans of liberationism is "Gay is not all there is." Liberationists are concerned to move beyond the binary oppositions of "straight-gay" or "heterosexual-homosexual"; for them, gender is a variable reality that does not fit neatly into oppositional categories.[28]

Second, the liberationist emphasis on culture is combined with a recognition of new scientific insights into the complexities of gender formation in gender-varied persons.[29] We know that at least one in a thousand infants are born with a physical anatomy that cannot be clearly designated male or female.[30] These infants are often assigned a gender by parents or medical professionals arbitrarily. We also know that some people are born genetically male but are anatomically female — and vice versa.[31] A different kind of phenomenon, but one that also matters to liberationists, is that of cross-dressers, or transvestites: these are heterosexual men who derive sexual pleasure from wearing women's clothing. One of the goals of the liberationist perspective is to promote compassion and justice for all individuals who diverge from society's gender norms.

Third, liberationists usually employ a more complex understanding of power than do celebrationists. Celebrationists have tended to accept what is known as the "repressive hypothesis": the idea that religious society operates to repress natural human sexual drives that are essential and normal. The goal of celebrationists is to eliminate these repressive mechanisms in order to allow people's true sexuality to emerge and receive affirmation. Liberationists are equally committed to challenging societal control of gender-varied persons; but they tend to regard the repressive hypothesis as much too simple. Informed by the work of Foucault, liberationists argue that sexuality has not so much been repressed by society as it has been transformed into something constantly being investigated. Foucault argues that, in premodern society, sex did not occupy center stage the way it does today. The constant attention focused on sex in modern culture by clergy, physicians, psychiatrists, and police has created an "incitement" to talk about or reflect on sex all the time. Liberationists are less concerned with celebrating sexuality as such and more concerned with pointing out how society has assigned pariah roles to gays and lesbians in a drama not of their own choosing. Moreover, liberationists contend that the categories of "gay" and "lesbian" do not exhaust the gender identities that actually exist. This is one reason that liberationists have also championed the concerns of bisexual and transgender people. Within the realm of legal scholarship, they have been concerned that the strategy of appealing to the fixed nature of sexual orientation in order to gain legal rights for gay people may have the unwanted side effect of causing society to look on gender-varied persons with pity rather than respecting the integrity of their life choices.[32]

Reading Romans

Liberationists consider gender to be an ambiguous social construction. They are also attuned to ways in which gender roles serve as a form of social control. Therefore, when it comes to interpreting Paul's letter to the Romans, the liberation perspective homes in not only on what the text says but on what it leaves unsaid. Paul describes gentile women as having given up the "natural way" in sexual intercourse (the phrase in Greek, *phusikēn chrēsin*, literally means "natural use").[33] It implies that sex is something that men are supposed to do, not so much *with* women as *to* them. According to Roman conventions of sexuality, a true man was always supposed to be in control of the sex act.[34] From a liberationist perspective, then, we cannot glean the authoritative meaning of this text without disentangling that meaning from the Roman cultural norms that we wouldn't want to perpetuate today.

Another issue is to determine precisely what the conduct is that Paul refers to in a derogatory way in Romans. Not only does Paul's reference to women assume female submission to males, but it is ambiguous: many take the term that has been translated "unnatural" *(para phusin)* to be a reference to female homoeroticism.[35] This is a possible meaning but by no means the only possible meaning. In Paul's day the term *para phusin* was sometimes used of lesbian sexuality; but it could also refer to female heterosexual behavior that was overly aggressive or violated sexual conventions. For example, the historical record indicates that some of Paul's contemporaries looked down on women who performed oral sex on a man, considering that to be against nature.[36] Others questioned what they perceived as female aggressiveness when women adopted a more active role in sexual relations with men.[37] As a typical Jew, Paul would have considered all of these behaviors to exceed the "natural way" for heterosexual intercourse. It is thus impossible to say with certainty what female behavior Paul had in mind.

As modern interpreters, we have imposed our binary grid of gay-straight and homosexual-heterosexual on the text. Paul's language does not assume these binary oppositions. He may be referring more generally to women who engage in sexual libertinism of any kind, whether hetero- or homoerotic. We need to recognize, therefore, that surface readings of the text are not helpful. As I have noted above, liberationists influenced by Michel Foucault would want to emphasize the way power is at work in the dominant discourse of a society, including Paul's society. Power operates not only in the ways that cultural elites define sexuality but also through the subtle and often hidden resistance to the dominant discourse of a society.

A. Creation

We will recall that celebrationists tend to mirror prohibitionists in focusing on the doctrine of creation. Celebrationists argue that gay sexuality is a part of natural created life, thus opposing the prohibitionist claim about a fixed order of nature by putting forward a fixed category of their own — namely, sexual orientation. In contrast, liberationists think of sexuality less as a matter of natural life and more the result of nurtured life. Some liberationists follow the work of theorist Judith Butler in conceiving of gender not as a given but as something performative.[38] For Butler, gender is not innate but arises when people act out the "script" written by custom and cultural expectations. Imagine a dinner party where, at the end, the women swing into motion to clear the table, make ready dessert, pour coffee, and begin the process of cleaning up, while the men remain seated, continue their conversation, and are content to be waited on by the women. Both the women and the men in this picture are doing "what comes naturally"; but what they are doing is determined not by biology but by social custom. A person's sense of what is expected of him or her as male or female is encoded through countless social interchanges and the lifelong acting out of roles that are sometimes more implicit than explicit. Many people assume that sex is biological and gender is sociological. For Butler, however, our sexual desires — and even the very sensations we consider to be sexual — are not simply biological givens but arise through cultural conditioning.

Accordingly, a major claim of the liberationists is that the other positions do not adequately appreciate the complexity of human sexuality. Liberationists especially want to problematize the claim that there is a fixed order of creation that dictates a clear-cut definition of what is legitimately male and female. For them, the very existence of gender-varied persons contests the idea that we can neatly divide the world up into categories of male and female, heterosexual and homosexual. In this regard, biologist Anne Fausto-Sterling has spoken of five genders.[39] In addition to the categories of males (having testes plus male genitalia) and females (having ovaries plus female genitalia), there are also "herms" (those having one ovary, one testis, and either male or female genitalia, or both), "ferms" (having ovaries plus male genitalia), and "merms" (having testes plus female genitalia).

Thus, liberationists claim that the "male and female" of the Bible's account of creation should be read as a trope that includes all forms of the human and not as a marker for fixed gender identities or roles.

B. Reconciliation in Christ

Reconciliation is about coming into right relationships with God and with one's fellow human beings. Reconciliation is the pivotal category for liberationists, because one of the chief ways reconciliation happens is by standing in solidarity with the poor, the outcast, and the oppressed. For gender liberationists, this solidarity includes an openness to gender-varied persons. Argentinian theologian Marcella Althaus-Reid makes a theological case for this solidarity through a radicalization of the basic Christian doctrine of the Incarnation.[40] If God embraces our humanity in Jesus Christ, she reasons, then God must embrace the humanity of *all* human beings, including those whose sexuality falls outside traditional norms. Our God is one whose love for us is not bound by human categories of what is decent or indecent, which means that theology itself must risk defying conventional categories and thus becoming "indecent."[41] It must strive for something more revolutionary than a church that is grudgingly inclusive of gays and transgender persons; it longs for a church that embodies Jesus' own solidarity with those whom the world casts off. Rather than reaching out to the outcast, the gospel calls us to *become* outcasts for God's sake.

I have observed above that prohibitionists call on gays to repent of their desires and their life choices. We have seen that advocates of toleration seek to balance this by calling on straight people to repent of homophobia. For celebrationists, by contrast, the idea of repentance was very different: gays must put aside the negative stereotypes imposed on them by society in order to become reconciled to the goodness of their own sexuality. Liberationists carry this claim made by celebrationists a step further: not only must gays put aside society's negative stereotypes, but all of us must recognize that our gender categories, especially the binary opposition between gay and straight, homosexual and heterosexual, are social constructs that can operate in oppressive ways.

C. Redemption in the Spirit

A vision of redemption provides a road map for how life ought to be lived in the power of the Spirit. We have seen that the legitimationist position advocates a form of justice in which a person's differences from "the norm" will no longer make a difference in how we treat him or her. For liberation-

Table 4. Comparison of Viewpoints Five and Six

Welcoming and Affirming Viewpoints

	Creation	Reconciliation	Redemption
Celebration	*Essentialist:* being gay is a fact of "natural" life.	Gays and lesbians need to be reconciled to the goodness of their sexual orientation.	Live into one's sexual orientation as God's good gift.
Liberation	*Social construction:* a fact of nurtured life	Challenge binary gender categories (male/female).	Affirm complexity of gender choices.

ists, this is a worthy goal at one level, but it is too limited at another level. Liberationists do not want us to simply cover over our differences. We need to strive for a world where being different does not trigger ill treatment but where differences are not ignored either — indeed where differences are valued for what they are.

For liberationists, the fact that gays and lesbians are vilified and condemned as part of an elaborate social construction of reality requires special scrutiny. That these negative evaluations are social constructions means that they can be deconstructed and also reconstructed. One pathway toward reconstruction is the adoption of a new usage of the word "queer," a word often used in the past as a derogatory and offensive reference to gay people. In contrast to this derogatory usage, many gay people today have turned the tables and assumed the label "queer" as a matter of pride. Some Christian theologians have likened this to the early Christian transformation of the shameful symbol of the cross into a positive and powerful image of the Christian faith, or the appropriation of the word "slave/servant" as a vital metaphor for what it means to be a Christian.

Reflection

The strength of the liberationist position is its passionate concern for those who reside on the margins of society, not only sexual minorities in general but even those on the margins of the gay and lesbian community itself. The crux of the liberationist position is that gay, lesbian, bisexual, and transgender persons need to be freed from the social expectations of binary gender categories. The net result is that this position levels a critique in two directions: it not only contests the suppression of gay identity by prohibitionists, but it also problematizes the particular one-dimensional portrayal of gay identity put forward by some celebrationists.

In order to carry on this twofold critique, liberationists have generated intricate criticisms of many of the foundational assumptions of Western culture; but they have also registered objections to the standard appeal to sexual orientation as a justification for gay rights. Since liberationists are not willing to base their theological judgments on the uncritical givenness of tradition, their position is sometimes hard to pin down. In challenging stark, binary oppositions, they insist that the categories ordinarily used to define gay, lesbian, bisexual, and transgender persons are not adequate. But one may ask whether the very paradigm of liberation versus oppression presents a similar binary opposition that would itself need to be problematized.

In its approach to gender, the liberationist movement has so far been more deconstructive than constructive or reconstructive. It has emphasized "liberation from" more than "liberation for," and this has led some who are otherwise sympathetic to liberationist goals to criticize the liberationist methods of reaching those goals. A common complaint is that some of today's gay liberationists use jargon that is not easily understood by ordinary people, including the very people they wish to help. A classic example of this complaint is feminist philosopher Martha Nussbaum's sharply critical review of the work of Judith Butler.[42] Nussbaum objects that Butler's impenetrable and self-referential jargon makes a pretense to sophistication but is in fact sophistry. Nussbaum pulls no punches: "Hungry women are not fed by this, battered women are not sheltered by it, raped women do not find justice in it, gays and lesbians do not achieve legal protections through it."

This is a powerful objection. It makes one wonder how liberationists hope to succeed in making a place for gays and lesbians within the established social order. The liberationist rejoinder, of course, is that securing one's place in the established order is of no help if the established order itself is the problem. But this poses the question of precisely what the problem is and how it is to be remedied. It is not enough merely to criticize the status quo. One must put forward a positive vision of what a rightly ordered social world would look like.

That is what the final position seeks to do. The goal of the consecration position is to transform the established order in a way that makes a place for gay, lesbian, and other gender-varied people. By consecrating gay unions, advocates of this position hope to affirm the best features of each of the other positions. They hope to emulate the call to moral clarity of the non-affirming positions while at the same time to follow the welcoming and affirming positions in honoring the moral integrity of committed gay unions.

VII. Consecration

"I am about to do a new thing; now it springs forth, do you not perceive it?"

(Isa. 43:19)

Discerning the Ways of God

The consecration position centers on the God who does surprising new things in the world. A consecration approach to gay unions has much to commend it, and this is the perspective that I adopt and set forth in more detail in the next chapter. To speak of consecrating a committed relationship is to refer to a liturgical act of extending God's blessing to a committed couple within the context of a worshiping and believing community. Marriage is clearly an act of consecration, but so too would be the ecclesial blessing of a civil union. I am using consecration, then, as an encompassing term that includes both traditional marriage and the blessing of gay unions.

Blessing gay commitments either through expanding the definition of marriage or through the creation of civil unions is definitely a new thing. Yet the Christian church itself began as one of those surprising new things of God. If our God is the living God, then we surely can expect this God to be at work in unexpected ways to accomplish human flourishing and to enable people to embody God's purposes. The consecration of gay unions is a new thing, but those of us who are advocates of this position appeal to some of the church's deepest convictions about the nature of God's grace.

The Case for Consecration

Consecration makes a biblical and theological case not only for *affirming* same-sex unions but also for *consecrating* such unions when they are exclusive, committed, and intended to be for life. According to the consecrationist view, the church today needs something more than the current policy that most mainline churches have of merely welcoming gay men and lesbians into membership as individuals but refusing to affirm their relationships. Within the rhythm of its life and worship, the church should not only open its arms to gay men and lesbians but also provide its blessing on their committed relationships.

Although since becoming Archbishop of Canterbury he has said that his personal views must take second place, the most formidable advocate of the consecrationist position to date is Rowan Williams, formerly a theology professor at both Oxford and Cambridge.[43] In approaching human sexuality, Williams does not see the first question as "Am I keeping the rules?" (as it is for the prohibitionists) or "Am I being sincere and not hurtful?" (as it is for the celebrationists). Rather, he sees the first question as this: "What does my relationship signify or demonstrate concerning the faithfulness and grace of God?"[44] In an important essay on this subject, "The Body's Grace," Williams argues that we need to take a step back and ask ourselves what the purpose of sexual desire is in the first place.[45] What place does sexuality have within God's economy of salvation? The answer Williams gives is that human sexual desire, especially when rightly ordered, reflects God's own desire for God's people. Just as God makes a covenant with God's people, so also they should order their sexual relationships in committed, covenantal ways that give glory to God.

Therefore, for Williams, the focus needs to shift from sex acts to relationships. Sex acts may serve to bring a certain physical release, but living in a conjugal relationship that is exclusive, committed, and long-term can go much further: it can bring joy. One of Williams's major constructive moves is to declare that, for one person's body to experience sexual joy, it must be open to becoming the occasion of joy for another. It requires more than physical, sexual performance for this to happen; it requires that the couple be willing to give time to one another in "a commitment without limits." Only with the gift of time does the gift of sexuality blossom into all that God intends it to be. The arguments Williams makes are based on a resolutely Christological foundation. The Christian gospel is about the Savior who "made his entire life a sign that speaks of God."[46] Williams follows Karl Barth in declaring that Jesus Christ is the greatest sacrament between God and human beings.[47] The sacramental quality of God's salvation in Jesus Christ in turn provides human life with a promise. By the grace of the Spirit, we, too, can become signs of God. And our committed, conjugal relationships in particular "can speak of mercy, faithfulness, transfiguration, and hope." Just as God has demonstrated love to the world through the gift of Jesus Christ (John 3:16), so also do two people commit themselves to each other in Christian love and give themselves sacrificially to each other, thereby becoming a sacramental sign of God's love in Christ (Eph. 5:21-22). In this way, committed, covenantal relationships not only remind us of God's deep desire for God's people, but they become a gift to the wider community: "The life of the Christian community has as its rationale . . . the task of teaching us to so order our relations that human beings may see themselves as desired, as the occasion of joy."[48]

Building on Rowan Williams's reflections, theologian Eugene Rogers argues that the commitment of marriage is a means of grace that nurtures Christians in the ways of the gospel.[49] The purpose of sexual desire, when properly understood and practiced, is to lift us up into that covenantal desire that God has for people in Jesus Christ by the Spirit's power. When we think of it that way, the church not only can but should reach out to honor, support, nurture, and ritually bless gay and lesbian couples whose exclusive commitments are deliberately structured as a means of grace. Gray Temple, a charismatic Episcopal priest in Atlanta, has argued that reaching out in this way to support gay unions flows from the church's discernment of the Spirit and would constitute a proper exercise of the "keys to the Kingdom."[50] Rogers goes a step further: because marriage is a means of grace, and because being excluded from marriage may lead some to leave the church, denying gays and lesbians the rite of marriage is nothing less than to deny them the gospel itself.

The consecrationist approach has the potential, I believe, to draw on the best of the other six positions. It agrees with the welcoming and affirming viewpoints we have discussed above that the gospel is calling on the people of God to embrace gay life and love. At the same time, consecration agrees with the non-affirming viewpoints that human sexuality needs to be ordered in a covenantal context with the intention of being exclusive and lifelong. For this reason, consecration is best described not only as welcoming and affirming but as welcoming, affirming, and *ordering*.

Reading Romans

It is not enough to marshal every biblical text that speaks of homoerotic activity and fool ourselves into thinking that we have thereby uncovered all that the gospel has to say on the subject. Merely citing Scripture is not enough, any more than citing every biblical passage on "kingship" or the "reign of God" would automatically yield a blueprint for governing the nations and peoples of a globalized world, or that cataloguing every biblical reference to war and peace would thereby give us a workable foreign policy for the nuclear, post-9/11 world.

Moving beyond the textualism of the non-affirming positions, and agreeing with the contextualism of the welcoming and affirming positions, consecrationism asks us to take a step further and consider what the gospel is bringing into being in our own context. In order to do this, we must not rest content reading the first chapter of Romans. Instead, we must continue reading Romans to the end: if we do, we discover that, in Romans 11, Paul once again picks up the language of unnatural acts from Romans 1 — but with a surprising twist.[51] Paul's argument in Romans 9-11 is that the gentiles (that is, those from the non-Jewish nations whom Jews considered to be ritually and morally unclean) have been grafted into the covenant God originally made with Israel. This is an astonishing teaching. It is one thing for God to act graciously toward the ritually and morally unclean; it is quite another thing to include them in the covenant and, in effect, make them full members of one's family of faith. It turns out that, from Paul's perspective, this was one of God's aims for the original covenant to begin with — that is, for Jews and non-Jews to be a blessing to one another. God's making this happen defied all the religious expectations of Paul's Jewish contemporaries.

To put it another way, God defies our ordinary religious categories in order to bless the whole people of God. Paul explains it this way:

> For if you [gentiles] have been cut from what is by nature *(kata phusin)* a wild olive tree and grafted, contrary to nature *(para phusin)*, into a cultivated olive tree, how much more will these natural *(kata phusin)* branches be grafted back into their own olive tree. (Rom. 11:24)[52]

Notice what is happening here. In Romans 1, Paul says that the gentiles have sexual habits that are unconventional or contrary to nature *(para phusin);* in Romans 11, Paul uses the very language from chapter 1 to describe God's own action of including these gentiles within the covenant of grace. God acts contrary to what seems natural *(para phusin)* in order to graft these very same gentiles into God's original covenant with the Jews. We must remember that Paul constructed the argument of Romans in the first place precisely to defend God's gracious activity among these gentile people whom Jews considered ritually and morally — indeed sexually — unclean.[53]

If we view it from this perspective, the noteworthy thing about the letter to the Romans is not that it has a negative view of homoeroticism in the gentile world. All Jews did in those days. The amazing thing is that this did not prevent Paul from reaching out to them. His goal as an apostle, in fact, was to reach *all* the gentiles (Rom. 1:5). He wrote to all God's people in Rome (1:7), thanking God for them all; he considered the gospel to belong to all, both Jew and Gentile (1:16); in order to defend his mission, Paul tells us that all have sinned — Jews as well as gentiles (Rom. 1:18; 2:12, 16; 3:9). But then, in God's mercy, all have been included so that there is no longer any distinction between Jew and gentile: "There is no distinction between Jew and Greek; the same Lord is Lord of all and is generous to all who call on him" (10:12). And all this is part of God's own mysterious plan for the world. Paul's argument is that "God has imprisoned all in disobedience" for the very reason that God wanted to "be merciful to all" (Rom. 11:32).

That God shows mercy to the gentiles does not, of course, mean they are entitled to continue their sexual hedonism. Paul's ethical advice to them is clear: "Let us live honorably as in the day, not in reveling and drunkenness, not in debauchery and licentiousness, not in quarreling and jealousy. Instead, put on the Lord Jesus Christ, and make no provision for the flesh, to gratify its desires" (Rom. 13:13-14). In other words, members of the body of Christ are to shun their former ways of immorality. Nevertheless, the ethical life to which Paul calls them is one of discernment from the heart and not mere external conformity to convention. In Romans 12 he admonishes them to "present your bodies as a living sacrifice, holy and acceptable to God, which is your spiritual worship" (Rom. 12:1). They are to obey God's commandments, such as "You shall not commit adultery; You shall not murder; You shall not steal; You shall not covet." Yet, as I have observed above, he also says that these "and any other commandment, are summed up in this word, 'Love your neighbor as yourself'" (Rom. 13:9).

From the consecrationist perspective, living a gay or lesbian life in covenant partnership is in keeping with the ethical discernment that the new life in the Spirit requires. It is important to look at the reason for a rule as one interprets that rule. The reason behind Paul's admonition is to enable one to live a holy life, and living in a consecrated relationship furthers that end. As we shall see in the next chapter, consecrationism similarly looks at the scriptural purposes of marriage between a man and a woman in order to find scriptural reasoning for supporting unions — even marriages — between gay couples who are ready to commit their lives to one another. But before doing so, let us consider how the consecrationist position envisions the place of gay life within the drama of creation, reconciliation, and redemption.

A. Creation

Creation is not an end in itself but finds its fulfillment in redemption. All the positions that we have considered so far agree with this in principle. But the consecrationist position takes this insight and makes it the chief principle on which everything turns. If prohibitionism and celebrationism focus mainly on the order of creation, and if the tolerationist and legitimationist positions focus more on the doctrine of reconciliation, then accommodation and consecration cast their primary gaze on redemption: it is only from the standpoint of redemption that the truth about creation becomes clear. Accordingly, consecrationists Rowan Williams and Eugene Rogers, for example, say very little about the status of homoerotic desire within creation. For them, such desire apparently presents itself as a fact of nature, having the potential for sin but also the potential to partake in the goodness God intends for all of creation. The main thing is that they do not think of sexuality as good in itself, as the celebrationist approach does. It is not sex but rather humans who are God's good gift. The goodness or badness of sexuality is to be judged on the basis of the context in which it occurs, and thus sexuality needs to be rightly ordered to be what God would have it be.

This means, among other things, that one cannot learn about the meaning of sexuality merely from examining nature. Hence the prohibitionist claim that we can understand the purpose of sexuality merely from examining the sex act is a profound theological mistake. It is not just that consecrationism disagrees with those who are non-affirming here; the problem goes much deeper: consecrationists see nothing distinctively *theological* about the non-affirming argument. Consecrationists want arguments that are firmly rooted in the character of God and the reality of God's grace, and this requires more than a selective quoting of Scripture.

This conviction leads consecrationists to reject both the claims of some prohibitionists that gay and lesbian sexuality violates nature and the claims of some celebrationists that gay and lesbian sexuality is good in and of itself. Consecrationists are inclined to say that nothing is good "in and of itself" except God. The question really is: How do we relate our lives to God's life in ways that are life-giving for ourselves and others?

B. Reconciliation in Christ

In keeping with their contextualist understanding of sexuality, consecrationists have a contextual understanding of sin. They disagree with prohibitionists and advocates of mere toleration that homosexual orientation is sinful per se, or that it is always and invariably the result of sin. Sin does not reside in sexual orientation per se, but in whether or not one rightly orders one's life. Failure to reach out and support gay and lesbian couples when they display real integrity in their relationships is not only a failure of pastoral care, as the accommodationists insist, but it is a failure of the gospel itself. The gospel does not merely accommodate itself to our weakness; it also brings transformation and wholeness.

Because the consecrationist approach wishes to situate gay and lesbian life concretely within the community of faith, it insists that the primary identity we have as Christians is not our sexual identity but the identity we acquire in baptism. Baptism defines us as belonging to Christ, which means that, even though we still struggle under the power of sin, our principal identification is no longer that of "sinner" but "child of God." Being baptized means being incorporated into the body of Christ, so that all who are in Christ are of one family. Therefore, to make sharp divisions between "straight" and "gay" is not only wrong, it is to miss the true meaning of the gospel. Because we are brothers and sisters in Christ, we all bear responsibility for living into our baptism together. This is a responsibility we carry out by ordering our earthly desires so that they reflect God's deepest desire for us, which is embodied in the covenant of grace. This gives us a larger context within which to read the biblical condemnations, and thus a reason to read them narrowly. If the church decides to consecrate the committed unions of gay and lesbian people, it will not be just for their sakes but for the sake of the whole community. This is true because the way we order our lives is not just a private matter but a matter that affects everyone.

Stanley Hauerwas has suggested that, rather than becoming overly exercised about staking out an abstract position on something called "homosexuality," what Christians really need to do is rely on their traditional teachings against promiscuity and against adultery.[54] Hauerwas suggests that the way forward depends on serious conversations with gay and lesbian people who are in exclusive and committed relationships. It may be that the church will conclude that particular gays and lesbians in committed partnerships are neither promiscuous nor adulterous. In other words, examining concrete practices is a better way forward than arguing over abstractions.

C. Redemption in the Spirit

Like the pastoral accommodationist position, consecrationism places the emphasis on redemption — but with a critical difference. Both approaches try to extend acceptance to gay and lesbian couples; yet most accommodationists are not willing to extend the church's blessing to gay couples in an official way. At best they will offer a blessing to a gay couple privately and discreetly. Those who favor consecration, by contrast, would create a public affirmation that is an analogy to marriage. Some would even expand the definition of marriage to include gay and lesbian couples.

In contrast to prohibitionism, consecrationism construes marriage not as a fixed order of creation but as a dynamic order of redemption. Gender complementarity by itself never made a marriage, for marriage is about a relationship that has depth, contour, and mystery. To consecrationist ears, much of the church's rhetoric today seems to reduce marriage to a license to engage in sex. As we shall see in the next chapter, marriage is much more than this: it is the "bone of my bone" hailed by Adam; it is the "where you go, I will go" of Ruth's devotion to Naomi; and it is the "love is strong as death" of the Song of Songs. Rowan Williams, in arguing in favor of the church's blessing same-sex unions, points out that the purpose of committed sexual faithfulness — whether gay or straight — is to create a context where grace can abound, a context in which two people are consecrated to one another for the sake of their mutual transformation by the ongoing work of the Spirit.

Table 5. Comparison of Viewpoints Five, Six, and Seven

Welcoming and Affirming Viewpoints

	Creation	Reconciliation	Redemption
Celebration	Essentialist: being gay is a fact of "natural" life.	Gays and lesbians need to be reconciled to the goodness of their sexual orientation.	Live into one's sexual orientation as God's good gift.
Liberation	Social construction: a fact of nurtured life	Challenge binary gender categories (male/female).	Affirm complexity of gender choices.

Welcoming, Affirming, and Ordering Viewpoint

	Creation	Reconciliation	Redemption
Consecration	Sexual orientation not to be condemned, but also ambiguous and needing to be rightly ordered	Sin does not reside in orientation or behavior per se, but in whether one's life is rightly ordered. Our relationships are a means of grace.	One's sexuality is to be consecrated through an exclusive, committed covenant blessed by the church. People, not sexuality, are the objects of our celebration.

Reflection

Because it shares features of both the non-affirming and affirming positions, the consecrationist approach may have potential to serve as a bridge between them. On the one hand, consecrationists agree with celebrationists that same-sex desire should be affirmed; but consecrationists insist that such desire be monogamously ordered within the covenantal community of the church. The consecrationists challenge the celebrationists by asking them to move in a direction that runs from affirmation to order. Now that we have good reasons to affirm such relationships, let's also see to it that they are rightly ordered. Many consecrationists also agree with the liberation position that gender and sexuality are ambiguous and that ideals of sexual complementarity are sometimes used to suppress difference. They may also recognize that the institution of marriage has a patriarchal and hierarchical past. The point of the consecration position is not to perpetuate patriarchy, to deny ambiguity, or to render difference invisible. Instead, the point is that within the ambiguity of human experience, there are possibilities for redemption that the blessing of committed relationships is meant to symbolize. In addition, including gay and lesbian couples within the traditional blessing of the religious community has the potential to challenge patriarchal forms from the past.

On the other hand, consecrationists agree with the non-affirming positions about the importance of moral order. The challenge they issue to the non-affirming is to move in the opposite direction — from order to affirmation. That is, consecrationists challenge the non-affirming to recognize the moral ordering of gay relationships that gays themselves have already undertaken. The recognition of this moral ordering, then, would give the church good reason to offer its affirmation of that ordering.

It may be possible that many in the church, especially those who have found the accommodationist argument compelling, will be open to a consecrationist position if it is styled not as consecration of gay relationships per se but as consecration of the commitment that two people have made to each other. Perhaps previously non-affirming folks will be open to the ordination of gay and lesbian people if it is framed, not as consecration of a gay lifestyle, but as a recognition of the gifts of gay people for ministry. Would such a reframing of the issue leave accommodationists and others who hold non-affirming views free to have "scruples" concerning the character of homoerotic desire itself? Or would such a reframing remain offensive to gays and lesbians themselves? Would they see it as no more than a grudging acceptance?

Arguably, the full church should affirm people's commitments that are made in concrete terms even if the full church has come to no agreement about homoeroticism in the abstract. In short, consecrationists ask the non-affirming types to move from a recognition of order to an affirmation of relationships; and they ask celebrationists to move from an affirmation of gay sexuality toward a provision for the ordering of that sexuality.

But by what authority would the church embark on this bold new step of blessing committed same-sex love? We tend to forget that Jesus gave tremendous authority to the church in governing its affairs. In fact, Jesus said that whatever the church "binds" on earth will be "bound" in heaven, and whatever the church "looses," or "sets aside," on earth will be "set aside" in heaven (Matt. 16:19; 18:18). The word Jesus uses here for "to loose" or "to set aside" (*luō*; λύω) is the same word he uses in the Sermon on the Mount to speak of his attitude toward the law:

> Do not think that I have come to abolish the law or the prophets; I have come not to abolish but to fulfill. For truly I tell you, until heaven and

earth pass away, not one letter, not one stroke of a letter, will pass from the law until all is accomplished. Therefore, whoever breaks (*luō;* λύω) one of the least of these commandments, and teaches others to do the same, will be called least in the kingdom of heaven; but whoever does them and teaches them will be called great in the kingdom of heaven. (Matt. 5:17-19)

We know that Jesus' way of keeping the law defied convention. When he was accused of breaking the Sabbath, his retort was that humans were not made for the Sabbath, but the Sabbath was made for humans (Mark 2:27). Thus Jesus admonishes his disciples to "do" and "teach" the commandments, but to do so with an eye toward the coming of God's reign (Matt. 5:19). In fact, in the same passage where he tells them to "bind" and "loose," he also tells them that they have been given the "keys to the kingdom" (Matt. 16:19). This means that the church, in judging ethical cases, has a certain amount of sanctified discretion. When we keep this in mind, there is every reason to use that discretion to create a sanctified context in which faithful, exclusive, and committed gay and lesbian relationships may receive the church's blessing.

About this one thing we should all be clear: consecrationists are not trying to do away with the church's traditional teaching about marriage, fidelity, and chastity; rather, they wish to take that teaching to a deeper level. According to consecrationists, denying gays and lesbians the church's blessing and support when the couples covenant together to live in exclusive faithfulness is denying them the opportunity to grow in grace. Consecrationists argue that, in a real sense, denying gays and lesbians this means of grace is denying them their place at the family table, the table where Jesus is host and where none is worthy to gather but by the invitation of God's grace.

Summary

What should be clear from the discussion thus far is that the controversies over same-sex unions are theologically quite complex. There is a spectrum of positions, and only by attending to the full range of religious belief on this subject will we be able to move forward successfully in our search for truth. As a way of summing up the distinctive features and the pivotal differences that exist among the seven viewpoints discussed in Chapters One and Two, imagine that you are playing a card game. It turns out that each of the viewpoints we have been considering understands the rules of the game differently when it comes to people who are gay. But let's imagine that, in every version of the game, if you find a two of clubs in your hand when the cards are first dealt, it means you have been dealt a same-gender sexual orientation: you have been dealt the gay card. If this happens, what are you going to do?

Three of the viewpoints, each of which was covered in Chapter One, treat the phenomenon of being dealt the gay card as a huge problem. In the prohibitionist version of the game, you should discard the two of clubs as soon as possible — because it is a very, very bad card. If, instead of discarding it, you choose to play it, the game is over for you: you lose. The toleration rules are different: as this is embodied in the policies of some churches, if you are dealt the gay card, you are not to be condemned. But you have a dilemma: you cannot get rid of the card, because it is now considered to be a part of who you are; so the best you can do about it is hide it. You don't want anyone to know you have it, especially if you are seeking to be a leader in a church. As long as you hide it, you will still be allowed to play the game. If you choose to show the card, you are permitted to stay in the game, but attitudes toward you will change. You will be forced to remain on the fringes. If you choose to play the card, you can still remain in the game, but you are never, ever permitted to be one of the game's leaders.

There is little good news for gay people in these first two non-affirming versions of the game. A glimmer of hope appears in the accommodationist position, whose rules say that if any one of us, or our neighbors or friends, are dealt the gay card, it creates a situation that affects all the other players: they need to find a way to support and help the one who holds the card in deciding *whether* to play it and *how* to play it in a way that is responsible. Gay people will receive a certain kind of acceptance from accommodationists, but it is still a grudging acceptance — something less than a full welcome and affirmation. As with prohibitionists and tolerationists, accommodationists still consider the two of clubs an unfortunate card to have. It will make it very difficult for you to play the game, but not impossible.

Four of the viewpoints, the ones considered in this chapter, consider the gay card in a completely different way: they treat the fact of receiving it as an occasion of grace. Accordingly, the legitimationist position thinks that the way the game has been played previously is all wrong. This viewpoint believes that the other players should regard the gay card as no different from any other card, nor should they treat its recipient any differently. Advocates of this strategy will cry foul if other players insist that the old rules should still apply. As for becoming church leaders, this should not rest on what cards we have been arbitrarily dealt but on what gifts we exhibit as we play all our other cards. Simply to be gifted is to be eligible for church office. From the celebrationist viewpoint, if you are dealt the gay card, you should be glad; in fact, you are encouraged to show it to everyone, for it is a very good card to have. If you are dealt this card, you need not hide it, and you need not create an alternative game in which to play it. The key is to learn how to play it in the most fulfilling and responsible way within the present game. The liberationist position takes legitimation a step further: it insists that there is nothing intrinsic in the gay card as such that should be causing all this fuss. We make such a fuss over it because of the random decisions in earlier versions of the game to treat it negatively. There are many such unfair aspects of this game, liberationists believe, and they argue that we should consider remaking all the rules of the game from the ground up.

From the consecrationist perspective, this is more than just a game; it is an exercise in person formation. In ways that are sometimes hidden, the act of playing the game is meant to be a journey into redemption. When anyone is dealt the gay card, the key is to play it in a way that is redemptive both for the player who receives the card and for the community playing the game. Those playing by these rules should find a way to consecrate the card within the game itself. The consecration viewpoint, more than all the others, desires that persons who have received the card may find a life companion who shares the card and who also wants to share the playing of the game in lifelong fidelity and commitment.

It is my belief that the consecrationist viewpoint has the potential to change how religious communities approach same-sex couples. At the present moment, prohibitionists, tolerationists, and accommodationists have joined to form a slim non-affirming majority in most mainline religious bodies. Legitimationists have led the charge in attempting to change this, but so far they have only managed to rally a strong minority to their side. The consecrationist position approaches the topic in a new way: it offers a way forward that is welcoming and affirming, but because of the value it places on the moral integrity of exclusive commitment to another, it insists that the way forward must be welcoming, affirming, and *ordering*. It is likely that others along the theological continuum — especially accommodationists — will find the consecrationist position increasingly attractive. If so, a new consensus in favor of blessing same-sex unions

Table 6. Same-Sex Relationships in the Church: Seven Theological Viewpoints

Non-affirming Viewpoints

	Creation	Reconciliation	Redemption
Prohibition	Same-sex desire and behavior = *perversion*	Repent of gay *identity;* the church prohibits gay desire and behavior.	Return to true heterosexual nature
Toleration	Same-gender sexual orientation = *a tragic burden*	Repent of gay *choices;* welcoming of persons, non-affirming of deeds	Stoic acceptance of one's tragic fate through abstinence
Accommodation	Same-sex desire = tragic burden, but open to traces of grace	Focus: gay and lesbian *relationships*. While these are disobedient in form, they may be obedient in substance, if monogamous.	Exclusive, same-sex partnerships are better than promiscuity — i.e., they are the lesser of the evils.

Welcoming and Affirming Viewpoints

	Creation	Reconciliation	Redemption
Legitimation	Same-sex desire = like all other sinful conditions	Focus: *ordination.* Repent of singling out gay sins and ignoring other sins.	Create a just world in which differences no longer make a difference.
Celebration	*Essentialist:* being gay is a fact of "natural" life.	Gays and lesbians need to be reconciled to the goodness of their sexual orientation.	Live into one's sexual orientation as God's good gift.
Liberation	*Social construction:* a fact of nurtured life	Challenge binary gender categories (male-female).	Affirm complexity of gender choices.

Welcoming, Affirming, and Ordering Viewpoint

	Creation	Reconciliation	Redemption
Consecration	Sexual orientation not to be condemned, but also ambiguous and needing to be rightly ordered	Sin does not reside in orientation or behavior per se but in whether one's life is rightly ordered. Our relationships are a means of grace.	One's sexuality is to be consecrated through an exclusive, committed covenant, blessed by the church. Humans, not sexuality, are the objects of our celebration.

could emerge. What is needed is more biblical and theological reflection on the consecrationist option, and the goal of the next chapter is to provide a starting point for just such an ongoing reflection.

CHAPTER THREE

Becoming Family:
The Consecration of Same-Sex Love

Scripture progresses along with those who read it.

Gregory the Great[1]

When two people give themselves to one another in a mutual act of loving and lifelong commitment, something transformative happens: they become family. Becoming family is the kind of thing that religious communities should honor, nurture, and support. With that in mind, my aim in this chapter is to make a constructive biblical and theological case for the religious blessing of exclusively committed same-sex unions. The case I wish to make here builds on the insights of the consecrationist viewpoint that I have set forth in the preceding chapter. The question is this: How do religious communities honor the integrity of gay families while also honoring the integrity of their own deepest traditions? I believe that both of these honorings are possible, and that is why I base my argument squarely within a biblical and theological framework. And I want to underscore the possibility of doing that and the need to do it. For too long now, our religious communities have been told that taking a supportive stance toward gay people somehow violates everything our religious traditions hold dear. That is not the case. Supporting exclusively committed gay unions represents not a departure from our biblical and theological traditions but rather a deepening of them.

For Christians, Scripture is the unique and authoritative witness to Jesus Christ, the divine Word mediated and spoken through inspired human words.[2] Christians always look to Scripture to be a reliable guide in matters of faith and morals. Unfortunately, the plain fact is that nowhere does Scripture explicitly address the question of mutually committed same-sex unions. This is simply one of those cases where we have to read *with* Scripture in order to see *beyond* what the biblical writers themselves could envision. We do not approach Scripture as a collection of abstract propositions, for Scripture is a living Word as well as a living conversation partner that we engage time and again. When we demand of it answers to questions its writers never anticipated, as we are doing here, we must approach it with a special measure of wisdom and grace.

On what biblical and theological basis might the blessing of a religious community be given to a gay or lesbian couple? And what would such a blessing signify? My perspective is deeply informed by the traditional purposes of marriage. Marriage is primarily about transformation: it functions as a "means of grace." Moreover, as Rowan Williams has argued, the mutual delight of the couple symbolizes something important about God: God delights in the human beings God has created. Not only does God delight in us, but God has determined to remain committed to us through thick and thin. Both this delight and this divine dedication are symbolized for human experience in the love between spouses. Marriage is born of two people knowing themselves as desired by one another and determining to stand by one another for better or for worse.

What are we to make of same-sex couples who embody the same kind of dedication and desire we see in heterosexual marriage? The best way to answer this question is to look at the traditional purposes of marriage and then ask what light these traditional benchmarks shed on gay unions. In general, the tradition has conceived of marriage as a context for embodying three fundamental realities: companionship, commitment, and community.[3] Upon investigation, I think we will see that gay couples are just as capable as straight couples of embracing all three of these ideals. Not only are they capable, but many gay and lesbian couples are already living out these three values in exemplary ways.

Companionship

The desire to enter into an exclusive bond with a "significant other" is a powerful feature of human experience. This desire is affirmed in the biblical story of creation, when Adam sees Eve for the first time and rejoices, saying, "This at last is bone of my bones and flesh of my flesh" (Gen. 2:23). Being in communion with a significant other is something Scripture deeply affirms. We encounter the power of this desire later on in Scripture, in the Song of Songs, where the woman exclaims of her lover in the opening lines, "Let him kiss me with the kisses of his mouth" (Song 1:2). The rest of the Song is a passionate tribute to the power of erotic love. So explosive is the ardor expressed between the two lovers here, so emphatic the fusion that is occurring between their lives, that it is sometimes impossible to tell which lover is speaking.[4] It is hard to imagine that this poetic intermingling of voices is accidental. For that matter, neither lover is ever clearly identified as such; this is an ambiguity that invites the reader to regard his or her own desire for a significant other as poetically validated and blessed.

This all-too-human desire for a significant other is both biological and cultural, and it is a mistake to reduce it to one or the other. Biologically speaking, we are programmed as a species to desire an intimate companion. This is not only for reasons of propagating the species; there are tangible communal advantages that result from the life-giving character of human love. One does not need to have children for nuptial life to be a blessing. In addition to the biological reasons for conjugal love, there are powerful cultural forces at work in the experience of this human desire for the other.[5] One such force is the structure of marriage itself. In the past, marriage served as a way to forge ties of kinship, political power, and wealth between family groups. It provided privileged families a way of solidifying their power and less powerful families a way of providing their children a chance to ascend the social ladder. In contrast to this model of marriage based on kinship networks, ours is a society whose ideals for erotic coupling have evolved toward a model of companionate marriage, involving equality, mutual love, and affection. In an earlier time, when men were educated and privileged in a way that women were not, the notion of marriage as a friendship between equals was rare. Given today's new emphasis on nuptial companionship, it is not surprising that people in our culture place great emphasis on finding a romantic partner who suits them. If gays and lesbians desire such a companion, they desire no less than what most of the rest of us do.

This is not to say that no one in the past married for love. Nor is it to deny that even today, with companionate marriage as an ideal, people marry in part to gain economic and social advantage. Rather, it is simply to remind us that the purposes and functions of marriage are complex and ever-changing.[6]

One of the major self-deceptions engaged in by those who oppose marriage equality for gay couples is the assertion that marriage is an institution that has remained the same for millennia. This is simply not true. Even something as basic as the ideal of monogamy has not always been a part of traditional marriage. Men in the Bible, just to name one obvious example, were permitted more than one wife provided they had the wealth to support them all (1 Kings 11:1-13). In fact, only 174 of the 1,154 past and present human societies have had monogamy as a goal.[7] Even in that 15 percent of human societies where monogamy has been the norm, the actual meaning of monogamy has changed over time. Monogamy can be defined either as the practice of marrying only once or the practice of being married to only one person at a time. The difference between these two ideals can be captured by comparing their divergent views on divorce. If monogamy means marrying only once, then divorce is by definition prohibited. Or where divorce is grudgingly allowed, this first view of monogamy prohibited remarriage after divorce. This view has enjoyed much support among traditional Christians. It is sobering to remember that, a generation ago, Protestant churches were arguing not over gays but over whether divorced persons should be allowed to remarry. Today, of course, remarriage after divorce has become routine. But for that to happen, it required a shift in our understanding of marriage itself. Today monogamy has acquired the second meaning, namely, being committed to only one person at a time. Under this understanding, then, remarriage after divorce becomes permissible — and more than permissible. People can even celebrate remarriage as an act of affirming marriage as an institution. In fact, in our culture most people respect marriages entered into between previously divorced persons.

In short, the claim that we need to preserve a history of marriage that has remained unchanged for thousands of years or more does not match the facts. Not only has marriage changed dramatically through the centuries, but marriage has meant things in the past that we definitely would not want it to mean today. In biblical times, when a man wanted to "marry" a woman, he did so simply by "taking" *(laqah)* her.[8] This "taking" of a woman connoted male initiative, dominance, supremacy, and possession. It's true that male authority carried with it male responsibility to care for the woman; but even this male obligation to provide care was a tenuous one from the woman's point of view. In some understandings of the biblical law, if a woman displeased a man for any reason, he could simply divorce her. Coincident with the "taking" of the woman by the man was the fatherly act of "giving" her away *(nātan).*[9] This exchange of giving and taking is something that is the supreme prerogative of men, something that happens *to* women in the Old Testament. That women were treated as if they were some sort of property can be further seen in the fact that, in order to acquire a woman, a man had to pay a "purchase price," a term that has been sanitized in the English Bible to read "marriage present" (e.g., Gen. 34:12; 1 Sam. 18:25). Surely these are elements of a system of inequalities that we no longer want to perpetuate in our contemporary understanding of marriage.

The inequalities woven into ancient patterns of marriage also made their way into the laws of the Western world. Under the common law of England and the United States, for example, when a woman married a man, she ceased to have the right to enter into contracts for herself, and the power over all of her property was vested in the man. This law of *coverture* endured well into the nineteenth century. The philosopher and statesman John Stuart Mill spoke of a threefold patriarchy that needed to be overcome. The church lorded it over the state; the state lorded it over the couple; and the husband lorded it over his wife and children. Mill argued that on the domestic front we should replace this patriarchy with an equality of male and female. He insisted that men should no longer be allowed to rape their wives without accountability; that women as well as men should be able to obtain a divorce; that child custody should no longer be presumed to belong to the father; and that women should have the right to hold property, enter into contracts, and freely conduct business without direction from their husbands.[10] All these changes to traditional marriage were resisted at the time, but most people today would agree the changes were salutary.[11]

Unless we intend to perpetuate such holdovers from the past, we must interpret and apply biblical insights in a way that makes sense with everything else we know about God and God's still-unfolding way with humanity. It is necessary to discern the deeper purpose of biblical norms and then to ask how those norms can be embodied in a way that has integrity for us today. With that as a goal, let us look at the creation accounts in Genesis. These accounts are often invoked to reject same-sex love, but in fact they contain elements that support gay and lesbian couples' quest for committed companionship.

Genesis: The Priority of Human Companionship

A biblical inquiry into the importance of marital companionship must begin with the two creation accounts in the opening chapters of Genesis. The first account, Genesis 1:26-31, comes from the so-called Priestly source: it focuses on the creation of humanity as male and female. The second account, which appears in Genesis 2:4-25, derives from what is called the Yahwist tradition: it centers on the story of Adam and Eve in the Garden of Eden.

Traditional prohibitionist readings of these early texts see them as laying down a fixed and unalterable structure of heterosexual marriage, ruling out any form of sexuality that does not comply with that structure. But does this prohibition really make sense? What we need to consider is whether the attention given to heterosexual marriage in Scripture sets up an absolute prohibition against same-sex couples. Is it really true that gay couples who want to commit themselves in exclusive, lifelong partnerships should be prevented from doing so? If gay people are giving themselves to one another in marriage-like commitments, are they not embodying the very act of self-giving for the other that lies at the heart of biblical religion? Since the first two chapters of Genesis have been used so often to argue against gay and lesbian unions, we need to consider these passages in some detail.

Genesis 1

The first verse of the Priestly account of human creation in Genesis 1 reads as follows:

> Then God said, "Let us make *humankind* [*hā 'ādām*] in our image, according to our likeness; and let *them* have dominion over the fish of the sea, and over the birds of the air, and over the cattle, and over all the wild animals of the earth, and over every creeping thing that creeps upon the earth." (Gen. 1:26 [NRSV], emphasis added)[12]

What can we learn about our humanity from this verse, and especially about the humanity of people who are gay?

First, we need to recognize that the emphasis is on the creation of human beings as a whole ("let *them* have dominion").[13] The first human being serves as a microcosm for all human beings; and the blessing God applies to this one human being applies to all subsequent human beings, no matter who they are. By sheer virtue of being human, so Genesis proclaims, we are loved by God — and this is true no less of gay people than of any other people.

Second, in telling us that human beings are created in God's image, the verse does not spell out precisely what the "image" means. Some have thought it refers to the human soul or to human reason. Others have thought it may mean the capacity for language. Still others have focused on the human ability for self-transcendence, that is, being able to reflect on oneself and one's circumstances. Perhaps being in the image of God means all these things, but it also certainly includes something that is central to the biblical narrative itself, namely, the capacity and desire to enter into deep and enduring relationships — both with one another and with God. As creatures who bear God's image, human beings have a status and a calling to live a life beyond mere animal existence. In other words, the desire for intimate companionship that all of us feel so deeply, whether we are gay or straight, is an important part of our humanity. The nurturing and ordering of this desire is what marriage seeks to accomplish.

Third, not only are human beings made in God's image, but the image includes both "male and female." For same-sex couples, much depends on the theological meaning of this phrase. Some interpreters have suggested that the phrase "male and female" refers to the anatomical "fit" between male and female body parts. In this view, a certain understanding of body parts becomes the bedrock reason for rejecting same-sex relationships.[14] But this is not a claim that has any explicit grounding in Genesis or anywhere else in Scripture. For that matter, biblical Hebrew does not even have specific words for genitalia.[15] It is true that the passage goes on to urge human beings to "be fruitful and multiply" (Gen. 1:28), a fact that obviously contemplates sexual intercourse. Yet this is a commandment that belongs to the species as a whole, not to each individual. If the commandment to have children applied to each individual, the Christian interpreter would be in the anomalous position of having to view those who are single, celibate, or who for whatever reason do not have children — including Jesus of Nazareth — as being disobedient sinners.[16]

A better way of interpreting this comes to us if we pay attention to the grammatical structure of the biblical passage. Consider Robert Alter's expert rendering of the Hebrew in Genesis 1:27 (emphasis added): "And God created *the human* in his image, in the image of God He created *him, male and female* He created *them*."[17] Notice that the first two lines form a chiasm, a structure in which the thoughts in the second line (image/him) are presented in the reverse order of the thoughts in the first (the human/ in his image).[18] Right off the bat, the arrangement of the first two lines sets up an interpretive question: How do we read the ordering of the words in the third line?[19] There the phrase "male and female" sits in apposition to the phrase "in the image of God" ("in the *image of God* He created him/ *male and female* He created them"). This establishes a literary equivalence between the two phrases. Why this equivalence? It is telling us that we should equate *both* male and female with the image of God. This interpretation squares with the rest of the Hebrew Bible, where the trope "male and female" usually functions to convey the Hebraic sense of the whole.[20] In short, both male and female are created in God's image whether or not they conform to culturally conditioned norms. They were *all* created in God's image regardless of gender, gender orientation, or any other condition on which anyone might choose to lessen their humanity.

In summary, therefore, the first creation account in Genesis underscores not the peculiarities of anatomy, or the wonders of gender complementarity, but the comprehensiveness and communal character of all humanity being created in God's image. The point is the sanctity and importance of every human being. And this sanctity applies regardless of a person's gender identity.

Genesis 2

The second biblical account of human creation is located in Genesis 2:7-21. Whereas God, in the first account, repeatedly declares that creation is "good" (Gen. 1:4, 10, 12, 18, 21, 25; and very good, 1:31), we are suddenly confronted in this second account with the idea of an evil that does not live up to the good. God creates a garden in which there are two forbidden trees: one is the tree of life, which is set in the very middle of the garden; the other is the tree of "knowing good and evil" (Gen. 2:9). The name of this second tree is significant, for acquiring the knowledge of good and evil becomes important as the narrative unfolds.

Now, for the first time, we hear the story of two concrete individuals, Adam and Eve; and we learn of their fateful choice to disobey God in the Garden of Eden. To understand this story, we must recognize that even though the world is created good, this created goodness can be subjected to misuse — that is, it can be put to ends that are less than good. Following Augustine, theologian H. Richard Niebuhr characterized it this way: everything in the world is *good;* but not everything with the world is *right.*[21] Everything was created for goodness, but there is still the need to live into that goodness.

For our purposes, the key verse is Genesis 2:18. Here, for the very first time in the Bible, God declares that something is "not good."[22] Having created the first earth creature *(hā 'ādām)* and placed him in the garden, here God solemnly declares, "It is *not good* for the human being to be alone." This is the most important verse in all of Scripture for the gay marriage debate. Let me repeat it: "It is *not good* for the human being to be alone."

The theological point is clear: the God of the universe expresses concern about the human being who finds himself or herself dwelling in nuptial loneliness. As in the first creation account, what God says of this one earth creature applies to them all. Just as Adam's loneliness merited God's attention, so all human beings need and long for intimate companionship. This "not good" is an objective evaluation rooted in the very wisdom of God. It is God who looks, who sees, and who announces that human beings are created not for isolation but for community. This does not mean that individuals who live without a conjugal partner are somehow living a less than human existence; there are many ways to be in relationship with others. But it does mean that the desire for intimate companionship is something God recognizes, something God affirms as a fundamental aspect of being human. When gay and lesbian people desire to give and receive love from another person, they are expressing a deep feature of their God-given humanity — a feature that God understands.

In this biblical narrative, not only does God recognize the human need for companionship, but God also responds. God steps in to remedy the situation. Listen to the way Robert Alter translates Genesis 2:18: "And the Lord God said, 'It is not good for the human to be alone, I shall make a sustainer beside him.'"[23] The phrase that Alter nicely renders as "a sustainer beside him" *('ēzer kĕnegdō)* could also be understood to mean a "help suitable," a "fit helper," or an "appropriate partner."[24] This implies something more than an "anatomically correct" sexual companion. The one whom God supplies for the earth creature is a life-giving, nurturing, and sustaining presence. This is clear from the Hebrew word that is used here: *'ēzer* has the connotation of someone performing a redemptive — even a salvific — function.[25] Often in the Old Testament, an *'ēzer* intervenes to render deliverance, as in the case of decisive military support. Frequently, it is actually God who steps in to be humanity's *'ēzer* (e.g., Gen. 49:25; Ps. 121:1). Indeed, when Christian worship services begin with the invocation "our help [*'ēzer*] is in the name of the Lord," we are testifying that to have one's divine "sustainer beside one" connotes redemption, liberation, and release from the bare givenness of creation.

We need to underscore this last point. Even God is not satisfied with creation "as it is" as a basis for ordering human existence. From this verse it seems that God is constantly thinking of creation "as it ought to be." The need to redeem creation, the need for a better world, appears in the very first verses of the Bible, even before the recording of human sin. God sees the need for a suitable companion, and God provides.

So then, what kind of suitable, redemptive companion is appropriate for a person who is gay or lesbian? There are good reasons — pastoral and otherwise — not to push such a person into an opposite-sex marriage. Such a move would be a double affront: on the one hand, it would deny to the gay or lesbian person the intimate companion that he or she needs and desires; on the other hand, it would also frustrate the reasonable expectations of the unwitting heterosexual spouse. I am well aware that some people have lived in such marriages and have made them work. I also know that some people have entered into such marriages in good faith, while others have married a member of the opposite sex knowing that they were gay and not revealing their orientation to their spouse. The number of such marriages has not been small: it is estimated that at least 1.7 million American women are married to or have been married to a man who is gay.[26] Many such marriages are full of emptiness and despair, and many end in tragedy. Does it really make sense for church and society, as a matter of policy, to advise gay people to marry straight people? Does it not make more sense for a gay or lesbian person to find a companion suitable to his or her own sexual orientation?

The argument against this, of course, is that it denies the traditional understanding of marriage as a divinely established "order of creation." The idea of "orders of creation" holds that certain social relationships, such as marriage, family, race, and nationhood, are written into the fabric of existence. But there are serious problems with this idea. To claim that there is only one divinely ordained structure for government, family, and the economy is to ignore the diversity in these structures that Christians themselves have advocated over the centuries. Moreover, these supposedly timeless "orders" have been conceived too often in a hierarchical way — for example, the domination of men over women, of whites over blacks, of certain nations over others. We can see that such notions were especially dangerous when they were used in the twentieth century to support Hitler's racist ideologies in Nazi Germany and the decades of apartheid in South Africa. And in the nineteenth century, a similar form of biblical interpretation was used to support slavery in the American South. Surely it is up to those who invoke the "orders of creation" to show why the talk of "orders" that has been used so egregiously in these other contexts will not lead us to similarly unfortunate consequences on this issue as well. One begins to suspect that in the end this talk about orders of creation is actually more ideological than theological.

This leads to a final criticism that is perhaps the most telling, namely, that the Bible itself nowhere talks about "orders of creation."[27] God creates the world (e.g., Gen. 1:1), but the creative work of God's Spirit remains ever at work to transform and renew all things (e.g., Ps. 104:30). Indeed, God's creative work and redemptive work are intimately linked (Isa. 43:1), and the sanctification of human beings is always an act of dynamic new creation (e.g., Jer. 31:31-33). It is true that, in bringing about the conditions that sustain life, God does not leave us with chaos (Gen. 1:2; Isa. 45:18). But this is not the same thing as seeing creation as a network of fixed and unalterable "orders." What is most objectionable about this invoking of "orders," from a Christian point of view, is that it misrepresents one of the basic teachings of the gospel: it poses a false separation between what God has done in creating the world and what God continues to do in working to redeem the world.

The fact that creation is not yet complete is built into the very narrative we are called on to interpret here. This second creation account — the same one that has been invoked to support so-called "orders of creation" — suggests that marriage is not merely an order of creation but most especially an order of *redemption*. What do I mean by this? We do not encourage people to marry in order to help them remain the same but to help them to become better. To think of one's spouse as one's ʿēzer (i.e., as a redemptive presence) is precisely to move beyond the notion of marriage as a fixed order of creation: marriage becomes a vehicle of redemption. From a Christian point of view, then, marriage already gives a foretaste of the divine reordering that is breaking into the world. It is no accident that both Jesus and Paul use images of the wedding feast (Matt. 22:1-14; 25:1-13; Luke 12:36; 14:7-11; cf. John 2:1-11) and of man and wife (Mark 2:19, par.; John 3:29; Eph. 5:31-32) to describe the destination toward which our redemption is headed.

What do we make of the cry of delight that comes from the lips of Adam when he first catches sight of Eve? He exclaims: "This at last is bone of my bones and flesh of my flesh; this one shall be called Woman, for out of Man this one was taken" (Gen. 2:23). Sometimes it is claimed that the joy expressed by Adam arises because he has found his sexual "other," and from this claim it is reasoned that only opposite-sex relationships are sanctioned by God. Once again, there is nothing explicit in the text that supports this view; indeed, what the text itself actually says points the other way: there is no emphasis here on "difference" or "complementarity" at all — in fact, just the opposite. When Adam sees Eve, he does not celebrate her otherness but her sameness: what strikes him is that she is "bone of my bones, flesh of my flesh." If achieving anatomical complementarity were the primary point, then, ironically, Adam would not really need Eve. Mere anatomical complementarity already existed between the male human animal and the female animals.[28] Reducing what is going on here to a crude theology of "parts that fit" will simply not do. The very fact that we are created in the image of God requires a more human and more holy form of theological thinking.

The key point is that God sees the plight of this first human being and steps in and does whatever it takes to provide him with a life-giving, life-sustaining companion. For gay and lesbian people, a person of the opposite sex is simply not best able to provide this sort of fitting companionship. The best way for a gay or lesbian person to find a "help suitable," an "appropriate partner," is in a committed union with a person of the same gender. There is nothing explicit in the Genesis texts that prohibits this and much there that actually supports it.

Commitment

The second traditional purpose of marriage, as noted above, is to provide a context within which to live out a structured commitment to another person. From the standpoint of biblical religion, the reason we honor the commitment of two spouses is that their commitment serves as a tangible witness to the commitment God makes to God's own people. The Hebrew prophets, in fact, portrayed God as one whose passion for the people is like that of a husband who remains ever faithful despite the unfaithfulness of his bride.[29]

The joy of companionship leads to commitment. We catch a glimpse of this in the biblical poem discussed above, the Song of Songs. There are many indications that the two lovers who are exulting in one another's bodily charms are young and unmarried. The text even hints at society's disapproval of the couple's love, for the woman finds herself at various points verbally reproved (e.g., Song 1:6) and even physically beaten (Song 5:7) because of her passion for the man. Whether the obstacles faced by the woman were real or merely metaphorical, her love is of a kind that will not allow itself to be quenched. Passion and commitment here are intimately conjoined.

This tells us something important about the committed love of one human being for another. Quite often, when the Song speaks of "love," it refers to the physical, erotic love captured in the Hebrew word *dodîm* — a sensual love that speaks in the intimate cadences of the I-thou exchange. It unashamedly revels in the pleasure of love even as it seeks to give pleasure in return. In these poems, the lovers speak to each other face to face. On the other hand, this same love points us to something beyond the passions of the moment. Having exchanged their declarations of desire throughout the Song, the woman and her lover step back from the intensity of their passion in the Song's last chapter to speak in a different way. Now, suddenly, they speak of their love no longer in the I-thou vocabulary but objectively in the third person: "Love is strong as death," the woman insists, its "passion fierce as the grave" (Song 8:6). Here the vocabulary shifts to the Hebrew word *'ahăbâ* — not a purely sexual love any longer but the selfless love that freely pours itself out for the sake of the other, always seeking more to give than to receive. In other words, the sexual energy of the Song of Songs points to something beyond itself, something more enduring and more holy.

Many gay and lesbian couples have bound themselves to one another in stable, long-term commitments. Many of them are raising children. Many have nursed a partner, or perhaps a member of a partner's family, through long months of physical illness, demonstrating that they know as well as heterosexual couples do what it means to love another "for better or for worse, in sickness and in health." The question that currently faces our churches, our synagogues, our mosques, and our other religious communities is whether we can recognize as genuine the caliber of love that is so clearly expressed by gay and lesbian people. I believe that there is so much evidence of its genuineness that those who deny its authenticity risk bearing false witness against their neighbors. Despite stereotypes to the contrary, we know from surveys that many gay people desire to commit themselves to a significant other.[30] As I write these words, the first legal partnerships between gay couples in the United Kingdom are being celebrated.[31] Indeed, in some Scandinavian countries, where openness to gay commitments has a longer track record, over 90 percent of gays and lesbians have expressed a desire for a committed relationship; furthermore, in those countries the divorce rate for gays is even lower than it is for heterosexual couples.[32] In the United States today, even though there is only a very short-lived history of legally supported gay unions, we know that approximately 30 percent of gay people are living in partnership relationships.[33] Were society to approve of gay marriage or civil unions, this number would only increase. The figures for those raising children are equally impressive: over 30 percent of lesbian couples in America and some 22 percent of gay male couples are raising children. Just as same-sex couples desire conjugal happiness, they are also making commitments to one another whose integrity is no less than that of their opposite-sex counterparts.

Within a Christian context, the commitment a person makes to his or her spouse is meant to be a reflection of God's own gracious commitment to be for and with humans through Christ. We are told in the Epistle to the Ephesians that marriage is a mystery that mirrors the love of Christ, the bridegroom, for his spouse, which is the church (Eph. 5:21-32). When we say that God's love for God's people has a spousal character, what exactly do we mean? Ephesians characterizes the nature of spousal love as follows: "Christ loved the church and gave himself up for her" (Eph. 5:25). Notice that this text does not invite us to picture the presence or absence of particular kinds of sexual acts between Christ and the church. The text is happy to have men in the church as well as women consider Christ to be their bridegroom. The biblical focus is squarely on the act of self-giving love for the other: "He gave himself up for her." It is the quality of the commitment — the purity of the love itself — that is elevated to first importance, and this has been true throughout the Christian tradition. One need look no further than the teachings of Augustine on the love of God and the love of neighbor.[34] Though love of God is to be valued above all else, says Augustine, it is through the love of neighbor that love of God becomes real. In fact, when one loves another person, one is also loving God; and such love unites us together with God, who is our supreme good.[35]

Genuine love should be celebrated and supported. That should be the fundamental lens through which we view same-sex commitments. Is there really anything in Scripture that would lead us to think otherwise?

Interlude: What the Bible Does and Does Not Say about Same-Sex Commitments

Within the context of this discussion about marital commitment, it is time to reflect more specifically on the fact that no biblical passage says anything explicit about same-sex unions that are exclusively committed and covenantal in character. In the introductory chapter I distinguished three types of homoeroticism: intergenerational, status-defined, and egalitarian. The biblical passages reject the first two types, but they say nothing about egalitarian, covenantal commitments. What Scripture does say positively about the nature of our nuptial commitments, moreover, provides a good theological basis for supporting and blessing gays and lesbians who bind themselves together in exclusively committed unions. True, a few passages speak negatively about some homoerotic acts; but again, the acts in question are not of the nuptial kind. As Scott Black Johnston has argued, it makes no more sense to take these acts as indicative of what it means to be gay today than it does to take the ribaldry of Mardi Gras as the best indicator of marital love. Furthermore, when considered in context, the biblical prohibition passages actually point us implicitly to a still more excellent way for gay couples. They point us to a life of consecrated commitment to one another. With this in mind, let us consider some of these pivotal biblical passages.

Leviticus: Consecration to Holiness

I shall begin with the book of Leviticus because all subsequent evaluations of same-gender sex acts in Judaism and Christianity flow directly from what is said there. Because of the vast divide that separates the modern interpreter from the cultural context of Leviticus, some Christian interpreters make the mistake of simply dismissing the witness of Leviticus entirely. They seem to believe that its prohibitions belong to a bygone age.[36] It is true that Leviticus includes a number of commandments that, if carried out literally, would have little applicability in a modern society. These include the injunction against wearing garments with mixed fibers (19:19); the prohibitions against sowing fields with two kinds of seed (19:19); and the ban on charging interest (25:36-37). Other commandments appear to be matters of convention with little mandatory force today, such as the rules for priests cutting their hair and beard (19:27) or the strict prohibition against the "abomination" of eating ostrich (11:13-19), a meat praised by some today for its health benefits.

However, the key is not to dismiss the texts of Leviticus outright as though they no longer have the status of Scripture. Instead, we must ask what these texts were trying to achieve in their own day in order to discern what they still have to say to us today. Not paying heed to these texts would be a serious mistake. Leviticus captures with compelling moral clarity a number of the grand themes of biblical faith, themes such as showing mercy toward the poor (e.g., Lev. 19:10, 15), justice for the foreigner (19:33-34), and integrity in all one's dealings with others (19:11-14, 16-18, 35-36; 25:16-17).[37] Above all, there is the central command in Leviticus 19:18 to "love your neighbor as yourself," which is the command that Jesus himself places at the center of his ethical teaching.[38] This same admonition is reiterated elsewhere in the New Testament, by both Paul (Rom. 13:9; Gal. 5:14) and James (Jas. 2:8). In short, there is no way for those crafting a biblical moral vision to get around the texts of Leviticus.[39] Instead, we must proceed through them.

Two texts that we need to examine carefully are Leviticus 18:22 and 20:13.[40] These two texts are directed to the male leaders of Israel.[41] The New Revised Standard Version renders these texts as follows:

> You shall not lie with a male as with a woman; it is an abomination. (Lev. 18:22)[42]

If a man lies with a male as with a woman, both of them have committed an abomination; they shall be put to death; their blood is upon
them. (Lev. 20:13)[43]

These two passages clearly prohibit certain male homoerotic acts. But
which ones? And why? We must consider these questions in the light of Leviticus as a whole. It seems strange that anti-gay polemicists have put so
much weight on these two individual verses when, in the last hundred
years, the number of comprehensive, critical commentaries devoted to the
book of Leviticus as a whole can be counted on one hand.[44] Why so much
selective focus on two texts and so much neglect of all the rest? In order to
decipher these sexuality commands, we must immerse ourselves in the
context from which they arose, remembering that the categories of a particular culture spring forth and derive their intelligibility from the lived
experience of the culture itself.[45] Some of the admonitions of Leviticus
had an obvious purpose in their original context, but thinking through
their applicability for today requires cultural discernment. For example, in
many ancient societies the penalty for seducing a man's wife was death.
Why? Because it was an affront to the honor of the man. By contrast, the
act of raping an unmarried woman was punishable only by a fine. Clearly,
a crime perpetrated against a woman was a crime of a lesser degree. This
discrepancy tells us that notions of law, status, gender, and social boundaries intersect in ways that are not neatly portable from one society to another. In fact, simply to repeat the past conventions of an ancient society
without discernment would constitute moral folly. Thus, when we approach the text of Leviticus, how do we take its call to holiness seriously
without falling prey to the blind spots that inevitably accompany any historical text? As faithful religious interpreters today, how do we appropriate
the enduring teaching of this text?

The way *not* to appropriate the text is to expect all its ancient reckon-
ings of what was clean and unclean, approved and not approved, to have a
one-for-one correspondence with how life should be ordered within the
theological community today. We need to inquire further and determine
the reason for the rule. Learning the reason for an ancient rule helps us re-
formulate what that rule might mean in a new day with a new set of moral
issues.

One reason for the rule in Leviticus 18:22 and 20:13 is that the act in
question was of the kind that a socially superior man usually imposed on a

social inferior. In ancient society such acts were sometimes performed on a slave or other subordinate person merely as a form of sexual gratification. That is, the perpetrator of the act did not have what we think of today as an exclusively same-gender sexual orientation; instead, he was merely looking for a way to release sexual tension. But there were sometimes even more ominous reasons for such acts; they were commonly performed on people, especially prisoners of war, as a form of sexual humiliation. Not only had the enemy been conquered, but the victors wanted to further defeat their captives through sexual abuse. In the ancient culture in which Leviticus arose, it was an indignity to a man's masculinity to be sexually penetrated by another man. By its very nature, then, we are speaking of a one-sided, asymmetrical act, one that had the effect in the eyes of ancient culture of symbolically turning the man who was penetrated and had thus become sexually subservient into a woman.

It is in this context of dominance, exploitation, and humiliation that these two Leviticus texts need to be read. This interpretation is further bolstered when we note what is *not* explicitly prohibited here: there is nothing here that explicitly prohibits forms of sexual expression such as mutual touching, holding hands, kissing, or even oral sex.[46] I am not claiming that ancient Israel would have explicitly approved of these other forms of sexual expression; I am simply pointing out that the focus was on one particular kind of behavior, a behavior that in its day would have been seen as an act of humiliating another person. Moreover, the text issues no prohibition whatsoever of sexual expression between women. This silence about what we call lesbianism is telling: it underscores the fact that the concern is with protecting male dignity and not protecting women or any particular marital ideal.

We gain another clue into the meaning of these prohibitions by observing the socio-historical context in which they occur. The prohibitions were issued to males who exercised authority within the ethos of an extended kinship system.[47] At least some of the males to whom these commandments were addressed were sexually polygamous: they were men whose sexual partners included not only wives but also concubines and slaves.[48] Under the conventions of the day, concubines and slaves would have been expected to be sexually available to the master.[49] (Incidentally, the very fact that slavery was an accepted institution in the book of Leviticus tells us that we need to do some important interpretive work before we can apply the worldview and laws of Leviticus directly to our life today.)[50]

Even though the head of a household was allowed to seek sexual gratification in a wide number of ways, Leviticus specifically prohibits Hebrew men from a certain kind of sexual activity: they are to refrain from "uncovering the nakedness" of certain persons within the extended household. Hebrew men were prohibited from having sexual relations with "any flesh of one's flesh" (*kol-shě'ēr běsārô* [Lev. 18:6]).[51] The term "flesh" here connotes close kinship.[52] The phrase "uncovering the nakedness" can be taken as a euphemism for sexual intercourse; but it can also mean any act of exposing a person to sexual vulnerability. A man was not allowed to even gaze on the nakedness of a female near relative (Lev. 18:6). In short, the point of the Leviticus prohibitions was to admonish powerful men in an ancient Near Eastern society — men who, for the most part, were used to having their way with sexual partners — not to bring themselves or others into sexual dishonor.

We can shed additional light on the two texts when we focus on the Hebrew words themselves. The key prohibition may be rendered in this way: "And with a male you shall not lie as one lies with a woman," where the crucial idiom is the phrase "to lie with."[53] In virtually every case in which Hebrew Scripture uses this idiom to speak of sexual relations, the usage refers not to the *manner* of the act itself but to the specific *context* in which the act is performed. Conservative exegetes of both Christian and Jewish conviction have long noted that the phrase "to lie with" almost always connotes a sex act being performed within a specific context that departs from permissible, consecrated, and covenantal norms.[54] The idiom operates as something like a euphemism for fornication, much as the vulgar English expression "to get laid" almost always connotes a promiscuous, extramarital, heedless sexual liaison. Examples of this usage in narrative contexts bolster the point: Lot's daughters "lying with" their father (Gen. 19:32-36); the case of Rebekah being given to "lie with" another man (Gen. 26:10); Shechem's forcible "lying with" Dinah (Gen. 34:2, 7); Reuben's "lying with" his father's concubine Bilhah (Gen. 35:22; 49:4); Potiphar's wife asking Joseph to "lie with me" (Gen. 39: 7, 10, 12, 14); the multiple sexual escapades of the sons of Eli (1 Sam. 2:22); David's forcing himself on Bathsheba (2 Sam. 11:4); the punishment meted out to David for "lying with" Bathsheba (2 Sam. 12:11, 24);[55] and Amnon's rape of Tamar (2 Sam. 13:11, 14).[56] Similarly, in every single mention of this idiom in the book of Leviticus, the phrase has to do with a sexual event that renders one ritually or morally unclean.[57] It seems, then, that context is everything.

Let us pause for a moment to ask, since the text specifically speaks of only one kind of sexual act, by what authority do some claim that the Leviticus prohibition is absolute, sweeping, and universal? The only way to arrive at that conclusion is to read the two prohibitions more broadly than they are literally written.[58] Merely repeating in a loud voice that Israel considered it to be an "abomination" does not tell us what this label meant or why it was invoked.[59] After all, "abomination" is merely a word for a strong, culturally restricted boundary. Since the Bible tells us that some considered the mere act of socially associating with shepherds to be an "abomination" (Gen. 46:34), we need a fuller sense of why this boundary existed. The best explanation is that Leviticus prohibits powerful men from taking sexual advantage of other men; this prohibition is possibly in support of the command to be "fruitful and multiply," or to keep Israelites from joining in pagan sexual customs, but primarily to preserve the sense of what it meant to be a man in Israelite society.[60]

Focusing on the reason for these prohibitions is important, but it still does not take us to the heart of what Leviticus is trying to say. We must remember that Leviticus is a collection of laws, and laws by their very nature must be interpreted. There are few laws — in either ancient Israel or contemporary America — that operate without reasonable exceptions. One is not permitted to kill another human, but one will not be prosecuted for killing someone in self-defense. In Anglo-American law we distinguish between written statutes and the legal opinions of judges: both are binding law, but the pronouncements made by judges in case law are always subject to interpretation, to exceptions, and to the reflective act of distinguishing one case from another. The laws set forth in Leviticus are more analogous to our case law, meaning that they are subject to being reinterpreted and modified, and to distinctions being made when new and different circumstances present themselves.[61] This act of reinterpretation, modification, and distinction has been going on for centuries in the interpretation of Leviticus, which is why we no longer worry about the supposed "abomination" of eating ostrich or the named sin of planting different kinds of seed in the same field.[62]

Rather than absolutizing two isolated texts from the past and ignoring the rest, we might better approach Leviticus by asking what its text as a whole may be trying to teach us. The most important lesson of Leviticus is about what it means to live a holy life. In order for life, including nuptial life, to become holy, it needs to be set apart and consecrated to God.

According to the biblical perspective, sex is a part of the world that God created to be "good" *(tôv)*.[63] Though our sexuality is "good," it must be set within boundaries if it is to become "holy" *(qādôš)*.[64] This is a key point of the biblical witness: in order for sexuality to be "holy," it must be set apart. Set apart for what? A classic answer is that it is set apart from sin and set apart for God. Perhaps a more nuanced answer is that sexuality needs to be set apart to bear witness to something beyond itself. It needs to be set apart to show that, in order to reach true fulfillment, the goodness of creation requires context, commitment, and constancy — in short, covenant. The reason why such covenantal love is blessed by religious communities is to give thanks for God's faithfulness and to lift up the hope that this same faithfulness will be reflected, however inadequately, in human covenant relationships. The goodness of sexuality finds its purpose in the particularity of sexuality within a covenantal context. Goodness seeks holiness as its fulfillment.

If love must be consecrated to be considered holy, then finding a consecrated context for the love of gays and lesbians should become a moral imperative. Especially if we conclude that the prohibitions in Leviticus were aimed at a specific cultural context, then withholding consecration from exclusively committed gay and lesbian couples in our new and different context becomes less and less defensible.

The Apostle Paul: Becoming a Living Sacrifice

The other important cluster of biblical texts on homoeroticism appears in works either written by or attributed to the apostle Paul.[65] The most noteworthy of these is Paul's Letter to the Romans, which we have already discussed in Chapters One and Two. What we discovered there was a difference between textual and contextual approaches to Paul. Textual approaches read what appears on the face of the text and apply it uncritically to today. When Paul speaks about Greco-Roman homoeroticism, a textualist approach assumes that what he says about some forms of homoeroticism must apply to all homoeroticism. By contrast, a contextualist approach interprets Paul's meaning squarely in reference to the Greco-Roman milieu to which he was addressing his admonitions. Paying attention to context allows us to make appropriate distinctions between one situation and another.

The Law

One key thing to remember in reading Paul is that he is always speaking as a faithful Jew. The notion of a separate religion known as "Christianity" had not fully emerged at the time Paul wrote. To be sure, Paul was a Jew who followed Jesus of Nazareth; but he was a Jew nonetheless. Thus, when Paul speaks of "law," he is speaking quite specifically of the Jewish Torah.[66] As Richard Hays has noted, Torah performs three discrete functions for Paul.[67] First, Torah establishes Jewish identity, both revealing the will of God and establishing the Jews as God's elect people. Second, it demonstrates that all human beings have sinned and fallen short of God's will. Third, it is a revealing witness to God's coming action in Jesus Christ.[68] Though Paul does not reject the law, he maintains that one must interpret it in the light of the outpouring of the Spirit: the gift of the Spirit to the community brings with it a new kind of freedom. It is the freedom not to be enslaved to the letter of the law but to discern the Spirit behind the law. The apostle says: "For freedom Christ has set us free. Stand firm, therefore, and do not submit again to a yoke of slavery" (Gal. 5:1). If there is freedom in Christ, and if this freedom is grounded in the power of the Spirit (Gal. 5:18), then the primary ethical question is not one of adhering to a list of rules; rather, the question is one of living a life of freedom and integrity in relationship to God's commandments. Quoting Leviticus 19:18, Paul declares: "The whole law is summed up in a single commandment, 'You shall love your neighbor as yourself'" (Gal. 5:14; cf. Rom. 13:8-10).

Since love is the key, how does a person know whether he or she is following this love commandment? The apostle Paul's answer is to live by the Spirit and not by the flesh (Gal. 5:16-26). What does this mean? Paul clarifies it by enumerating the works of the flesh as "fornication, impurity, licentiousness, idolatry, sorcery, enmities, strife, jealousy, anger, quarrels, dissensions, factions, envy, drunkenness, carousing, and things like these" (Gal. 5:19-21a). By contrast, he says that the fruits of the Spirit are "love, joy, peace, patience, kindness, generosity, faithfulness, gentleness, and self-control" (Gal. 5:22-23). Paul then adds this remarkable insight: with regard to the fruits of the Spirit, "there is no law" (Gal. 5:23). There is no law! In other words, since living by the Spirit is by its very nature living according to the purpose of the law, the individual features of the law (such as circumcision, dietary restrictions, and Sabbath observance) must be applied in a way that effects the law's overriding purpose.

This raises an important point. When we consider the case of exclusively committed same-sex unions, it can be argued that we should be guided by the spirit of the law rather than being slavishly bound to the letter. We should interpret the law in a way that is life-giving and redemptive rather than dehumanizing and punitive. The controlling question should be, Does the exclusive commitment of a gay or lesbian couple give evidence of the "fruit of the spirit," or does it more closely resemble the kinds of vices that Paul calls "works of the flesh"? If we approach this question honestly, the answer is clear. Today gays and lesbians are committing themselves to one another "for better or worse, in sickness and in health." I submit that equating exclusively committed same-sex love with such things as "fornication, impurity, licentiousness, idolatry," and so forth makes neither common sense nor Christian sense. Exclusively committed love between equals, especially when it is a love that reflects Christ's own self-giving for the other, fits more appropriately under the list of virtues, not the list of vices.[69]

Some may object that same-sex love by definition should be in the category of "fornication" *(porneia)*, which Paul places first in the list of vices in Galatians. But this argument merely begs the question: by definition, fornication is a sexual encounter that falls outside the covenantal context that Jews believed was blessed by God. Yet this is precisely what is in dispute today: may we, or may we not, establish a covenantal context in which same-sex unions may be blessed? The anti-gay argument really boils down to this: "You need a covenantal context, but we aren't going to give you one." Again, we must push beyond merely citing the various vice lists to understand the whys and wherefores of these lists, beyond finger-wagging and toward compassionate, redemptive care.

1 Corinthians 6 and 1 Timothy 1

There are two New Testament vice lists that refer to certain forms of homoerotic activity. The first one is in 1 Corinthians 6:9-10, where Paul admonishes his audience:

> Do you not know that wrongdoers will not inherit the kingdom of God? Do not be deceived! Fornicators, idolaters, adulterers, *male prostitutes, sodomites,* thieves, the greedy, drunkards, revilers, robbers — none of these will inherit the kingdom of God.

On the one hand, this list itself speaks in generalities (for that matter, the list is not specifically Christian in origin but is a standard enumeration of actions that many in the Greco-Roman world considered unacceptable). In New Testament days, authors cited such lists in order to "hook" their audience rhetorically. When the New Testament authors use these lists, they are making a general appeal for the community to aspire to upright conduct and shun behaviors that would bring them shame (e.g., 1 Cor. 5:10, 11; 6:9-10; Rom. 1:29-31; Gal. 5:19-23; Col. 3:5-8; 2 Tim. 3:1-5). On the other hand, the mention of homoerotic conduct is quite specific. It refers to a particular kind of hedonistic sexuality that falls outside a committed, covenantal context. It does not refer to all sexuality but to a hedonistic, uncommitted kind of sexuality. In order to see this, we must look carefully at the language Paul uses.

In 1 Corinthians the term translated by the NRSV as "sodomites" is more literally "males who go to bed with males." This has a specific kind of practice in mind. The Greek word *arsenokoitai* appears to have been coined directly from the Greek Septuagint translation of Leviticus 20:13 (the Greek Septuagint translation of the Hebrew Bible was read by most Jews in Paul's day). That word combines the Greek words *arsēn* ("male") and *koitē* ("bed"), both of which appear side by side in Leviticus 20:13.[70] The word translated by the NRSV as "male prostitutes" is *malakoi*, which literally means "soft ones."[71] Though some correctly point out that the meaning of *malakoi* is obscure, many believe it refers to the receptive, penetrated partner in male-on-male sexual intercourse, probably in the context of male prostitution. The linking of *arsenokoitai* and *malakoi* here suggests precisely the hedonistic homoerotic practices that were widespread in the Roman Empire. Such practices were almost always performed by social superiors upon social inferiors; that is, there was nothing essentially loving, exclusive, or covenantal about these encounters.[72] They were premised on Roman understandings of class and status.[73] As I have noted in the preceding chapter, a Roman citizen could sexually penetrate his wife, a woman of lower social standing, his slave, a prostitute — anyone who was his social inferior.

In specifically linking "male prostitutes" and "men-who-have-sex-with-men" *(arsenokoitai)*, Paul is referring to the sort of male prostitution in which men who were not slaves, but free, sold themselves to other men who were seeking sexual gratification. To sell oneself in this way was considered demeaning, and in denouncing such behavior Paul was not being especially countercultural.[74] Many Romans themselves, especially those influenced by Stoicism, had come to question such sexual hedonism and exploitation.[75]

Interpreting *arsenokoitai* as referring to heedless and hedonistic behavior is confirmed by 1 Timothy 1:9-10 (one of the so-called Pastoral Epistles), which reads:

> This means understanding that the law is laid down not for the innocent but for the lawless and disobedient, for the godless and sinful, for the unholy and profane, for those who kill their father or mother, for murderers, *fornicators, sodomites* [*arsenokoitai*], *slave traders,* liars, perjurers, and whatever else is contrary to the sound teaching.[76]

In addition to male prostitution, an especially pernicious — though controversial — feature of Roman life was the lively trade in boys who were sold into sexual slavery. I have referred to this briefly in the Introduction, but now it merits further comment. Slave boys were usually captured during military campaigns, when the Romans took many prisoners of war. It was commonplace for the Romans to castrate their young male prisoners to preserve their soft features for as long as possible. If they survived this mutilation, they quickly went to market as sexual slaves. Eventually, enough Romans came to consider slave boy castration problematic that they crafted laws banning the practice, though it persisted despite those efforts. This fact alone testifies to the lucrative nature of slave boy castration and thus the difficulty of stamping it out. This is almost certainly the situation that prompted 1 Timothy to place in the very same phrase "fornicators, men-who-have-sex-with-men, and slave traders." This is hardly the kind of behavior involved in exclusively committed same-sex love.

1 Thessalonians

Given the profligacy of sexual standards throughout the Roman Empire, it is no wonder that the apostle Paul insisted that his followers abide by high standards of sexual purity. This is clear from his earliest extant work, 1 Thessalonians. What he says there anticipates what he will later say in the letter to the Romans:

For this is the will of God, your sanctification: that you abstain from fornication [*porneia*]; that each one of you know how to control your own body [*skeuos*] in holiness and honor, not with lustful passion [*epithumias*], like the Gentiles who do not know God; that no one wrong or exploit [*pleonektein*] a brother or sister [*ton adelphon*] in this matter, because the Lord is an avenger in all these things, just as we have already told you beforehand and solemnly warned you. (1 Thess. 4:3-6)[77]

As we think about this passage in relationship to same-sex couples, we can see that four things are immediately apparent.

First, Paul's teaching is in the service of promoting a positive spiritual goal, namely, that his hearers become more holy — or, in the language of the tradition, that they be sanctified. In other words, Paul is not issuing prohibitions for prohibition's sake, but he's aiming rules at correcting social ills and bringing holiness into sexual relations. If exclusively committed same-sex unions actually help gay and lesbian people live more holy lives, then at least this much of Paul's vision for the ordering of Christian life has been satisfied.

Second, Paul frames his prohibition of sexual immorality as a task of knowing how to control one's own body.[78] Again, we must interpret the naming of specific prohibitions in light of the overarching goal for which the prohibition has been issued. In this case, sexual standards exist for the purpose of the ordering of life in relationship to God. An exclusively committed same-sex union is by its very nature a way of controlling one's body and ordering one's life to avoid promiscuity.

Third, the prohibited practices are connected with a practical test: Paul is concerned to promote a way of life that keeps people from being sexually exploited *(pleonektein)*. This specific mention of exploitation in 1 Thessalonians helps make sense of all Paul's other statements on the subject. It is hardly surprising when we keep in mind that so much of the sexual practice of the Roman world was exploitative by design.

Fourth, Paul is operating here with a stereotype that was widespread in the Jewish world, namely, that the gentiles as a group were sexually promiscuous. The premise is that people in the non-Jewish world are driven by their passions and not by a mind that has been trained in the ways of following God. Playing on these stereotypes helped Paul score rhetorical points with his audience. In 1 Thessalonians, and then later in Romans,

Paul takes this Jewish stereotype about gentile promiscuity and weaves it together with Roman Stoic convictions about the need for self-control, discipline, and regulating the body.[79] This is an important point to remember when we assess the later argument in Romans, where Paul cites pagan sexuality as one example of how the gentiles, because they do not know how to engage in a proper veneration of God, live idolatrously disordered lives. We can't blame Paul for attempting to craft an argument that would be persuasive. But does it really make sense to perpetuate these stereotypes taken from the practices of the Roman brothels when we seek to think through a very different issue — exclusively committed, marriage-like love?

Romans

Since I have treated Romans in detail throughout Chapters One and Two, I shall not engage in a lengthy treatment here. However, inasmuch as many Christians consider Romans to provide the final word on the issue, it is worthwhile to consider it yet again. It is not often noted that the argument about homoeroticism in Romans builds on the patterns of thinking already apparent in 1 Thessalonians. In both texts Paul advises his readers to refrain from the sexual practices engaged in by the kinds of gentiles "who do not know God." Paul does not provide a specific word for contemporary gays and lesbians who *do* know God. Chief among the sexual practices Paul condemns are those in which people are wronged or exploited.

This is clear from the language Paul uses. In both 1 Thessalonians and Romans, Paul defines what he is against as lustful passion (*epithumias* [cf. 1 Thess. 4:5 and Rom. 6:12; 7:7, 8; 13:14]). In fact, in Romans 7:7-8 and 13:9 (following the Greek Septuagint), Paul uses the very same word *(epithumias)* to translate the "Do not covet" commandment.[80] This underscores that it is lustful desire, as well as the sort of exploitative behavior that expropriates what is not one's own, that Paul has in mind here. Elsewhere, Paul is able to use the same word positively when he speaks of a godly desire to be with another (1 Thess. 2:17) or of a desire that is focused on Christ (e.g., Phil. 1:23). Thus it is not desire itself that is bad; the key is to have one's desires channeled in a godly direction.

What would a rightly channeled desire look like for gays and lesbians? In Romans, Paul speaks negatively of the kind of sexual desire that

seeks its own satisfaction while not caring for the other. He refers specifically to those who do not seek to honor God. It stands to reason, then, that
same-sex couples who *do* seek to honor God ought to be viewed in a different light. Paul's own mode of argumentation allows for this result. His ethical advice to those who seek a godly life is clear: "Let us live honorably as
in the day, not in reveling and drunkenness, not in debauchery and licentiousness, not in quarreling and jealousy. Instead, put on the Lord Jesus
Christ, and make no provision for the flesh, to gratify its desires" (Rom.
13:13-14). The ethical life to which Paul calls his readers is one of discernment from the heart and not mere external conformity to convention.
Again, he admonishes them: "Present your bodies as a living sacrifice, holy
and acceptable to God, which is your spiritual worship" (Rom. 12:1). They
certainly are to obey God's commandments, such as "You shall not commit adultery; You shall not murder; You shall not steal; You shall not
covet." But he also says that these and all the other commandments "are
summed up in this word, 'Love your neighbor as yourself'" (Rom. 13:9).
How anomalous it would be, in the light of this instruction, to slavishly
treat Paul's comments on a specific kind of pagan homoeroticism as a law
to be interpreted woodenly and without discernment! In addition to these
pieces of advice from Romans, Paul also specifically praises loving relationships in which the parties look not merely to their own interests but
also to the interests of the other (see Phil. 2:4).

What we have here, then, is a classic case of interpretation. Should we
read Paul's gloss on homoeroticism broadly to cover every conceivable
kind of conduct imaginable, or narrowly to speak only to a specific kind of
conduct in a specific context? There are many things about the Romans
text that argue for interpreting it narrowly within the specific cultural context in which it was written. The immorality, debauchery, and licentiousness that Paul complains about bears no resemblance to the exclusively
committed relationships we are being asked to assess today.

Community

The institution of marriage serves a community-building function. It con-
nects the new family formed by the mutual love of two people to a wider
family, a community of the faithful to which the couple contributes and
from which it draws strength. This is the third traditional purpose of mar-

riage, to integrate two people into a wider community that sustains them and in which they meaningfully participate. Becoming family involves much more than the tired old claim that the crux of marriage is procreation.[81] In the Bible, the passionate young couple in the Song of Songs can celebrate their physical, sexual love without any hint of procreative intent. To be sure, having children is an integral part of most marriages, and openness to having children is part of the stewardship of life that God entrusts to the human species (Gen. 1:28).[82] Still, today we never consider a marriage invalid merely because the couple, for whatever reason, does not produce children. Significantly, in American law the inability to have children is not typically a grounds for divorce. It is not even a legal requirement of marriage today that the couple engage in sexual relations.[83] In current law the main thing required to make a marriage valid is the desire to give oneself in exclusive commitment to another person.

Nevertheless, even though companionship and commitment are at the heart of marriage, all couples are connected, whether directly or indirectly, to a wider community. Even though a couple may not be rearing children, every couple has connections to the generations that will follow them and the generations that preceded them. Every couple is indebted to the past and looks forward into the future. In Christian doctrine, this interface between the couple and the community, between the nuclear family and the extended family, has a doctrinal name: we call it "the communion of saints." In terms of political thought, the point I am making here resonates with communitarian critiques of individual autonomy. That is, our individual choices have implications for the life of the society. In anthropology this insight is captured in the observation of Claude Levi-Strauss: "There would be no society without families, but equally there would be no families if society did not already exist." No family could sustain itself apart from the wider community that makes cooperative existence possible. This is as true of gay and lesbian families as it is of all other families. Like everyone else, gay and lesbian families do their part to make the community what it is, and they are as deserving of the community's support as is anyone else.

The intimate link between family and society is easy to see when we turn to the Bible. The importance of nurturing a vital connection to one's own people is at the heart of biblical religion. In Hebrew Scripture adherence to the ways of one's people is encapsulated in obedience to the law. Being remembered by one's people, moreover, is an integral part of being connected to a community. Thus it was said of the patriarch Abraham that he "breathed his last and died in a good old age, an old man and full of years, and was gathered to his people" (Gen. 25:8).

In the New Testament the understanding of marriage, family, and community receives a new twist. Unlike some contemporary "family values" teaching that almost makes an idol out of marriage, Jesus teaches that marriage and family are not ends in themselves but exist for the sake of something much bigger.[84] In fact, Jesus would not score very high on a test measuring commitment to today's notion of "family values": he tells his disciples that when they *leave* their traditional families for the sake of God's family they will receive an abundant reward (Mark 10:29-30; Matt. 19:29). Indeed, unless they are willing to *subordinate* the family to higher goals, they cannot be true disciples (Luke 14:26). In defining one's sense of belonging, Jesus acknowledges traditional notions of kinship only to see to it that they are thoroughly *transformed*. In the light of Jesus' teaching concerning God's reign, one's sense of family loyalties is changed (Luke 21:16), for now one's family extends in every direction (Matt. 25:40; Luke 14:12-13), especially to those who attend to the things of God (Matt. 12:49-50; Luke 8:21). What is valued is not biological procreation but godly association. Being Jesus' follower has little to do with whether one's family follows conventional patterns of family ties and everything to do with what and who one is living *for*.

It is interesting that, when questions are posed to Jesus about the nature of family, his answers contest the conventional understandings held by his opponents. In Jesus' day people assumed that a woman was the property of a man. Therefore, some of Jesus' opponents asked him about a situation where a woman had been "taken" (Luke 20:31) by seven brothers in succession: "Whose woman" would she be in heaven (Matt. 22:28)? Jesus' response to their question is quite stern: "You are wrong, because you know neither the scriptures nor the power of God" (Matt. 22:29). He goes on to explain that women are not "given" or "taken" in the day of resurrection, for a new order is dawning and a new understanding of belonging is being set in motion.[85] Belonging to the family of God, it turns out, is more important than the conventions of the biological family (Mark 3:34-35; Matt. 10:34-39; Luke 14:26).

This raises an important question. Jesus' vision of God's reign includes calling into question certain societal conventions concerning marriage. So then, why are those same conventions being used by some of his followers today to exclude gay and lesbian people from the full benefits of community? The great irony in this exclusion is that, while many make accommodations for heterosexual divorce, they are not willing to make similar accommodations for gays and lesbians being included within the covenant of marriage. And yet Jesus' teachings against divorce are quite strict. Many in Jesus' day assumed that a man could divorce his wife on any whim; but Jesus took a different view, no doubt in part because divorcing a woman in that culture meant that she was left vulnerable because she had no support. A deeper reason was that being bound together in community was a sacrosanct value. Jesus reminds his interrogators of the Genesis passage we discussed earlier about God having made human beings male and female, and about the two spouses coming together to become one family (Matt. 19:3-5; cf. Gen. 2:24). Jesus cites this verse, not to dwell on the sexual complementarity of male and female, but to speak out against the act of breaking one's family ties through divorce. He is quite clear about that: "Therefore what God has joined together, let no one separate" (Matt. 19:6). Breaking a family covenant is serious business, according to Jesus, because being family has implications both for the individual and for the broader community.

How are we to square the laxity with which today's churches treat Jesus' teachings on divorce with the strictness the church applies to gays and lesbians, a subject about which Jesus never said a word? If anything, Jesus' explicit teachings should invite us to push beyond legalisms in dealing with gay and lesbian people. In all his dealings, Jesus pushed beyond the surface in order to embrace the humanity of each person whom he encountered. This is clear from what Jesus says immediately following his teaching on divorce. Jesus' disciples, having heard the seriousness with which Jesus spoke of divorce, blurt out that it must be better, then, not to marry a woman at all. If they found Jesus' teaching on divorce exasperating, how much more what he said next? Listen to Jesus's enigmatic response:

> But he said to them, "Not everyone can accept this teaching, but only those to whom it is given. For there are eunuchs who have been so from birth, and there are eunuchs who have been made eunuchs by others, and there are eunuchs who have made themselves eunuchs for the sake of the kingdom of heaven. Let anyone accept this who can." (Matt. 19:11-12)

Why does Jesus, all of a sudden, make a proclamation about eunuchs? At one level, this is merely a statement of the degree of religious devotion demanded by Jesus. Some (though not all) are called to put aside sexual relations for the sake of following God's reign. To this extent, it is a statement of ethical rigor. Yet there is something more in this statement that should catch our attention: according to Jewish law, a eunuch was a sexually nonconforming person. In the conventions of the day, a eunuch was a person who was neither male nor female and thus was excluded from the "male and female" community of Genesis. Because of this perceived lack of purity, such a person was barred from the religious assembly (Deut. 23:1; Lev. 21:20). Now it becomes clear that two further things are going on in Jesus' statement, and both are revolutionary.

First, we must remember the social context in which Jesus operated. As I have observed before, Rome thrived on sexual hedonism, and the most common version of eunuchs in this context were those "who have been made eunuchs by others." These were people who had been castrated and turned into servants and sex slaves. These people were by definition near the bottom of the social and sexual hierarchy. True, they sometimes rose to become high-ranking officers who were entrusted with important responsibilities. But in the process they had been robbed of their sexual identity; indeed, their sexuality was often appropriated violently for the benefit of others. Lest anyone think that Jesus, in rural Galilee, was ignorant of the sexual profligacy of the Roman world, we should note that Herod the Great built a gymnasium in Jerusalem that was a notorious place for exploitative sexual liaisons.[86] So it is not likely that Jesus was naive about the ways of the Roman world. Notwithstanding the inferior status of eunuchs, Jesus speaks here of these sexually nonconforming persons in a remarkable way. Not only does he defy convention by including them within the religious community; he also considers them a symbol of the highest and best devotion that individuals in that community could achieve.

Second, Jesus implicitly makes good here on a promise that was articulated in the book of Isaiah. Isaiah utters a prophecy to those Israelites who have been carried off and made eunuchs by foreign captors, holding out to them the promise that they will have a heritage greater than the children they are now unable to sire (cf. Isa. 39:7). If they hold fast to the covenant, they will be given a name that will never be cut off (Isa. 56:4-5). Surely this is part of the background for the story of the Ethiopian eunuch in Acts 8, who is reading from the book of Isaiah. The apostle Philip has been directed by the Spirit to this eunuch, and he explains to him that the passage about the suffering servant from Isaiah 53:7-8 refers to Jesus. Responding to what Philip says, the eunuch points to some water and asks Philip whether there is anything keeping him from being baptized (cf. Isa. 55:1). The answer is that, under a strict reading of the law, there is everything to prevent his baptism: his nonconforming sexuality bars him from the covenant. But under the new dispensation of the Spirit, this man's sexuality and his personhood are able to be blessed. If gays and lesbians hold fast to the covenant today, are we willing to stand with Isaiah in promising them that they will not be cut off from their community?

This is not the only instance where Jesus pushes the envelope regarding Jewish sexual mores. In Matthew 8:5-13, a professional Roman commander, a "centurion," comes to Jesus, saying, "Lord, my servant [*pais*] is lying home paralyzed, in terrible distress."[87] Why this no-nonsense, seasoned military officer, a gentile, comes to Jesus is not clear; but in response Jesus offers to come to his home — in itself a boundary-breaking gesture. The soldier demurs: as a person under command, he knows that Jesus need only say the word and his *pais* (his "boy") will be healed. The parallel version in Luke 7 makes it clear that the soldier's *pais* does not mean his son, as some interpretations have it, but his slave (*doulos* [Luke 7:2]). Like the historic usage in the American South, a "boy" — both in the Greek (Septuagint) version of the Old Testament and in the common Greek parlance of Jesus' day — was a diminutive word for a slave.[88] As we know from our previous brief sketch of slavery in Rome, one of the functions a slave would perform for a Roman soldier was sexual gratification. Thus, this "boy" may have been not only a slave but more specifically a sex slave.[89] We cannot know for sure what the nature of the centurion's relationship with his slave was, and it doesn't matter for the purposes of the argument. What matters is that Jesus does not rebuke the centurion, either for having a slave or for how he treated the slave. This is astonishing in itself. Instead, Jesus' focus is on something else altogether: he praises this pagan centurion's faith and uses it as an object lesson for the ways of the "kingdom." He tells all those assembled that, first of all, he has not found a faith as it is exhibited by this gentile soldier in all of Israel. He then pronounces an eschatological, end-time vision of gentile inclusion into God's family: "I tell you, many will come from east and west [i.e., gentiles] and will eat with Abraham and Isaac and Jacob in the kingdom of heaven, while the heirs of the kingdom will be thrown into the outer darkness, where there will be weeping and gnashing of teeth." Finally, in response to the centurion's faith, Jesus heals the boy.

It becomes clear, then, that belonging to the covenant is about more than conforming to social conventions — even to sexual conventions. It is about allegiance to God and to the people of God.[90] In the Sermon on the Mount, Jesus claims that he does not want to set aside *(luō)* any of the commandments, but he does call on the disciples to "do" and "teach" the commandments with an eye toward the redemptive coming of God's "kingdom," or reign (Matt. 5:19). This teaching has direct bearing on the question of ethics for gay and lesbian Christians. The dynamism in the life lived before the biblical text means that the church is empowered to exercise a sanctified discretion in ordering its corporate life. Having been given the "keys to the kingdom," the church is empowered to judge ethical cases with wisdom as they arise. They are encouraged to make decisions with "binding" and "loosing" *(luō)* effect in the community.

An eminent example of this communal discretion occurs in the Acts of the Apostles. In the 1990s some Christians, among them New Testament scholars Luke Timothy Johnson and Jeffrey Siker, began to ask whether the movement of the Holy Spirit among gay and lesbian people was analogous to the early church's experience with gentiles, among whom God was performing "signs and wonders."[91] The earliest Jewish Christians had assumed that, if gentiles were to enter the fellowship of the church, they could do so only by first becoming Jews, that is, by observing the Jewish laws concerning circumcision, dietary requirements, and so forth. This assumption was based on texts such as Genesis 17:9-14, which demands circumcision of all males, including foreigners. From their experience of gentile conversion, both Peter and Paul came to a different conclusion: gentiles were permitted to enter the church as gentiles without being circumcised and conforming to kosher laws, though they were of course expected to put aside immorality. Critics have countered that there is no analogy between being a gentile, which is involuntary, and homoerotic practice, which one chooses to engage in voluntarily. Critics have also countered that listening to the Spirit never contradicts the plain meaning of Scripture. But these criticisms miss the point. The proper analogy is not one of voluntary or involuntary behavior but of the presence of the Spirit. Because of the visible work of the Spirit, the early church saw fit to include gentiles in the community, even though it meant countermanding the plain meaning of the circumcision texts. Similarly, the covenantal love being expressed between committed gays and lesbians has been kindled by the same Spirit that inaugurated the gentile mission.

This may be one of those times when asking ourselves "what would Jesus do?" makes eminent sense. Do we really believe that Jesus would condemn gay couples who are sincerely seeking to live a life committed to one another? After all, Jesus was the one who taught his followers that the promises of Scripture were being brought to completion in his own life and ministry, and he also admonished them to bring the law to completion in their own lives by loving their neighbors (Matt. 5:43-45).[92]

In order to gain further understanding into the dynamic nature of loving community, let us conclude by looking at three more pivotal stories. Two are from Hebrew Scripture, the story of a foreigner named Ruth, and that of David and Jonathan. The other is the New Testament announcement in Galatians 3:28 that in Christ there is no more "male and female."

Ruth and Naomi, David and Jonathan

It turns out that Jesus' seemingly innovative approach to issues of family is not so new after all. It taps into one of the Bible's deepest veins. Throughout the Bible unconventional people are empowered to contribute to God's redemptive story in amazing ways. Consider the biblical story of Ruth.[93] It tells of an Israelite family that moves to a foreign country, the land of Moab, in order to escape a time of massive famine in Israel. The fact that the story concerns a woman who is a Moabite is significant. Jewish law absolutely prohibited a Moabite from being part of Israel's religious community (Deut. 23:3; Neh. 13:1).[94]

At first things seem to go well. The family prospers long enough for the two sons to marry Moabite women. But before long, the head of the household dies, followed shortly by the death of his two sons as well, making widows of all three of the women — Naomi and her two daughters-in-law. Bereft of male protection and now with no means for her own provision, the matriarch of the family, Naomi, confronts her daughters-in-law with the crisis they all face. Proposing a plan that seems eminently sensible, Naomi frees the two younger women to seek new families with new husbands among their own people, while she herself resolves to journey home alone to the land of Israel. In tears, the first daughter-in-law, Orpah, follows Naomi's advice and departs. At this point in the story a good Isra-elite might be thinking, "It serves these people right for consorting with Moabites. Be done with them. Let them part ways."

Nevertheless, the second daughter-in-law, Ruth, will hear none of leaving her mother-in-law. Despite not being an Israelite, and despite the fact that staying with Naomi involves substantial risk and an uncertain fu-ture, she feels bound to Naomi by covenant loyalty — in Hebrew, *hesed*.[95] The word *hesed* is used frequently in the Hebrew Bible to mean God's own bond of covenant loyalty to God's people.

"Covenant" is a term we have used a number of times throughout this study. It is a category with overlapping religious, social, and political connotations. A covenant is the solemn, public enactment of a reciprocal relationship in which the parties bind themselves to undertake certain mu-tual obligations and provide certain mutual benefits to one another. A typ-ical example of a covenant in ancient times was a treaty that two kings would enter into. This reminds us that, from its origins, covenant-making had a political character. Accordingly, the quintessential example of covenant-making in modern times is the written constitution. As we shall see in the next chapter, the United States Constitution establishes a kind of political covenant in which various rights, duties, and obligations are ob-served among a diverse citizenry. Because they have implications for the broader society, covenants are public in character, often stipulating clear consequences if the terms are broken. The breaking of a treaty alters the balance of power between nations and can lead to the forfeiture of privi-leges; in dire cases, it can even lead to retaliation or war.

In the theological realm, covenant-making is an important way of speaking of God's basic determination to be our God. God reaches out to human beings in grace and invites our faithful response. Although there are many forms of covenant in Scripture, the paradigmatic idea is centered in God's covenant with Israel at Sinai, where God became bound to Israel as a people, and Israel became bound to obey and embody God's law. This is expressed well by the prophet Jeremiah: "I will be your God, and you will be my people" (Jer. 30:22).[96] God's covenant with the people always arises at God's own gracious initiative, and God always remains faithful to the covenant, even when human beings let God down.

One of the most important covenants in our society, of course, is the relationship made between one human being and another in the cove-nant of marriage. Spouses are called on to be faithful to one another as a sign of God's faithfulness to us. And like other covenants, marriage has a public character: it not only affects the two spouses, but also their children, their wider families, and society as a whole. This is why society, upon the death of one of the spouses, steps in and provides significant support. This is also why, if the marriage breaks down, the law steps in to provide rules concerning child custody, support payments, and the division of property.

The book of Ruth is a story about what happened to one such family when calamity struck and about how the bonds of family were not only nurtured by individuals but honored by the society in which they lived. The language used in the book of Ruth gives us a clue that covenant loyalty, as conceived within the precepts of biblical religion, is about something other than the narrow construct of "gender complementarity." The bond described in Ruth is between two women. There is nothing overtly sexual about it, and yet the story being told uses the very same words that appear in the famous summary statement about the meaning of marriage from the book of Genesis: "Therefore a man leaves [*'āzab*] his father and his mother and cleaves [*dābaq*] to his wife, and they become one flesh" (Gen 2:24, RSV).[97] Many contemporary interpreters take "one flesh" in Genesis to signal sexual intercourse; but, as we shall soon see, this is too constricted a reading. It more properly means that the two become "one family." This is in keeping with the fact that in the Genesis text the word "leave" (*'āzab*) connotes a shift in loyalty. Formerly, the allegiance of the parties ran to their families of origin; but now they embark on a new loyalty to one another. This new-found loyalty is gathered up in the word "cleave" (*dābaq*). The intensity of marital "cleaving" no doubt flows in part from the natural, erotic desire that exists between a man and a woman in love. Nevertheless, there is more to it than that, as the story of Ruth makes clear.

In the book of Ruth these identical words also signal something far more enduring than the passions of sexuality. In an echo of Genesis, Ruth refuses to "leave" Naomi (*'āzab* [Ruth 1:16]) and insists on "cleaving" to her (*dābaq* [Ruth 1:14]). Though her words do not pertain to marriage, Ruth's statement is often quoted or sung in wedding ceremonies:

> Entreat me not to leave [*'āzab*] you or to return from following you; for where you go I will go, and where you lodge I will lodge; your people shall be my people, and your God my God. (Ruth 1:16, RSV)

In keeping with this pledge, Ruth follows Naomi back to Israel, where, in order to secure both her livelihood and that of Naomi, she marries Naomi's kinsman Boaz. In keeping with the rules for honoring family in Israelite society, Boaz steps in and becomes the protector of both Ruth and Naomi. In other words, Ruth's reaching out to Boaz results in Boaz's reaching out to Naomi. Ruth's loyalty pays huge dividends, and the ramifications of her faithfulness spread well beyond the resolution of the immediate crisis she and Naomi have faced. By the end of the book, the specter of famine has been replaced by a bountiful harvest, and Ruth gives birth to a son who will become the grandfather of Israel's King David, who himself will be an ancestor of Jesus of Nazareth. Here the faithfulness of one whom convention considered to be an inappropriate marriage partner leads to redemption. It even leads to the birth of Jesus.

In short, becoming family arises from the personal act of individuals, yet such individual acts also have implications for the broader social ordering of the world. Sexuality conduces to sociality; and sociality, in turn, has implications beyond the conjugal love of the particular couple. This point is illustrated not only in the language of leaving and cleaving but in the usage of the biblical word "flesh," a word we have encountered several times now. The book of Genesis describes Eve as having been formed from one of Adam's ribs (Gen. 2:22). As I have noted above, Adam was alone and without a companion with whom to share his life; but on first seeing Eve, Adam cries out with joy, "This at last is bone of my bones and flesh of my flesh" (Gen. 2:23). The emphasis here is on the fact that Adam and Eve are of the same flesh. A verse later, the importance of being of the same flesh is invoked in the Priestly writer's summation of what marriage means: "Therefore a man leaves his father and his mother and clings to his wife, and they become one flesh" (Gen. 2:24).

Again, it is a mistake to read these idioms concerning the flesh as though they applied solely to sexual intercourse. As we saw in Chapter One, some Roman Catholic philosophers are fond of speaking about the "two-in-one-flesh union" of man and woman in marriage. They might just as well speak of the "three-in-one-flesh union" of man, woman, and child, or the "twenty-in-one-flesh union" of the extended family. This is made perfectly clear later in the Genesis narrative, when Jacob meets his uncle Laban for the first time. Laban greets Jacob with precisely Adam's words to Eve: "Surely you are my bone and my flesh" (Gen. 29:14).[98] Here the meaning obviously is not sex but kinship: to be "one flesh" with another is to become part of the same family. When two men or two women find each other and make this one-flesh commitment to one another, there is just as much reason to rejoice as when Adam first beheld Eve. When anyone finds a suitable life partner, it is appropriate for the community to give them its blessing. For they have become one bone, one flesh — united in the same family.

Another instructive story of becoming family is the friendship of David and Jonathan. Ruth's great-grandson, David, rose from being a humble shepherd boy to become one of Israel's most honored kings. David is celebrated as the boy hero who defeated the Philistine giant, Goliath, with a slingshot. It was David who supplanted King Saul, ruled over a united Israel, and established Jerusalem as its capital. During David's ascent to power he was befriended by Saul's son, the young warrior Jonathan. So strong was this friendship that Jonathan gave David his own armor, his bow, his belt and, in the ups and downs of palace intrigue, sided with David against his own father Saul.

A few commentators have suggested that the bond between David and Jonathan was homoerotic. We are told, for example, in 1 Samuel 18:1 that "the soul of Jonathan was bound to the soul of David, and Jonathan loved him as his own soul" (cf. 18:3). The language here may echo the amorous declarations of the young woman in the Song of Songs to her beloved (Song 1:7; 3:1-4). David's wife, Michal, and Jonathan are each said to love David and both risk their lives to save him from Saul's anger, a parallel that some commentators see as portraying Jonathan as wifelike and subordinate to David. In addition, when Jonathan is finally killed in battle, David mourns and says of Jonathan, "greatly beloved were you to me; your love to me was wonderful, passing the love of women" (2 Sam. 1:26).[99] Other scholars find it unlikely that a venerated king of Israel would be depicted in homoerotic terms.

One need not accept the thesis that David and Jonathan were male lovers, however, in order to find meaning in their story for a contemporary theology of gay marriage. Like the Ruth and Naomi story, this is another example of covenant loyalty that informs our understanding of what it means to be family. Because of his loyalty to David, Jonathan put himself on the line for David, risking his political capital and his very life. After all, Jonathan was in line to become king himself and was willing to relinquish this possibility for David's sake. Even if theirs is not a story of sexual union, it exemplifies the kind of self-giving upon which covenant love depends.

That David and Jonathan became "family" to one another is further evidenced by David's actions when he ascends to the throne. Jonathan is killed in battle, but leaves a male heir. Ordinarily, one might expect a new monarch to eliminate any potential rivals. Instead, David declares that Jonathan's physically challenged son, Mephibosheth, would always be treated as family. He would always have a place at the king's table and his progeny would be provided for (2 Sam. 9:1-13).

In both Ruth and Naomi and David and Jonathan, we have examples of covenant belonging that brings benefits to others. The bonds of family, and the obligations of covenant, extend beyond sexuality. They are rooted in faithfulness to the other and serve as tangible signs of God's faithfulness to us.

Galatians 3:28: Belonging and Baptism

It is belonging, not biology, that is important for the family of God. Thus it is no accident that, within the fellowship of the church, disciples are made by baptism, not by procreation. Baptism bestows on each person a new identity: child of God. Being a child of God constitutes an identity more enduring and more significant than any that we ourselves or others may assign us. For people who have been given a pariah status in a community, which has certainly been the historic case for gays and lesbians, the birthright of baptism is good news indeed.

The broad implications of this new identity are set forth with compelling clarity in Paul's letter to the churches in Galatia. What Paul says here is particularly pertinent for the controversy concerning same-sex relationships:

> [F]or in Christ Jesus you are all children of God through faith. As many of you as were baptized into Christ have clothed yourselves with Christ. There is no longer Jew or Greek, there is no longer slave or free, there is no longer male and female; for all of you are one in Christ Jesus. And if you belong to Christ, then you are Abraham's offspring, heirs according to the promise. (Gal. 3:26-29)[100]

In Christ, all who are baptized become "heirs" to the promises of God; and in accordance with this new status, they are to live their lives in the confidence born of being children of God.

The most striking claim, for purposes of thinking about sexual orientation in the church, is the one made in verse 28: *"There is no longer Jew or Greek, there is no longer slave or free, there is no longer male and female; for all of you are one in Christ Jesus."*

This verse mentions three sets of human characteristics, each of which is framed as a polarity: Jew/Greek, slave/free, male/female. The breadth of these three polarities is clear, in that they comprise the most basic features of our human existence: (1) ethnic, political, cultural, and religious identity (Jew/Greek); (2) legal status, social location, economic and class distinctions (slave/free); (3) sexuality and gender roles (male/female). What the biblical witness is saying here is remarkable: the most basic features of our created human existence — features that are used constantly to define a person's place and significance in the religious, social, and political order — no longer define the identity of people who are in Christ. What does this teaching of Galatians 3:28 mean for gays and lesbians?

I believe that careful attention to the text of Scripture at this point can yield ground-breaking insights. The Greek word for "or" *(oude)* that appears in the first two declarations ("there is no longer Jew *or* Greek" and "there is no longer slave *or* free") suddenly shifts in the final declaration to the conjunction "and" *(kai):* "There is no longer male *and* female."[101] Previous English translations of the Bible have not paid much attention to this grammatical shift. The Revised Standard Version, which was published in 1952 and followed the King James Version, made the mistake of using the construction "neither/nor" for all three declarations. Thus it translated the first two polarities as: "There is neither Jew nor Greek, there is neither slave nor free." It then went on to mistranslate the third polarity: "There is *neither* male *nor* female." In doing so, the RSV was perpetuating a mistranslation that had cropped up unnoticed in English versions of the Bible from the earliest days.[102] It was not until 1989, when the New Revised Standard Version finally rendered the passage literally and more accurately ("there is no longer male *and* female"), that the English-speaking church finally got the text right.

This is not just a grammatical point; it is a profoundly theological point. And it is a point that has implications for how we view the reality of gender in general and same-gender sexuality in particular. Scholars from across the spectrum agree that Galatians 3:28 makes far-reaching theological claims.[103] This text says that the religious, social, and gender realities that define the world at large do not ultimately define the identities of those who are baptized in Christ. Here Paul is quoting a prior baptismal formula: he is appealing to words that both he and the Galatians had inherited from the earliest Christian believers.[104] And Paul invokes words that emerged from the vision of God's reign that Jesus himself had bequeathed to the early Christian community — words the Galatian believers would have heard when they were first baptized, and words they would have remembered as defining a new way of being in the world.

In other words, the content of Galatians 3:28 is not merely an idiosyncratic statement of the theology of Paul; rather, it is a powerful statement of the theology of the *church*. The meaning and significance of this statement reside not just within the mind of Paul, but they belong to the wisdom of the whole church as discerned through the ages. This means that it is the whole church, and not Paul alone, that has the responsibility for making sense of this baptismal declaration and living it out. This is a process, in fact, that has taken the church many centuries, and is still ongoing. Let us consider some prominent examples.

The text of Galatians 3:28 speaks specifically to the issues of slavery and gender, and yet it has taken the church centuries to wrestle with both of these issues. The biblical text says that slavery and gender should no longer define the identity of Christians. And yet it was not until 1865, almost 250 years after Africans were brought to America in chains, and after a long civil war, that America finally abolished slavery.[105] Even today, there are an estimated 27 million people who live in slavery around the world.[106] It is one thing for the biblical text to announce that "there is no longer slave or free"; it is another thing to live out the implications of that announcement.

Likewise, it is only in the last seven or eight decades that the church has dared to explore the full implications of Galatians 3:28 for the equality of women. And only recently has the church acknowledged male domination, female subordination to men, and sexual exploitation as serious ethical and theological problems. These are problems that reside not only in our culture but in the long-standing theological traditions that have influenced our culture. For far too long now, texts that supported women's subjugation by men have been used to trump the broader, more positive testimony about women and men in Galatians 3:28 — and elsewhere in the Bible. Statements about women keeping silent in specific circumstances were used to negate the more general baptismal declaration of male and female parity. This is a telling example of how the more general statements of biblical principle, rather than the prohibitions addressed to specific circumstances, should guide our interpretation of the biblical text. If the Galatians passage is given the interpretive priority, then equality in both church and world flows as a logical consequence.

But there is even more to Galatians 3:28 than an endorsement of equality. If all the text had said was that in Christ "there is *neither* male *nor* female," then it would constitute an admirable articulation of the equality of men and women as individuals. Yet, taking it further, the phrase "male *and* female" is a religious "term of art" — in this case a precise theological rubric that comes from another biblical text that we have previously examined. The "male and female" in Galatians 3:28 is an exact quotation of the Greek version of Genesis 1:27, which says: "So God created humankind in his image, in the image of God he created them; *male and female* he created them."[107]

Notice what is happening here. In Galatians 3:28, it is not just one's status as male *or* female that is declared irrelevant for one's identity in Jesus Christ; it is also the foundational reality of gender itself, the pairing of male *and* female, that has no ultimate hold on the new community seeking to live out the gospel. Invoking "gender complementarity" or even "gender identity" as a fundamental basis for drawing ethical distinctions of status or worth within the body of Christ has no support in the gospel according to Galatians 3:28.[108] Gender roles and expectations need no longer determine the ultimate identity of the baptized, for all are now "Abraham's offspring, heirs according to the promise."[109] This is good news for all people, and especially for those whose manhood, womanhood, or sexual orientation has been scorned either within the church or in society at large.

It would be wrong to claim that the early Christians who first announced the new reality in Galatians 3:28 could have imagined blessing same-sex relationships. That is not my claim — any more than these early Christians could have explicitly anticipated the abolition of slavery in the early nineteenth century or the establishment of women's social and legal equality in the early twentieth. Still, the limits of a past generation's imagination need not constrain the limits of our own generation's commitment to compassion or justice. Past generations could not have predicted the end of slavery, but in our day it has come. Past generations could not have predicted a world of gender equality, but in our day it has come and is still coming. Past generations could not have predicted that gay and lesbian people would step forward to enter marriage-like commitments and raise families; but finding a way to support such commitments is the challenge we face in our own time.

Even though slavery's abolition and gender equality were not explicitly contemplated by the biblical writers, they nonetheless planted seeds that eventually blossomed into these results. Take slavery, for example: earlier we saw that, under Roman law, a slave was one who by definition was captive to the will of the master. Not only was the slave's labor, but also the slave's body, subject to the master's control. Male slaves were routinely forced to submit to same-sex intercourse with the master.[110] The very word "slave" was synonymous with being a sexual object. If we keep this in mind, we will see how subversive the apostle Paul's message was: Paul took the very metaphor of slavery, with all its ugly and inhuman connotations, and turned it into one of his most vivid ways of speaking about what it means to be a Christian disciple.[111] Paul tells us that Jesus himself took the form of a slave (Phil. 2:7), and thus are his followers to join him in slavery. In one of his most shocking images, Paul even compares the Christian life to that of a defeated prisoner of war being led in a slave parade (2 Cor. 2:14). In that passage Paul refers to the Roman "triumph," a processional in which Rome's defeated enemies were led away either to slavery or to ritual death, as sacrifices to the pagan gods.[112] Paul's readers would have seen these bleak processionals and would have known that, before being put on parade, those prisoner-slaves were routinely sexually humiliated by their captors. John Calvin even found Paul's imagery so abhorrent that he assumed the apostle must have meant something different, namely, that Christians themselves are the triumphant ones rather than those who are subdued and defeated.[113]

Given the typical treatment shown toward slaves — abusive by our standards, accepted by Roman standards — how do we interpret some of Paul's other admonitions, such as, "Slaves, obey your masters" (Eph. 6:5)? Or his advice to enslaved people, "Remain as you are" (1 Cor. 7:26)? These imperatives are not meant to endorse the sexual abuse of slaves any more than "children, obey your parents in the Lord" (Eph 6:1) is meant to approve the parental abuse of children. Rather, the point is that baptism announces and anticipates a new situation in which the condition of slavery — even with the profound sexual stigma attached to it — can be redeemed through the power of the death and resurrection of Christ.[114] This is a radical redemption indeed. Even if one is living the life of an abused slave, one's life is still redeemed in Christ! And this is a redemption that has come to social fruition in the modern world with the abolition of slavery.

With a redemption so radical, who is in a position to place limits on the scope of a text like Galatians 3:28? To limit it to what past generations have thought of it is to misunderstand the very nature of Scripture. Scripture is not merely to be read backward; if it is to be a living word for today, we must read it forward through our own history.[115] Scripture is always saying far more than any of us can imagine because it is pointing us to the unfolding reality of the reign of God and inviting us to live into that reality. If the meaning of Scripture is limited to what ancient minds could have imagined, there is no such thing as a Word of God that is living and active (Heb. 4:12). Nonetheless, some will persist in objecting that this text has "always been read" not to have any explicit implications for gender complementarity and sexual orientation. As is usually the case with the "it's-always-been-read-that-way" argument, it is not true. Long ago, one of the chief architects of the doctrine of the triune God, Gregory of Nyssa, made the connection between Galatians 3:28 and Genesis 1:27 a chief plank in his own understanding of gender. His argument was that gender itself is something that needs to be redeemed. In fact, he held that gender distinctions did not exist prior to the Fall, would not exist in the resurrected state, and could be transgressed in the present age — for example, in women exercising the gender roles of men — as an anticipation of the age to come.[116]

Of course, it is important to be very clear about what Galatians 3:28 is saying and what it is not saying. It is not saying that, once one is baptized, the fact that she or he is a woman or a man living in a particular time and place suddenly disappears — any more than the empirical reality that one is a gentile or a slave, a banker or a chimney sweep, suddenly vanishes. Yet it is equally important to hold fast to what Galatians 3:28 *is* saying: it signals that gender roles and definitions, even the venerable pattern of "male and female," do not establish the ultimate reality within which Christians are called to live. We cannot reduce who a person is to his or her gender. Galatians 3:28 is an expression of liberation for us all, but especially for gays and lesbians. What first-century Christians were empowered to imagine was a new, post-Resurrection world in which sexuality and gender roles placed no ultimate limit on the redemption that was possible for those who are in Christ. The early Christians caught a glimpse, there and then, into a distant, new, and redeemed world. And we have been permitted by grace, here and now, to take one step closer to that world. There and then, they began to live out a new, redeemed existence; here and now, we seek by grace to make that redemption even more real. There and then, they could only envision those things darkly, as through a glass, and so they walked by faith. Here and now, we walk no less by faith, grateful that their initial vision still shows us the way.

Summary

Much of the opposition to gay and lesbian people in our culture has been fueled by biases that purport to be of a biblical and theological nature. It is important to challenge these biases if we are to make progress in church and society concerning the consecration of exclusively committed same-sex relationships. In this chapter I have made a biblical and theological case for a stance toward same-sex couples that is not only welcoming and affirming, but that is welcoming, affirming, and ordering. I have made this case based on marriage as a context for companionship, commitment, and community.

First, regarding companionship, I have based my support of same-sex couples on the divine declaration in Genesis that it is not good for the human being to be alone. It is of great theological importance that God is the one who created the human desire for otherness. It is also important that in the biblical narrative God responds to this human desire by providing a companion who is suitable. For gays and lesbians, a suitable companion is one whose sexual orientation matches their own. Does this, then, give the church permission to bless gay and lesbian unions? I believe that it does. I have argued that marriage is not a fixed order of creation but an order of redemption. We encourage people to unite in marriage, not on the merits of who the people already are, but with expectations of who we hope they will become. Marriage is a means of transformation and grace; when it is, the couple's mutual desire and devotion are meant to reflect God's own desire for us and devotion to be our God. There is every reason to believe that, by the grace of God, gay and lesbian couples are just as capable as heterosexual couples of modeling a desire and devotion worth consecrating.

Second, companionship should lead to commitment. Spousal love is an engaged and self-giving love. Today the exclusively committed love of gay couples raises questions about the relationship of such love to traditional marriage. It also raises the question of how to read the biblical prohibitions against certain forms of homoeroticism in the ancient world. In every case, these biblical prohibitions refer to one-sided and exploitative and culturally distinct forms of behavior, not to nuptial love. And that is true both for Leviticus in Hebrew Scripture and for the teachings of Paul in the New Testament. It is important to interpret the prohibitions in Leviticus correctly because all later prohibitions flow from the Leviticus texts. Yet Leviticus 18:22 and 20:13 do not prohibit every form of same-sex expression imaginable; instead, they prohibit a form of emasculating sexual behavior marked by dominance, exploitation, and humiliation. This does not mean that we should reject what Leviticus aims to say. In truth, its teaching is extremely important: Leviticus tells us that sexuality is created good but needs to be consecrated in a covenantal context if it is to become holy.

A similar approach makes sense in reading the New Testament. 1 Corinthians and 1 Timothy speak of male prostitution and the sale of people into sexual slavery; 1 Thessalonians and Romans speak of hedonistic sexual practices engaged in by pagan peoples who do not acknowledge God. Reading these New Testament texts presents us with a classic case of whether to read narrowly or broadly. Should we read Paul's statements broadly to cover every conceivable kind of conduct imaginable, or should we read them narrowly to point only to a specific kind of conduct in a specific context? I have argued for the latter, and I believe that my argument gains strength when we consider Paul's approach to law in general. In Galatians, Paul invites us to consider whether a person's ethical conduct exhibits the "fruit of the spirit" or whether it more closely resembles the kinds of vices Paul calls "works of the flesh." The immorality, debauchery, and licentiousness about which Paul complains bears no resemblance to the exclusively committed same-sex relationships we are being asked to assess today. Gay and lesbian couples who are living lives of integrity, including in many cases the rearing of children, deserve our support and blessing.

Third, companionship and commitment come to fruition in community. Obviously, one way that married couples contribute to community is by bringing children into the world. Yet procreation is by no means a prerequisite for marriage; for that matter, current law does not even make sexual intercourse a prerequisite for marriage.[117] Couples participate in the wider community in a variety of ways, not just by rearing children. The teaching of the biblical story of Ruth makes clear that the "one-flesh union" of which the Bible speaks is not about sex alone but about kinship. Ruth and Naomi, two women who are daughter-in-law and mother-in-law, are bound to one another as one family, just as Laban and his nephew Jacob consider one another to be "bone of bone" and "flesh of flesh." Perhaps the most striking teaching concerning the nature of family, community, and belonging is the baptismal declaration in Galatians 3:28, that in Christ "there is no longer Jew or Greek, there is no longer slave or free, there is no longer male and female; for all of you are one in Christ Jesus." This means that it is wrong for Christians to draw distinctions among the baptized based on ethnicity, social status, gender, or sexual orientation. Galatians 3:28 has implications for the full inclusion of gay and lesbian couples that the church is only just now beginning to see.

For a long time now, prohibitionists have argued that, if there is to be any change from traditional moral and religious strictures against gay and lesbian practice, then the burden of proof should rest on those advocating for change. This seems fair enough: tradition deserves respect, and those who claim that the tradition is wrong, as do I, need to construct well-grounded arguments. Nevertheless, this burden runs in two directions. Sustaining the burden of proof for change does not require that I actually succeed in convincing all who disagree. It is enough that I make arguments in good faith that have biblical, theological, and moral integrity. I believe that I have done this. My arguments in favor of consecrating same-sex unions are steeped in the traditions of Western Christianity; they take seriously the objections of traditionalists; and they provide reasoned responses cast within the terms honored by the tradition itself.

Once a good-faith argument of this kind has been put forward, the burden of proof should shift back to the other side. The burden is now on them to show why society and the church should continue to treat gays and lesbians as pariahs. They should have to demonstrate why gay and lesbian families should not receive the same recognition and support as do non-gay families. At the very least, the arguments I have presented here should convince people of good will that we need to find a way to live together on issues of this kind — even when we disagree.

The time has come, indeed is long overdue, for religious communities — and especially the Christian church — to move toward the full consecration of exclusively committed same-sex love. In this chapter we have seen that there are compelling biblical and theological reasons to do so. In the chapters that follow we shall see that there are very good legal and political reasons to do so as well.

PART TWO

LAW AND POLITICS

CHAPTER FOUR

Freedom and Equality under the Law

> [T]imes can blind us to certain truths and later generations can
> see that laws once thought necessary and proper in fact serve
> only to oppress. As the Constitution endures, persons in every
> generation can invoke its principles in their own search for greater
> freedom.
>
> Justice Anthony Kennedy, United States Supreme Court,
> Lawrence v. Texas (2003)[1]

Anthony M. Kennedy has been a Supreme Court Justice since 1988.[2] A traditional Republican, a devout Roman Catholic, and a jurist with impeccable conservative credentials, Justice Kennedy was appointed to the high court by President Ronald Reagan. The appointment was stoutly opposed by a number of liberal interest groups.[3] As a measure of Justice Kennedy's conservatism, his record is tough on crime, is strong on states' rights, and employs a careful case-by-case approach to jurisprudence. Moreover, in every gay-rights decision that Kennedy had participated in as a federal circuit court judge prior to being appointed to the Supreme Court, he had ruled against the gay litigant.[4]

And yet Justice Kennedy is the author of the two most important Supreme Court opinions to date supporting civil rights for gay and lesbian people.[5] The first, *Romer v. Evans* (1996), declared it impermissible for the government to target gay and lesbian people for discrimination merely because of their identity.[6] In effect, it declared that the United States is a country that refuses to brand certain people as outcasts. The second decision, *Lawrence v. Texas* (2003), invalidated the so-called sodomy law in Texas and twelve other states, laws that criminalized same-gender sexual activity. When a conservative justice such as Anthony Kennedy declares that the rights being afforded gay and lesbian people are based on bedrock American values, we need to pay attention.

As might have been expected, for these decisions Justice Kennedy has been viciously attacked for engaging in what anti-gay groups are now calling "judicial tyranny." So many on the right wing have pummeled Kennedy that he has become a "judicial piñata."[7] Some have even suggested that Kennedy be impeached, even though he is a justice with a reputation for working cooperatively with others on the Supreme Court and for writing opinions crafted in language that ordinary people can understand.[8] When Justice Kennedy wrote these opinions on gay rights, had he suddenly abandoned his plainspoken commitment to conservative judicial values? Or is a more plausible explanation that he had come to see that assuring civil rights to gays and lesbians is very much in keeping with traditional legal values?

My aim in this chapter is to demonstrate that (1) from a legal point of view, extending basic civil rights to gay and lesbian individuals is the right thing to do, and (2) that there are also good reasons for going a step further and extending some form of relationship rights to exclusively committed same-sex couples. Both of these gestures are in keeping with long-standing principles of liberty and equality. A principle of liberty is inherent in our political system, and it is embodied constitutionally in the right of the due process of law. The Due Process Clause provides a simple guarantee that individuals will be treated fairly: no citizen of the United States may be "deprived of life, liberty, or property without due process of law."[9] In other words, governmental actions that impinge on a person's life, liberty, or property must not be arbitrary. This right of due process is both procedural and substantive in character. *Procedural* due process requires that, before a person is arrested or subjected to any other deprivation of liberty, the government must have acted according to fair procedures. For example, before a person may be convicted of a felony, he or she has a right to be represented by an attorney. *Substantive* due process is more difficult to define and has a more controversial history.[10] It includes certain fundamental rights that are considered to be essential to the very concept of ordered liberty. These rights, including the right to self-determination, are deeply embedded in our legal history.

In addition to liberty, there is an inherent right of equality under the law. This inherent right has been made explicit in the "Equal Protection" Clause of the Fourteenth Amendment, which was written into the Constitution as a response to the inequalities imposed on African Americans because of slavery. Nevertheless, the language of the Equal Protection Clause is not limited to race but applies to every kind of inequality.

In short, principles of both equality and liberty are central to Western jurisprudence and are the basis for the rights enjoyed by both individuals and couples in our system of government. In the next two chapters I shall argue that, based on our society's commitment to liberty and equality, civil rights for gay individuals and recognition of committed gay relationships are in keeping with the highest and best of democratic values.

Equality: Protecting Gay Identity

The landmark decision of *Romer v. Evans* declared that targeting gay and lesbian people for special discrimination is impermissible.[11] Doing so, the Supreme Court said, violates the constitutional right of equal protection under the law.[12] The right of equality under the law, in addition to being written specifically into the U.S. Constitution, is actually an implicit principle of all Anglo-American jurisprudence: it requires that the benefits and the burdens of the law should apply to everyone, irrespective of power, privilege, or station in life. In response to the experience of slavery, this implicit principle of equality was made explicit in the Constitution, thus assuring that henceforth the government may not "deny to any person . . . the equal protection of the laws."[13]

As we shall explore in more detail in the next chapter, equality is also a basic principle of a democratic polity. Perhaps the most distinguished theoretical defense of equality in our time is John Rawls's classic 1971 book, *A Theory of Justice*. Rawls conceives of justice fundamentally as fairness, and fairness entails two things: a commitment to basic liberties and to equal opportunity for all, and especially for society's least advantaged.[14] In order to show how important equality is, Rawls asks us to imagine that everyone comes together at the beginning of a society to create a basic structure they all would be willing to live with. But imagine, too, that in carrying out this exercise, people must retire behind a "veil of ignorance," not knowing in advance anything about the advantages or disadvantages they will have in real life once the principles of justice are established. They will not know, for instance, whether they will be born male or female, rich or poor, intelligent or mentally disabled. Faced with this situation, Rawls suggests, wouldn't people want to structure society in a way that would minimize the potential negative effects of inequality? Would they not want equality for women, for example, since any one of them might end up being female? Would they not want some social safety net, since there is a chance that any one of them might be born into poverty? This principle also implies that positions and offices should be open to all; and it implies that society should work to encourage the equal distribution of social goods, and that social and economic inequalities can be tolerated only if they work to the advantage of everyone — and especially to the least advantaged.[15]

This discussion of equality puts us in a position to consider the significance of the *Romer* decision. At issue in *Romer* was so-called "Amendment 2," a 1992 voter referendum in Colorado that would have amended the state constitution to invalidate all existing antidiscrimination laws protecting gay and lesbian people.[16] Not only that, but Amendment 2 would have forever prohibited the passage of any future antidiscrimination laws concerning gays and lesbians. A moment's reflection reveals that, in seeking to eliminate every conceivable antidiscrimination law both now and forever, Amendment 2 intended to make discrimination against gays and lesbians legitimate.

What kinds of discrimination are we talking about? As in many other states, certain city and county governments (e.g., in Aspen, Boulder, Denver), as well as the state executive branch, had enacted laws that protected gay and lesbian people from discrimination in housing, employment, education, the use of public facilities, and the receipt of public services. One example would be a regulation that prevented life insurance companies from denying coverage simply because of a person's sexual orientation. Another made it unlawful to deny housing to a person simply because he or she was gay or lesbian. These ordinances obviously were based on basic liberties and equal opportunities for all.

Who, then, proposed Amendment 2, and what was their agenda? The fact that gays had received the benefit of these antidiscrimination protections had infuriated a number of anti-gay groups, including James Dobson's evangelical organization "Focus on the Family." While many Christians have found themselves edified by the positive message of Focus on the Family — that is, providing support for traditional family values —

there is also a more negative, more questionable side to this group's advocacy. In 1991, Focus on the Family joined with other anti-gay organizations to create a political coalition called "Colorado for Family Values" (CFV). This coalition began gathering signatures to provoke a statewide constitutional referendum that was designed to repeal all legislation offering any antidiscrimination protection to gays and lesbians. This is one of those cases in which the analogy to race and gender becomes both appropriate and illuminating. Imagine how you would react to being denied housing merely because of the color of your skin, or denied equal pay for equal work merely because of your gender. Martin Luther King Jr. spoke of his dream that people would be valued for the content of their character and not devalued simply because of what race they belonged to.[17] Amendment 2 was designed to take antidiscrimination protection away from all gay people — regardless of character and regardless of conduct. A gay person might be living a celibate life, but Amendment 2 removed from that person, as well as all other gay persons, the antidiscrimination protections that other Americans take for granted.

What advocates of Amendment 2 did not understand is that antidiscrimination laws exist to guarantee the basic civil rights all Americans expect to receive. The CFV claimed, instead, that gays and lesbians were being accorded "special rights" they did not deserve. This rhetoric of "special rights" was merely a roundabout way of trading on the usual stigma against gays and lesbians — a stigma the CFV was intent on keeping in the public eye. The campaign literature of CFV accused gays and lesbians of being child predators who "target . . . children"; it alleged that they desire to legalize sex in public; it implied that all gays are "sex addicted and tragic" with a desire to "destroy the family"; and it suggested that gays were bent on promoting "homosexual indoctrination in the schools." They cited some evidence that gays on the whole make more money than do American citizens at large. The truth, incidentally, is that gay men earn at least 15 percent *lower* wages than do heterosexual men with similar education, training, and experience (lesbians do earn slightly more on average than do heterosexual women).[18] The CFV made a special effort to target African Americans with their campaign literature to convince them that gays do not deserve civil rights.[19]

Amendment 2 won by a majority of 53.4 percent to 46.6 percent. Pro-gay action groups immediately filed suit to have the law set aside as a violation of equal protection. Rather than creating a level playing field, they argued, Amendment 2 did just the opposite. As Yale law professor Akhil Reed Amar has summed it up:

> Under Amendment 2, Aspen could pass an ordinance preventing a gay apartment complex owner from posting a "For Rent — No Straights" sign; but Aspen could not likewise prevent a straight apartment complex owner from posting a "For Rent — No Queers" sign. Indeed, in its larger social meaning Amendment 2 itself was a kind of "No Queers" sign writ large — a targeting of gays, lesbians, bisexuals, singling them and them alone out for disfavored treatment.[20]

The Colorado Supreme Court struck down the law, and Governor Roy Romer appealed the decision to the United States Supreme Court.

Writing for a majority of six justices, Justice Kennedy began with a quote from the famous dissent of John Marshall Harlan from the notorious *Plessy v. Fergusson* decision that legitimated segregation throughout the South:

> One century ago, the first Justice Harlan admonished this Court that the Constitution "neither knows nor tolerates classes among its citizens. . . ." Unheeded then, those words now are understood to state a commitment to the law's neutrality where the rights of persons are at stake. The Equal Protection Clause enforces this principle and today requires us to hold invalid a provision of Colorado's Constitution.[21]

With this quotation, Justice Kennedy implicitly drew an analogy between the effort in Colorado to disenfranchise gays and lesbians and the pernicious "separate but equal" scheme once imposed on African Americans. Noting the "sweeping and comprehensive" effect of Amendment 2, Justice Kennedy summarily rejected the claim that it simply denied gay and lesbian people "special rights."[22] Instead, the rights it denied to gay and lesbian people were those that all other citizens take for granted. Amendment 2 placed gays and lesbians in a "solitary class" of those who were denied antidiscrimination protection and on whom alone were imposed a special legal disability.[23] If Amendment 2 had been allowed to stand, argued Justice Kennedy, then gays, lesbians, and their supporters would have been effectively barred even from advocating antidiscrimination legislation. If we are to be a nation governed by the rule of law, he said, the law must be fair and impartial in its administration. Singling out one group for special legal disfavor is a violation of our deepest constitutional principles.[24]

In order to understand this decision, we must take account of the way the Equal Protection Clause has been interpreted over the decades. As it has been interpreted since World War II, this clause bans forms of discrimination that unfairly deny equality under the law, especially discrimination as to race, ethnicity, and national origin.[25] One issue at stake in gay-rights cases is the extent to which discrimination on the basis of gender orientation is sufficiently analogous to these other kinds of discrimination. To determine whether a form of discrimination violates equality, the Supreme Court has employed a three-tiered analysis: minimal, intermediate, and strict scrutiny. I pause to give a brief survey of this three-tiered approach because it comes into play in all the major gay-rights cases we shall consider.

Most laws are in the first and lowest tier: they receive the lowest level of scrutiny — what the Court calls "minimal scrutiny" or "rational basis review." Under rational basis review, laws are presumed to be constitutional: a law will be struck down as unconstitutional only if its provisions are "not rationally related to a legitimate state interest." This is true because the Court usually gives significant deference to the decisions of the legislature. Rational basis review does not second-guess the state interest in the law; it only explores whether the law is a rational implementation of that interest. Under minimal scrutiny, then, most classifications employed by the legislature will be upheld, so long as they are reasonable. After all, not every classification made by the law is an invidious form of discrimination. For example, it is not unfair or arbitrary to prohibit persons classified as nearsighted from driving without their lenses. Such classifications as these are necessary for public safety.

Still, there are some laws that raise suspicion and invite a more rigorous inquiry. In the third and highest tier, the Court employs its most stringent level of analysis — that is, "strict scrutiny." Laws that will be subjected to strict scrutiny are those that either (a) target a "suspect classification" or (b) threaten to impinge on the "fundamental rights" of a certain group of citizens.[26] In these two situations the Supreme Court will not allow legislative majorities to ride roughshod over the rights of minorities. In such cases, the Court is not squelching democracy at all, as critics claim, but just the opposite: in its "referee" function, it is assuring that the democratic process operates by rules that are fair.

A law employs a "suspect classification" when it singles out people of a particular race, ethnicity, national origin, or religion for unfair treatment. The paradigmatic example would be the old South's Jim Crow laws that implemented racial segregation. Such laws deny equality under the law per se, and the Court will almost always declare them unconstitutional. Since the language of the Equal Protection Clause is not limited to matters of race, a classification may be considered "suspect" if it targets *any* group of people in an arbitrary or unfair way simply because of who they are. We will return to this point in a moment, for it is a principle that obviously could have implications for classifications based on gender orientation.

In addition to suspect classifications, the Court will invalidate laws that unfairly impinge on the "fundamental rights" of certain citizens. Fundamental rights are the rights "implicit in the concept of ordered liberty."[27] They include the right to vote, the right of access to the democratic process, and the rights guaranteed by the Bill of Rights.[28] For example, the Supreme Court has ruled that the states may not criminalize the use of contraceptives, because their use is protected by one's fundamental right of personal integrity or privacy.[29] Or again, in 1942 the Court considered a law that required the forced sterilization of habitual felons.[30] Because it impinged on the fundamental right to procreate, the Court applied strict scrutiny to the way the law was written and declared it unconstitutional.

Whereas laws prejudicial to people of a single race are always unfair, other legislative categories may or may not be fair, depending on the circumstances. Thus the Court has created a second tier of analysis known as "intermediate scrutiny." In contrast to strict scrutiny, which is invoked to analyze suspect classifications and fundamental rights, intermediate scrutiny is applied to "quasi-suspect" classifications and rights that are "important," though perhaps not fundamental. The most prominent example of cases receiving intermediate scrutiny concerns discrimination on the basis of gender.[31] (In addition to gender, the Court has added the marital status of one's parents to the list of protected classifications.)[32] The Court has insisted that, while these classifications need to be scrutinized, the standard of scrutiny for these cases ought to be different from that in cases of race and ethnicity. Thus, in order for a gender classification to pass constitutional muster, it "must serve important governmental objectives and must be substantially related to the achievement of those objectives."[33]

There is a clear trend in international law toward treating sexual orientation as a "suspect classification" and thus applying some sort of height-ened scrutiny.[34] The United States Supreme Court, however, has refrained from taking this step. Indeed, since the 1970s, the Burger and Rehnquist Courts took a noticeable turn away from adding to the list of suspect classi-fications. Justice Rehnquist even went so far as to claim that race is the only classification the Equal Protection Clause was meant to cover, even though the clear language of the provision itself indicates otherwise.[35]

Thus, when the constitutionality of Colorado's Amendment 2 reached the Supreme Court, the Court determined to handle the case us-ing something less than strict scrutiny. In doing so, it declined to follow the lead of the Supreme Court of Colorado, which had bucked the trend and declared that sexual orientation did call for "strict scrutiny." The Colorado Court reasoned that Amendment 2 violated a fundamental right, namely, the right to participate meaningfully in the political process. Although he did acknowledge this argument, Justice Kennedy hung the case on a differ-ent rationale, one that has guided all the major gay-rights cases since then — both state and federal. Because gays and lesbians had been singled out in such a peculiar way, the justices ruled, there was in effect no need to in-voke heightened scrutiny. Here the law in question did not even meet the *minimal* standard that a law must meet, namely, that a classification must bear "a rational relationship to an independent and legitimate legislative end."[36] Instead, Amendment 2 targeted one group of citizens in a way that was simply irrational, and this for two distinct but related reasons.[37]

First, Kennedy noted that Amendment 2 was an "unprecedented" kind of provision that imposed a unique legal disability on gays and lesbi-ans and them alone that no one else in the state of Colorado was forced to endure. It did this through a legislative classification that was "at once too narrow and too broad."[38] It was too narrow because it singled out one group of citizens from among all others; it was too broad because it denied protection to this group "across the board." Referring to an argument made by law professors Lawrence Tribe, John Hart Ely, Gerald Gunther, Philip Kurland, and Kathleen Sullivan in an amicus brief before the Court, Justice Kennedy concluded that this law effected a denial of equal protec-tion "in the most literal sense."[39] The law professors had argued that a law such as Amendment 2 creates a "literal" denial of equal protection because it effectively bars a particular class of persons from even having the oppor-tunity to seek protection in the legal process.

The second reason was that the referendum had no other motivation than to pursue an "animus" against gays themselves. Amendment 2 targeted gays and lesbians "not to further a proper legislative end but to make them unequal to everyone else."[40] Justice Kennedy and the majority found it unpersuasive that such a law was necessary to protect freedom of association for those who do not approve of gays. To support this line of reasoning based on "animus," Justice Kennedy relied on the following principle from the *Department of Agriculture v. Moreno* case (1973):

> If the constitutional conception of "equal protection of the laws" means anything, it must . . . mean that a bare . . . desire to harm a politically unpopular group cannot constitute a legitimate governmental interest.[41]

In the *Moreno* case, Congress had fashioned a law subtly aimed at so-called hippies, making it unlawful for food stamps to go to any household in which a non–family member resided.[42] Like hippies, gays and lesbians form a politically unpopular group that the advocates of Amendment 2 were trying to harm.

A similar rationale was used by the Supreme Court in a case Justice Kennedy did not cite, *City of Cleburne v. Cleburne Living Center, Inc.* (1983).[43] In *Cleburne,* a city government denied a permit to a home for the mentally retarded. The Court found that the real reason for the denial was an irrational prejudice against mentally retarded people.[44] Professor Cass Sunstein has suggested that *Romer* belongs to a line of cases, what he calls the "Moreno-Cleburne-Romer trilogy," in which the government may have had some interest in regulating the matter at hand — food stamps *(Moreno),* land use permits *(Cleburne),* and perhaps public morals *(Romer)* — but in which mere prejudice or animus formed the reason for the law in question and thereby invalidated it.[45]

The net effect of *Romer* has been that, even without declaring sexual orientation to be a "suspect classification," the Supreme Court has held that laws directed against gay and lesbian people simply for who they are cannot sustain constitutional challenge. The notion of "minimal scrutiny," in other words, does not mean "no scrutiny." Laws such as this one, which perpetuate an invidious "we-versus-they" distinction, are motivated only by irrational prejudice and animosity and violate equal protection.[46]

Justice Antonin Scalia filed a scathing dissent, taking first aim at the "animus argument." To attribute animus to those who voted in favor of

Amendment 2, he said, was nothing short of "insulting."[47] There was no animus in play here at all, he contended, but only a clash of philosophies — yet another round in the so-called culture wars. Besides, Scalia continued, the citizens of Colorado were "*entitled* to be hostile toward homosexual conduct (emphasis in the original)."[48] Why? Because opposition to "homosexuality" is a moral opposition and hence is not impermissible. Being against same-gender sexual conduct, he insisted, is not on the same plane as racism or sexism.

Justice Scalia's first point is, of course, true at one level. People are permitted to hold whatever moral opinions they wish, including harboring moral scruples about same-gender sexual activity. But this is a fairly superficial observation; people differ about all kinds of things. The deeper question is: Where does one person's morality end and another person's begin? Justice Scalia's suggestion that the moral or religious nature of one's opposition to a group entitles one to do tangible harm to the group in the public arena is not only illogical, but is itself of questionable moral validity. The problem with Justice Scalia's argument is that it does not take adequately into account the significance of the right being infringed on here, namely, the right of equality under the law. Majorities are not entitled to turn a particular group of people into a pariah.[49]

Justice Scalia argued, in the second place, that a referendum of the people is the most democratic of all processes and that enshrining the results of such a vote in a state constitution is not a violation of federal constitutional law; instead, it is merely a "reasonable effort to preserve traditional American moral values."[50] This argument is flawed at two levels. First, it is not at all clear that a referendum that takes away rights from a minority group is democratic in the fullest sense of that term. As I shall argue more fully in the next chapter, democracy means more than majority rule. If a majority chooses to act in an undemocratic or unjust way, the fact that more than 50 percent of the people vote in favor of that injustice does not thereby legitimate it. Second, the example of polygamy as a majoritarian exercise in defining morality is an interesting one that turns up repeatedly in these arguments over gay rights. How can it be impermissible for government to take a stand against homoeroticism, Justice Scalia asks, when it *is* permissible for the government to prohibit polygamy?

Justice Scalia poses this question without mentioning any of the clear and obvious answers that distinguish polygamy from the case at hand. Prohibiting polygamy has to do with the definition of marriage, which poses a different kind of legal question than discrimination against individuals because of their identity. Justice Scalia's response, no doubt, would be that both polygamy and gay rights present questions about whether the law can prohibit immorality. This is true, but the question remains: By what public criterion of morality are such cases to be decided? Polygamy is a way of life that does demonstrable harm to women and children.[51] No such similar harm has been demonstrated regarding relationships between gays. Another concern that anti-gay advocates have brought forward is that, if one cannot prohibit spousal recognition for gays, then one cannot deny it to polygamous couples. This does not follow. The right to marry the person you love is not the same as the right to marry as many persons as you love.[52] Because state and federal governments provide significant economic benefits to married couples, there is a strong governmental interest in limiting those benefits to one significant other and not more.

Third, Justice Scalia argued that the Court's *Romer* decision was inconsistent with the 1986 decision of *Bowers v. Hardwick*.[53] This was Scalia's most substantive legal claim. Because of its importance to current controversies, the *Bowers* decision merits a brief discussion. *Bowers* was a closely decided (5-4) decision that upheld the constitutionality of a sodomy law in Georgia. According to that law, it was unlawful to have anal or oral sex, no matter whether the act was engaged in by a gay or straight couple.[54] The particular facts in the *Bowers* case show how sodomy laws, while written to cover both homosexual and heterosexual behavior, have often been used simply to harass gay people, especially gay men. The facts were these: a gay man, Michael Hardwick, was seen by a police officer exiting a gay bar in Atlanta, where he worked as a bartender. As he walked out the door of the club, Hardwick threw a bottle of beer he was just finishing in a dumpster. The officer, who seems to have taken an interest in pursuing gay men, gave Hardwick a citation for drinking in public. Then, because of an administrative error, Hardwick was given the wrong date for his court appearance and failed to appear. Eventually he did pay the court's fine, but not before a warrant had been issued for his arrest. The same officer who had given him the ticket decided to serve this warrant, and he chose to do so at 3:00 a.m. When the officer entered Hardwick's apartment, he found him engaging in an act of consensual sex with an adult male. He arrested Hardwick and charged him with sodomy. Whereas many gays who have been subjected to this kind of charge in the past have simply paid the fine, Hardwick decided to challenge the law's legitimacy.

Eventually, Georgia would eliminate its sodomy law, but in the meantime the U.S. Supreme Court upheld the law in a decision written by Justice Byron White. Justice White argued that, though the Court has recognized a fundamental right to make decisions about marriage, family, and procreation, there was no constitutional right to engage in sodomy. How could there be such a right, he argued, when sodomy was considered a crime in all fifty states until the 1960s and was still outlawed in twenty-four states and the District of Columbia in 1986? To contend that a right to engage in sodomy is rooted in the fundamental traditions of the nation and thus deserves constitutional protection, scoffed White, is simply "facetious." Chief Justice Warren Burger agreed and also weighed in with a concurring opinion that argued that sodomy violates long-standing Judeo-Christian values on which Western Civilization was based.[55] Justice Sandra Day O'Connor, who had been on the Court for under five years at the time, voted with the majority. Justice Lewis Powell was torn about which way to vote; at the very last minute he reluctantly provided the deciding vote in favor of the Georgia law.[56]

Justices Harry Blackmun and John Paul Stevens (joined by Justices Brennan and Marshall) filed strong dissents, portions of which they read aloud from the bench. Justice Blackmun, a Republican appointed by Richard Nixon, protested that this case was not at all about a "fundamental right to engage in homosexual sodomy" but about the right of all people, including gay people, to be free to live their own lives.[57] Justice Blackmun quoted the famous saying of Oliver Wendell Holmes:

> [I]t is revolting to have no better reason for a rule of law than that it was laid down in the time of Henry IV. It is still more revolting if the grounds upon which it was laid down have vanished long since, and the rule simply persists from blind imitation of the past.[58]

Blackmun then went on to make a number of substantive legal arguments, of which I highlight two. First, he charged that the majority had "distorted" the issue being presented through an "obsessive focus on homosexual activity."[59] In fact, the statute prohibits certain intimate activity of a homosexual or heterosexual nature, he said, and thus it violates the right of privacy. Second, Justice Blackmun argued that privacy in intimate sexual matters is necessary to protect the integrity of individual personhood. Only a "willful blindness," he said, could deny this.[60] Blackmun continued:

The Court claims that its decision today merely refuses to recognize a fundamental right to engage in homosexual sodomy; what the Court really has refused to recognize is the fundamental interest all individuals have in controlling the nature of their intimate associations with others.

To deny individuals the right to determine their own intimate sexual conduct, Justice Blackmun concluded, is a betrayal of deep-seated American values of tolerance.[61]

Justice Stevens based the reasoning of his dissent not on Justice Blackmun's "right to privacy" but on what he considered the more basic right of individual "liberty." That is, it was not so much about the place where the intimate activity occurred (i.e., the home) but about respecting the individual integrity to decide to engage in the activity. (This subtle distinction will become important in just a moment, when we turn to the case of *Lawrence v. Texas*.) Justice Stevens also picked away at the majority's thin grasp of the history of sodomy laws, reiterating that such laws have historically not distinguished between homosexual and heterosexual conduct, nor have such laws made an exception for married couples. If a married couple engaged in oral sex, this was considered a crime against nature according to the Georgia law. Since states are willing to allow heterosexual sodomy, Stevens asked, what is the basis for denying non-heterosexual sodomy? The Court's precedents were clear that a state may not proscribe intimate activity between husband and wife, and Justice Stevens insisted that neither should it be able to do so regarding gay and lesbian couples. To hold otherwise, he argued, would mean that gays and lesbians were being accorded a lesser liberty interest. It would also be allowing Georgia to enforce its laws against some and not others — a clear violation of the principle of equality under the law.

This excursion into the reasoning of the *Bowers* case has been necessary for me to shed light on a central plank of Justice Scalia's dissent in *Romer v. Evans*. Scalia draws what would seem to be the logical conclusion from *Bowers*. If it is lawful to criminalize same-gender sexual activity, Scalia asks, then why is it not lawful for the state of Colorado (or any state) to enact laws that are unfavorable to persons who desire to engage in such activity? On its face, this is a reasonable argument; but there are two answers to it. First, Colorado Amendment 2 was not focused on criminal conduct; it was focused on personal identity. Any person may self-identify as gay without regard to particular acts, and the principle proclaimed by the *Romer* majority is that no person should be deprived of equality under the law simply because of who he or she is. Second, *Bowers v. Hardwick* was one of the most criticized cases to come out of the Burger Court. The holding of *Romer v. Evans* called both the holding and the rationale of *Bowers* into question, though without explicitly overruling it. By quoting Justice Harlan's dissent in *Plessy v. Ferguson*, Justice Kennedy was firing a shot across the bow that indicated *Bowers v. Hardwick* was in trouble. Subsequently, in fact, the *Bowers* decision was overruled in *Lawrence v. Texas*.

Liberty: Protecting Gay Self-Determination

In the late evening of September 17, 1998, the Harris County (Texas) sheriff's department responded to a phony report of a "weapons disturbance" at the apartment of John Geddes Lawrence. The report had been called in by a neighbor with a grudge (who later served jail time for filing a false report). Based on this report, the sheriff's deputies entered the apartment and found Lawrence, a fifty-five-year-old white male, and Tyrone Garner, a thirty-one-year-old black male, engaging in a consensual sex act. The deputies arrested the two men and charged them with sodomy. Texas law made oral or anal sex between persons of the same gender a crime, but it did not criminalize such activity between a man and a woman.[62]

In *Lawrence v. Texas,* Justice Kennedy for the second time delivered a landmark gay-rights opinion, striking down the Texas sodomy law as a violation of due process and thus rendering all such laws unconstitutional as between consenting adults.[63] The Court argued that gay and lesbian people are entitled to "retain their dignity as free persons."[64] Moreover, the Court overruled the earlier sodomy decision of *Bowers v. Hardwick,* and in so doing it invalidated similar laws in twelve other states. The Supreme Court majority situated the case squarely within the understanding of rights that I have defended in both this chapter and the introductory chapter, namely, as limits on the power of the majority. Even though a large number of people may have qualms about same-sex relationships, the Court made it clear: "The issue is whether the majority may use the power of the State to enforce these views on the whole society through operation of the criminal law."[65]

In one sense, this legal result was long overdue and was far from radical. As early as 1774, the British philosopher Jeremy Bentham had realized that same-gender sexuality did no harm at all to society and should not be subject to criminal sanction.[66] Similarly, in 1955, the American Law Institute had argued for decriminalization of consensual same-sex acts performed in private; and the Wolfenden Commission in Great Britain followed suit in 1957.[67] By the time the U.S. Supreme Court overruled *Bowers* in 2003, most states had done away with their sodomy laws.

Justice Kennedy, writing as he had done in the *Romer* case for a 6-3 majority, opened with a paragraph concerning the importance of a person's individual "liberty" interest under the Due Process Clause of the Fourteenth Amendment:

> Liberty protects the person from unwarranted government intrusions into a dwelling or other private place. In our tradition the State is not omnipresent in the home. And there are other spheres of our lives and existence, outside the home, where the State should not be a dominant presence. Freedom extends beyond spatial bounds. Liberty presumes an autonomy of self that includes freedom of thought, belief, expression, and certain intimate conduct. The instant case involves liberty of the person both in its spatial and more transcendent dimensions.[68]

This appeal to the centrality of individual liberty has deep roots in the American political tradition. Drawing on the classical political thought of John Stuart Mill, it considers each individual to be a center of moral value and judgment. Since each person matters for who he or she is, this aspect of political liberalism has an affinity with the standard biblical idea that all humans are created in the image of God. In its secular form, this focus on the centrality of the individual requires that all persons be treated with respect and dignity as human beings.[69] This broad principle of respect for individuals means that each person — whether gay, straight, or otherwise — should be accorded proper dignity and should be allowed to live the life of his or her own choosing.

The extent of this constitutional interest in liberty, declared Justice Kennedy, had been underestimated by the Supreme Court in *Bowers*. Kennedy situated the right of liberty belonging to gay and lesbian people within the line of cases granting constitutional protection to the intimate lives of married couples;[70] extending that protection to unmarried couples and minors;[71] and granting a qualified liberty protection to women choosing to have an abortion.[72] The right of liberty is broad enough that one should be able to exercise it without fear of criminal sanction; and it should certainly include one's choice of a sexual partner, so long as both parties are consenting adults.[73] Gays and lesbians should have the right and the freedom to live out their gay identity without being branded as criminals. In furtherance of this goal, the role of the Court is to define liberty for all and not to impose a moral code favored by the majority: "At the heart of liberty is the right to define one's own concept of existence, of meaning, of the universe, and of the mystery of human life."[74]

Kennedy noted that, contrary to what was claimed in *Bowers*, "there is no long history in this country of laws directed at homosexual conduct as a distinct matter." In fact, the laws targeting gay sex date only from the 1970s and later.[75] To be sure, there were laws against "sodomy," but the definition of "sodomy" included nonprocreative sex of any kind — whether heterosexual or homosexual. And, as a practical matter, prosecutions were aimed not at consensual acts in private but against sexual acts of a violent, predatory, or exploitative character, especially against minors.

Even though the two men in the *Lawrence* case were not in a long-term, committed relationship, the Court still determined that the integrity of their lifestyle decision merited legal protection.[76] "To say that the issue in *Bowers* was simply the right to engage in certain sexual conduct demeans the claim the individual put forward, just as it would demean a married couple were it to be said marriage is simply about the right to have sexual intercourse."[77] Though the Supreme Court is typically slow to overturn precedent, Justice Kennedy's language could not have been more decisive: *Bowers*, he said, "was not correct when it was decided, and it is not correct today."

Justice Sandra Day O'Connor concurred in the result of *Lawrence* but would have based the outcome on a different and narrower legal footing. For her, since the Texas sodomy statute targeted gays alone, it obviously violated the right of equal protection: a gay-only sodomy statute, she reasoned, was different from a sodomy statute applicable to everyone. By arguing in this way, Justice O'Connor was attempting to draw short of overruling *Bowers v. Hardwick*, the case in which she had voted with the majority in 1986.[78] Still, her opinion agrees that mere moral disapproval of gay and lesbian people is not a rational basis on which to treat them unequally under the law.[79] The problem with the Texas sodomy statute was that it did more than proscribe conduct, she said. "It is instead directed toward gay persons as a class."[80]

Justice Kennedy gently but firmly rejected O'Connor's attempt to limit the scope of *Lawrence.* While acknowledging the plausibility of her equal protection approach, he countered that the *Bowers* case needed to be overruled — if for no other reason than the indelible stigma it imposed on gay and lesbian people. In perhaps the most poignant statement of what is really at stake in the gay-rights debate, Justice Kennedy declared that allowing *Bowers* to stand "demeans the lives of homosexual persons."[81] This is so because the protection of one's intimate conduct is closely linked to the protection of one's personhood itself:

> When homosexual conduct is made criminal by the law of the State, that declaration in and of itself is an invitation to subject homosexual persons to discrimination both in the public and in the private spheres.[82]

As if this social stigmatization were not enough, conviction under the sodomy law carries with it such consequences as a permanent criminal record, the possibility of being barred from certain professions, and the requirement in some states to register as a sex offender.[83]

In anticipation of the inevitable dissent by Justice Scalia, the majority opinion made it clear that the ruling in *Lawrence* only applies to the liberty interests of consenting adults. It does not sweep away all so-called "morals legislation," and it specifically leaves open the question of whether constitutional law ought to *compel* the legal recognition of same-sex marriage or civil unions:

> The present case does not involve minors. It does not involve persons who might be injured or coerced or who are situated in relationships where consent might not easily be refused. It does not involve public conduct or prostitution. It does not involve whether the government must give formal recognition to any relationship that homosexual persons seek to enter.[84]

But these assurances did not dissuade Justice Scalia from registering another scathing dissent.[85] The core of Scalia's dissent was his view that there is no fundamental right, deeply rooted in the Anglo-American legal tradition, to engage in same-gender sexual activity. In addition, he argued that the *Lawrence* decision would cast doubt on all efforts to promote "majoritarian sexual morality." He mentioned specifically "fornication, bigamy, adultery, adult incest, bestiality, and obscenity."[86] To Scalia, overturning *Bowers* would be nothing less than a "massive disruption of the current social order" and nothing more than a "result-oriented expedient."[87] One of Justice Scalia's major concerns was that the Court had not followed the three-tiered structure required for heightened scrutiny. In other words, if the Court is going to protect gay and lesbian sexual activity from state interference, then under standard due process analysis it must declare such activity a "fundamental right" (or under equal protection analysis, it must declare sexual orientation a "suspect classification").

What Scalia misses is that the human claim to liberty does not depend on the Constitution alone for its existence.[88] The difference here is between two different kinds of conservative jurisprudence. For Justice Scalia, the Constitution protects only those rights that are deeply embedded in our nation's history. Justice Kennedy, by contrast, espouses a more libertarian brand of conservatism and links it with a more dynamic and evolving understanding of the Constitution. For Justice Kennedy, the right of liberty possessed by individuals is prior to and a limit to the power of the state, even in new circumstances not previously recognized. Thus, Justice Kennedy tells us, the drafters of the Bill of Rights and the Fourteenth Amendment intended the search for freedom to be ongoing, for they "knew that times can blind us to certain truths and later generations can see that laws once thought necessary and proper in fact serve only to oppress. As the Constitution endures, persons in every generation can invoke its principles in their own search for greater freedom."[89]

Another palpable difference between the two views of jurisprudence is that, throughout his dissent, Justice Scalia insists on describing the activity in question pejoratively as "homosexual sodomy." Whereas Scalia focuses on sex acts, Justice Kennedy and the majority focus on the integrity of the relationship. It is clear that the real issue in Scalia's dissent is gay marriage. Though Kennedy specifically disavowed that *Lawrence* opens the door to gay marriage, Scalia snapped back in his dissent, "Do not believe it." What led Justice Scalia to this conclusion? The *Lawrence* decision speaks of constitutionally protecting "personal decisions relating to marriage, procreation, contraception, family relationships, child rearing, and education." Scalia perceives a constitutional springboard to gay marriage lurking in Kennedy's assertion that "persons in a homosexual relationship may seek autonomy for these purposes, just as heterosexual persons do."[90]

Perhaps he is correct.

The Equality Argument Extended:
Civil Unions and the Benefits of Marriage

The first American jurisdiction to come close to extending full equality to couples in committed, exclusive same-sex relationships was the state of Vermont.[91] On April 26, 2000, Governor Howard Dean signed legislation creating a new institution for committed same-sex couples — the "civil union." Unlike the registered or domestic partnership, which calls for only limited benefits and obligations, the civil union provides to committed gay and lesbian couples all the benefits and protections — as well as the full obligations — of marriage, but without the name and symbolic prestige of the word "marriage" itself. The civil union is, in effect, a compromise between the power of the courts and the power of the legislature, between the interests of equality for all citizens and the interests of the democratic majority in sustaining deeply held communal values.

The civil union was created in response to a lawsuit filed in July 1997 in which three same-sex couples — Stan Baker and Peter Harrigan, Holly Puterbaugh and Lois Farnham, and Nina Beck and Stacy Jolles — objected to their exclusion from the "benefits and protections" of Vermont's marriage laws. At the time they filed the suit, one of the couples had been living together in a committed relationship for twenty-five years; two of the couples had raised children together; and all of the couples were respected members of their communities.[92]

In asking the state of Vermont for all the "benefits and protections" of the marriage laws, the three couples were invoking the so-called Common Benefits Clause of the Vermont Constitution. The "Common Benefits" Clause provides that government exists for "the common benefit, protection, and security of the people."[93] Therefore, they argued, all citizens must be afforded the same benefits and protections under the law. This provision of Vermont's Constitution originated in 1777, well before the United States Constitution was adopted and almost a century before the Equal Protection Clause of the Fourteenth Amendment was added. With this venerable pedigree, the Common Benefits Clause sets forth a broad principle of inclusion, whereby government exists for the benefit of all Vermonters. Though this clause is unique to the constitution of Vermont in its specific terms, the principle it enunciates is a fundamental belief of all American jurisprudence, namely, that each person is equal in the eyes of the law.

On the basis of this principle of equality, the Supreme Court of Vermont responded to the claims of the three plaintiffs with the 1999 landmark decision in *Baker v. State*.[94] With the full weight of a unanimous opinion, which was written by Chief Justice Amestoy, the court held that same-sex couples had been discriminated against by being excluded from the benefits of marriage. The argument presented against the gay and lesbian couples by the state attorney general was that excluding same-sex couples from the benefits of marriage promoted a legitimate state interest, namely, the nurturing of child-bearing and the protection of children. The court firmly rejected this contention. In the first place, they noted, the law extends the cloak of marital benefits and protections to many couples who are incapable of or have no intention of having children. There must be more to marriage, then, than having children. Furthermore, since Vermont had passed a law allowing same-sex couples to adopt and rear children, for the state then to turn around and withdraw the protections of marriage from same-sex families would be contradictory. For the court to allow this would be to remove from children who lived with same-sex parents the legitimacy accorded to all other children. As the court put it,

> The laudable goal of promoting a commitment between married couples to promote the security of their children and the community as a whole provides no reasonable basis for denying the legal benefits and protections of marriage to same-sex couples, who are no differently situated with respect to this goal than their opposite-sex counterparts.[95]

Notwithstanding their unanimity and their strong statement about the injustice being visited on committed same-sex couples, the court split over both the rationale for their decision and how to provide these couples with a remedy. As to rationale, two members of the court, Justices Dooley and Johnson, would have invoked heightened scrutiny.[96] For Justice Denise Johnson, the case presented a "straightforward case of sex discrimination." This is true, she argued, because it is the sex of the parties that determines whether they are to be issued a marriage license. In essence, her argument was that gays and lesbians were being excluded from marriage on the basis of an overly "thin" notion of equality. The state had argued that since men and women are equally prohibited from entering into same-sex marriage, there is no violation of equal justice. The problem with this truncated conception of equality is that it is the very same argument used to define blacks as separate but equal: it was reasoned in *Pace v. Ala-*

bama that antimiscegenation laws were permissible because they applied to both blacks and whites.[97] In order to defeat this argument, Justice Johnson posed the following hypothetical:

> Dr. A and Dr. B both want to marry Ms. C, an X-ray technician. Dr. A may do so because Dr. A is a man. Dr. B may not because Dr. B is a woman. Dr. A and Dr. B are people of opposite sexes who are similarly situated in the sense that they both want to marry a person of their choice. The [marriage] statute disqualifies Dr. B from marriage solely on the basis of her sex and treats her differently from Dr. A, a man. This is sex discrimination.[98]

The court was also divided as to the remedy. Justice Johnson advocated a court-imposed solution. Reasoning that the practice of excluding same-sex couples was unconstitutional per se, she would have directed county clerks to immediately begin issuing marriage licenses, just as the California Supreme Court had done in 1948, when it opened the doors of marriage to interracial couples.[99] But the majority took a more cautious approach, voting to defer to the legislature in shaping a remedy.

This deference to the legislature shows that, far from engaging in "judicial activism," the Vermont Supreme Court actually was attempting to implement the plain terms of the state's constitution in a way that was sensitive to the potential divisiveness of the issue.[100] The majority reasoned that fairness demands that gay and lesbian couples receive equal benefits and protections; but it did not necessarily demand their inclusion in the institution of marriage itself. Retaining jurisdiction of the case to assure compliance, the majority left it to the legislature to decide through a democratic process whether to expand the definition of marriage or create a new civil institution for those who do not fit the current definition. The court said:

> The State is constitutionally required to extend to same-sex couples the common benefits and protections that flow from marriage under Vermont law. Whether this ultimately takes the form of inclusion within the marriage laws themselves or a parallel "domestic partnership" system or some equivalent statutory alternative, rests with the Legislature. Whatever system is chosen, however, must conform with the constitutional imperative to afford all Vermonters the common benefit, protection, and security of the law.[101]

The political aftermath of the *Baker* decision is instructive. Pro-gay advocates argued for expanding the definition of marriage to include same-sex relationships; anti-gay forces explored the feasibility of a constitutional amendment that would, in effect, overrule the *Baker* decision via voter referendum. In the end, the Vermont legislature opted for a compromise: it declined to expand the definition of marriage, creating instead civil unions as a parallel institution for committed same-sex couples.[102] Even this compromise, which was signed into law by then-Governor Howard Dean on April 26, 2000, provoked strong reactions from some Vermont residents at the time. In the next election, a number of legislators who had supported civil unions lost their seats. Nevertheless, once same-sex couples started entering into civil unions, the rancor subsided. A mere four years later, according to Howard Dean,

> [W]e wonder what the fuss was all about. Civil unions were never an issue in Vermont in the 2002 election and will not be [in 2004]. The intensity of anger and hate has disappeared, replaced by an understanding that equal rights for groups previously denied them has no negative effect on those of us who have always enjoyed those rights. My marriage has not become weaker.[103]

Five years later, more than 7,000 couples had joined themselves in civil unions in Vermont. In 2009, the Vermont legislature enacted gay marriage, overriding a later Republican governor's veto.

What does a civil union entail? It is a legal contract in which couples pledge a lifelong union to one another. This pledge is supported by benefits and obligations that are equivalent to those of marriage, including obligations of maintenance and support.[104] Commitment in civil union is open to persons of the same gender who are over eighteen, otherwise mentally competent, not related to one another, and not already parties to a marriage or other civil union.[105] Dissolution of a civil union is handled in the same way as a divorce is, with jurisdiction vesting in the family court.[106]

The civil union was designed to be parallel to marriage. But is it? While same-sex couples may have gained equal benefits under the law of Vermont, they are still not considered equal for purposes of federal law. Civil unions provide partners with none of the famous 1,138 federal benefits that accrue to married couples — benefits that include survivorship rights under Social Security, medical benefits under Medicare, Medicaid spend-down provisions, rights to continue insurance under COBRA, eligibility under medical and family leave acts, certain tax benefits regarding retirement plan pay-outs, and on and on.[107] Perhaps the most significant disadvantage is that this new legal regime smacks of the old Jim Crow doctrine of "separate but equal." After all, marriage is not only a bundle of benefits, but it also grants a unique social status; under civil unions, this status is still withheld from gay and lesbian couples.

Nonetheless, whatever the limits of the civil union arrangement, one must acknowledge that its creation was a considerable political achievement. In addition, one can only agree with the Vermont Supreme Court that extending recognition to gay and lesbian people in their commitments to one another "is simply, when all is said and done, a recognition of our common humanity."[108]

The Liberty Argument Extended:
The Right to Marry the Person One Loves

In addition to the equality-based argument for the recognition of same-sex relationships, there is also a "liberty argument." The equality argument, while powerful in its own right, has sometimes been used to avoid reaching the liberty argument, with its affirmation of gay personhood. For example, Justice Johnson's sex-discrimination argument, which was based on equality, had been used earlier by the Hawaii Supreme Court in *Baehr* precisely because that court was not prepared to recognize that gay people have a right to marriage. The court admitted:

> [W]e do not believe that a right to same sex marriage is so rooted in the traditions and collective conscience of our people that failure to recognize it would violate the fundamental principles of liberty and justice which lie at the base of all our civil and political institutions.[109]

In other words, the court rendered no opinion concerning the status of gay and lesbian people as such. As constitutional lawyer Evan Gerstmann has perceptively observed, "To rule in favor of the gay and lesbian plaintiffs, the *Baehr* court first had to render their homosexuality invisible."[110] One way to honor gay personhood would be to grant gay people the right to marry on their own merits. The first American court to declare that the fundamental right to marry extends to same-sex couples was a trial court in Alaska in *Brause v. Bureau of Vital Statistics* (1998).[111] This case has not received much attention, partly because the decisions of trial courts do not carry the weight of precedent, but more specifically because the Alaska legislature acted quickly to invalidate the ruling by amending the state constitution.[112]

On August 4, 1994, two men, Jay Brause and Gene Dugan, who had been in a committed relationship for more than nineteen years, sought and were denied a marriage license in the state of Alaska.[113] They challenged the constitutionality of that denial in court, arguing that the gender-neutral language of the marriage law should already allow same-sex marriage. Very quickly, a bill was introduced in the Alaska legislature to restrict marriage to one man and one woman. Crafted not only in response to the gender-neutrality argument of Brause and Dugan, but also as a reaction to the litigation going on in the *Baehr* case in Hawaii, the bill became law in March 1996. Brause and Dugan appealed, claiming a violation not only of their equal protection rights but also of their right of privacy. The Alaska constitution contains a specific acknowledgment of a right to privacy, and because of that, Judge Peter A. Michalski reasoned that he could not simply accept the argument of the state that marriage is by definition between a man and a woman; nor could he accept at face value the statutory ban of same-sex marriage that was in effect in Alaska.[114] Said Judge Michalski:

> It is not enough to say that "marriage is marriage" and accept without any scrutiny the law before the court. It is the duty of the court to do more than merely assume that marriage is only, and must only be, what most are familiar with. In some parts of our nation mere acceptance of the familiar would have left segregation in place.

Accordingly, Brause and Dugan had raised a legitimate constitutional issue: specifically, whether the right to marriage is so fundamental as to demand heightened scrutiny when the right is denied. The judge reasoned that "[t]he relevant question is not whether same-sex marriage is so rooted in our traditions that it is a fundamental right, but whether the freedom to choose one's own life partner is so rooted in our traditions." Relying on *Loving v. Virginia,* the judge found as a fact "that marriage, i.e., the recognition of one's choice of a life partner, is a fundamental right," and hence that the appropriate analysis is "strict scrutiny," requiring the state to show a compelling state interest in order to justify the exclusion of gay and lesbian people from the institution of marriage. Judge Michalski pointed out that, in construing the right of privacy, the Supreme Court of Alaska had recognized that determining the length of one's own hair is a fundamental right.[115] Surely, if personal appearance is a fundamental right, then choosing one's life partner is a fundamental right as well.

Within days of Judge Michalski's decision, however, the Alaska legislature had passed a resolution to amend the Alaska Constitution and placed it before voters. In November 1998, Alaskans adopted the constitutional amendment to turn aside Judge Michalski's finding with a 68 percent majority.

The first court to succeed in recognizing a right to marry for gay and lesbian people was the Supreme Judicial Court of Massachusetts in its 2003 decision in *Goodridge v. Department of Public Health*.[116] In contrast to the *Baker* opinion in Vermont, *Goodridge* was a closely decided 4-3 vote, with the opinion rendered by Chief Justice Margaret H. Marshall. The majority concluded that the state had presented no evidence of a rational basis for denying civil marriage to same-sex couples. Although its holding was based on both equal protection and due process grounds, the court spent considerable time defending the fundamental right to marry. Its conclusion was that the definition of civil marriage needed to be expanded to include same-sex couples. Thus the *Goodridge* decision prompted the legislature to rewrite the marriage statute, making Massachusetts the first state in the United States to recognize same-sex marriage.

Chief Justice Marshall began the opinion for the majority by acknowledging the presence of religious and moral opposition to same-sex marriage. She also pointed out that many others have moral and religious reasons for favoring same-sex marriage. However, neither of these perspectives, she argued, impacts the constitutional question, which is to determine the law as it applies to all citizens of the state of Massachusetts. Fulfilling Justice Scalia's prediction, the opinion then moved immediately to situate itself within the rationale of the U.S. Supreme Court's *Lawrence* decision. Although *Lawrence* left open the question of gay marriage, Justice Marshall read it as affirming a "core concept of common human dignity" as well as a recognition that the decisions whether to marry or have children play a central role in shaping one's identity. To deny someone the right to make such decisions and to build a life around them is an arbitrary violation of basic principles of human dignity.

After broadly staking out this principle, the court then moved to take account of the lives of the seven same-sex couples who in April and May 2001 had sought publicly to affirm their commitments to one another by seeking marriage licenses from the state of Massachusetts and were denied. One of the couples had been together for thirty years; many of them were rearing children; like the plaintiffs in so many other cases, some had cared for one another's aging parents. Together they had filed suit alleging that the denial of a marriage license violated their rights under the Massachusetts constitution.

Chief Justice Marshall made clear her intention to treat the parties as persons with integrity and not just another abstract "issue" to be dispensed with.[117] On the basis of their commitments to their partners, she noted, each of the plaintiffs had used the legal means available to them to secure their relationships — such as wills, powers of attorney, and contracts of various sorts. But none of these was able to provide the couples all the governmental protections afforded by marriage. Next, the court noted that both the common law and statutory definitions of marriage exclude same-sex couples. Still, the court argued, a history of exclusion does not, by itself, justify more exclusion. Marriage is a wholly secular institution, never having required a religious ceremony to legitimate it, and as such it must be judged by the laws that govern civil society and not the dogmas of religious tradition. Marriage is an "evolving institution," and the redefinition the court was bringing about was no different from many other such changes through the years.

Finally, marriage holds a unique place in our society, conferring significant legal, financial, and social benefits — not only on the couple but also on the children they are rearing. The court spent several pages enumerating those benefits, which included medical benefits, predictable rules of child support and property division, and the ability to visit one's sick child or partner in the hospital. To be denied participation in this institution is to be denied an important human right. The court also spoke of the "joy and solemnity" that attend marriage. Not only is a couple excluded from an important societal institution when the partners are denied marriage, but an individual is impeded in his or her exercise of individual liberty when same-sex marriage is denied. Drawing on the now-familiar analogy between the ban on same-sex marriage and the earlier prohibition against interracial marriage, the court concluded that "the right to marry means little if it does not include the right to marry the person of one's choice, subject to appropriate government restrictions in the interests of public health, safety, and welfare."[118]

The Massachusetts Supreme Court implied that, since the right to marry is a fundamental right, it should invite "strict scrutiny." However, there was no need to apply strict scrutiny, since the court concluded that excluding gays and lesbians from marriage failed even the "rational basis" test. In essence, the Massachusetts Court decided that discrimination against gays and lesbians is irrational. Said the court: "The marriage ban works a deep and scarring hardship on a very real segment of the community for no rational reason."[119]

In declining to apply heightened scrutiny, the *Goodridge* court was following the U.S. Supreme Court's lead in *Romer v. Evans* and *Lawrence v. Texas*. And, just as in *Romer* and *Lawrence*, it was this move that provoked the ire of the three *Goodridge* dissenters. Justice Martha Sosman presented the same complaint that Justice Scalia had voiced — that is, the three-tiered analysis had been violated. "As a matter of constitutional jurisprudence," she argued, "the case stands as an aberration. To reach the result it does, the court has tortured the rational basis test beyond recognition."[120] Justices Spina and Cordy contended that the court had arrogated to itself the prerogative of the legislature. "The power to regulate marriage lies with the Legislature," Justice Spina lectured the majority, "not the judiciary. The court has transformed its role as protector of individual rights into the creator of rights."[121] Similarly, Justice Cordy maintained that "[t]he Legislature is the appropriate branch, both constitutionally and practically, to consider and respond to same-sex marriage. The issue presented here is profound, deeply rooted in social policy, that must, for now, be the subject of legislative not judicial action."[122]

Like Justice Scalia, the three dissenters were so focused on the technicalities of the three-tier framework that they missed the most obvious meaning of the *Romer, Lawrence,* and *Goodridge* majorities. These decisions are in accord on one basic issue: to discriminate against gay and lesbian people is irrational, and that is why it fails to survive even the lowest level of scrutiny — rational basis review.

Perhaps it was in partial deference to the legislature that the majority refrained from making its decision effective immediately. On the one hand, the court's remedy for gays and lesbians was to redefine marriage in

Massachusetts as "the voluntary union of two persons as spouses, to the exclusion of all others." Since the common law is judge-made law, the majority reasoned, it may also be modified by judges in accordance with principles of equity. On the other hand, the then-current definition had been enacted by the legislature. Instead of making the order effectively immediately, therefore, the court gave the Massachusetts legislature 180 days to revise the law as it deemed appropriate in light of the opinion.[123]

The political response at first was heated. As soon as the decision was announced, Chief Justice Marshall was pilloried by anti-gay groups: they alleged that she was biased in favor of gays and lesbians, and that this bias tainted her opinion. Governor Mitt Romney sought ways to circumvent the judicial decision. Politicians were pressured by anti-gay activists to reject the Supreme Court's ruling. The legislature toyed briefly with a compromise that would have rejected gay marriage in favor of a civil-union-type statute as modeled on the compromise achieved in Vermont.[124] They adopted a proposal on December 11, 2003, and submitted it to the Supreme Judicial Court the next day for an advisory ruling as to whether civil unions would meet the constitutional standards.

The answer from the four-justice majority was swift and uncompromising: resorting to civil unions would create a regime of second-class citizens, and this the Massachusetts Constitution will not tolerate.[125] According to the majority, this inferior and discriminatory second-class status obtains even if same-sex couples are provided the same tangible benefits as married couples. Tangible benefits, though important, are not enough, for there are also "intangible," or symbolic, benefits to marriage. Even though the civil union law was specifically declared by the Massachusetts legislature to be an "equivalent to marriage," merely saying that does not make it so. In an attempt to fend off the charge of judicial activism, the court insisted that the reason for the ruling arose not from a desire to take sides in the culture wars but from a commitment to heed the requirements of fairness under the Massachusetts Constitution. Besides, argued the majority, changing the civil definition of marriage does not prohibit religious dissenters from defining marriage in any way they wish for religious purposes. But it does prevent such groups from effectively excluding one class of people from constitutional protection under the guise of "traditional" values that are not necessarily held by all. Referring to the separate status of African Americans under the Jim Crow laws, the court declared: "The history of our nation has demonstrated that separate is seldom, if ever equal."

This emphasis on gays and lesbians being made "second-class citizens" was especially poignant coming from the pen of Chief Justice Marshall, who is a native of South Africa and opposed the regime of apartheid as a young woman. Moreover, Marshall's role as only the second woman in 300 years to serve on Massachusetts's Supreme Judicial Court — and the first to serve as chief justice — gave an added significance to her opinion.

As one might expect, the three original dissenting justices disagreed and sharply criticized the reasoning of the majority. Justice Martha Sosman made clear her exasperation that the court was raising to a constitutional level "as insignificant an issue as what a statutory program is to be called." In Justice Sosman's mind, as long as same-sex couples were receiving all the benefits, rights, and privileges of marriage, there was no constitutional issue at stake. Since same-sex couples were being given all the legal benefits of marriage but without the name, the dispute now boiled down to "a pitched battle over who gets to use the 'm' word."[126] As we shall see in the final chapter, democratic debate over the "m" word has implications not only for gay couples but for the kind of society we want to live in.

Summary

How should society treat an individual who self-identifies as gay? The status of individual rights for gay people has been addressed in two landmark cases by the United States Supreme Court. The *Romer v. Evans* case provided constitutional protection for gay identity: it held that it is impermissible to target gay people for exclusion from participation in the civil polity simply because they are gay. The *Lawrence v. Texas* case established the constitutional need to respect gay self-determination: it invalidated all laws that criminalize gay relationships between consenting adults. In both cases the Court held that there was no rational connection between the legislative end in view and the means employed. What the Court, in essence, was signaling is that laws aimed at discriminating against gay identity or refusing to respect gay liberty are simply irrational. They discriminate for discrimination's sake, and they take away rights of self-determination that everyone else enjoys.

In addition to valuing gay identity, recent state court decisions have underscored the need to support gay families. First, in *Baker v. State*, the Supreme Court of Vermont held that gay couples must receive the same le-

gal benefits as married couples do. The result was the creation by the legislature of a new legal institution in America, the "civil union."[127] A similar
result was reached in 2006 in the New Jersey case of *Lewis v. Harris,* which
paved the way for New Jersey civil unions.[128] Second, in *Goodridge v. Department of Public Health,* the Supreme Judicial Court of Massachusetts
insisted that gays and lesbians have a constitutional right to marry the person of their own choice. As a result, Massachusetts became the first state in
America to allow full-fledged gay marriage. In all these cases, the courts
appealed to long-standing principles of equality and liberty. Equality arguments assume that gays and lesbians should receive the very same legal
benefits that other people in our society take for granted. Liberty arguments presuppose that, like all other people, gays and lesbians have a right
to personal self-determination that the laws will protect.

The more one examines the legal arguments against expanding
spousal rights to include gay couples, the more one watches them collapse
like a house of cards. The truth is that there are no cogent legal arguments
of a secular nature for refusing to grant some form of relationship rights to
gay couples.[129] What form those rights should take is still very much a subject of debate. In the next chapter I examine the implications of that debate
for the fabric of democracy.

CHAPTER FIVE

Toward a Welcoming Democracy:
Marriage Equality in the Civil Polity

Injustice anywhere is a threat to justice everywhere.

Martin Luther King Jr.,
"Letter from Birmingham Jail," April 16, 1963

Marriage in the United States is a civil institution. As such, it belongs to all citizens regardless of their particular moral beliefs or religious creed. That's why there is no requirement in law that marriage be approved by the church or any other religious community. The consent of the two parties is all it takes to enter a marriage. Beyond licensing requirements, no approval of the state or of any other authoritative body is necessary. Religious officials — whether priests, rabbis, ministers, imams, or others — may preside at weddings, but in no sense do religious communities define what counts as marriage in the civil arena. Moreover, there is no requirement that couples adhere to any particular code of moral conduct while married. There is no action the couple can engage in that automatically dissolves a marriage, because the marital bond can be ended only by death, annulment, or divorce.

Contrary to claims made by anti-gay marriage advocates, the right to marry in the American context has never been conditioned on or based in procreation. As a matter of constitutional law, the right to use contraception *to avoid procreation* was held in *Griswold v. Connecticut* to be a fundamental right of the married couple. Marriage is open to the sterile, to those who are past procreation age, and even to one who is in prison with no prospects for conjugal visits. There is no legal requirement that the couple must have children or even that they must engage in sexual relations. The couple may conduct their marriage relationship in any way they see fit, so long as both are in agreement. Given all this, there is nothing inherent in the structure or content of marriage in the secular arena that can justify using procreation to bar gay couples from getting married.[1]

The idea that marriage must be governed by some particular religious or moral framework from the past ignores the history that gave us a secularized understanding of marriage in this country in the first place. It was the Protestant church, after all, that insisted marriage is best governed by the secular state.[2] Prior to the Protestant Reformation, marriage had been conceived as a sacrament administered by the church. However, reformers such as Luther and Calvin insisted that the covenant of marriage is made by the two parties themselves, not the church, and that it should be regulated, not by the church, but by the civil authority. From colonial days until the present, people have married one another by mutual consent. There was not even a requirement for a wedding ceremony; rather such celebrations originated as rituals of the wealthy and were not necessary for a marriage to be valid.[3]

So then, in a democratic society, should gay men and lesbians have the right to enter into the institution of marriage? In the previous chapter I explained how that proposal first came into being. In this chapter I describe how the idea has steadily progressed in the United States since *Goodridge v. Department of Health* brought gay marriage to the state of Massachusetts and *Baker v. State* brought civil unions to Vermont. I will next turn to the significance of this progress for the health and integrity of our pluralistic democracy.

The Continued Contest over Marriage Equality

When the first edition of this book was published in 2006, Massachusetts was the only state in the United States to provide for gay marriage; Vermont and Connecticut were the only ones to allow for civil unions. In the previous chapter I discussed the background that brought these two different legal frameworks, gay marriage and civil unions, into existence. In the book's first edition, I predicted that the number of gay-marriage states would increase. I also noted that in some locales civil unions would offer a more politically palatable compromise that would serve as a stepping stone to full marriage equality. I argued, too, that despite their short-term political advantages civil unions still discriminate and treat same-sex couples as second-class citizens.

Today these predictions have proved correct. Seven jurisdictions in the United States now give gay and lesbian couples full access to the institution of marriage: Connecticut, Iowa, Massachusetts, New Hampshire, New York, Vermont, and the District of Columbia.[4] My predictions about the role of civil unions have also proved accurate. The civil union laws in Vermont and Connecticut served as stepping stones to gay marriage. The same was true in New Hampshire, which approved civil unions in 2007 (effective January 1, 2008) and then quickly passed a gay marriage law in 2009.[5] Five more states now provide for civil unions: Delaware (effective January 1, 2012), Hawaii (effective January 1, 2012), Illinois (effective June 1, 2011), New Jersey (2006), and Rhode Island (effective July 1, 2011). For a complete, state-by-state account of the status of same-sex couples in the United States, see the chart on pages 238-242.

Nevertheless, the road to gay marriage has also faced challenges. In California, by an action of the courts, gay marriage was legal for a few months in 2008 before being rescinded in a voter referendum, a story to which I will return later. Similarly, the state of Maine passed a gay marriage bill that was signed into law on May 10, 2009, but before it could take effect, a voter referendum, passing by a 53 percent to 47 percent margin, made gay marriage illegal. Proponents have succeeded in placing a new referendum on the ballot for November, 2012, to reinstate gay marriage. In 2012, the state of Maryland passed a gay marriage law easily, allowing same-sex couples to marry beginning in January, 2013.[6] However, the law faces a likely referendum challenge. In the state of Washington, a same-sex marriage bill was signed into law on February 13, 2012, to take effect on June 7, 2012. However, it too faces a likely electoral challenge by referendum.

Given the sort of backlash that gay marriage often provokes, why not opt for civil unions and put full marriage equality on the back burner? This is the tactic many shrewd politicians, including President Barack Obama, have taken.

Yet civil unions have significant drawbacks. In Rhode Island, where a civil unions bill has been pending, some pro-gay activists have actually opposed civil unions because they create a second-class citizenship for gay couples. Also, experience is now starting to show that civil unions are not able to guarantee all the rights and privileges they claim to provide. For example, in 2006 the New Jersey legislature passed a civil unions bill in response to the New Jersey Supreme Court decision of *Lewis v. Harris.*[7] Since then it has become clear that in the workplace, in the hospital, in the insurance and pension arenas, and elsewhere, civil unions do not provide equal benefits. For example, instances were reported of corporate employers denying benefits on the grounds that gay couples were not technically "spouses." In December 2008 a New Jersey commission charged with monitoring the results of the civil unions law concluded that it should be changed to provide for gay marriage.[8]

The inequalities implicit in civil unions had already been anticipated by New Jersey Chief Justice Deborah T. Poritz in her dissent in *Lewis v. Harris,* rejecting the majority's claim that the "m" word was irrelevant:

> What we name things matters, language matters. . . . Labels set people apart surely as physical separation on a bus or in school facilities. . . . By excluding same-sex couples from civil marriage, the State declares that it is legitimate to differentiate between their commitments and the commitments of heterosexual couples. Ultimately the message is that what same-sex couples have is not as important or as significant as real marriage, that such lesser relationships cannot have the name of marriage.[9]

About the same time, a similar dissent was registered by Chief Justice Judith Kaye of the highest court in New York. Because the state of New York has long nurtured a tradition of equality, it came as a surprise to many when the state's highest court rejected the appeal of forty-four gay couples for marriage equality in the case of *Hernandez v. Robles.*[10] The justices implied that though they might personally favor gay marriage as a matter of public policy, creating a new right of this sort was not a decision for the courts but for the state legislature. In her dissent, Chief Justice Judith Kaye argued that the right to marry the person of one's choice is a fundamental right, which calls for strict scrutiny by the courts. It is not a "new" right gays and lesbians are invoking but the same long-standing liberty interest recognized by the United States Supreme Court in *Lawrence v. Texas.* That a group of people has historically been denied its rights is no reason for allowing injustice to be perpetuated. "Simply put, fundamental rights are fundamental rights. They are not defined in terms of who is entitled to exercise them." Just as there was a "deep history" of denying rights to interracial couples — and doing so on the grounds that such marriages are "unnatural" and a "violation of God's will" — so too gay and lesbian couples have suffered a similar discriminatory history. Since definitions of marriage have evolved over time, to declare that marriage excludes gays and lesbians by definition is to ignore this changing history and to argue in a circle. Even if the court declined to apply strict scrutiny, she argued, the marriage exclusion does not even pass the "rational basis test," because forbidding gay marriage does nothing to promote procreation nor does it hurt heterosexual marriages. Justice Kaye concluded:

> It is uniquely the function of the Judicial Branch to safeguard individual liberties guaranteed by the New York State Constitution, and to order redress for their violation. The Court's duty to protect constitutional rights is an imperative of the separation of powers, not its enemy.
>
> I am confident that future generations will look back on today's decision as an unfortunate misstep.[11]

Misstep or not, the result of the *Hernandez* case was to throw the issue back to the state legislature where it became embroiled for several years in partisan politics. In 2009 a committee of the New York Bar Association surveyed the situation of gay couples nationwide and recommended New York adopt a gay marriage law.[12] Gay marriage was finally approved in New York on June 24, 2011.

The negative results for gay marriage in the New Jersey and New York courts might well have raised serious doubts about the short-term prospects for marriage equality. But then in 2008 a dramatic shift on the judicial front began to take place. In quick succession the Connecticut, California, and Iowa Supreme Courts all ruled for gay marriage, essentially agreeing with the rationales of the dissenters in New Jersey and New York. Prior to 2008, courts focusing on the propriety of gay marriage analyzed its prospects using "rational basis review." Usually rational basis review results in the court deferring to the legislature. As it was explained in the previous chapter, the exception is when government adopts a classification that discriminates for discrimination's sake against a politically unpopular group — hippies in *Moreno*, unmarried birth-control users in *Eisenstadt*, the mentally challenged in *Cleburne*, and homosexuals in *Romer* and *Lawrence*. In these cases the statute in question may not survive rational basis review. Thus in *Baker v. State* the Vermont Supreme Court unanimously struck down the statutory discrimination against gay couples but divided 4 to 1 on the marriage question, thus giving birth to civil unions. In *Goodridge v. Department of Public Health,* the Massachusetts Supreme Court struck down discrimination on a split vote and called for gay marriage. In *Lewis v. Harris,* the New Jersey court struck down discrimination and called for civil unions but voted 4 to 3 against mandating marriage.

The major shift in 2008 came when courts began to acknowledge for the first time that gays and lesbians constitute a class suffering from a level of discrimination that requires the protection of the courts. To qualify as a protected class under constitutional law, gays and lesbians need to show that (1) they have suffered a history of discrimination based on their sexual orientation, (2) their orientation does not keep them from contributing to society, and (3) their orientation is "immutable" or not subject to change. Some also argued for an additional criterion, (4) that gays must prove they are politically powerless. By 2008, lawyers for states seeking to prohibit gay marriage were routinely conceding points (1) and (2) — a history of discrimination and the benign nature of sexual orientation. The central dispute usually boiled down to whether sexual orientation was immutable — can it be changed? And to what extent did gays and lesbians need judicial protection? The California, Connecticut, and Iowa Supreme Courts all decided that sexual orientation is such a core part of any person's identity that it cannot be changed without difficulty, and in any event it is something the state should not be in the business of requiring one to change. Each of these three decisions is worth briefly summarizing.

A Landmark California Case

The California Supreme Court in 2008 became the second (after Massachusetts) to rule that same-sex couples must be granted access to the secular institution of marriage.[13] In the 6 to 3 decision known as *In re Marriage Cases,* the California court also raised the stakes, holding that (a) sexual orientation is a "suspect" classification requiring strict scrutiny, and (b) the right to choose a marriage partner is a fundamental right even if the person one chooses to marry is of the same gender.[14] As noted, the key question regarding the appropriate level of judicial scrutiny was whether sexual orientation is immutable. Writing for the majority, Chief Justice Ronald George reasoned that if religion, which one adopts by choice, can be considered an immutable characteristic (which it can in constitutional law), then so can sexual orientation. One's sexual orientation is not something one ordinarily chooses. And even if one thinks gay and lesbian people can change their identity, the court insisted that one's sexual orientation is not something the government can force you to alter or disown. Therefore, the court concluded, "statutes that treat persons differently because of their sexual orientation should be subjected to strict scrutiny."

Regarding marriage as a fundamental right, Chief Justice George relied in part on California's famous 1948 *Perez* decision, which held that the prohibition of interracial marriage infringed upon the fundamental right to marry the person one chooses.[15] The question for *In re Marriage Cases,* then, was whether the fundamental right to marry the person one chooses should include the right to choose a member of the same gender. Chief Justice George argued that in *Perez* the right was not a "right of interracial marriage," nor in the present case was the right in question a right of "same sex marriage." Rather, the right was simply the right "to join in marriage *with the person of one's choice.*" Chief Justice George quoted precedents to the effect that marriage is "the most socially productive and individually fulfilling relationship that one can enjoy in the course of a lifetime." It is a right recognized in Article 16 of the United Nations Declaration of Human Rights and many other similar declarations. He noted, furthermore, that at the time at least seventy thousand children were being raised by gay couples in California and that "gay individuals are fully capable of entering into the kind of loving and enduring committed relationships that may serve as the foundation of a family and of responsibly caring for and raising children." The Chief Justice concluded that whether the "m" word in the abstract is part of the constitutional right to marriage, certainly it includes "the right of same-sex couples to have their official family relationship accorded the same dignity, respect, and stature as that accorded to all other officially recognized family relationships." Civil unions and domestic partnerships do not do this any more than creating a "trans-racial union" would have done it for interracial couples.

Based on this analysis, the court ruled that gay couples should have access to the institution of marriage. It also pointed out that providing such access does not prohibit or undermine the marriages of opposite-sex couples. In dissent, Judge Marvin Baxter repeated the objection that there is no long-standing right to same-sex marriage in American law. The problem with

Judge Baxter's argument, however, is that this was the very same one used in *Bowers v. Hardwick* to uphold the criminalization of homosexual practice. In *Bowers*, the court insisted there was no longstanding constitutional right to engage in "sodomy." In overruling *Bowers*, the *Lawrence v. Texas* majority responded that the longstanding right needing to be protected is the right to liberty. In *Lawrence* the liberty right was considered broad enough to extend to casual sexual liaisons. The claim in *In re Marriage Cases* went a step further, arguing that the right includes access to the institution society has created to recognize permanent nuptial bonds. To say that no such right has existed in the past is to beg the very question at issue. As with the right of interracial marriage, the question is not whether such a right has existed in the past but whether justice demands it should exist right now.

Gay Marriage Comes to Connecticut

A few months later, the Connecticut Supreme Court weighed in with a similar line of reasoning. The Connecticut state legislature had enacted a civil unions law in 2005 modeled on the original Vermont statute. In the meantime, a 2004 lawsuit brought by eight gay couples protesting their exclusion from the right to marry had been making its way through the Connecticut court system. Initially, a trial court rejected the claim of these couples, reasoning that the couples were done no harm and that providing equal benefits under the civil unions law was sufficient to satisfy the constitutional right of equality. On October 10, 2008, the Connecticut Supreme Court rejected this reasoning — the same reasoning that had prevailed in many court cases prior to 2008. In a 4-3 decision in *Kerrigan v. Department of Public Health,* the court invalidated the civil unions law, declaring it unconstitutional to deny gay and lesbian couples access to the secular institution of marriage.[16] Again, the major issue was a recognition of a specific form of discrimination aimed at gay couples. Judge Richard N. Palmer explained the majority's perspective as follows:

> Gay persons have been subjected to and stigmatized by a long history of purposeful and invidious discrimination that continues to manifest itself in society. The characteristic that defines the members of this group — attraction to persons of the same sex — bears no logical relationship to their ability to perform in society, either in familial rela-

tions or otherwise as productive citizens. Because sexual orientation is such an essential component of personhood, even if there is some possibility that a person's sexual preference can be altered, it would be wholly unacceptable for the state to require anyone to do so. Gay persons also represent a distinct minority of the population. It is true, of course, that gay persons recently have made significant advances in obtaining equal treatment under the law. Nonetheless, we conclude that, as a minority group that continues to suffer the enduring effects of centuries of legally sanctioned discrimination, laws singling them out for disparate treatment are subject to heightened judicial scrutiny to ensure that those laws are not the product of such historical prejudice and stereotyping.[17]

Notice here that Connecticut called for "heightened scrutiny," something shy of California's "strict scrutiny." Heightened scrutiny, you may recall from the preceding chapter, is the level of inquiry often applied to sex discrimination cases. The idea is that, unlike race (the usual arena of "strict scrutiny"), some distinctions based on sex may be appropriate (e.g., his and her bathrooms). In rejecting strict scrutiny for heightened scrutiny, the court is leaving its options open for other cases down the road. In a dissenting opinion, however, Judge David M. Borden argued that sexual orientation should not trigger any heightened scrutiny on the grounds that gay and lesbian people already have political clout and do not need the protection of the courts. But if this were true, then why do sexual orientation and gay marriage provoke such controversy, so much political and even violent activity targeted at gay and lesbian people, and so much continued stigmatization? In his majority opinion, Judge Palmer responded that whatever political clout gays and lesbians may have, it has not been sufficient to stop the prejudice and discrimination.

Iowa Moves Forward by Returning to Its Roots

Then on April 3, 2009, the Iowa Supreme Court handed down *Varnum v. Brien,* adding its voice to the growing judicial opinion that same-sex couples have a right to marry.[18] A long-standing principle of justice and the rule of law is that similarly situated persons should be treated in the same way. The Iowa Constitution enshrined this principle in the following provision:

[T]he general assembly shall not grant to any citizen or class of citizens, privileges or immunities, which, upon the same terms shall not equally belong to all citizens.[19]

Writing for a unanimous court, Justice Mark Cady underscored that in Iowa the "absolute equality of all" before the law provides "the very foundation principle of our government." He reminded Iowans that they had a long history of taking stands for justice before the rest of the country. The very first case it heard, the supreme court in Iowa had refused to enforce a contract for the sale of a slave. Similarly, as early as 1868 the Iowa court rejected segregation, many decades before *Brown v. Board of Education*. Iowa was also the first state to admit women to the bar in 1869. Justice Cady then pointed out that gay couples are similarly situated to heterosexual couples. Both are in committed, loving relationships, in some cases raising children. The argument put forward by those defending the traditional law was that gay and lesbian people are not barred from the institution of marriage at all, so long as they marry someone of the opposite sex. Yet Justice Cady responded that "the right of a gay or lesbian person . . . to enter into a civil marriage only with a person of the opposite sex is no right at all." It would require them to deny their very identity. By putting marriage beyond the reach of gay and lesbian people seeking to live out their choice of life partners, the law in practical effect discriminates.

Backlash in Iowa and California

In Connecticut the transition to gay marriage happened with little turmoil, but in both Iowa and California, there was a backlash. In Iowa it was directed personally at the justices themselves. Even though supreme court justices in Iowa are appointed by the governor, they must periodically make themselves subject to a "retention" vote of the electorate. In this retention vote, judges run unopposed, and since retention voting was instituted in 1962 no retention vote had become politicized. In response to the same-sex marriage case, however, interest groups from outside the state of Iowa spent hundreds of thousands of dollars smearing three justices whose terms were up for renewal in 2010, including warnings that further judicial decisions concerning handguns and the like would be forthcoming. Warnings were also issued by some of these interest groups to judges around the country that they would be held accountable for their votes.

A major premise of American law is that we need a free and impartial judiciary that is not subject to political influence or coercion. Based on their conviction that the judiciary should not become politicized, the three targeted Iowa justices refused to campaign on their own behalf. When the election was held, all three were removed from office. In response to media efforts to draw them further into the vortex of controversy, the justices mostly remained silent and returned to private life. Yet the incident raises questions about the type of judicial system we want to have. An impartial judiciary is put at risk if the office of judge becomes politicized. In many other cases, judges decided against the gay or lesbian candidate without being subject to similar intimidation or reprisal.[20]

In California the backlash came in the form of a state-wide voter referendum placed on the November 2009 ballot to make same-sex marriage unconstitutional. By order of the California Supreme Court, marriage licenses for same-sex couples had become available on June 16, 2008. In a hotly contested vote, the provision known as "Proposition 8" passed with a 52 percent majority, eliminating gay marriage beginning November 5, 2011. Much of the money funding the media campaign on both sides of Proposition 8 came from outside the state of California, and much of the pro-Proposition 8 funding came from the Church of Jesus Christ of Latter Day Saints. After the new gay marriage ban passed, lawsuits were filed to overturn the ban. The California Supreme Court issued a May 25, 2009, opinion, *Straus v. Horton*, upholding the legitimacy of the new ban, though also ruling that approximately eighteen thousand California same-sex marriages entered into between June 16, 2008, and November 5, 2008, were still valid.[21] I will return to this decision in the discussion of voter referenda below.

A Trial in California That Changed Everything

On May 22, 2009, a potentially game-changing lawsuit filed in federal court in California by two same-sex couples dramatically raised the stakes. This new lawsuit, filed with the express intention of reaching the United States Supreme Court, could potentially change laws on gay marriage nationwide. At the trial level this new case was known as *Perry v. Schwar-*

zenegger and is now known as *Perry v. Brown.*[22] While the previous California lawsuit, *Straus v. Horton,* addressed the question of whether Proposition 8 violated the California Constitution, this new federal lawsuit argued that Proposition 8 violates the United States Constitution.

The legal team pressing the case was headed by two lawyers who are usually on opposing sides: the conservative litigator Theodore B. Olson, who represented President George W. Bush in the 2000 case of *Bush v. Gore,* and David Boies, who represented Al Gore in the same case.[23] Together they filed suit on behalf of two couples, Kris Perry and Sandy Stier, and Paul Katami and Jeff Zarrillo, who love each other and seek to be married but were prevented from doing so by Proposition 8.

By the luck of the draw, the case was assigned to Federal District Judge Vaughn Walker, a conservative jurist, once active in Republican politics, who was first appointed to the bench by Ronald Reagan. Walker's nomination had to be withdrawn, however, when it became known he had represented the United States Olympic Committee in its effort to prevent the use of the term, "Gay Olympics." This resulted in charges made by Representative Nancy Pelosi and others that Walker was insensitive to gays. Ironically, as it turns out, Walker himself happens to be gay, though he never spoke about it publicly until after he retired from the bench. After his first nomination was withdrawn, Walker was reappointed to the bench by President George H. W. Bush and was approved.

Perry v. Schwarzenegger began with a high-profile trial in which both sides had the opportunity to present evidence for and against the state's interest in banning same-sex couples from the institution of marriage.[24] Faced with this opportunity, the anti-gay advocates of Proposition 8 presented a case that simply fell apart. They were asked to offer concrete, empirical evidence to establish the harm that would be caused by same-sex marriage. On this question, the Proposition 8 advocates offered no empirical evidence at all other than a single witness, David Blankenhorn, founder of a conservative advocacy group. Not only did Blankenhorn have no empirical evidence to support his opinions, but he also actually made statements on cross-examination that supported the gay couples' claim, namely that same-sex marriage would improve family stability and offer benefits to the children of gay couples. At a pre-trial hearing, Judge Walker asked whether the Proposition 8 case for banning gay marriage boiled down to a claim about procreation. If so, he asked the Proposition 8 advocates for evidence to substantiate their claim. The following exchange took place:

JUDGE: "I'm asking you to tell me how [same-sex marriage] would harm opposite-sex marriages. . . ."

PROPOSITION 8 ATTORNEY: "Your Honor, my answer is: I don't know. I don't know."[25]

In contrast to this, lawyers for the gay couples presented evidence by three psychologists, an economist, an academic historian, and a social epidemiologist. Drawing on academic studies, these witnesses testified that same-sex couples are as loving and as capable of raising well-adjusted children as opposite-sex couples. Lawyers for the Proposition 8 proponents cross-examined the plaintiffs' expert witnesses but could provide no contrary evidence whatsoever to rebut the empirical case they were making.[26]

In order to be evenhanded, Judge Walker encouraged the Proposition 8 lawyers to provide more evidence for their case but to no avail. The Proposition 8 lawyers offered legal conclusions about same-sex marriage, but none were based on empirical data. Given the testimony at trial, Judge Walker ruled that the plaintiffs had established a long list of facts. Some of these included:

- that marriage is a secular institution;
- that California (like other states) imposes no requirement that married couples procreate or be willing to procreate;
- that the nature of marriage has changed over time (including elimination of interracial marriage prohibitions, rules that subordinate women's property rights to their husbands, expectations regarding male and female gender roles, advent of no-fault divorce laws, etc.);
- that certain harms accrue to same-sex couples due to their inability to marry (including harms pertaining to immigration and citizenship, taxation, rules of property and inheritance, and social services benefits);
- that same-sex couples are deprived of the support obligations of marriage as well as the material benefits and sense of well-being that marriage often brings;
- that children of same-sex couples are deprived of many of these same benefits;
- that sexual orientation is a non-chosen, enduring pattern of object affection that comprises a fundamental part of a person's identity;

- that there is no difference between same-sex and heterosexual couples regarding their ability to form successful marital unions;
- that marrying a person of the opposite sex is not a realistic option for most gay and lesbian people;
- that the California domestic partnership law does not bestow on same-sex couples the same status as marriage;
- that Proposition 8 stigmatizes same-sex couples and treats them differently from heterosexual couples;
- that Proposition 8 eliminates the right of same-sex couples to marry, whereas the creation of same-sex marriage does not eliminate the right of proponents of Proposition 8 to express their First Amendment rights against same-sex marriage;
- that the public campaign for Proposition 8 traded upon and perpetuated stereotypes about gay and lesbian people, including that they are not capable of long-term relationships and are not good parents;
- that Proposition 8 had the effect of making same-sex couples feel as though their relationships were not as highly valued by the state of California;
- that the children of same-sex couples are as likely to be well-adjusted as the children of heterosexual couples;
- that children do not need both a male and a female parent to be well-adjusted;
- that a child's adjustment and well-being does not depend on having a genetic connection with his or her parents;
- that the Proposition 8 campaign relied on the erroneous suggestion that being exposed to same-sex marriage could turn a child into a gay or lesbian person.

No matter what the ultimate legal outcome of the case may be, the establishment of these facts is important. People are free to draw different legal conclusions from the facts, but the facts are what they are. The trial transcripts are available to the public, and everyone with an interest in the subject should read them in their entirety, especially the expert testimony.

Based on these facts, Judge Walker was driven to the legal conclusion that Proposition 8 violates the due process and equal protection rights of same-sex couples. It violates due process by infringing on the fundamental right to marry and does so without a legitimate (and thus not a compelling) state interest. Lawyers for both sides agreed that the right to marry is fundamental. The question was whether the same-sex couples were trying to exercise that right or to create a new right. The evidence presented at trial showed that the couples loved each other and wished to choose each other as spouses and to build a life together, including all the marks of marriage as defined by law. Since procreation is not a requirement for marriage, excluding same-sex couples from marriage for that reason is a relic of a bygone era. Even if in the past gender roles were distinct and woven into the cultural understanding of marriage, that is no longer the case today. Yet Judge Walker suggested a core belief remains constant beneath the cultural changes in marriage: "The right to marriage has been historically and remains the right to choose a spouse and, with mutual consent, join together and form a household."[27] Same-sex couples are in the identical situation as different-sex couples in their ability to perform marital rights and obligations under California law. In short, the plaintiffs are not seeking same-sex marriage, they are simply seeking marriage.

According to Judge Walker, Proposition 8 violates equal protection because it discriminates on the basis of sexual orientation. Many laws create classifications that distinguish people for various reasons. In order not to violate equal protection the classification must promote some governmental interest. Judge Walker considered a list of possible governmental interests the law could serve. If, for example, the governmental interest of Proposition 8 is supposedly to promote procreation, there is nothing in the prohibition that actually advances this interest. Stopping gays from marrying will do nothing to make people procreate. If, to take another example, the purpose is to promote stable families, the law actually thwarts that purpose by not promoting stability for same-sex families. It is only moral and religious views (understood in particular ways) that give a basis for distinguishing between same-sex and different-sex couples, but such views are not the proper basis for secular laws. In short, the overwhelming evidence at trial showed that Proposition 8 singled out gays for exclusion from marriage simply because they were gay, and thus the law was unconstitutional.

Advocates of Proposition 8 appealed.[28] At that point, however, the governor and the attorney general of the state of California declared their unwillingness to defend Proposition 8 in court, leaving the defense of the case to the civilian (mostly religiously-based) supporters of the measure. With California no longer willing to defend Proposition 8 in court, the question arose concerning who is in a legal position to mount a defense.[29] However, the California Supreme Court ruled on Novemeber 7, 2011, that nongovernmental supporters of Proposition 8 had legal standing to defend it.[30] On February 7, 2012, a three-judge Ninth Circuit panel ruled two to one that Proposition 8 is unconstitutional.[31] Further appeals are pending, and it is likely the case will be appealed all the way to the United States Supreme Court, where a ruling could affect anti-gay marriage provisions throughout the country.

After they lost and Judge Walker retired from the bench, advocates of Proposition 8 filed a motion claiming that Judge Walker should have refused to hear the case because he is gay. They claimed that the judge's own sexual orientation meant that they did not get a fair trial. However, it is an established principle of law that a hypothetical interest in the outcome of a case is not cause for a judge to remove himself or herself. If this were so, then judges who are racial minorities would be prohibited from ruling in civil rights cases, and judges who have religious affiliations would be prohibited from hearing cases involving religion. Would supporters of Proposition 8 think the same-sex couples could claim unfairness if the judge had been straight? The very fact that Proposition 8 advocates could even make this argument sound plausible is another demonstration of the bias against gays in our society. The judge who heard the motion immediately rejected it.[32]

Marriage, Deliberation, and the Making of a Welcoming Democracy

Current debates over marriage extend beyond establishing winners and losers in a culture war; the deeper issue is nothing less than what it means to be a democracy.[33] Democracy is a way of political life in which all are invited to participate as free and equal citizens. The word "democracy" refers literally to the political empowerment *(kratia)* of the people *(dēmos)*. In its highest and best sense, this means *all* the people — the weak as well as the strong, the few as well as the many, the popular as well as the unpopular. Thus, there is more to democracy than simply following the principle of majority rule. It is true that democracy frequently arrives at decisions through honoring the will of the majority. At the same time, however, our democracy has mechanisms for balancing power, protecting the interests of the minority, and upholding the fundamental rights of individuals. The rights of some will always be in tension with the rights of others, but this much is clear: the aim of the Bill of Rights and constitutional jurisprudence is to guarantee that the fundamental rights of individuals cannot be taken away by majority power.

This interplay between majoritarian power, on the one hand, and the rights of individuals and unpopular minorities, on the other, is at the heart of the continuing debate over same-sex marriage. The answer to the same-sex marriage question has implications for the sort of democracy we wish to be.

Democracy has assumed different forms in diverse contexts.[34] In the American context it has taken the form of a democratic republicanism. Republicanism is a form of representative democracy that is grounded in a written constitution and governed by the rule of law.[35] It is a form of limited government that espouses the separation of powers, a balance between the interests of competing factions, with the goal of liberty and equality for all. Through a system of checks and balances — in which the legislative, executive, and judicial powers operate in complementary and mutually circumscribing ways — republicanism attempts to prevent the arbitrary exercise of power, whether it is the arbitrariness of the central government imposed on the people or the arbitrariness that people themselves impose on groups that are unpopular.

At its best, the American form of government has sought to be what I shall call a "welcoming democracy,"[36] that is, one that reaches out to the "other" — for example, to the immigrant, the outcast, or the neighbor in need.[37] This openness to the other works itself out through bedrock principles we have already encountered in Chapter Four, those of equality and liberty. According to these principles, all people share an equal right to participate in the responsibilities and benefits of government as free and equal citizens. All people have a liberty interest with which no others may unduly interfere. These principles function both as present realities and as ongoing ideals.[38] That is to say, equality and liberty as actual achievements depend on the ideals of equality and liberty against which success or failure is constantly being measured. These ideals ought to be preserved by the official institutions of government, but the ultimate guardians of these ideals are democracy's citizens themselves. It is we who nurture the practices of democracy, and it is only we who can make a welcoming democracy come more fully into being.[39]

Commitment to equality and liberty requires that we be especially zealous to protect groups that happen to be unpopular. A welcoming democracy will go out of its way to protect the rights even of its critics and nonconformists. A classic example occurred in 1943, in the middle of World War II, when the United States Supreme Court met to decide the landmark case of *West Virginia State Board of Education v. Barnette*. The *Barnette* case enunciated a principle that, by analogy, has a crucial bearing on the gay-rights disputes today. The case was about how to relate the rights of the minority to the deeply held sentiments of the majority. Was it permissible to force the children of Jehovah's Witnesses who were enrolled in public schools to salute the American flag, a gesture that violated their consciences?[40] In *Barnette*, the court upheld the right of the Jehovah's Witnesses to preserve their consciences by not saluting the flag. In this way *Barnette* affirmed principles of interest to both sides in the gay-rights struggles. On the one hand, it affirmed the rights of a persecuted minority to constitutional protection, which is important to proponents of gay rights; on the other hand, it also underscored the expressive freedom of religious groups to disagree with behaviors they considered morally offensive.

Given the values of a welcoming democracy, the result in *Barnette* is obviously correct. But less than three years earlier, in a 1941 case known as *Minersville School District v. Gobitis*, the Supreme Court had actually decided against the Jehovah's Witnesses, upholding a flag-saluting statute in a lopsided 8-1 vote and allowing the Jehovah's Witnesses' children to be expelled from public school if they did not comply.[41] The harsh result in *Gobitis* was based on the perceived need at the time for patriotism and national unity. The problem with this reasoning is that unity should not become a pretext for coercing *uniformity*. It is no wonder, then, that many legal scholars and civil libertarians were sharply critical of the *Gobitis* case.[42] Forcing a person to violate his or her conscience is a serious matter, from both a political and a theological point of view. Politically speaking, it contravenes the respect that is owed to the individual; theologically speaking, it ignores one of the most compelling rubrics to emerge from the Protestant Reformation, namely, that God alone is Lord of the conscience. This implies that people must be left free to determine their own minds and hearts about important moral and religious matters. One may think of democracy as an ongoing conversation in which majorities coalesce to decide elections and determine policy; but when it comes to practices of criticism and dissent, minority views are protected and preserved — not only for the sake of the critics and dissenters but for the strengthening of democracy itself.

In addition to nurturing a logic of equality and liberty, democracy encourages respect for the "other" through the concrete practices that make democracy what it is. These practices include the open give-and-take of negotiation and compromise. Princeton philosopher Jeffrey Stout has recently argued that the norms of democracy are derived from these democratic practices themselves. They are not derived, as some liberal ideologies proclaim, from generating principles in the abstract or from the fiction of a social contract. Instead, they emerge from the ongoing experience of embodying the democratic ideal in lived experience. In answering ideologues on the right, who argue that democracy is corrosive of traditional values, Stout maintains that democracy itself *is* an ongoing tradition that centers on a moral core. It is a mediating tradition that requires us to attend to the perspectives of all. By cultivating the practices of democracy, we may be able to avoid the extremes of an antidemocratic authoritarianism, on the one hand, and an antitraditional form of liberalism, on the other. Certainly, the gay-rights debates have seen their share of authoritarian advocates of religious tradition pitted against secular detractors of those same traditions. When issues are framed in this way, Stout argues, the two sides feed off each other, each amplifying the other's threats and demonizing the other side. If this either-or situation is left unchecked, and even more if it is allowed to escalate, there is a danger that the impasse will become permanent. The perception of unrelenting animosity will become reality.[43]

Naturally, if democracy operates by fostering an ongoing conversation among participants with diverse perspectives, clashes of conscience are inevitable from time to time. In the *Gobitis* and *Barnette* cases, the clash concerned how to square freedom with order: the freedom of conscience demanded by the Jehovah's Witnesses with the patriotic order favored by society's majority. And a similar conflict is at work in the current controversies over same-sex relationships. The right of gay couples to be included as a part of the civil polity is clashing with the desire of many to oppose what they regard as an immoral lifestyle. The result is a profound irony: one group, in exercising its democratic right to express opposition to another group's behavior, is undermining the other group's democratic right to equal citizenship. It is one thing to uphold the freedom of one group to disagree with another; it is another thing to allow one group to perpetuate a status hierarchy in which members of the other group are treated like second-class citizens.

One key to resolving the conflict is to gain greater precision concerning the two very different kinds of rights that are in question here. On the one hand, there is the right of all people, including gay people, to equality under the law. This right should include equal access to crucial societal institutions and equal participation in the benefits of government. Today even some anti-gay groups are beginning to acknowledge that fairness calls for some form of societal support for gay and lesbian families.[44] (As we shall see, precisely what kind of support this calls for is where the real debate lies.) On the other hand, there is the right of all people, including the religious opponents of homoerotic behavior, to advocate their views vigorously in the public square.[45] Whereas the first is a right of free and equal participation, the second is a right of free expression. Both rights need to be honored, but both rights lie within certain parameters and need to be construed in ways that minimize conflict.

First, we should honor the right of gay couples to inclusion, but, as I shall explain below, we will not all agree on the best means to accomplish that inclusion. Second, we should also honor the right of anti-gay groups to espouse their convictions, but these groups should not be allowed to deprive gay couples of their rights as citizens. Just as no one has a right to yell "fire" in a crowded building when there is no fire and call that utterance free speech, so one's freedom of speech should not be allowed to do demonstrable harm to others.[46] This is one reason the proof of harm to same-sex couples that was demonstrated in the *Perry v. Schwarzenegger* trial is so important. Causing harm should be prohibited even if a majority has been persuaded that the group in question — in this case, gay people — deserves the harm.

The importance of not allowing the majority to erase the rights of the minority was another important principle reinforced in the Jehovah's Witnesses cases. Not long after the first case *(Gobitis)* was decided, the United States was drawn into World War II. Those refusing to salute the flag came under even greater popular condemnation, and a wave of violent persecution broke out against the Jehovah's Witnesses, including beatings and the burning of their church buildings. This persecution formed the backdrop of the subsequent case *(Barnette)*, which had reached the Supreme Court review when a lower court took the highly unusual step of simply refusing to apply the *Gobitis* decision. In *Barnette* the Supreme Court reversed itself, holding for the Jehovah's Witnesses on freedom-of-speech grounds; it was one of the quickest turnarounds in Supreme Court history. Speaking for the majority, Justice Robert Jackson, who later would serve as chief counsel for the United States at the Nuremberg trials, stated the bedrock democratic principle that "fundamental rights may not be submitted to vote; they depend on the outcome of no elections."[47] In short, in a democratic society the rights of the minority must be protected even if the majority finds those rights objectionable or repugnant, and even if the majority considers the people asserting those rights unpopular.

216

How, then, can the controversy over gay marriage be reframed in a way that moves society forward with the rights of all being honored? One way for this to happen is through the cultivation of deliberative modes of discourse based on respect for the other.

This implies that how we advocate our positions is as important as the content of the positions themselves. Arguing for a more welcoming democracy requires that our own approach to the problem be welcoming in its turn. It will not do to argue for inclusion of same-sex couples while demonizing and thus rhetorically excluding those who disagree. We must strive for a mode of advocacy that itself models the kind of society we want to see. In arguing for the acceptance of social and political differences, we must handle such differences gracefully ourselves. In short, we must make our case in a way that builds up the civil polity instead of tearing it down; we must work for a better democracy and do so in a way that is itself truly democratic. The best way to do this is by committing ourselves to a form of deliberative democracy.

Deliberative Democracy and Disputes over Gay Relationships

Respecting the democratic process is at the heart of an approach to politics known as "deliberative democracy." In a deliberative democracy, citizens resolve to reason together about their differences, and all citizens — of all convictions — are invited to participate on equal footing. The key feature that makes deliberative democracy work is the practice of giving reasons to one another for positions taken, reasons that are framed in ways that everyone can appreciate and understand. If I am debating the merits of same-sex marriage with a person who believes in "family values," it makes sense for me to give my reasons for my position in a way that resonates within a family-values framework. If I do not do so, this person will never be persuaded. One argument in favor of gay marriage or civil unions, for example, is that legalizing gay commitments provides ways to support the *families* of people who are gay. A case can be made that genuine "family values" supporters should go beyond advocating family values for themselves alone. They should endorse all families, even those families that are nontraditional. Even if no full agreement is ultimately possible on this issue, there is a greater chance of agreement if people attempt to speak each other's language.

How does a deliberative form of democracy become a reality?

Among the many versions of deliberative democracy being advocated today, I find the one developed by Amy Gutmann and Dennis Thompson to be especially accessible and worthwhile.[48] Gutmann, the former Provost of Princeton University, is now President and professor of political science at the University of Pennsylvania. Thompson is the Alfred North Whitehead Professor of Philosophy at Harvard University. They define deliberative democracy succinctly as follows:

> [A] form of government in which free and equal citizens (and their representatives) justify decisions in a process in which they give one another reasons that are mutually acceptable and generally accessible, with the aim of reaching conclusions that are binding in the present on all citizens but open to challenge in the future.[49]

As conceived by Gutmann and Thompson, deliberative democracy is marked by six basic features, each one of which, I will seek to show, has implications for the marriage equality debate. Three of these features are procedural, and three are substantive. Procedurally, deliberative democracy is guided by a process that depends on *reciprocity, publicity,* and *accountability;* substantively, it seeks to promote *basic liberty, opportunity,* and *fairness.*

First, if deliberation is to be authentic, it must embody *reciprocity.*[50] When citizens reason together concerning gay marriage or any other social issue, they should give each other not only reasons for their positions but reasons that are intelligible to their opponents and that can help reach results that are fair for all concerned. In a sense, the process of seeking reciprocity is the basis from which all the other deliberative principles flow.[51] One implication of reciprocity is that citizens will respect the integrity of each other's deeply felt convictions. This does not just mean agreeing to disagree; it means giving all sides a way to live out their disagreements. For example, in places where gay marriage becomes a reality (such as in Massachusetts), the winners must not require religious communities to accept what they find offensive. A minister in a gay-marriage jurisdiction should be free not to perform gay weddings; he or she must be free to voice conscientious objections to gay marriage without fearing prosecution or reprisal. By the same token, where gay marriage is prohibited, the winners might see their way clear to endorse substitutes for marriage, such as domestic partnerships or civil unions. In terms of the typology discussed in Chapter One, opponents of gay marriage might offer civil unions as an "accommodation" to the other side. To put it another way, a minister in a non-gay-marriage jurisdiction needs to have a life-giving alternative to offer his or her gay and lesbian parishioners.

Second, deliberation must be *public*.[52] Only public reasons command public assent, build public confidence, foster mutual respect, and are open to the critique that moral deliberation demands.[53] This means that, whether someone is religious or secular in perspective, he or she should make arguments framed in the language of the public good. If one's audience is Jewish, quoting the New Testament is not going to be persuasive. If one's audience is Christian, one's reasons should connect with significant features of the Christian gospel — such as compassion for the outcast or giving one's life in service to others. Public deliberation requires that we speak a language that others will understand. A season of communicating in this way is likely to open doors to understanding that decades of shouting and posturing never could.

Third, democratic deliberation requires a many-sided *accountability* from elected officials. Gutmann and Thompson speak of accountability as "universal" in the sense that it runs in more than one direction.[54] Representatives are accountable not only to those who elected them but also to their political party, to the colleagues with whom they serve, and, most of all, to the deliberative process itself. One reason that the deliberative process depends on a representative form of government is that deliberation is not practicable for the body politic as a whole. All the people can vote, but not all the people can occupy the same room to reason together. Because of this, Gutmann and Thompson are sharp critics of the referendum process. Elected representatives are in a position to take into account information and viewpoints that might never occur to their constituents, who are simply being asked to vote up or down on a controversial matter. Elected representatives are also in a position to — and should — consider the impact of their decisions on future generations. Even though our descendants are not here to vote now, their interests should be considered in decisions that could affect their lives. Moreover, elected representatives may consider compromises, propose alternatives, offer amendments, and seek creative outcomes in which neither side wins everything but neither side loses everything either.

Fourth, authentic deliberation can happen only if people are accorded *basic liberties*. These include the right of self-determination and the right to vote.[55] But democratic liberty goes deeper than being able to live one's life free from coercion and being free to cast votes. It includes protecting the integrity of each person, including "freedom of speech, religion, and conscience, and due process and equal protection under the law."[56] I would want to add that it includes the basic freedom to live out one's sexual orientation without threat of being made to conform to the majority. Gutmann and Thompson argue that liberty must also include allowing even the opponents of liberty to make their case in the public arena.

Fifth, it is difficult for deliberation to happen in the absence of *equality of opportunity*.[57] Ideally, according to Gutmann and Thompson, this would mean that all the people have a threshold level of health care, education, and economic livelihood. They claim that a democratic society as a whole cannot thrive unless all its individual citizens thrive. One task of a deliberative democracy, then, is to find ways to meet these goals. How to do so may not be obvious, and here the value of deliberation becomes all the more important. Some will favor a welfare state, while others will argue for solutions rooted in the mechanisms of a market economy. For the marriage-equality debate, the important point is that a democracy should seek the economic well-being of all families, whether gay or straight. If equality of opportunity is an agreed-upon social goal, then gay couples and their families should receive the same support as non-gay families.

Sixth, deliberative democracy must also embody principles of *fair opportunity*.[58] Among other things, this entails a commitment not to discriminate on the basis of factors that should be morally irrelevant, such as race or gender. What about sexual orientation? If equality is a fundamental premise of democracy, then institutionalized inequality must be wrong. Today racial discrimination is ruled out of bounds as beyond rational argument, as is discrimination on the basis of gender. These are principles that were not clear to our forebears, but they have become clearer to us today. Could it be that we may one day, through the deliberative process, reach a consensus concerning fairness for gays and lesbians as well?

A key presupposition underlying deliberative practices is the importance of conscience and the need to honor and respect one another's deeply held convictions. The process of deliberation elevates democracy to something more than merely reading opinion polls or bargaining among interest groups. Indeed, democracy itself is more than majority rule, more than the aggregation of economic interests, more than the winner-take-all of electoral battles. Rather, it is about reaching substantive conclusions that possess a moral persuasiveness. In the process of deliberating, the participants come to acquire a sense of ownership regarding the results.

An immediate objection, of course, is that democracy is messy and does not always run in a straight line. Some pro-gay advocates have worried that a deliberative process may lead to results unfavorable to gay couples; others have challenged the model of deliberative democracy, saying that sometimes democracy has to be advanced through nondeliberative means. Strategies such as boycotts, protests, and the pressures applied by interest-group politics are all part of what makes democracy work. For example, the 1969 Stonewall riots in New York City and the tactics employed by the gay liberation group Act Up have been as important to advancing the cause of gay rights as the deliberative efforts of courts and legislatures. The answer to this objection is that deliberative democracy need not dismiss or discount the value of such nondeliberative practices. Protests sometimes carry powerful moral force. Still, the efficacy of these practices must at some point be judged by their ability to produce deliberative results. Perhaps the Stonewall riots helped to put gay rights on the map, but the real test is the social and political results that were eventually obtained.

Advocates of deliberative democracy believe that, when we submit to the discipline of reasoning together, our chances of knowing truth are thereby enhanced. That is, the process of deliberation is by its very nature productive of truth: the whole is greater than the sum of its parts. There is synergy in the act of deliberating, and the perspectives of each person or group contribute to the whole. This is true because no one's perspective is totally void of truth. Human beings, though always fallible, are seldom simply diabolical. And we have reasons for what we believe. When what we believe turns out not to be the whole truth, it may still contain an element of truth. Truth emerges from a complex process of give and take, of trial and error. Thus, when dialogue is genuine, there is always something to learn from one another.

This is one of the lessons that emerged in Part One of this book, where we considered a range of viewpoints on same-sex relationships. It is from the wealth of viewpoints in the community that a way forward eventually emerges. Because we never arrive at the perfect attainment of knowledge, the quest for truth is ongoing. After all, why do religious communities read Scripture week in and week out if it is not to hear a new Word from God? If biblical meaning were something straightforward and obvious, why do we have so many commentaries with so many different takes on what the texts are saying?

The ideal of deliberation is not always greeted warmly. Those who believe they already have all the answers are not quick to allow themselves to be challenged. Ironically, this refusal to listen usually reflects a deep, underlying uncertainty: it tells us more about what a person fears than about what he or she knows for sure. This can be seen frequently in the debates concerning gay rights. About twenty years ago, I was invited to speak on gay and lesbian issues at a forum in which positions from across the spectrum were being represented. When I agreed to participate, letters demanding my resignation started coming in to the seminary where I taught at the time. They were not objecting to the content of what I would say at the forum; the writers of those letters, in fact, had no idea what I planned to say, since at the time I had very little idea of what I would say myself. Instead, their stated objection was to the fact that I had even agreed to discuss the issue at all. This is revealing. So great was their fear that even a willingness to discuss the matter of gays and lesbians in the church was anathema.

The refusal to engage one another in deliberation creates a serious problem in a democratic society. When religious fundamentalists refuse to deliberate with others because they believe they already have a monopoly on revealed truth, political results that are welcoming to all become impossible. By the same token, when secular hardliners simply assert their positions without making an effort to respect or enter into the worldview of their religious opponents, then the parties talk past each other and get nowhere. Of course, this is precisely what has been happening in many of the debates — or really nondebates — over sexuality. By contrast, when opponents come together for the purpose of mutual understanding, the emergence of a new consensus becomes more likely, even if it is not guaranteed.

Some may harbor suspicions about deliberative democracy because they associate this approach with the political left, but this is not necessarily the case. It is true that deliberative democracy places a premium on the participation of excluded or marginalized groups, and that fact alone may appear to favor the interests of gays and lesbians. But the commitment to be inclusive means that we should welcome all kinds of groups, including conservative groups, to the table. In fact, some liberals have raised objections to deliberative democracy precisely because they fear a deliberative outcome that does not match their own view of justice.[59] Certainly, individual rights should not be revocable just because the majority engaged in deliberation. But when it comes to the process of deliberating over spousal equality for gays, conservative, liberal, and communitarian values may sometimes overlap. Hence, posing the question as a war between liberalism and conservatism is a mistake. The strengths and weaknesses of all these various "isms" can be tested and refined in the process of deliberation.

The Interplay between Liberalism and Conservatism

Let us consider the interplay between liberalism and conservatism a bit more. More than any other political perspective, classical liberalism has provided the philosophical framework that is most often invoked to support gay rights. This liberal tradition is a venerable one, for, as we have seen in Chapter Four, the classical liberal values of liberty and equality now stand as hallmarks of American jurisprudence, revered by progressives and conservatives alike. In fact, the usual opposition posed between liberalism and conservatism hides the fact that what many conservatives today are precisely seeking to "conserve" is the old-line liberal emphasis on the centrality of the individual and the necessity of limited government.[60] In this classical view, it is not justifiable for governments to treat individuals coercively except when it is necessary to avoid harm to others. Based on this so-called "harm principle," which was famously articulated by John Stuart Mill, there is emerging support in American society for a tolerant approach to gay life. In fact, as we have seen in Chapter One, toleration is the predominant policy adopted by mainline religious groups toward gay people. And it is just such a position of liberal tolerance that even many conservatives now espouse. Indeed, this helps to explain why it was a conservative Republican, Anthony Kennedy, who wrote the two most important Supreme Court decisions on gay rights: *Romer v. Evans*, which upheld equality for gay individuals, and *Lawrence v. Texas*, which made it clear that gay individuals have a liberty interest in being free to live the lifestyle they choose. Nor is Justice Kennedy an anomaly. Charles Fried, who served as Solicitor General under President Ronald Reagan, has argued that same-sex couples ought to be free to pursue their own lives without government interference.[61] However, Fried does not accept that government has any positive obligation to recognize same-sex couples as married. Gay marriage is where many conservatives draw the line. Contrast this view with that of the conservative lawyer Ted Olson, who is co-leading the legal team seeking gay marriage in California.

In taking liberalism only so far, contemporary conservatives are following a path first set forth in Great Britain in the 1950s by Lord Patrick Devlin. Responding to the Wolfenden Commission, which had argued for the decriminalization of consensual same-gender sex acts, Lord Devlin argued that, if society is empowered to protect people from civil harm, as liberalism asserts, then it should also be entitled to protect people from moral harm.[62] While Lord Devlin agreed that criminalizing same-gender sex acts was not called for, he did believe society could and should do everything in its power to discourage such acts. Something akin to this blend of liberalism and conservatism is behind Justice Antonin Scalia's dissent in *Lawrence v. Texas*. Justice Scalia argues that society should be able to embody its moral convictions in law, and with his typical bluntness, he complains:

> Many Americans do not want persons who openly engage in homosexual conduct as partners in their business, as scoutmasters for their children, as teachers in their children's schools, or as boarders in their home. They view this as protecting themselves and their families from a lifestyle that they believe to be immoral and destructive.[63]

To political conservatives of this stripe, neither gay marriage nor civil unions would be appropriate because creating such institutions could send a societal signal that homoerotic conduct is just as acceptable and appropriate as heterosexual marital conduct.

One problem with this position is that it does more to conserve traditional prejudice than it does to preserve traditional morals. It completely ignores the possible moral value that could accrue from consecrating same-gender relationships. After all, instituting gay marriage would reinforce the concept that marriage is the norm — as opposed to more transient forms of sexual involvement. Another problem with this brand of conservative reaction is that it depends on a quite specific vision of the moral good that not everyone in society shares, not even all conservatives. And even if the vast majority in a society were to agree with this particular vision of what constitutes morality, how are we to preserve the freedom of conscience of the minority that disagrees?

It is to combat a narrow brand of conservatism that many liberals insist that the government should take no position that seeks to advance a vision of the good. Rather, the proper governmental posture is one of neutrality, one in which citizens afford each other a benign tolerance and in which all are free to pursue their own version of the good life. Nevertheless, this neutral form of liberalism carries with it certain liabilities for gays and lesbians. As a case in point, neutral liberalism has had little success — either in the churches or in society at large — in convincing people of the wisdom of gay marriage. Classical liberalism has laid a solid foundation for affirming individual rights for gays and lesbians, but it has been less successful in grounding relationship rights for gay couples. Liberalism has succeeded in arguing for tolerance but not for true acceptance. Why is this?

One reason is that, instead of trying to resolve issues of religion and morality, liberalism historically has sought to defuse them. Instead of presenting a moral case for one way of life over another, liberalism has tried to accommodate various ways of life within a neutral framework. This neutral approach is so ingrained in liberals that they are at a loss to understand what drives the traditionalist aversion to gay marriage. As Andrew Sullivan has noted, the issues of gender and family values that are at stake in the gay-marriage debates are "simply too deep, too emotional, too visceral to be resolved by the calm voice of liberal legalism."[64] For decades, moral traditionalists (for whom "morality" in effect means sexual morality) have become alarmed about the increase in sexual experimentation, about abortion, about the rate of divorce, about children born out of wedlock, and so forth — and they have decided to draw a line in the sand when it comes to gay marriage.[65] Never mind that the choices made by gay men and lesbians have little direct bearing on these other social issues. Never mind that for gays and lesbians to favor marriage is, ironically, a move in the direction of traditional morality. Stanley Hauerwas has suggested that, among traditionalists within the Christian churches, pointing the finger at alleged gay unfaithfulness helps to deflect attention from the many areas in which the church itself has been unfaithful.[66]

Another reason for liberal ineffectiveness is that traditional opponents of gay marriage are able to use liberalism against itself. If the state is supposed to remain morally neutral, as many versions of liberalism claim it should, then the state, traditionalists argue, should not favor the "gay agenda" and force citizens who find gay life and conduct offensive to acquiesce. In this sense, the traditionalist backlash against gay rights relies on a subtle appropriation of individualistic, liberal reasoning. Traditionalists of this persuasion argue that gays as individuals should be free to do as they wish, but others should not be forced to give the tacit approval that gay marriage would imply.

Liberalism, of course, has a response to this argument. Protecting the rights of a minority group against the prejudices of the majority, say liberals, is a major function of government. Besides, as I have noted above, there is currently no moral screening for heterosexuals before they may procure a marriage license: a marriage license is obtainable in a matter of minutes by the most morally upstanding and the most immoral heterosexuals alike. This makes the screening of gays appear quite arbitrary. But this liberal argument, which is certainly true, leads to other problems. It leads to a rhetorical impasse: prohibitionists label gays as perverse, and liberals respond by labeling traditionalists as bigots. Some forms of liberal rhetoric can thus actually perpetuate the same kind of dismissiveness that liberals claim they receive from traditionalists. Such name-calling is not conducive to fruitful deliberation.

Another standard liberal argument, that of depicting gays as a persecuted minority, also has drawbacks. It is certainly true that gays have been targeted for abuse. But the problem with portraying them as needing paternalistic protection is that, ironically, it reinforces their second-class status. In a subtle way it invites society to continue to look down on gays — and worse, to pity them. Instead of feeling the need to demand a place in the military, in business, in schools, and in religion and culture, commentator Sullivan insists that the gay response should be:

> We *are* your military and have fought your wars and protected your homes. We *are* your businessmen and -women, who built and sustained this economy. . . . We *are* your teachers; we have built your universities and trained your scholars. We have created your art and designed and built your buildings. We *are* your civic leaders, your priests and rabbis, your writers and inventors, your sports idols and entrepreneurs. We need nothing from you, but we have much to give back to you. Protect us from nothing, but treat us as you would any heterosexual.[67]

A third reason for liberal inadequacy in the marriage debates is that laws concerning marriage and family are as much about the effects on society and the community as they are about individual couples. Defining marriage and promoting family are community-building in their basic rationale, and the theme of building up community is one that liberalism has tended to neglect in recent years. This was not always true. One can think of liberals such as John Dewey, for whom the formation of community was very important. One can also think of countless liberal organizations that work tirelessly for the good of all. But these values do not always remain prominent in liberal political rhetoric. As Sullivan puts it, liberalism insists on "using the language of rights in an area where it is impossible to avoid the language of goods."[68]

These concerns about recent liberal arguments have been pointed out by communitarians for quite some time.[69] Harvard's Michael Sandel, a leading communitarian critic of liberalism, has taken liberalism to task for its inability to make a positive case for the integrity of gay lives rooted in moral tradition.[70] Accordingly, gay liberals such as Carlos Ball and Jonathan Rausch have begun of late to insist on a *moral* case for gay marriage. In the same vein, the philosopher Martha Nussbaum argues that liberal freedom means more than the ability to engage in the unfettered use of reason. It also includes a broad understanding of human flourishing and emphasizes the importance of the body, the emotions, and the intimate bonds of companionship that go to make human life worth living. According to Nussbaum, society has an obligation to support individuals in making a life that is truly human. Drawing on Nussbaum's arguments, Carlos Ball says:

> [I]f society uses the institution of companionate marriage as a way of encouraging and supporting individuals in the exercise of their basic capabilities . . . but then denies some of its members the opportunity to marry without adequate justification, it would fail to meet its moral obligations to account for all the capabilities of its citizens.[71]

Andrew Sullivan and others suggest that this moral case is actually a *conservative* case, because allowing gays to marry would promote the very sort of fidelity, commitment, and care for the other that traditionalists claim they want to see. In this view, making marriage the norm for gays would actually strengthen marriage as an institution, whereas civil unions or domestic partnerships may contribute to the idea that marriage is just one option among many.

One of the chief complaints against liberalism is its emphasis on the autonomous self as the basic building block of society. In opposition to this view, communitarian philosopher Charles Taylor has argued that we are beings who are "dialogically constituted," social animals who are embedded in particular traditions and practices.[72] Communitarians object to the idea advanced by some liberals that the best way to reach moral judgments in the public realm is to downplay the importance of tradition. Allowing people to act freely is the right thing to do, they say, but this by itself does nothing to give content to that freedom. How does one know what is worth doing and what is not? Since there is no context-independent thought, we must recognize that tradition, habit, and custom play a large role in all political thinking. Accordingly, the good of individuals is inextricably linked to the good of society, and our identities as individuals depend on the influences of society. We are shaped by our language, our communities, our families, and our other social attachments. Instead of a neutral state that refuses to take a position on what is good, communitarians favor a politics that self-consciously works for the common good. We need to build up civil society, which means we need norms of justice that flow from the community and that serve the community.[73] To sum it up, communitarianism advocates that we focus not so much on the individual as on the community; not so much on rights as on the common good; not so much on freedom *from* community as on freedom *for* community.

No resolution of the gay-marriage impasse can succeed unless it draws on the best of our political traditions — liberal, conservative, libertarian, communitarian, and so on. The competition among these traditions runs throughout American history and permeates our constitutional jurisprudence.[74] Sometimes, as in the aforementioned *Gobitis* decision, the priority of the community is emphasized; other times, as in the overruling of *Gobitis,* the need to lift up individual rights becomes paramount. It is difficult to imagine the American system of democracy working without holding both individual liberty and communal values in careful balance. An unfettered communitarianism divorced from a commitment to liberty stands in deep tension with the principles of American constitutionalism.[75] Yet a constitutional polity with no commitment to communal values shall not long endure.[76] Liberty without community is empty; community without liberty is blind.

What can we say, then, about gay marriage within the framework of deliberative democracy? Gutmann and Thompson offer the following solution. First, they argue that, on equality grounds, both straight and gay unions should be legally recognized; we should not create second-class citizens. Second, they call for the same legal rights and benefits to accrue to both. Yet, in keeping with the reciprocity principle of deliberative democracy, they maintain, third, that religious organizations should not be required to accept any particular form of union that violates their religious convictions. In other words, even as society moves to welcome gays and lesbians, it must remain welcoming toward those for whom gay sexuality still presents a stumbling block. Gutmann and Thompson take no position on whether the best way to achieve these goals is through civil unions or gay marriage. Whether gay unions should be considered "marriages" in name is not as important to them as the concrete social goals of basic recognition and equality of rights.

On this last point, I respectfully differ. As I have argued in earlier discussions, without the imprimatur that marriage connotes in our society, the basic recognition gay couples seek will always be compromised. Moreover, without being able to claim the status of "spouse," full equality of rights for gay families will remain elusive. And, as we are about to see, even when courts and state legislatures move to confer recognition and benefits on gay families, there are still other mechanisms at work by which they may be taken away.

DOMA, Voter Referenda, and the Shape of Democracy

Even in states that provide for gay marriage, the federal Defense of Marriage Act (DOMA) was enacted to prevent gay couples and their children from receiving any of the family benefits provided by federal law, including Social Security, the Family and Medical Leave Act, an Estate Tax Marital Deduction upon death, and many others. The law was passed in 1996 as a reaction to the fear that Hawaii was about to allow for gay marriage in the aftermath of its supreme court's *Baehr* decision. DOMA does two things: first, it defines marriage as "a legal union between one man and one woman as husband and wife";[77] second, it provides that states without gay marriage would not be forced to recognize gay marriages contracted in states that do.[78]

The effect of DOMA goes beyond mere definitions. In reality, DOMA was a preemptive strike against states that might possibly expand the definition of marriage; and its effect was punitive against gays. Some 1,138 federal benefits apply to married couples. The net effect of DOMA was to assure that, no matter what the law of a particular state was, the gay and lesbian couples in that state would receive no *federal* benefits for their marriage-like commitments.

Since the passage of DOMA, a number of individual states have passed their own versions of DOMA, sometimes known as "junior DOMAs." In addition, some states, such as Nebraska, have enacted so-called "super-DOMAs," which ban not only gay marriage but also civil unions and other marriage-like arrangements. From 1996 until 2010, having a DOMA, or a super-DOMA, or similar voter referendum on the ballot come election time had been an effective way to bring conservative voters to the polls in large numbers.

After DOMA, some in Congress have also taken the extraordinary step of proposing a so-called Federal Marriage Amendment, which would make any recognition of spousal rights for gays and lesbians impossible throughout the United States. It purports to cover only gay marriage, but it is so broadly written that, were it enacted, it would have the effect of eliminating both gay marriage and civil unions.[79] Although this proposal has little political chance of passing, the very fact that reasonable legislators could propose such an unprecedented measure is ominous.

Efforts such as DOMA and the Federal Marriage Amendment aim to capitalize on the fears of the many by taking away the rights of the few. Fear can be a potent fuel for injustice. This is the reason that in 2001 constitutional lawyer Cass Sunstein warned that if the courts were to move too quickly to mandate gay marriage before the majority was ready, such action could provoke a destructive backlash. For this reason he recommended incremental steps forward.[80] At the same time, in the often chaotic mix of the democratic process, judges must occasionally step in to act as referees. A little-remembered but important example is the role played by the judiciary in making possible Martin Luther King Jr.'s historic march from Selma to Montgomery, Alabama, in 1965. It was only when Federal District Court Judge Frank M. Johnson Jr. saw to it that the Alabama National Guard accompanied the civil rights protesters to protect them that the march was successful.[81] Those who decry what they derisively call "judicial activism" or even "judicial tyranny" are mistaken when they claim that judicial protection of rights is antidemocratic. On the contrary, the judiciary is an integral part of the democratic process: every law needs to be interpreted, and the judicial system offers a proving ground where the meaning and scope of the law are tested. Sometimes laws are struck down because they stand in opposition to important constitutional protections.

Not only are judicial rulings part of the democratic structure of government, but the content of those rulings actually promotes the democratic process. Those rulings may spur the citizenry and its legislative bodies to deliberate on important issues of liberty, equality, and justice that may have been previously overlooked or lost in the heat of conflict. In this, courts perform a role without which democracy could not reasonably function. The courts preserve a long tradition of inquiry into what is fair and just. By upholding constitutional rights, courts prevent the arbitrary power of the broader community from riding roughshod over the rights of those whose status in the community is controversial or marginal.

A number of courts have now ruled that DOMA constitutes unconstitutional discrimination against gay couples. The Obama administration has indicated it will no longer defend the constitutionality of DOMA in court. It is likely that the days of DOMA are numbered. If individual states have recognized a right of gay couples to marry, it is unfair for the federal government to deny those couples the federal benefits of marriage.

A related question is the legal propriety of the various state constitutional amendments that forbid gay marriage. As explained earlier, a constitutional challenge to one such amendment — Proposition 8 — has been filed in federal court in the California case of *Perry v. Schwarzenegger*. The question at issue is whether in a democratic society such as ours the majority may act to remove constitutional rights from the minority.

At stake in this debate is the very meaning and shape of constitutional government. In analyzing the stakes in Proposition 8, Yale Law School Professor William N. Eskridge Jr. has helpfully lifted up several classic models of conceiving what a constitution does.[82] The first model is one inspired by Plato and Aristotle whereby the constitution mirrors the soul of a people, or as Aristotle put it, "the constitution speaks the life of the city." Eskridge points out that this model was visible in the death of Socrates, who knew his death sentence was unjust but accepted it because Athenian democracy had nurtured him and made him who he was, warts and all. On this model, the original version of the United States Constitution, which allowed neither freedom for slaves nor the voting franchise for women, nevertheless embodied the essence of the patriarchal culture at that time and had to be accepted since the constitution embodies the traditions that make a people who they are. So, on this logic, if the patriarchal family is one of our core values, then it is appropriate for it to be enshrined constitutionally even if it works for some and not for others. This seems to be the model implicitly adopted by advocates of Proposition 8.

In the second model a constitution is a social contract that also preserves certain inalienable rights. This is the model advanced by Thomas

Hobbes and John Locke, and it is undeniably the model that prevailed among those who wrote the United States Constitution. This model has a long history in American jurisprudence, and it was revitalized most powerfully in the court rulings of the civil rights era.[83] On this model there are rights that exist apart from majority rule and apart from what may be found in a written document. These rights are inherent in personhood, necessary for the well-being of the individuals protected, and essential to the integrity of a democratic polity. The claim here is not that Hobbes or Locke or the framers of the constitution would have been thinking of fundamental rights for gay couples; rather, the claim is that as society evolves it recognizes fundamental human rights that inhere in individuals and which the majority should not infringe. This is the theory being invoked by those who oppose Proposition 8.

A third model, says Eskridge, operates according to an ideal of practical reasoning. This model has roots in the utilitarianism of Jeremy Bentham and the pragmatism of William James. And of course, it also has certain roots in Aristotle. The art of practical reasoning trusts that one can arrive at the right decision without necessarily having a universal theory of what is right. It balances the constitution as soul (Aristotle) with the constitution as conscience (Locke). This sort of balancing act is always happening in the democratic process, especially among executives and legislatures. But it also happens among judges. When the California Supreme Court refrained from overturning Proposition 8, this may have been the sort of balancing act the majority was undertaking. In a constitutional polity like California's, in which referenda can play such a pivotal and frequent role and in which judges themselves can be ousted in retention votes, courts will naturally tread more softly.[84]

So then what are we to say about the twenty-nine states (see accompanying chart) that have written into their constitutions exclusions of gay couples and their families from the institution of marriage, depriving them of all the benefits, obligations, and societal recognition inherent in that institution? Are these exclusions simply acceptable statements of community values (à la Aristotle)? Or do they violate the meaning of a democratic community (à la Locke) and infringe the fundamental rights of gay couples?

My answer is clear: the state constitutional amendments violate fundamental rights. This becomes clear when one considers the punitive effects of these amendments. In Michigan, for example, public employers, such as the city of Kalamazoo, which prior to the constitutional amendment had provided same-sex domestic partner health insurance benefits, are now prohibited from doing so.[85] In promoting the anti-gay marriage amendment to the public before the referendum, advocacy groups testified in public hearings that the amendment would have no effect on health care benefits and the like. Then when the amendment was passed, they argued that health benefits for gay couples were forbidden and the courts agreed.[86]

This is the sort of dirty political pool that goes on in the world of government by public referendum. Some will argue that because these state constitutional amendments were validated by a direct vote of the people, they represent the most rudimentary and reliable form of democracy. It is hard to take this claim seriously. First, it ignores the political realities that surround voter referenda in our current interest-group-driven and media-dominated age. These advocacy groups certainly are within their rights to advocate their point of view. But by their very nature, these groups — on both the right and the left — do not exist for the purpose of seeking the common good. Rather, they exist for one reason only, and that is to rally their supporters to oppose those on the other side of an issue. Such a tactic is polarizing, and it accentuates a growing "us-versus-them" mentality in politics. Moreover, the fund-raising efforts of many of these groups use the tactic of manufacturing a sense of crisis to spur donations. If a crisis does not already exist, it is in the financial interests of these groups to stir one up, or else the interest group could face financial cutbacks. Frequently, when it comes time to vote on any given referendum, popular sentiment has been disproportionately influenced by the blitz of media campaigns and unduly affected by the funds raised by these political interest groups. As I mentioned previously, often the money used to drive the referenda comes from outside the state where the vote is taking place. The outcome is predictable: like the shifting results of opinion polls, the result of a voter referendum will depend to a great extent on the way the question is framed and on which of the interest groups has been more successful at "spinning" the question in its direction.

Second, extolling the results of voter referenda misunderstands the genius of our representative, constitutional democracy. Our democracy is based on the idea that elected representatives are in a better position to make informed, considered judgments than is the population at large. This is not an elitist claim but a practical one. As I have argued above, a truly deliberative assembly is more likely to take into consideration more facets of an issue and thereby effectuate better outcomes. Furthermore, the best results are least likely when questions are posed to the whole electorate in a stark either-or form, with no possibility of amendment, no room for compromise, and no incentive for dialogue between the competing sides.[87] It is little wonder that the referendum option has been used time and time again in gay marriage disputes: the principal reason legislators have handed the issue off to voters is that it keeps them from having to go on record concerning the "gay issue," which many of them regard as a no-win situation.[88] Why else are highly volatile decisions such as these relegated to a popular vote — when few others are? Of all the decisions made in a democracy, these deeply divisive ones are the last ones we should toss out to the electorate at large. To look at this from another angle, if direct democracy is so superior, then why are all democratic decisions not decided by e-mail? It is because direct democracy seldom results in true democracy. True democracy is a welcoming democracy that takes the interests of all into account, including the interests of the minority. True democracy ought to give us something more than the results of a popularity contest. It should promote true belonging for all of its citizens.

As I observed in the preceding chapter, in 1996 the U.S. Supreme Court in *Romer v. Evans* struck down a state constitutional amendment in Colorado that, in one sweeping gesture, would have eliminated all present and future antidiscrimination laws protecting gays and lesbians. In just the same way, these other state constitutional amendments impose varying degrees of prohibition on same-sex relationships — both now and in the future. *Romer* was an equal protection case based on two arguments: first, that it is unfair for a law to impose a unique disadvantage on gays and gays alone; and second, that the law should remain neutral and not be based on a societal "animus" against gay people. The net effect of both the Colorado law and this new phalanx of anti-gay constitutional amendments is "to impose a broad disability on a single group," thus preventing them from seeking — and the legislature from granting — any legal protection in perpetuity.[89] As one federal judge has summed it up, "A blanket prospective prohibition on any type of legal recognition of a same-sex relationship not only denies the benefits of favorable legislation to these groups, it prohibits them from even asking for such benefits."[90]

Let us be clear about the broad and antidemocratic implications of these sorts of prohibitions: if a group of people is prohibited from even petitioning the legislature on a matter, then this group in effect has been excluded from the ordinary democratic process and, at least regarding the matter in question, has been turned into a group of noncitizens. Even prisoners in penitentiaries are free to petition the legislature for better living conditions. It is true that gay couples still have the freedom to petition for new constitutional amendments to overturn the ones that now exclude them. Yet this was also true of the Colorado amendment struck down in *Romer:* to argue that an amendment is fair simply because it might someday be changed misses the deeper constitutional point. So long as the exclusionary amendments remain in place, these gay couples are denied their democratic voices *within the existing constitutional framework.* To put it another way, in these states with anti-gay marriage constitutional amendments, the existing framework has been amended *precisely* to exclude them, and it is only by going *outside* the existing framework to advocate for a new constitution that there now exists any place for their voices to be heard and their complaints registered. Therefore, these constitutional amendments do not merely withhold the benefit of marriage, they also operate to prohibit persons in a same-sex relationship from working within the ordinary system to ever obtain governmental benefits or legal recognition. This is a right they possessed before the amendments were passed, and so the amendments are designed for the specific purpose of depriving them of their rights.[91]

Here the sevenfold framework set forth from Chapters One and Two helps us see what is going on with these amendments. In terms of their moral or spiritual base, these amendments emanate from nowhere else than the hard core prohibitionist side of the spectrum. There is no place in them for tolerance, even less for accommodation or legitimation. These amendments enact a categorical ban on the most meaningful forms of recognition for gay families. They enact this ban on gay couples and gay couples only. And for this reason, such constitutional provisions are antithetical to the deepest streams of American constitutional government and should be struck down.

The very purpose of a constitution is to craft provisions of government that are fundamentally fair to all. This the state anti-gay marriage amendments clearly fail to do.

The electoral success of these state constitutional amendments tells us something important about the politics of gay marriage. It underscores the fact that traditional ideas of marriage and family have deep symbolic significance for some people — significance that may be difficult to articulate but that will assert itself forcefully when challenged. To make changes in an institution that holds so much symbolic capital for so many requires more than the assertion of principles of equality and liberty. As important as equality and liberty are, bringing about deep change requires time for three things to occur.

First, the politics of gay marriage requires time for people to hear the stories of gay couples and to come to know these couples as part of their community. This is perhaps the single most important factor. Experience shows that the more people become familiar with gay families, the more open they become to adopting a welcoming and affirming stance. Second, it requires time for people to acquire new ways of thinking — biblically, theologically, and ethically — about same-sex couples. I have attempted to make a contribution to these new ways of thinking throughout this book. My goal has been to demonstrate that there are good arguments for moving beyond stark prohibition, beyond mere toleration, and even beyond a grudging accommodation of same-sex couples. Indeed, there are compelling arguments for a welcoming and affirming stance toward gay couples, who themselves are seeking to order their lives in praiseworthy ways. Third, it requires time for the continuing formation of a way of political life that is welcoming to all citizens, including gay, lesbian, and gender-varied citizens.

The good news is that time is on the side of those of us advocating for change. A majority of all Americans now approves of gay marriage. Among those under the age of 34, the approval rating is 70 percent. The recent passage of gay marriage in New York through a deliberative process in the legislature bodes well for the future. There is every reason to hope that acceptance of gay families will grow stronger and that together we will move closer to the promise of a truly welcoming democracy.

Summary

Gay marriage is now the law in Connecticut, Iowa, Massachusetts, New Hampshire, New York, Vermont, and the District of Columbia. Civil unions are allowed in Delaware, Hawaii, Illinois, New Jersey, and Rhode Island. Other states will follow in due course. In addition, in 2008 the Supreme Courts of California, Connecticut, and Iowa indicated that classifications based on sexual orientation demand a higher level of scrutiny by the courts and a greater measure of protection against discrimination.

This does not mean that progress on marriage equality has proceeded in a straight line. Gay marriage came for a brief time in California and Maine but was overturned by voter referenda. In California, however, federal district court judges overturned the voter referendum — known as Proposition 8 — declaring that it was an unconstitutional violation of the equal protection and due process rights of gay and lesbian couples wishing to marry. It is possible the case could reach the United States Supreme Court and affect the law on this issue nationally.

Amid all these controversies, this chapter has argued that we should aspire to be a welcoming democracy, one that reaches out to invite the participation and full ownership of all citizens. The best tool for achieving a welcoming democracy is that of good-faith deliberation. In a deliberative democracy, the goal is consensus, not coercion; it proceeds via persuasion, not pugnacity. In contrast to other models, a deliberative democracy does not exclude the contribution of religion. In a deliberative democracy both the community-forming commitments provided by religion and the community-sustaining values nurtured by the law are allowed to play their proper roles. Moving beyond a strict "neutrality" that divides the religious from the secular, a deliberative democracy is one in which all citizens — those with religious convictions as well as those who spurn religion — participate as equals.

One of the problems in the marriage equality debate is that some citizens in some states, through the means of referenda and constitutional amendments, have engaged in a majoritarian power move aimed at ensuring that the minority — in this case gay couples — are unable to obtain or even advocate for marriage equality within the existing constitutional framework. This same majoritarian impulse inspired a federal law, DOMA, that deprives couples in gay marriages and civil unions of all the federal rights of marriage. As long as this is the case, gay couples remain second-class citizens no matter what nomenclature we attach to their commitments.

Progress on this issue will take place only when we, the citizens of the United States, are able to take a step back and ask what kind of society we want to live in. Do we really want to construct a society in which the majority forces members of one group to live their lives as second-class citizens? Is this what democracy is supposed to be about? The truth is this: if we are to *have* a welcoming democracy, we will need to *want* a welcoming democracy — and want to do what it takes to bring it into being.

STATE-BY-STATE LEGAL STATUS
OF SAME-GENDER RELATIONSHIPS

Same-Sex Marriage Allowed
Connecticut (2008)
District of Columbia (December 18, 2009)
Iowa (April 3, 2009)
Maryland (2013, pending possible voter referendum)
Massachusetts (2004)
New Hampshire (2010)
New York (2011)
Vermont (2009)
Washington (2012, pending possible voter referendum)

Same-Sex Marriage Allowed Then Disallowed
California: Same-sex marriage was allowed by court order from June 16, 2008, to November 5, 2008, when constitutional prohibition enacted by voter referendum. On August 4, 2010, federal judge Vaughn Walker declared the ban unconstitutional, and on February 7, 2012, the Ninth U.S. Circuit Court of Appeals upheld Walker's decision. The resumption of same-sex marriages in the state was stayed pending further appeals.
Maine: A same-sex marriage law was passed by the legislature and signed into law by the governor on May 6, 2009. The law was invalidated by voter referendum before going into effect. A new voter referendum to reinstate the law is scheduled for November, 2012

Civil Unions Allowed (all marriage benefits and obligations but without the "m" word)
Delaware (2012)
Hawaii (2012)
Illinois (2011)
New Jersey (2006)
Rhode Island (2011)

Domestic Partnerships Allowing Most
State-Level Benefits of Marriage
California (1999)
Nevada (2009)
Oregon (2008)

Domestic Partnerships Allowing Some
Enumerated Benefits of Marriage
Colorado (2009). Civil unions failed in 2011.
Maine (2004). State employees in same-sex partnerships have had benefits since 2001.
Maryland (2008). Same-sex marriage law passed but pending voter referendum.
Wisconsin (2009)

States Not Currently Allowing Same-Sex Marriages but
Recognizing Them When Entered in Other Jurisdictions
California: Family Code 308 recognizes benefits accorded such relationships but will not designate them as "marriages."
Hawaii: recognized as "civil unions"
Illinois: recognized as "civil unions"
Maryland
New Jersey: recognized as "civil unions"
New Mexico: recognized by virtue of a 2011 Attorney General opinion.
Nevada: recognized as "civil unions"
Rhode Island
Washington: recognized as "domestic partnerships"

Constitutional Provision Allowing Legislature
to Prohibit Same-Sex Marriage
Hawaii (1998). However, civil unions allowed as of January 1, 2012.

Constitutional Provision Prohibiting Same-Sex Marriage
Alaska (1998). However, the state Supreme Court ruled unanimously in 2005 that the state of Alaska may not discriminate regarding employment benefits for same-sex couples (*Alaska Civil Liberties Union v. Alaska*, 122 P.3d 781 [Alaska Supreme Ct. 2005]).
Arizona (2008)

States allowing same-sex marriage, civil unions, or domestic partnerships

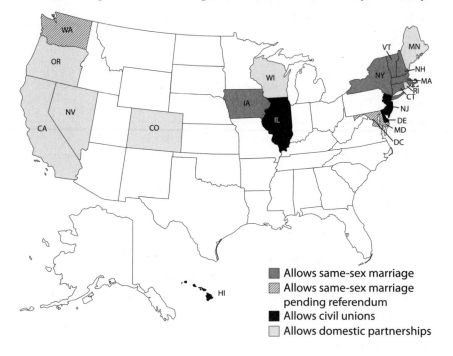

California (2008). However, the prohibition was ruled unconstitional by federal judge Vaughn Walker on August 4, 2010, and that decision is currently being disputed in court. The state allowed same-sex marriage June 16, 2008, to November 5, 2008, and currently allows domestic partnerships.

Colorado (2006). Allows designated beneficiary agreements (2009)

Mississippi (2004)

Missouri (2004)

Montana (2004)

Nevada (2002). Allows domestic partnerships (2009)

Oregon (2004). Allows domestic partnerships (2008)

Tennessee (2006)

Constitutional Provision Prohibiting Same-Sex Marriages *and* Civil Unions

Alabama (2006)

Arkansas (2004)

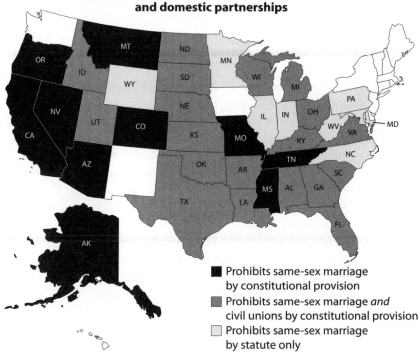

States prohibiting same-sex marriage, civil unions, and domestic partnerships

■ Prohibits same-sex marriage by constitutional provision

■ Prohibits same-sex marriage *and* civil unions by constitutional provision

□ Prohibits same-sex marriage by statute only

Florida (2008)

Georgia (2004)

Idaho (2006)

Nebraska (2000). The prohibition was briefly overturned in federal court in 2005 but reinstated on appeal in 2006.

Kansas (2005)

Kentucky (2004)

Louisiana (2004)

North Dakota (2004)

Ohio (2004)

Oklahoma (2004)

South Carolina (2006)

South Dakota (2006)

Texas (2005). However, *Littleton v. Prange*, 9 S.W.3d 223 (Tex. App. San Antonio Cir. 1999) allows a transgender woman (i.e., a person

born a man) to marry a woman; i.e., the law declares birth gender
to be legally unchangeable.

Utah (2004)

Wisconsin (2006). Allows domestic partnerships (2009)

Constitutional Provision Prohibiting Same-Sex Marriages, Civil Unions, *and* Private Contracts

Michigan (2004). The Michigan Constitution, Article I, Section 25,
states that "To secure and preserve the benefits of marriage for our
society and for future generations of children, the union of one
man and one woman in marriage shall be the only agreement recognized as a marriage or similar union for any purpose."

Virginia (2006). The Virginia Constitution, Article I, Section 15-A,
states "That only a union between one man and one woman may
be a marriage valid in or recognized by this Commonwealth and its
political subdivisions. This Commonwealth and its political subdivisions shall not create or recognize a legal status for relationships
of unmarried individuals that intends to approximate the design,
qualities, significance, or effects of marriage. Nor shall this Commonwealth or its political subdivisions create or recognize another
union, partnership, or other legal status to which is assigned the
rights, benefits, obligations, qualities, or effects of marriage."

Same-sex Marriage Prohibited by Statute Only

Illinois

Indiana

Maryland (same-sex marriage pending voter referendum)

Minnesota

North Carolina

Pennsylvania

Washington (same-sex marriage pending voter referendum)

West Virginia

Wyoming

Neither Prohibit nor Permit Same-Sex Marriage

New Mexico

Rhode Island

A Time to Embrace

Gay marriage is here to stay. Support for gay marriage rose in 2011 by nine percentage points, the largest increase for this issue the Gallup poll has ever recorded.[1] The first reason for this surge is *relational:* more people now have friends and family who are openly gay. The second reason is *factual:* people now have better information about sexual orientation, about how marriage policy has changed over time, about the data on children raised by gay and lesbian couples, and about the harm withholding marriage inflicts on committed gay and lesbian couples and their families. The third reason is *logical:* people are starting to realize that the arguments mounted against gay marriage simply do not add up. Nothing about a gay or lesbian couple's marriage detracts from a heterosexual couple's marriage. Fear-based arguments that gay marriage will lead to state-sponsored polygamy or polyamory are groundless.[2] The right to marry the person you choose does not include the right to marry as many persons as you choose. Ironically, the more opponents of gay marriage insist on the importance of marriage as an institution, the more unreasonable depriving gays and lesbians access to it seems. The fourth reason is *moral.* Greater numbers of straight people are coming to respect the love and commitment they see in their gay and lesbian friends and to recognize that the quality of family life enjoyed by same-sex couples is no different from that of other families.

I believe there is also a fifth reason that is starting to emerge, namely a sense of affirmation for gay couples that is *religious* in character. When people make deeply felt, public commitments to one another, it evokes a sense of the *sacred*. For many people, marriage is solemnized with ancient vows exchanged in a holy place of worship. But even for people with no institutional religious affiliation at all, marriage is usually a serious business. It brings to mind the things that matter most in life. Until now religion has been the major source of the scorn leveled against gay and lesbian relationships. If that scorn is to be fully lifted, then there must be religious reasons given for a welcoming and affirming stance that can overcome the religious reasons given for being non-affirming. People who care about their religious faith need to see that there are good and faithful reasons to give their full blessing to committed same-sex couples.

I have tried to give such reasons in the welcoming, affirming, and *ordering* stance I have set forth in these pages. Readers are invited to review the summaries at the end of each chapter of the book. The reason same-sex marriage should be consecrated within our religious communities, validated in law, and welcomed gladly into our democratic way of life is not simply an accommodation to a changing culture. It is because doing so draws from the deepest wells of moral, religious, and political traditions.

So now religious communities face a choice. In the rest of my concluding remarks I shall be speaking as a Christian believer, pastor, and theologian addressing the church. Will we, the church, stand in solidarity with gay and lesbian couples as they make their sacred vows to one another? And if so on what grounds will we take that stand?

As Christians we stand in solidarity with our gay and lesbian brothers and sisters because the gospel of Jesus Christ calls us to do so. We do not take this stand merely from a benign "inclusivism" that accepts all viewpoints as equally valid and invites people to "live and let live." Within the political arena, inclusivism and "live and let live" are solid virtues. But in the Christian church we have even deeper, more pressing reasons for taking this stance of solidarity. We respect the element of truth contained in the multiple viewpoints to be found in society and in the church. We even place a high value on exploring and valuing our differences, as I have tried to do throughout this book. But we are not moral relativists. We do not believe that all viewpoints are equally valid.

Nor do we adopt a welcoming and affirming stance merely to keep the peace or to shore up the unity of the institutional church. Make no mistake: in this book I have not been arguing that we should all just join hands and sing "Kumbaya." I believe that church unity is important — very important, for it rests in Jesus' own prayer that his followers may be one (John 17:11). However, unity without justice is not a unity that deserves the name Christian. As long as church and society continue to treat gays and lesbians as second-class citizens, any appeal to unity as the highest value rings hollow. I am reminded of the comment Abraham Lincoln famously made in response to Horace Greeley, to the effect that if he, Lincoln, could save the Union without freeing the slaves, he would do so. In the end, of course, Lincoln realized his original impulse was wrong. He realized that freeing the slaves was necessary *for the sake of* the Union. Similarly, finding a way forward on the issue of same-sex relationships in the church is necessary not simply to preserve an institutional unity but *for the sake of the gospel itself.*

And this is really the issue we as a church face: What is the gospel? And what does it demand of us? My claim throughout this book is that the church's traditional stand on "homosexuality" is wrong and hurtful, and does not accord with the best light of the gospel itself. As long as the church remains in the grip of its traditional anti-gay, anti-affirming message, it is at risk of losing its soul. Some people believe it already has. Many young people now equate being Christian with being anti-gay. At the very least, they wonder why the church has argued vehemently and without end about gay sexuality to the neglect of other pressing concerns. Many are familiar with Martin Luther King Jr.'s lament in Birmingham Jail. He was being pressed by good church people to go slower in is fight for civil rights. King asked why it is that the church is too often a taillight in the cause of justice and not a headlight leading the way. King's question continues to challenge us today.

Unless the church digs deeper to find a more solid gospel core for its stance of solidarity with gay and lesbian people, its witness is likely to remain like that of a dim and irrelevant taillight. The default mode for many in the church, going forward, will be what I have been calling "accommodation." They will go along with innovations like domestic partnerships and civil unions, but they will do so while harboring somewhere deep down the church's old grudging, non-affirming posture. They may even approve of gay marriage in the civil arena, but they will withhold their full blessing from gay couples in the church. Please let me be clear: I believe that a position which makes a gracious accommodation to gay couples is better than outright prohibition. But it falls short of what I believe the gospel is demanding of us.

For one thing, holding on to the old non-affirming stance has led to a practical acquiescence to the prohibitionist policies that still permeate church policies and the laws of many states. Prohibitionist sentiment still reigns in the policies of denominations that persist in categorically preventing gifted gays and lesbian leaders from being ordained. Even though we no longer criminalize same-gender sexual behavior, prohibitionism is still enshrined in public policies such as the Defense of Marriage Act and in the various state constitutional amendments that categorically disallow gay marriage. The spirit of prohibition still echoes in the pervasive rhetoric of disgust and shame that characterizes the arguments of some vocal Christian opponents of gay marriage. It lurks, for example, in the claim that to allow gays and lesbians to marry will somehow taint or diminish the marriages of heterosexuals. People who feel disgust when it comes to gay marriage may be expressing their sincerely held beliefs. But disgust provides no reasonable or sufficient basis for public policy.[3] It provides even less basis for the policy of the church.

No doubt some will respond that they do not feel disgust about gay sexuality but simply an ambivalence. Fair enough. But ask yourself about the source of this ambivalence. Even more, ask yourself what this ambivalence communicates. Is ambivalence the best we can come up with as we seek to live out the grace of the gospel? What does our ambivalence communicate in the face of gay teenagers who are driven to commit suicide? As I write these words, people are rejoicing in the passage of gay marriage in New York. But let us not forget the years of hand-wringing ambivalence that preceded the historic vote. Ambivalence is the stuff of taillights not headlights.

I cannot put it any more plainly than this. Making shame, disgust, or even ambivalence the centerpiece of the church's teaching has nothing to do with the gospel of Jesus of Nazareth. The gospel literally means good news. So where is the good news in the church's traditional disdain for gay and lesbian relationships? The gospel presents a radical message of welcome and hospitality for all. So why hasn't the Christian church been in the forefront of extending hospitality for same-sex couples? A hallmark of the ministry of Jesus was his counter-cultural solidarity with those who were regarded as immoral, unclean, and outcast. So isn't it time for the church to be second to none in coming alongside gay and lesbian people?

Jesus not only stood in a sort of theoretical solidarity with the outcasts of his day but he engaged in table fellowship with them — an unheard of act for a first-century Jew. In the mindset of Jesus' day, to eat with someone was to be joined with them. It implied that they shared a joint fellowship and blessing in the eyes of God. There was no ambivalence in Jesus' ministry of solidarity. One of the frequent charges his detractors made against Jesus was that he sat at table and ate with sinners. In engaging in this sort of radical solidarity, Jesus stood in deep continuity with one of the most pervasive strains of Hebrew Scripture. Emmanuel Levinas has called attention to the inescapable imperative of Scripture to extend hospitality to the "other" — the stranger, the sojourner, the neighbor in need. There is always the danger that in extending hospitality to the other, we will do so from a vantage point of paternalism or smug superiority. That is perhaps one reason that Levinas says we must treat the neighbor not as someone beneath us. Rather, we treat the neighbor as one who is elevated and comes into our presence "from on high." In other words, solidarity is never merely an accommodation. As one of the parables of Jesus puts it, when we encounter and extend fellowship to a neighbor, it is as though we were meeting Christ himself (Matt. 25:31-46). This is why the command to love one's neighbor is often interpreted not merely as "love *of* neighbor" but, as David Kelsey calls it, "love *as* neighbor."[4] In love *of* neighbor, we remain the arbiters of who is our neighbor and who is not. With love *as* neighbor, we are called to *be* a neighbor to everyone we meet.

Christian teaching has also long affirmed that all people are created in the image of God. This means that every human being has a sacred status in the world. Each person is fearfully and wonderfully made by God (Ps. 139:14), having been endowed with reason, a conscience, and the ability to make consequential decisions in the world. Each person has a unique story and a unique vocation within the economy of God's activity in the world. Not only that, but it takes all of us *together* to reflect God's image in the world. This means that the gifts, the desires, and the stories of gay and lesbian people are included in this vocation of reflecting God's light in the world. The stories of all of us — gay and straight alike — are taken up by God and blessed. It is true that all have sinned and have distorted the image of God. But there is nothing sinful in itself about being gay. The question for all of us is how are we living into the gifts and the calling God has given us.

In short, the integrity of the gospel is at stake in how we graciously confront the question of gay sexuality. We need to find a way forward that is faithful to our deepest convictions. The consecration position, which favors full religious and legal blessing for gay marriage, provides that way forward.

From Live and Let Live to Live and Let Love

With gay marriage now finding solid footing in our culture, the question for Christians is whether gay marriage will be celebrated as Christian marriage. Throughout this book, I have argued that the answer is yes. There is nothing in all of Scripture — not a word — that explicitly prohibits what we are debating today, which is the committed, covenantal love of same-sex partners who are seeking to become family. Jesus affirmed the covenant of marriage but also made comments about treating the kingdom of God as more important than family ties. He specifically included eunuchs — a type of person who did not conform to ancient standards of gender complementarity — among those finding favor in the kingdom of heaven. Jesus said nothing — not a word — about how to think about exclusively committed gay and lesbian couples. There is nothing in the collected sayings of Jesus — not a word — about excluding anyone who faithfully seeks the kingdom.

The consecration position values the full humanity of all people, both gay and straight. It honors the fact that when people give themselves to one another in nuptial commitment they are making a statement about their intention to enter into a covenant, to honor the humanity of their partner, and to live their lives as faithful parts of a broader community. In both secular and sacred contexts marriage is a cause for celebration and remembrance, communal gathering and societal protection.

Consecration, when practiced in a Christian context, is a furtherance of the affirmations and promises contained in baptism. Baptism bestows upon each Christian person a new identity. Through grace, a baptized person is now declared to be a child of God. But baptism does more than declare that gay and lesbian believers may gladly enter into the fellowship of the church if they wish. We are told in the early church's baptismal utterance in Galatians 3:28 that in Christ there is "no longer male and female" — a Christological reversal of the "male and female" of Genesis 1:27, reminding us that identity in Christ is not limited by gender hierarchies or gay or straight stereotypes. Just as it has taken centuries for the church to understand fully the baptismal declaration that there is no longer "Jew or Greek, slave or free," so it is taking a long time to fully realize the implications of there being "no longer male and female."

With this broad, baptismal declaration in mind, it is clear that a Christian understanding of marriage is about more than affirming gender complementarity as a fixed order of creation. Marriage points beyond creation to the fulfillment God promises in redemption. In the Catholic Church, for example, marriage is a sacrament. In Protestant tradition, marriage is one of the means of grace, that is, one of the earthly vehicles through which the grace of God is mediated. Pushing beyond the idea that marriage is a fixed order of creation, we have to say that marriage is also a dynamic order of redemption. To put it another way, we do not bless people's unions in the church because they have already perfectly conformed to some clear divine plan. We bless them because of their mutual promises to give themselves to one another in a life that seeks to grow in love and grace.

A Christian understanding of marriage also takes note of the divine declaration in Genesis 2:18 that "it is not good for the human being to be alone." This does not mean that people who are unmarried or widowed are not blessed or that there is something wrong with living outside the institution of marriage. Rather, it means that the desire to give oneself to another person is God-given. And as such, we need to honor it. In the biblical passage, God responds to this human desire by providing a companion who is "suitable." So then who is a suitable companion for someone with a same-gender sexual orientation? The answer is clear: a suitable companion is a person whose sexual orientation matches his or her own.

Consecration also honors the traditional purposes of marriage from the Western Christian tradition — mutuality, remedy for lust, and procreation — by re-framing them positively as companionship, commitment, and the strengthening of community. How does gay marriage fulfill these traditional purposes? Concerning companionship, the best companion for a gay or lesbian person is one whose sexual orientation matches his or her own. Concerning commitment, there is every evidence that gay and lesbian couples are giving themselves to one another without reservation, in sickness and in health, and with the intention of establishing a permanent household that often includes the raising of children. Concerning community, it is true that gay and lesbian unions do not in themselves involve procreation. But procreation is also impossible for many heterosexual couples. The broader test is whether the relationship builds family ties and contributes to the broader fabric of community life. On this score, permitting gay marriages underscores the importance of marriage as an institution, while also enhancing the lives of gay and lesbian couples and their children.

Within the Christian tradition, marriage has a broader focus than

249

the couple and the family. Marriage provides a way for the love of a committed couple to bear witness to Christ's love for the church. The love of Christ was marked by self-giving and self-sacrifice, and this is what the love of committed couples, both gay and straight, should seek to emulate. From a Christian point of view, the commitment of gay couples is no less able than that of straight couples to point to Christ's love for the church as discussed in Ephesians and Revelation (Eph. 5:21-22; Rev. 19:7; 22:2, 9).

Rowan Williams, Archbishop of Canterbury, once pointed out that the key question regarding sexuality is not "Am I keeping the rules?" (a predominant concern for conservatives), or "Am I being sincere?" (a typical touchstone for liberals), but "What does my relationship signify?" The question of what a relationship demonstrates or signifies pushes beyond an external conformity to rules, and beyond the subjective feelings of the parties, to inquire about the substance of the relationship itself. If we use this test, then there are good moral reasons to take gay marriage seriously, because in increasing numbers gays and lesbians are giving themselves to one another in a quality of commitment that honors the covenant of marriage — and therefore by analogy *signifies* Christ's own love for the church.

This argument seems to me to be a strong one, so strong in fact that it prompts us to turn Rowan Williams's question back upon the church itself. What does it *signify* when the church continues to withhold its blessing from people who are making sacred commitments to one another? What does it *signify* when the church continues to teach — or to allow some to teach in its name — that the lives and loves of gay and lesbian couples are intrinsically inferior just because of whom they love? What does it *signify* when the church spends so much of its energy arguing against gays when there are so many other pressing moral and spiritual issues crying out to be addressed?

These are questions that people in religious communities, and especially the Christian church, must ask themselves. A watching world wants to see how the teachings of religious leaders are lived out in practice, how the "truth" they urge others to follow makes the world a better place to live. The truth that matters most is not confined to the pages of ancient texts but must take up residence in the lives of individuals and communities. It proves itself in relationships and is authenticated in human flourishing.

The time has come for society to grant same-sex couples full access to the institution of marriage. There are compelling legal and political reasons to do so. The time has come — indeed it is long overdue — for religious communities to abandon arguments that diminish their gay and lesbian brothers and sisters and diminish the moral credibility of the church. It is time to move with all deliberate speed, fortified by the grace of God, toward the full blessing and consecration of the committed relationships of same-sex couples. It is time to move beyond "agreeing to disagree" and to recognize the powerful moral and theological case for this welcoming, affirming, and ordering position. It is time to embrace those who for so many years have earnestly longed to be treated as equal and valued parts of the human family.

Select Bibliography

Ackerman, Susan. *When Heroes Love: The Ambiguity of Eros in the Stories of Gilgamesh and David*. New York: Columbia University Press, 2005.

Adam, Barry. "Age, Structure, and Sexuality." *Journal of Homosexuality* 11 (1986): 19-33.

Alison, James. *Faith Beyond Resentment*. New York: Crossroad, 2001.

―――. *On Being Liked*. New York: Crossroad, 2003.

Alter, Robert. *The Art of Biblical Poetry*. New York: Basic Books, 1985.

―――. *The Five Books of Moses: A Translation with Commentary*. New York and London: W. W. Norton, 2004.

Althaus-Reid, Marcella. *Indecent Theology: Theological Perversions in Sex, Gender and Politics*. New York: Routledge, 2000.

―――. *The Queer God*. London and New York: Routledge, 2003.

Altman, Dennis, Carole S. Vance, et al., eds. *Homosexuality, Which Homosexuality?* Amsterdam: Schorer Boeken, 1989.

Amar, Akhil Reed. "Attainder and Amendment 2: *Romer's* Rightness." 95 *Michigan Law Review* (October 1996): 203-235.

―――. "Justice Kennedy and the Ideal of Equality." 28 *Pacific Law Journal* (Spring 1997): 515-532.

American Pediatric Association Committee on Psycho-social Aspects of Child and Family Health. "Technical Report: Co-parent or Second-parent Adoption by Same-sex Parents." *Pediatrics* 109 (February 2002): 341-344.

American Psychological Association. *Lesbian and Gay Parenting: A Resource for Psychologists*. 1995.

Anonymous. *Miscegenation: The Theory of the Blending of the Races, Applied to the American White Man and Negro*. New York, 1863.

Appiah, Kwame Anthony. *The Ethics of Identity.* Princeton, NJ: Princeton University Press, 2004.

Aquinas, Thomas. *Summa Theologiae,* vol. 43, 2a2ae, qq. 153-154.

Atkinson, Jeff, et al. *The American Bar Association Guide to Family Law.* New York: Three Rivers Press, 1996.

Augustine. *De bono conjugali.*

———. *De doctrina Christiana.*

———. *In Epistulam Johannis ad Parthos tractatus.*

Badgett, M. V. Lee. *Money, Myths and Change: The Economic Lives of Lesbians and Gay Men.* Chicago: University of Chicago Press, 2001.

Bagemihl, Bruce. *Biological Exuberance: Animal Homosexuality and Natural Diversity.* New York: St. Martin's Press, 1999.

Bailey, J. Michael, David Bobrow, Marilyn Wolfe, and Sarah Mikach. "Sexual Orientation of Adult Sons of Gay Fathers." *Developmental Psychology* 31/1 (1995): 124-129.

Ball, Carlos. *The Morality of Gay Rights: An Exploration in Political Philosophy.* New York: Routledge, 2002.

Ball, Carlos, and Janice Farrell Pea. "Warring with Wardle: Social Science, Morality, and Gay and Lesbian Parents." 1998/2 *University of Illinois Law Review* (1998): 253-339.

The Barmen Declaration. 1934.

Barnett, Randy E. "Justice Kennedy's Libertarian Revolution: Lawrence v. Texas." *Boston University School of Law Working Paper* No. 03-13. http://ssrn.com/abstract=422564.

———. *Restoring the Lost Constitution: The Presumption of Liberty.* Princeton, NJ: Princeton University Press, 2004.

Barth, Karl. *Church Dogmatics,* III/1 and III/2. Edinburgh: T&T Clark, 1958, 1960.

Bawer, Bruce. *A Place at the Table: The Gay Individual in American Society.* New York: Simon and Schuster, 1993.

The Belhar Confession. 1984.

Bell, Alan P., and Martin S. Weinberg. *Homosexualities: A Study of Diversity Among Men and Women.* An Official Publication of the Institute for Sex Research founded by Alfred C. Kinsey. New York: Simon and Schuster, 1978.

Benhabib, Seyla. *Democracy and Difference: Contesting the Boundaries of the Political.* Princeton, NJ: Princeton University Press, 1996.

Bentham, Jeremy. "Offences Against Oneself: Paederasty, Part 1." Edited by Louis Crompton. *Journal of Homosexuality* 3/4 (Summer 1978): 389-405; "Offences Against Oneself: Paederasty, Part 2," *Journal of Homosexuality* 4/1 (Fall 1978): 91-107.

Berryman, Philip. *Liberation Theology: The Essential Facts about the Revolutionary Movement in Latin America and Beyond.* New York: Pantheon Books, 1987.

Black, Dan A., Hoda R. Maker, Seth G. Sanders, and Lowell J. Taylor. "The Earnings Effect of Sexual Orientation." 56/3 *Industrial and Labor Relations Review* (2003): 449-469.

Bocklandt, Sven. "Extreme Skewing of X Chromosome Inactivation in Mothers of Homosexual Men." *Human Genetics* 118/6 (February 2006): 691-694.

Boff, Leonardo, and Clodovis Boff. *Introducing Liberation Theology.* Maryknoll, NY: Orbis, 1987.

Boswell, John. *Christianity, Social Tolerance, and Homosexuality.* Chicago: University of Chicago Press, 1980.

———. *Same-Sex Unions in Premodern Europe.* New York: Random House, 1994.

Boykin, Keith. *Beyond the Down Low: Sex, Lies, and Denial in Black America.* Berkeley, CA: Carroll and Graf, 2005.

Bradley, Gerard V., and Robert P. George. "Marriage and the Liberal Imagination." 84 *Georgetown Law Journal* 301-320 (1995).

Bradley, K. R. *Slaves and Masters in the Roman Empire: A Study in Social Control.* New York and London: Oxford University Press, 1987.

Bradley, Keith. *Slavery and Society at Rome.* Key Themes in Ancient History. Cambridge: Cambridge University Press, 1994.

Bradshaw, Timothy, ed. *The Way Forward: Christian Voices on Homosexuality and the Church.* 2nd ed. Grand Rapids: Wm. B. Eerdmans, 2003.

Bray, Alan. *The Friend.* Chicago: University of Chicago Press, 2003.

———. *Homosexuality in Renaissance England* [with a new afterword]. New York: Columbia University Press, 1982; 1995.

Breslin, Beau. *The Communitarian Constitution.* Baltimore and London: Johns Hopkins University Press, 2004.

Brooten, Bernadette. *Love Between Women: Early Christian Responses to Female Homoeroticism.* The Chicago Series on Sexuality, History, and Society. Chicago: University of Chicago Press, 1998.

Browder, Brenda Stone. *On the Up and Up: A Survival Guide for Women Living with Men on the Down Low.* New York: Dafina Books, 2005.

Brown, Robert McAfee. *Liberation Theology: An Introductory Guide.* Louisville: Westminster John Knox Press, 1993.

Burguière, André, et al., eds. *A History of the Family.* Translated by Sarah Hanbury Tenison. 2 vols. Cambridge, MA: Harvard University Press, 1996.

Butler, Judith. *Gender Trouble.* 10th ann. ed. New York: Routledge, 1999.

Cabezón, José Ignacio. *Buddhism, Sexuality, and Gender.* Albany: State University of New York Press, 1992.

Cameron, Paul, and Kirk Cameron. "Homosexual Parents." *Adolescence* 31 (1996): 757-776.

Carey, Benedict. "Straight, Gay or Lying? Bisexuality Revisited." *The New York Times, Science Times,* Tuesday, July 5, 2005, F1, F6.

Chauncey, George. *Why Marriage? The History Shaping Today's Debate over Gay Equality.* New York: Basic Books, 2004.

Clarke, John. *Roman Sex: 100 B.C. to 200 A.D.* New York: Harry N. Abrams, 2003.

Coakley, Sarah. "The Eschatological Body: Gender, Transformation, and God." *Modern Theology* 16/1 (January 2000): 61-73.

Comstock, Gary. *Violence Against Lesbians and Gay Men.* New York: Columbia University Press, 1991.

Cott, Nancy F. *Public Vows: A History of Marriage and the Nation.* Cambridge, MA: Harvard University Press, 2000.

Crompton, Louis. *Homosexuality and Civilization.* Cambridge, MA: Harvard University Press, 2003.

Crossan, John Dominic, and Jonathan L. Reed. *In Search of Paul: How Jesus' Apostle Opposed Rome's Empire with God's Kingdom: A New Vision of Paul's Words and World.* San Francisco: HarperSanFrancisco, 2004.

Dahl, Robert A. *On Democracy.* New Haven and London: Yale University Press, 1998.

Davidson, Arnold I. *The Emergence of Sexuality: Historical Epistemology and the Formation of Concepts.* Cambridge, MA: Harvard University Press, 2001.

Davidson, James, *The Greeks and Greek Love: A Radical Reappraisal of Homosexuality in Ancient Greece.* London: Weidenfield and Nicholson, 2007.

Dean, Howard. "Vermont's Lessons on Gay Marriage." *Boston Globe,* May 17, 2004.

Delphy, Christine, and Diana Leonard. *Familiar Exploitation: A New Analysis of Marriage in Contemporary Western Societies.* Cambridge, MA: Polity Press, 1992.

D'Emilio, John, and Estelle B. Freedman. *Intimate Matters: A History of Sexuality in America.* 2nd ed. Chicago and London: University of Chicago Press, 1997.

Derrida, Jacques. *Adieu to Emmanuel Levinas.* Translated by Pascale-Anne Brault and Michael Naas. Palo Alto, CA: Stanford University Press, 1999.

Devlin, Patrick. *The Enforcement of Morals.* New York: Oxford University Press, 1965.

Diagnostic and Statistical Manual of Mental Disorders II. American Psychiatric Association. 1973.

Dover, Kenneth J. *Greek Homosexuality.* Cambridge, MA: Harvard University Press, 1978; 2nd ed., 1989.

Dworkin, Robert. *Taking Rights Seriously.* Cambridge, MA: Harvard University Press, 1977.

Ellison, Marvin M., ed. *Body and Soul: Rethinking Sexuality as Justice-Love.* Cleveland: Pilgrim Press, 2003.

Ely, John Hart. *Democracy and Distrust: A Theory of Judicial Review.* Cambridge, MA, and London: Harvard University Press, 1980.

Eskridge, William N., Jr. *The Case for Gay Marriage: From Sexual Liberty to Civilized Commitment.* New York: Simon and Schuster, 1996.

————. *Equality Practice: Civil Unions and the Future of Gay Rights.* New York: Routledge, 2001.

————. *Gaylaw: Challenging the Apartheid of the Closet.* Cambridge, MA: Harvard University Press, 1999.

————. "The California Proposition 8: What Is a Constitution For?" 98 *California Law Review* (2010): 1235-1252.

Eskridge, William N., Jr., and Darren R. Spedale. *Gay Marriage: For Better or for Worse? What We've Learned from the Evidence.* New York: Oxford University Press, 2006.

Eskridge, William N., Jr., and Nan Hunter. *Sexuality, Gender, and the Law.* Westbury, NY: The Foundation Press, 1997; 2nd ed., 2004.

————. *Sexuality, Gender, and the Law,* 2nd ed., 2009 Supplement. New York: Tomson Reuters/Foundation Press, 2009.

Faderman, Lillian. *Odd Girls and Twilight Lovers: A History of Lesbian Life in Twentieth-Century America.* New York: Columbia University Press, 1991.

————. *Surpassing the Love of Men: Romantic Friendship and Love from the Renaissance to the Present.* New York: Morrow, 1981.

Falk, Patricia J. "Lesbian Mothers: Psychological Assumptions in Family Law." *American Psychologist* 44 (1989): 941-947.

Fausto-Sterling, Anne. "The Five Sexes: Why Male and Female Are Not Enough." *The Sciences* 33/2 (1993): 20-25.

————. *Sexing the Body: Gender Politics and the Construction of Sexuality.* New York: Basic Books, 2000.

Finnis, John M. *Natural Law and Natural Rights.* Oxford: Clarendon Press, 1980.

Foucault, Michel. "Afterword: The Subject and the Power." In *Beyond Structuralism and Hermeneutics.* Edited by Hubert L. Dreyfus and Paul Rabinow. Chicago: University of Chicago Press, 1982.

————. *The History of Sexuality.* Translated by Robert Hurley. 3 vols. New York: Pantheon, 1978-1986.

Freire, Paulo. *Pedagogy of the Oppressed.* Translated by Myra Bergman Ramos. Rev. 20th ann. ed. New York: Continuum, 1993.

Fried, Charles. *Saying What the Law Is: The Constitution in the Supreme Court.* Cambridge, MA: Harvard University Press, 2004.

Furnish, Victor Paul. *The Moral Theology of Paul.* Nashville: Abingdon, 1979.

Gagnon, Robert A. J. *The Bible and Homosexual Practice: Texts and Hermeneutics.* Nashville: Abingdon, 2001.

George, Robert P. *The Clash of Orthodoxies: Law, Religion, and Morality in Crisis.* Wilmington, DE: ISI Books, 2001.

Gerstmann, Evan. *The Constitutional Underclass: Gays, Lesbians, and the Failure of Class-Based Equal Protection.* Chicago: University of Chicago Press, 1999.

————. *Same Sex Marriage and the Constitution.* Cambridge, UK: Cambridge University Press, 2003.

Glancy, Jennifer. *Slavery in Early Christianity.* New York: Oxford University Press, 2002.

Goody, Jack. *The European Family: A Historical Anthropological Essay.* The Making of Europe. Oxford: Blackwell Publishers, 2000.

Greenberg, David F. *The Construction of Homosexuality.* Chicago and London: University of Chicago Press, 1988.

Grenz, Stanley J. *Welcoming but Not Affirming: An Evangelical Response to Homosexuality.* Louisville: Westminster John Knox Press, 1998.

Grisez, Germain. *The Way of the Lord Jesus,* vol. 2, *Living a Christian Life.* Quincy, IL: Franciscan Press, 1993.

Gutiérrez, Gustavo. *A Theology of Liberation: History, Politics, and Salvation.* 15th ann. ed. Maryknoll, NY: Orbis, 1988.

Gutmann, Amy. *Identity in Democracy.* Princeton, NJ, and Oxford: Princeton University Press, 2003.

Gutmann, Amy, and Dennis Thompson. *Democracy and Disagreement: Why Moral Conflict Cannot Be Avoided in Politics, and What Should Be Done about It.* Cambridge, MA: Harvard University Press, 1996.

————. *Why Deliberative Democracy?* Princeton, NJ: Princeton University Press, 2004.

Habermas, Jürgen. *Between Facts and Norms: Contributions to a Discourse Theory of Law and Democracy.* Translated by William Rehq. Studies in Contemporary German Social Thought. Cambridge, MA: The MIT Press, 1998.

————. *The Inclusion of the Other: Studies in Political Theory.* Edited by Ciran Cronin and Pablo De Greiff. Cambridge, MA: The MIT Press, 1998.

————. *Moral Consciousness and Communicative Action.* Translated by Christian Lenhardt and Shierry Weber Nicholsen. Cambridge, MA: The MIT Press, 1992.

Hall, Kermit L. *The Oxford Companion to the Supreme Court.* New York: Oxford University Press, 2005.

Hallett, Judith P., and Marilyn B. Skinner. *Roman Sexualities.* Princeton, NJ: Princeton University Press, 1997.

Halley, Janet E. "Sexual Orientation and the Politics of Biology: A Critique of the Argument from Immutability." 46/3 *Stanford Law Review* (February 1994): 503-568.

Halperin, David M. *One Hundred Years of Homosexuality and Other Essays on Greek Love.* New York: Routledge, 1990.

Hamer, Dean, and Peter Copeland. *The Science of Desire: The Search for the Gay Gene and the Biology of Behavior.* New York: Simon and Schuster, 1994.

Hamilton, Marci A. *God vs. the Gavel: Religion and the Rule of Law.* Cambridge, UK: Cambridge University Press, 2005.

Harrison, Verna. "Male and Female in Cappadocian Theology." *Journal of Theological Studies* 41 (1990): 441-471.

Hartzog, Hendrik. *Man and Wife in America: A History.* Cambridge, MA: Harvard University Press, 2000.

Hauerwas, Stanley. "On Gay Friendship: A Thought Experiment in Catholic Moral Theology." In *Sanctify Them in the Truth: Holiness Exemplified.* Nashville: Abingdon, 1998.

————. "Why Gays (as a Group) Are Morally Superior to Christians (as a Group)." In *The Hauerwas Reader.* Edited by John Berkman and Michael Cartwright. Durham, NC, and London: Duke University Press, 2001.

Hays, Richard B. *The Moral Vision of the New Testament: A Contemporary Introduction to New Testament Ethics.* San Francisco: HarperSanFrancisco, 1996.

Heinze, Eric. *Sexual Orientation — A Human Right: An Essay on International Human Rights Law.* Leiden: Brill Academic Publishers, 1995.

Held, David. *Models of Democracy.* 2nd ed. Palo Alto, CA: Stanford University Press, 1996.

Herdt, Gilbert H. *Guardians of the Flutes,* vol. 1, *Idioms of Masculinity.* Chicago: University of Chicago Press, 1994.

Herdt, Gilbert H., ed. *Ritualized Homosexuality in Melanesia.* Berkeley: University of California Press, 1984.

Hexter, Ralph, and Brent D. Shaw. "Samesex Unions in Premodern Europe: An Exchange." *The New Republic* 211 (October 3, 1994): 39-41.

Heyward, Carter. *Our Passion for Justice: Images of Power, Sexuality, and Liberation.* New York: The Pilgrim Press, 1984.

Hohfeld, W. N. *Fundamental Legal Conceptions as Applied in Judicial Reasoning.* Edited by W. W. Cook. Reprint. New Haven: Yale University Press, 1964. First published in 1919.

Holben, L. R. *What Christians Think about Homosexuality: Six Representative Viewpoints.* North Richland Hills, TX: Bibal Press, 1999.

Hooker, Evelyn. "The Adjustment of the Male Overt Homosexual." *Journal of Projective Techniques* 21 (1957).

Hunter, James Davison. *To Change the World: The Irony, Tragedy, and Possibility of Christianity in the Late Modern World.* New York: Oxford University Press, 2010.

Isay, Richard A., M.D. *Becoming Gay: The Journey to Self-Acceptance.* New York: Henry Holt and Company, 1996.

Jakobsen, Janet R., and Ann Pellegrini. *Love the Sin: Sexual Regulation and the*

Limits of Religious Tolerance. New York: New York University Press, 2003; Boston: Beacon Press, 2004.

Jenson, Robert W. *Systematic Theology.* New York: Oxford University Press, 1997.

Jewett, Paul K., with Marguerite Schuster. *Who We Are: Our Dignity as Human: A Neo-Evangelical Theology.* Grand Rapids: Wm. B. Eerdmans, 1996.

John Paul II. *A Theology of the Body: Human Love in the Divine Plan.* New York: Pauline Books, 1997.

Johnson, David K. *The Lavender Scare: The Cold War Persecution of Gays and Lesbians in the Federal Government.* Chicago: University of Chicago Press, 2004.

Jones, Stanton L., and Mark A. Yarhouse. *Ex-Gay? A Longitudinal Study of Religiously Mediated Change in Sexual Orientation.* Downers Grove, IL: InterVarsity Press, 2007.

——. *Homosexuality: The Use of Scientific Research in the Church's Moral Debate.* Downers Grove, IL: InterVarsity Press, 2000.

Jordan, Mark D. *The Invention of Sodomy in Christian Theology.* Chicago: University of Chicago Press, 1997.

Jung, Patricia Beattie, and Ralph F. Smith. *Heterosexism: An Ethical Challenge.* Albany: State University of New York Press, 1994.

Kelsey, David. *Eccentric Existence: Theological Anthropology.* 2 vols. Louisville: Westminster John Knox Press, 2009.

Kens, Paul. *"Lochner v. New York": Economic Regulation on Trial.* Landmark Law Cases and American Society. Lawrence: University Press of Kansas, 1998.

Kertzer, David, and Marzio Barbagli, eds. *The History of the European Family.* 3 vols. New Haven: Yale University Press, 2001-2003.

Keynes, Edward. *Liberty, Property, and Privacy: Toward a Jurisprudence of Substantive Due Process.* University Park: Pennsylvania State University Press, 1996.

King, J. L. *On the Down Low: A Journey in the Lives of "Straight" Black Men Who Sleep with Men.* New York: Broadway, 2004.

King, Martin Luther, Jr.. *A Testament of Hope: The Essential Writings and Speeches of Martin Luther King, Jr.* Edited by James M. Washington. New York: Harper and Row, 1988.

Kinnaman, David, and Gabe Lyons. *Unchristian: What a New Generation Really Thinks about Christianity and Why it Matters.* Grand Rapids: Baker, 2007.

Kinsey, Alfred C., Wardell B. Pomeroy, and Clyde E. Martin. *Sexual Behavior in the Human Male.* Philadelphia: W. B. Saunders Company, 1948.

Kinsey, Alfred C., Wardell B. Pomeroy, Clyde E. Martin, and Paul H. Gebhard. *Sexual Behavior in the Human Female.* Philadelphia: W. B. Saunders Company, 1953.

Kirtsoglou, Elisabeth. *For the Love of Women: Identity and Same-sex Relations in a Provincial Greek Town.* London: Routledge, 2004.

Kitzinger, Celia. *The Social Construction of Lesbianism.* New York: Sage Books, 1987.

Koppelman, Andrew. *The Gay Rights Question in Contemporary American Law.* Chicago: University of Chicago Press, 2002.

Koppelman, Andrew, with Tobias Barrington Wolf. *A Right to Discriminate? How the Case of Boy Scouts of America v. Dale Warped the Law of Free Association.* New Haven: Yale University Press, 2009.

Kotz, Nick. *Judgment Days: Lyndon Baines Johnson, Martin Luther King, Jr., and the Laws That Changed America.* New York: Houghton Mifflin, 2005.

Kvam, Kristen, Linda S. Shearing, and Valarie H. Ziegler, eds. *Eve and Adam: Jewish, Christian, and Muslim Readings on Genesis and Gender.* Bloomington: Indiana University Press, 1999.

Kymlicka, Will. *Contemporary Political Philosophy: An Introduction.* 2nd ed. Oxford: Oxford University Press, 2001.

LaCocque, André, and Paul Ricoeur. *Thinking Biblically: Exegetical and Hermeneutical Studies.* Translated by David Pellauer. Chicago and London: University of Chicago Press, 1998.

Laqueur, Thomas. *Making Sex: The Body and Gender from the Greeks to Freud.* Cambridge, MA: Harvard University Press, 1990.

Laslett, Peter. *The World We Have Lost: Further Explored.* 4th rev. ed. New York: Routledge, 2004.

Laumann, Edward O., John H. Gagnon, Robert T. Mitchell, and Stuart Michaels. *The Social Organization of Sexuality: Sexual Practices in the United States.* Chicago: University of Chicago Press, 1994.

Laycock, Douglas, Anthony R. Picarello, Jr., and Robin Fretwell Wilson, eds. *Same-Sex Marriage and Religious Liberty: Emerging Conflicts.* Lanham, MD: Rowman & Littlefield Publishers, Inc., 2008.

Lemire, Elise Virginia. *"Miscegenation": Making Race in America.* New Cultural Series. Philadelphia: University of Pennsylvania Press, 2002.

Leupp, Gary P. *Male Colors: The Construction of Homosexuality in Tokugawa Japan.* Berkeley: University of California Press, 1997.

Levinas, Emmanuel. *Totality and Infinity: An Essay on Exteriority.* Translated by Alphonso Lingis. Pittsburgh: Duquesne University Press, 1969.

Lofgren, Charles. *The Plessy Case: A Legal-Historical Interpretation.* New York: Oxford University Press, 1987.

Loughery, John. *The Other Side of Silence: Men's Lives and Gay Identities: A Twentieth-Century History.* New York: Henry Holt and Company, 1998.

Macedo, Stephen. "Homosexuality and the Conservative Mind." 84 *Georgetown Law Journal* 261-300 (1995).

————. *Liberal Virtues: Citizenship, Virtue, and Community in Liberal Constitutionalism.* Oxford: Oxford University Press, 1990.

Macedo, Stephen, ed. *Deliberative Politics: Essays on Democracy and Disagreement.* New York and Oxford: Oxford University Press, 1999.

Manbridge, Jane. *Why We Lost the ERA.* Chicago: University of Chicago Press, 1986.

McClure, Laura K., ed. *Sexuality and Gender in the Classical World: Readings and Sources.* Oxford: Blackwell Publishers, 2002.

Mendelsohn, Matthew, and Andrew Parkin, eds. *Referendum Democracy: Citizens, Elites, and Deliberation in Referendum Campaigns.* New York: Palgrave Macmillan, 2001.

Michael, Robert T., John H. Gagnon, Edward O. Laumann, and Gina Kolata. *Sex in America: A Definitive Survey.* Boston: Little, Brown and Company, 1994.

Milgrom, Jacob. *Leviticus 17–22.* New York: Doubleday, 2000.

Mill, John Stuart. *On Liberty.* Vol. 18, *Collected Works.* Toronto: University of Toronto Press, 1963-c1991.

———. *The Subjection of Women.* Edited by Susan M. Okin. Indianapolis: Hackett Publishing Company, 1988.

Moats, David. *Civil Wars: A Battle for Gay Marriage.* New York: Harcourt, 2004.

Mohr, Richard D. *Gays/Justice: A Study of Ethics, Society, and Law.* New York: Columbia University Press, 1988.

———. *The Long Arc of Justice: Lesbian and Gay Marriage, Equality, and Rights.* New York: Columbia University Press, 2005.

Mondimore, Francis Mark. *A Natural History of Homosexuality.* Baltimore and London: Johns Hopkins University Press, 1996.

Moore-Emmett, Andrea. *God's Brothel: The Extortion of Sex for Salvation in Contemporary Mormon and Christian Fundamentalist Polygamy and the Stories of 18 Women Who Escaped.* San Francisco: Pince-Nez Press, 2004.

Mosher, William D., Anjani Chandra, and Jo Jones. "Sexual Behavior and Selected Health Measures: Men and Women 15-44 Years of Age, United States, 2002." *Advanced Data from Vital and Health Statistics.* Centers for Disease Control, Number 362, September 15, 2005.

Murdoch, Joyce, and Deb Price. *Courting Justice: Gay Men and Lesbians v. the Supreme Court.* New York: Basic Books, 2002.

Murray, Stephen O. *Homosexualities.* Chicago and London: University of Chicago Press, 2000.

Murray, Stephen O., et al. *Islamic Homosexualities: Culture, History, and Literature.* New York: New York University Press, 1997.

Murray, Stephen O., and Will Roscoe, eds. *Boy-Wives and Female Husbands.* New York: Palgrave Macmillan, 1998.

Myers, David G., and Letha Dawson Scanzonia. *What God Has Joined Together: The Christian Case for Gay Marriage.* New York: HarperSanFrancisco, 2005.

Niebuhr, H. Richard. *The Meaning of Revelation.* New York: Macmillan, 1941.

————. *Radical Monotheism and Western Culture, With Supplementary Essays.* New York: Harper and Brothers, 1960.

Nissinen, Martti. *Homoeroticism in the Biblical World: A Historical Perspective.* Translated by Kirsi Stjerna. Minneapolis: Fortress Press, 1998.

Novkov, Julie. "Racial Constructions: The Legal Regulation of Miscegenation in Alabama, 1890-1934." 20/2 *Law and History Review* (Summer 2002): 225-277.

Nussbaum, Martha C. *From Disgust to Humanity: Sexual Orientation and Constitutional Law.* New York: Oxford University Press, 2010.

————. "The Professor of Parody." *The New Republic*, February 22, 1999.

————. *Sex and Social Justice.* New York: Oxford University Press, 2000.

Patterson, Charlotte J. "Adoption of Minor Children by Lesbian and Gay Adults: A Social Science Perspective." *Duke Journal of Law and Policy* 2/1 (1995): 195-205.

Pinello, Daniel R. *Gay Rights and American Law.* Cambridge, UK: Cambridge University Press, 2003.

Plant, Richard. *The Pink Triangle: The Nazi War Against Homosexuals.* New York: New Republic Books, 1986.

Posner, Richard A. *Law, Pragmatism, and Democracy.* Cambridge, MA: Harvard University Press, 2003.

————. *Sex and Reason.* Cambridge, MA, and London: Harvard University Press, 1992.

Preves, Sharon E. *Intersex and Identity: The Contested Self.* New Brunswick, NJ: Rutgers University Press, 2003.

Rapp, Claudia. "Ritual Brotherhood in Byzantium." *Traditio* 52 (1997): 285-326.

Ratzinger, Joseph Cardinal. *Letter to the Bishops of the Catholic Church on the Pastoral Care of Homosexual Persons.* Documents of the Congregation for the Doctrine of the Faith. San Francisco: Ignatius Press, 1987.

Rauch, Jonathan. *Gay Marriage: Why It Is Good for Gays, Good for Straights, and Good for America.* New York: Henry Holt, 2004.

Rawls, John. *A Theory of Justice.* Cambridge, MA: Belknap Press of Harvard University Press, 1971; rev. ed., 1999.

Rector, Frank. *The Nazi Extermination of Homosexuals.* New York: Stein and Day, 1981.

Report of the American Psychological Association Task Force on Appropriate Therapeutic Responses to Sexual Orientation. Washington, DC: American Psychological Association, 2009.

Report and Recommendations from the Task Force for Evangelical Lutheran Church in America Studies on Sexuality. January 13, 2005.

Richlin, Amy. *The Garden of Priapus: Sexuality and Aggression in Roman Humor.* Oxford: Oxford University Press, 1992.

Rieger, Gerulf, Meredith L. Chivers, and J. Michael Bailey. "Sexual Arousal Patterns of Bisexual Men." *Psychological Science* 16/8 (August 2005): 579-584.

Robinson, Paul. *Queer Wars: The New Gay Right and Its Critics.* Chicago: University of Chicago Press, 2005.

Rocke, Michael. *Forbidden Friendships: Homosexuality and Male Culture in Renaissance Florence.* Studies in the History of Sexuality. Oxford: Oxford University Press, 1996.

Rogers, Eugene F., Jr. *Sexuality and the Christian Body: Their Way into the Triune God.* Challenges in Contemporary Theology. New York: Blackwell Publishers, 1999.

Rogers, Eugene F., Jr., ed. *Theology and Sexuality: Classic and Contemporary Readings.* Oxford: Blackwell Publishers, 2002.

Roscoe, Will. *Changing Ones: Third and Fourth Genders in Native North America.* New York: St. Martin's Press, 1986; New York: Palgrave Macmillan, 2000.

Rowland, Christopher, ed. *The Cambridge Companion to Liberation Theology.* Cambridge, UK: Cambridge University Press, 1999.

Rudacille, Deborah. *The Riddle of Gender: Science, Activism and Transgender Rights.* New York: Pantheon, 2005.

Saikaku, Ihara. *The Great Mirror of Male Love.* Palo Alto, CA: Stanford University Press, 1990.

Sandel, Michael J. *Liberalism and the Limits of Justice.* 2nd ed. Cambridge, UK: Cambridge University Press, 1998.

———. "Moral Argument and Liberal Toleration: Abortion and Homosexuality." 77 *California Law Review* (1989): 521-538.

Satinover, Jeffrey, M.D. *Homosexuality and the Politics of Truth.* Grand Rapids: Baker, 1996.

Schmitt, Arno, and Jehoeda Sofer. *Sexuality and Eroticism Among Males in Moslem Societies.* Binghamton, NY: Haworth Press, 1991.

Scroggs, Robin. *The New Testament and Homosexuality: Contextual Background for Contemporary Debates.* Philadelphia: Fortress Press, 1983.

A Season of Discernment. Final Report of the Task Force on the Peace, Unity, and Purity of the Church to the 217th General Assembly (2006); with Study Guide (2006).

Sedgwick, Eve Kosofsky. *Epistemology of the Closet.* Berkeley: University of California Press, 1990.

Seidman, Louis Michael. *Constitutional Law: Equal Protection of the Law.* Turning Point. New York: Foundation Press, 2002.

Shaw, Brent D. "A Groom of One's Own?" *The New Republic* 211 (July 18-24, 1994): 33-41.

———. "Ritual Brotherhood in Roman and Post-Roman Societies." *Traditio* 52 (1997): 327-355.

Shilts, Randy. *And the Band Played On: Politics, People, and the AIDS Epidemic.* New York: St. Martins Press, 1987.

Sigmund, P. E. *Liberation Theology at the Crossroads: Democracy or Revolution?* Oxford: Oxford University Press, 1990.

Siker, Jeffrey, ed. *Homosexuality in the Church: Both Sides of the Debate.* Louisville: Westminster John Knox Press, 1994.

Skinner, Marilyn B. *Sexuality in Greek and Roman Culture.* Oxford: Blackwell Publishers, 2005.

Snyder, R. Claire. *Gay Marriage and Democracy: Equality for All.* Lanham, MD: Rowan and Littlefield, 2006.

Sollors, Werner, ed. *Interracialism: Black-White Intermarriage in American History, Literature and Law.* Oxford: Oxford University Press, 2000.

Stacey, Judith, and Timothy Biblarz. "(How) Does Sexual Orientation of Parents Matter?" *American Sociological Review* 66 (April 2001): 159-183.

Stein, Edward. *The Mismeasure of Desire: The Science, Theory, and Ethics of Sexual Orientation.* New York: Oxford University Press, 1999.

Stott, John R. W. *Homosexual Partnerships? Why Same-sex Relationships Are Not a Christian Option.* Downers Grove, IL: InterVarsity Press, 1985.

Stuart, Elizabeth. *Gay and Lesbian Theologies: Repetitions with Critical Difference.* Hampshire, UK: Ashgate Publishing Limited, 2003.

Sullivan, Andrew. *Love Undetectable: Notes on Friendship, Sex, and Survival.* New York: Alfred A. Knopf, 1998.

————. *Virtually Normal: An Argument about Homosexuality.* New York: Alfred A. Knopf, 1995; New York: Vintage Books, 1996.

Sullivan, Andrew, ed. *Same-Sex Marriage: Pro and Con.* Rev. and updated ed. New York: Vintage Books, 2004.

Sullivan, Kathleen M., and Gerald Gunther. *Constitutional Law.* 15th ed. New York: Foundation Press, 2004.

Sunstein, Cass. *Designing Democracy: What Constitutions Do.* New York: Oxford University Press, 2001.

————. *One Case at a Time: Judicial Minimalism on the Supreme Court.* Cambridge, MA: Harvard University Press, 1999.

Tasker, Fiona, and Susan Golombok. *Growing Up in a Lesbian Family: Effects on Child Development.* New York: Guilford Publications, 1997.

Taylor, Charles. *Multiculturalism and "The Politics of Recognition."* Princeton, NJ: Princeton University Press, 1992.

Temple, Gray. *Gay Unions: In the Light of Scripture, Tradition, and Reason.* New York: Church Publishing, 2004.

Ternus, Marsha. "Do Americans Still Value an Independent Judiciary?" In *Book of the States,* Forthcoming.

Thielicke, Helmut. *The Ethics of Sex.* Translated by John W. Doberstein. New York: Harper and Row, 1964.

To Set Our Hope on Christ: A Response to the Invitation of Windsor Report ¶135. New York: The Episcopal Church Center, 2005.

Traub, Valerie. *The Renaissance of Lesbianism in Early Modern England.* Cambridge, UK: Cambridge University Press, 2002.

Tribe, Laurence H. *American Constitutional Law.* Vol. 1. 3rd ed. New York: Foundation Press, 2000.

Tushnet, Mark V. *A Court Divided: The Rehnquist Court and the Future of Constitutional Law.* New York and London: W. W. Norton & Company, 2005.

Vicinus, Martha. *Intimate Friends: Women Who Loved Women, 1778-1928.* Chicago: University of Chicago Press, 2004.

Walker, Mark Clarence. *The Strategic Use of Referendums: Power, Legitimacy, and Democracy.* New York: Palgrave Macmillan, 2003.

Walzer, Michael. "The Communitarian Critique of Liberalism." *Political Theory* 18/1 (February 1990): 6-23.

———. "The Idea of Civil Society: A Path to Social Reconstruction." *Dissent* (Spring 1991): 293-304.

Wardle, Lynn. "Fighting with Phantoms: A Reply to Warring with Wardle." 1998/2 *University of Illinois Law Review* (1998): 629-641.

———. "The Potential Impact of Homosexual Parenting on Children." 1997/3 *University of Illinois Law Review* (1997): 833-920.

Watson, Alan. *Roman Slave Law.* Baltimore and London: Johns Hopkins University Press, 1987.

Williams, Rowan. "The Body's Grace" (1989).

———. *A Ray of Darkness: Sermons and Reflections.* Cambridge, MA: Cowley Publications, 1995.

Williams, Walter L. *The Spirit and the Flesh: Sexual Diversity in American Indian Culture.* Boston: Beacon Press, 1986.

The Windsor Report 2004. London: The Anglican Communion Office, 2004.

Wintemute, Robert. "International Trends in Legal Recognition of Same-Sex Partnerships." 23 *Quinnipiac Law Review* (2004): 577-595.

———. *Sexual Orientation and Human Rights: The United States Constitution, the European Convention, and the Canadian Charter.* Oxford: Clarendon Press, 1995.

Wintemute, Robert, and Mads Andenæs, eds. *Legal Recognition of Same-Sex Partnerships: A Study of National, European and International Law.* Oxford: Hart Publishing, 2001.

Witte, John, Jr. *From Sacrament to Contract: Marriage, Religion, and Law in the Western Tradition.* Louisville: Westminster John Knox Press, 1997.

Wolfenden, Sir John, et al. *Report of the Committee on Homosexual Offenses and Prostitution.* London: H. M. Stationery Office, 1957.

Wolfson, Evan. *Why Marriage Matters: America, Equality, and Gay People's Right to Marry.* New York: Simon and Schuster, 2004.

Wright, Robert. *The Moral Animal: The New Science of Evolutionary Psychology.* New York: Pantheon Books, 1994.

Young, Robin Darling. "Gay Marriage: Reimagining Church History." *First Things* 47 (November 1, 1994): 43-48.

Zimmerman, Bonnie, and George T. Haggerty, eds. *The Encyclopedia of Lesbian and Gay Histories and Cultures.* 2 vols. New York: Garland Books, 1999.

Table of Legal Cases

Acanfora v. Board of Education of Montgomery County, 491 F.2d 498 (4th Cir. 1973).

Alaska Civil Liberties Union v. Alaska, 122 P.3d 781 (Alaska Supreme Ct 2005).

Anderson v. King County, 138 P.3d 963 (Wash. 2006).

Baehr v. Lewin, 852 P.2d 44 (Haw. 1993).

Baker v. Nelson, 292 Minn. 310 (Minn. 1971), 409 U.S. 810 (1972).

Baker v. State of Vermont, 170 Vt. 194, 744 A.2d 864 (1999).

Beller v. Mittendorf, 632 F.2d 788 (1980).

Bolling v. Sharpe, 347 U.S. 497 (1954).

Bottoms v. Bottoms, 249 Va. 410, 457 S.E.2d 102 (1995).

Bowers v. Hardwick, 478 U.S. 186 (1986).

Boy Scouts of America v. Dale, 530 U.S. 640 (2000).

Bradwell v. Illinois, 83 U.S. 130 (1873).

Brause v. Bureau of Vital Statistics, Superior Court, Third Judicial District, case no. 3AN-95-6562 CI, Alaska, February 27, 1998.

Breese v. Smith, 501 P.2d 159 (Alaska, 1972).

Brown v. Board of Education, 347 U.S. 294 (1954).

Brown v. Board of Education II, 349 U.S. 294 (1955).

Bush v. Gore, 531 U.S. 98 (2000).

Carey v. Population Services Int'l, 431 U.S. 678 (1977).

Citizens for Equal Protection, Inc. v. Bruning, Memorandum and Order, May 12, 2005, case number 4:03-cv-03155.

City of Cleburne v. Cleburne Living Center, Inc., 473 U.S. 432 (1985).

Cole v. Arkansas, The Supreme Court of Arkansas, No. 10-840, April 7, 2011.

Conaway v. Deane, 932 A.2d 571 (Md.Ct. of Appeals 2007).

Craig v. Boren, 429 U.S. 190 (1976).

Douglas v. California, 372 U.S. 353 (1963).

Eisenstadt v. Baird, 405 U.S. 438 (1972).

Equality Foundation of Greater Cincinnati v. City of Cincinnati, 128 F.3d 289 (1998).

Fla. Dept. of Children & Families v. X.X.G., Florida Third District Court of Appeals (2010).

Frontiero v. Richardson, 411 U.S. 677 (1973).

Gaylord v. Tacoma School District, 88 Wn. 286, 559 P.2d 1340, *cert. denied* 434 U.S. 879 (1977).

Gill v. Office of Personnel Management, 699 F.Supp.2d 374 (D.Mass. 2010).

Goodridge v. Department of Public Health, 440 Mass. 309, 798 NE2d 941 (2003).

Griffin v. Illinois, 351 U.S. 12 (1956).

Griswold v. Connecticut, 381 U.S. 479 (1965).

Harper v. Board of Elections, 383 U.S. 663 (1966).

Hernandez v. Robles, 855 N.E.2d 1 (N.Y.Ct. of Appeals 2006).

Hurley v. Irish-American Gay, Lesbian, Bisexual Group of Boston, Inc., 515 U.S. 557 (1995).

In re Griffiths, 413 U.S. 717 (1973).

In re Marriage Cases, 43 Cal.4th 757, 76 Cal.Rptr3d 683, 183 P.3d 384 (California Supreme Ct. 2008).

Kerrigan v. Commissioner of Public Health, 289 Conn. 135, 957 A.2d 407 (Connecticut Supreme Ct. 2008).

Korematsu v. United States, 323 U.S. 214 (1944).

Kramer v. Union Free School District No. 15, 395 U.S. 621 (1969).

Labine v. Vincent, 401 U.S. 532 (1971).

Lawrence v. Texas, 539 U.S. 558 (2003).

Levy v. Louisiana, 391 U.S. 68 (1968).

Lewis v. Harris, 188 N.J. 415, 908 A.2d 196 (N.J. Supreme Ct. 2006).

Li v. Oregon, 338 Or. 383, 110 P.3d 91, 94 (Oregon Supreme Ct. 2005).

Littleton v. Prange, 9 S.W.3d 223 (Texas 4th Cir. 1999).

Lochner v. New York, 198 U.S. 43 (1905).

Lofton v. Kearney, 157 F.Supp.2d 1372 (SD Fla. 2001).

Lofton v. Sec'y of the Dep't of Children and Family Services, 358 F.3d 804 (11th Cir. 2004).

Loving v. Virginia, 388 U.S. 1 (1967).

Mapp v. Ohio, 367 U.S. 643 (1961),

Massachusetts v. United States Department of Health and Human Services, 698 F.Supp.2d 234 (D.Mass. 2010).

McLaurin v. Oklahoma State Regents for Higher Education, 339 U.S. 637 (1950).

Meyer v. Nebraska, 262 U.S. 390 (1923).

Minersville School District v. Gobitis, 310 U.S. 586 (1940).

National Gay Task Force v. Board of Education of Oklahoma City, 729 F. 2d 1270 (1985).

Select Bibliography

National Pride at Work v. Governor of Michigan, 481 Mich. 56, 748 N. W. 2d (Mich. 2008).

Opinions of the Justices to the Senate, 440 Mass. 1201, 802 NE2d 565 (Feb. 3, 2004).

Pace v. Alabama, 106 U.S. 583, 1 S.Ct. 637 (1883).

Palko v. Connecticut, 302 U.S. 319 (1932).

Perez v. Lippold, 198 P.2d 17 (Cal. 1948).

Perry v. Brown, No. 10-16696 (9th Cir., Feb. 7, 2012).

Perry v. Schwarzenegger, 702 F.Supp. 2d 921 (N.D.Cal., 2010).

Pierce v. Society of Sisters, 268 U.S. 510 (1925).

Planned Parenthood of Southeastern Pa. v. Casey, 505 U.S. 833 (1992).

Plessy v. Fergusson, 163 U.S. 537 (1896).

Poe v. Ullman, 367 U.S. 497 (1961).

Reed v. Reed, 404 U.S. 71 (1971).

Reynolds v. United States, 98 U.S. 145 (1879).

Roberts v. United States Jaycees, 468 U.S. 609 (1984).

Roe v. Wade, 410 U.S. 113 (1973).

Romer v. Evans, 517 U.S. 620 (1996).

Rotary International v. Rotary Club of Duarte, 481 U.S. 537 (1987).

Rumsfeld v. Forum for Academic and Institutional Rights (2006).

Shelley v. Kraemer, 334 U.S. 1 (1948).

Singer v. Barwick, 11 Wash. App. 247, 522 P. 2d 1187 (1974).

Singer v. United States Civil Service Commission, 530 F.2d 247 (9th Cir. 1976).

Skinner v. Oklahoma, 316 U.S. 535 (1942).

Snyder v. Phelps, 131 S.Ct. 1207 (2011).

Stanley v. Georgia, 394 U.S. 557 (1969).

Stanley v. Illinois, 405 U.S. 645 (1972).

Strauss v. Horton, 46 Cal.4th 364, 93 Cal.Rptr.3d 591, 207 P.3d 48 (Cal. 2009).

Sugarman v. Dougall, 413 U.S. 634 (1973).

Susan Stemler v. City of Florence, 126 F.3d 856 (6th Cir. 1997).

Sweatt v. Painter, 339 U.S. 629 (1950).

United States v. Carolene Products, 304 U.S. 144 (1938).

United States v. Smith, 574 F.2d 988 (1978).

United States v. Virginia, 518 U.S. 515 (1996).

University of Alaska v. Tumeo, 933 P.2d 1147 (1997).

U.S. Department of Agriculture v. Moreno, 413 U.S. 528 (1973).

Varnum v. Brien, 763 N.W.2d 862 (Iowa 2009).

Webster v. Reproductive Health Services, 492 U.S. 490 (1989).

West Coast Hotel, Co. v. Parrish, 300 U.S. 379 (1937).

West Virginia State Board of Education v. Barnette, 319 U.S. 624, 638 (1943).

Notes

Notes to the Preface to the Second Edition

1. Theodore B. Olson is a conservative attorney who served as Solicitor General of the United States from 2001 to 2004 under President George W. Bush. He represented President Bush before the U.S. Supreme Court in *Bush v. Gore*, which decided the 2004 presidential election in Bush's favor. He now favors same-sex marriage, and this quote is from his 2010 Closing Argument at the trial stage of the California District Court case, *Perry v. Schwarzenneger*. See Trial Transcript, p. 2971, lines 3-10.

2. At least four independent polls confirm these results. The Gallup Poll released the 53 percent figure in a study on May 20, 2011. http://www.gallup.com/poll/147662/first-time-majority-americans-favor-legal-gay-marriage.aspx.

The Gallup study confirmed a March 18, 2011, Washington Post-ABC News poll that also reported 53 percent approval for gay marriage. http://www.washingtonpost.com/politics/slim-majority-back-gay-marriage-post-abc-poll-says/2011/03/17/ABhMc7o_story.html. Similar results were obtained in CNN and AP polls conducted in 2010, both indicating a majority of Americans support same-sex marriage. http://politicalticker.blogs.cnn.com/2011/04/19/poll-more-americans-favor-same-sex-marriage/ and http://www.ontopmag.com/article.aspx?id=6428&MediaType=1&Category=26.

Even polling by the conservative Pew Research Center indicates that 58 percent of Americans say homosexuality should be accepted, with 45 percent favoring gay marriage. http://pewresearch.org/pubs/1994/poll-support-for-acceptance-of-homosexuality-gay-parenting-marriage.

3. In the poll from Gallup, this compared with only 39 percent for people over fifty-five.

4. The witness was David Blankenhorn, founder and president of The Institute

for American Values. Blankenhorn's highest degree is a master's in comparative social history from the University of Warwick, where his thesis focused on two nineteenth-century cabinetmakers. The other expert witness the attorneys called to testify against gay marriage was a political scientist, Kenneth P. Miller, of Claremont McKenna College; but Dr. Miller did not testify on the social effects of gay marriage as did Blankenhorn. Though Blankenhorn was allowed to testify, his credibility as an expert witness was eventually rejected.

5. Pub.L. 104-199, 110 Stat. 2419, enacted September 21, 1996, 1 U.S.C. § 7 and 28, U.S.C. § 1738C.

6. In 1996 when he was a candidate for the State Senate in Illinois, Obama responded to a questionnaire that he favored legalizing same-sex marriage, but as a presidential candidate he shifted his position to favoring civil unions.

7. The Mexican Supreme Court ruled in August 2010 that ceremonies performed in Mexico City must be recognized throughout Mexico. Bills are pending in various Mexican states to broaden the availability. http://www.nytimes.com/2010/08/11/world/americas/11mexico.html.

8. The proposed provision of the Nepalese Constitution reads: "All persons of full age, without any limitation due to race, nationality, religion, social order, gender, or sexual orientation have the right to marry. Such individuals are entitled to equal rights as to marriage, during marriage and at its dissolution." Title 10, Section 13, Rights and Freedoms of All Citizens, www.onlineconstitution.net. It was scheduled to go into effect on May 29, 2011, when the deadline for the Nepalese Assembly to reach agreement was extended by three months. http://www.nytimes.com/2011/05/30/world/asia/30nepal.html.

9. See, for example, Douglas Laycock, Anthony R. Picarello, Jr., and Robin Fretwell Wilson, eds., *Same-Sex Marriage and Religious Liberty: Emerging Conflicts* (Lanham, MD: Rowman & Littlefield Publishers, Inc., 2008).

10. *Snyder v. Phelps,* 131 S.Ct. 1207 (2011).

11. Douglas Laycock, "Afterword," in *Same-Sex Marriage and Religious Liberty,* p. 194.

12. http://www.nytimes.com/2009/07/16/us/16episcopal.html?_r=1.

13. http://www.nytimes.com/2009/08/22/us/22lutherans.html.

14. James Davison Hunter, *To Change the World: Irony, Tragedy, and Possibility of Christianity in the Late Modern World* (Oxford: Oxford University Press, 2010).

15. See my discussion of *Perry v. Schwarzenegger* and *Perry v. Brown* in ch. 5.

16. Those opposed to allowing gay marriage often raise the fear that it will lead to polygamy or incest. But freedom to marry the person you choose does not equal freedom to marry as many persons as you choose. Nor does it include the right to marry in violation of incest laws. There is no requirement that church or society must honor relationships that may do tangible harm.

17. For more on why I believe this is the case, see the response to conservative

critics of my position in William Stacy Johnson, "Response: Finding a Way Forward," in *Scottish Journal of Theology* 62/1 (2009): 81-90.

18. For a discussion of the attitudes of young people to the church's witness today, see David Kinnaman and Gabe Lyons, *Unchristian: What a New Generation Really Thinks about Christianity and Why it Matters* (Grand Rapids: Baker, 2007).

19. Regarding the New Testament in particular, I argued in the first edition that its statements must be situated within the brutal ideology of dominance and submission that accompanied most homoerotic liaisons in the Roman Empire. In an expanded section of the introduction, I elaborate on this point in greater detail. The argument has also been discussed at greater length in the following places: William Stacy Johnson, "Empire and Order: The New Testament and Same-Gender Relationships," *Biblical Theology Bulletin*, 37/4 (Winter 2007): 161-173; and William Stacy Johnson, "The New Testament, Empire and Homoeroticism," in *The Embrace of Eros: Bodies, Desires, and Sexuality in Christianity*, ed. Margaret D. Kamitsuka (Minneapolis: Fortress Press, 2010), pp. 51-66.

20. http://www3.law.ucla.edu/williamsinstitute/publications/USCensusSnapshot .pdf.

Notes to the Introduction

1. Alan Bray, *Homosexuality in Renaissance England* (New York: Columbia University Press, 1982; with a new afterword, 1995), p. 104.

2. The event, which took place at the church of San Giovanni a Porta Latina in Rome, is recorded by two sources: in 1578 by the Venetian ambassador Antonio Tiepolo, who was in Rome when the ceremony and arrests occurred (and who described the men as Portuguese and Spanish); and in 1580-1581 by the Renaissance scholar Michel de Montaigne, who heard about it upon visiting the city a few years later. See the discussion and sources cited in Louis Crompton, *Homosexuality and Civilization* (Cambridge, MA: Harvard University Press, 2003), pp. 286-287.

3. See John Boswell, *Same-Sex Unions in Premodern Europe* (New York: Random House, 1994); Alan Bray, *The Friend* (Chicago: University of Chicago Press, 2003). See also the discussion below, including the criticisms of Boswell.

4. As will become clear throughout this study, I avoid the word "homosexual" to speak of a type of person because of its pejorative connotations. For the most part, I have tried to use more neutral designators, such as "same-sex relationships"; I have followed contemporary usage in speaking of persons who want to own their same-sex desire as "gay" and/or "lesbian"; I will sometimes use the term "gay" to include both gay men and lesbian women. I will also speak from time to time of "gender-varied persons," which I take to include gay, lesbian, bisexual, and transgender persons. To me, "gender-varied" is a more natural way of speaking than the more technical acronyms

LGBT or GLBT. I should note, of course, that all such terms are contested on all sides of the debate. Some liberationists (see discussion in ch. 2 of viewpoint 6) argue that "gay" is too restrictive. Some prohibitionists (see discussion in ch. 1 of viewpoint 1) refuse to use the term "gay" for fear of legitimating its political connotations; they prefer the term "homosexual," which still carries with it the connotation of the pathological, as explained above. On the use of the term "gay," see Scott Speirs, "Gay," in George E. Haggerty, ed., *Gay Histories and Culture: An Encyclopedia*, vol. 2 of Bonnie Zimmerman and George E. Haggerty, eds., *The Encyclopedia of Gay and Lesbian Histories and Cultures* (New York and London: Garland Publishing, Inc., 2000), pp. 362-363.

5. Some of the best literature on this subject includes Richard D. Mohr, *Gays/Justice: A Study of Ethics, Society, and Law* (New York: Columbia University Press, 1988); Richard A. Posner, *Sex and Reason* (Cambridge, MA, and London: Harvard University Press, 1992), esp. ch. 11; Robert Wintemute, *Sexual Orientation and Human Rights: The United States Constitution, the European Convention, and the Canadian Charter* (Oxford: The Clarendon Press, 1995); Martha C. Nussbaum, *Sex and Social Justice* (New York: Oxford University Press, 2000), esp. ch. 7; William N. Eskridge, Jr., *Gaylaw: Challenging the Apartheid of the Closet* (Cambridge, MA: Harvard University Press, 2002); Daniel R. Pinello, *Gay Rights and American Law* (Cambridge, UK: Cambridge University Press, 2003); Janet R. Jakobsen and Ann Pellegrini, *Love the Sin: Sexual Regulation and the Limits of Religious Tolerance* (New York: New York University Press, 2003; Boston: Beacon Press, 2004).

6. For the gathering argument concerning marriage equality, see Andrew Sullivan, *Virtually Normal: An Argument about Homosexuality* (New York: Alfred A. Knopf, 1995; New York: Vintage Books, 1996); William N. Eskridge, Jr., *Equality Practice: Civil Unions and the Future of Gay Rights* (New York: Routledge, 2001); Andrew Koppelman, *The Gay Rights Question in Contemporary American Law* (Chicago: University of Chicago Press, 2002); Evan Gerstmann, *Same-Sex Marriage and the Constitution* (Cambridge, UK: Cambridge University Press, 2003); Jonathan Rauch, *Gay Marriage: Why It Is Good for Gays, Good for Straights, and Good for America* (New York: Henry Holt, 2004); Evan Wolfson, *Why Marriage Matters: America, Equality, and Gay People's Right to Marry* (New York: Simon and Schuster, 2004); George Chauncey, *Why Marriage? The History Shaping Today's Debate* (New York: Basic Books, 2004); Richard D. Mohr, *The Long Arc of Justice: Lesbian and Gay Marriage, Equality, and Rights* (New York: Columbia University Press, 2005); David G. Myers and Letha Dawson Scanzoni, *What God Has Joined Together: The Christian Case for Gay Marriage* (New York: HarperSanFrancisco, 2005); Jack Rogers, *Jesus, the Bible, and Homosexuality: Explode the Myths, Heal the Church* (Louisville: Westminster John Knox, 2006).

7. The states passing anti-gay-marriage amendments in 2004 were Arkansas, Georgia, Kentucky, Michigan, Mississippi, Montana, North Dakota, Ohio, Oklahoma, Oregon, and Utah. Prior to that, similar constitutional amendments had been enacted in Alaska, Hawaii, Louisiana, Nebraska, Nevada, and Missouri. Subsequently, two more

were passed in Kansas and Texas, making twenty-two states that have added anti-gay-marriage amendments to their constitutions as of the fall of 2005.

8. On April 28, 2004, the world learned of instances of abuse and torture perpetrated at Abu Ghraib prison in Iraq by American soldiers. Although many brushed this off as an aberration, it has since become clear that such mistreatment of prisoners found support at the highest levels of government (see Karen J. Greenburg and Joshua L. Dratel, eds., *The Torture Papers: The Road to Abu Ghraib* [Cambridge, UK: Cambridge University Press, 2005]; see also Mark Danner, *Torture and Truth: America, Abu Ghraib, and the War on Terror* [New York: New York Review of Books, 2005]). About a year later, major magazines and newspapers began publicizing the new American practice of "extraordinary rendition," a secret program carried out by the Central Intelligence Agency under broad authority from the White House to transfer suspected terrorists to foreign countries for forms of interrogation that included physical torture. One example was a man named Mahar Arar, a Syrian-born Canadian citizen whom the American government detained on September 26, 2002, as he was changing flights at Kennedy Airport. Based on the mere fact that Arar had a coworker whose brother was suspected of links with terror, Arar was whisked off to Jordan and then Syria, where he was imprisoned for a year and subjected to severe acts of physical torture. The Syrians concluded that Arar knew nothing (Jane Mayer, "Outsourcing Torture," *The New Yorker,* February 14, 2005). http://www.newyorker.com/fact/content/articles/050214fa_fact6 (posted Feb. 2, 2005; accessed Apr. 2005). Arar was exonerated in Canada and awarded an out-of-court settlement. He has not fared as well in the United States.

9. The first black indentured servants arrived in Jamestown, Virginia, in August 1619. The 13th Amendment, which abolished slavery in the United States, was passed by Congress on January 31, 1865, and ratified by the states on December 6, 1865.

10. Nancy F. Cott, *Public Vows: A History of Marriage and the Nation* (Cambridge, MA: Harvard University Press, 2000), p. 59.

11. Slavery was outlawed by the 13th Amendment (1865), equality granted by the 14th Amendment (1868), and the right to vote declared by the 15th Amendment (1870) to the U.S. Constitution.

12. These racial segregation laws applied in the fifteen former slave-owning states of the South, together with West Virginia and Oklahoma.

13. 163 U.S. 537 (1896). The *Plessy* decision upheld a Louisiana law that required railroads to provide separate but equal rail cars for whites and blacks and made it unlawful for one race to occupy the car of the other. Homer Plessy, who was seven-eighths white and one-eighth black, purchased a train ticket on the East Louisiana Railway and on June 7, 1892, took his seat in a whites-only car. Plessy was testing the law on behalf of a New Orleans–based group, the Citizens' Committee to Test the Constitutionality of the Separate Car Law. Learning of his black lineage, the railroad officials demanded that Plessy move to the "colored only" part of the train. When he refused to leave, Plessy was arrested, tried, convicted, and fined. In a seven-to-one majority opinion

(with one justice not participating), the U.S. Supreme Court argued that the Constitution prohibited slavery but not all distinctions based on race. In a famous dissent, Justice John Marshall Harlan argued that the 13th Amendment, which had banned slavery in the United States, also required the states to eliminate every "badge of servitude" left over from the slavery era: "[I]n view of the Constitution, in the eye of the law, there is in this country no superior, dominant, ruling class of citizens. There is no caste here. Our Constitution is color-blind, and neither knows nor tolerates classes among citizens" (163 U.S. at 555, 559). See Charles Lofgren, *The Plessy Case: A Legal-Historical Interpretation* (New York: Oxford University Press, 1987).

14. Prior to *Brown,* the Court had eliminated restrictive covenants based on race in real estate transactions (*Shelley v. Kraemer,* 334 U.S. 1 [1948]), because such covenants violate the Equal Protection Clause of the 14th Amendment and the Due Process Clause of the 5th Amendment, and had struck down segregation in graduate schools (*McLaurin v. Oklahoma State Regents for Higher Education,* 339 U.S. 637 [1950]), which required that an African American abide by such restrictions as occupying a separate row in class), because it violates equal protection; and it struck down segregation in law schools (*Sweatt v. Painter,* 339 U.S. 629 [1950]) when it found that establishing a separate law school for African Americans so as to deny them admission to the University of Texas violated equal protection.

15. So-called "Brown II," 349 U.S. 294 (1955), provided little in the way of concrete guidance about how to implement desegregation and left the ultimate responsibility to the local school boards, which meant that desegregation occurred slowly, episodically, and mostly ineffectually. In addition, the *Brown* decisions produced a powerful backlash. White flight to the nonblack suburbs became a basic feature of the American social landscape. From 1950 to 1960, the population of the suburbs increased by over 60 percent compared to a single-digit increase for urban areas (see Kenneth T. Jackson, *The Crabgrass Frontier* [New York: Oxford University Press, 1985], p. 238). For an exemplary study on the phenomenon in one southern city, see Kevin M. Kruse, *White Flight: Atlanta and the Making of Modern Conservatism: Politics and Society in Twentieth-Century America* (Princeton, NJ: Princeton University Press, 2005).

16. *Plessy v. Fergusson,* 163 U.S. at 559.

17. Appiah, *The Ethics of Identity,* ch. 1.

18. For example, from 1900 to 1914, some 1,100 lynchings were carried out in the American South.

19. King, Jr., "Letter from Birmingham Jail," April 16, 1963.

20. The number shipped to concentration camps is disputed, ranging from 5,000 to 15,000. For the lower number, see Gunther Grau, "Homosexuals," in Walter Laquer, ed., *The Holocaust Encyclopedia* (New Haven and London: Yale University Press, 2001), pp. 312-314. For the higher number, see Donald Niewyk and Francis Nicosia, *The Columbia Guide to the Holocaust* (New York: Columbia University Press, 2000), pp. 50-51. Most agree that the death rate of those thus consigned was about 60 percent. See also

Richard Plant, *The Pink Triangle: The Nazi War Against Homosexuals* (New York: New Republic Books, 1986); and Frank Rector, *The Nazi Extermination of Homosexuals* (New York: Stein and Day, 1981).

21. George Chauncey, *Why Marriage? The History Shaping Today's Debate over Gay Equality* (Chicago: University of Chicago Press, 2004), pp. 6, 174 n. 3, citing David K. Johnson, *The Lavender Scare: The Cold War Persecution of Gays and Lesbians in the Federal Government* (Chicago: University of Chicago Press, 2004), p. 166. See also John D'Emilio and Estelle B. Freedman, *Intimate Matters: A History of Sexuality in America,* 2nd ed. (Chicago and London: University of Chicago Press, 1997), pp. 295-298.

22. Ten years earlier, a judge reduced the sentence of two men convicted of murdering a gay man in Texas, making comments from the bench to suggest that the identity of a deceased homosexual did not warrant ruining the lives of the heterosexual accused. In a similar case, in 1984, three high school students beat a gay man to the point of unconsciousness in Bangor, Maine, and threw him into a river. The man drowned, but the students were released into the custody of their parents rather than being more severely punished. Ten years prior to that, Richard Heakin, a 21-year-old gay man was beaten to death by four teenagers; the teenagers were given probation but no time in jail. Just as there was a time when many blatantly regarded the life of an African American to be less valuable than that of a white person, the same sort of pernicious calculus has been applied to gays and lesbians.

23. Brandon was born Teena Renae Brandon on December 12, 1972. The story is the subject of the documentary film *The Brandon Teena Story* (1998) as well as the major motion picture *Boys Don't Cry* (1999). Advocates in the gay-lesbian-bisexual-transgender (GLBT) community have objected that these popular portrayals did not fully understand and thus distorted the struggle of transgender persons.

24. In addition to general abuse, 24 percent of gay men and 10 percent of lesbians reported some form of criminal assault on their persons during the previous year (see, generally, Gary Comstock, *Violence Against Lesbians and Gay Men* [New York: Columbia University Press, 1991]).

25. The best source for this is William N. Eskridge, Jr., *Gaylaw: Challenging the Apartheid of the Closet* (Cambridge, MA: Harvard University Press, 1999), pp. 57-97; see also pp. 373-380, which provide detailed records of the arrests in twelve American cities from 1875 to 1965, the reported sodomy cases from 1880 to 1995, the "degenerates" arraigned in New York City courts between 1915 and 1962, and the sex offense arrests in St. Louis from 1874 to 1946.

26. Consider the case of Susan Stemler. One night in Florence, Kentucky, a man named Steve Kritis began screaming at and hitting his girlfriend, Conni Black, in the bar of the Ramada Inn. Both Kritis and Black had been drinking heavily. As the conflict reached a crescendo, Kritis threw Ms. Black into a concrete wall in the hotel lobby, causing her to pass out. When she came to, Ms. Black asked Susan Stemler, whom she had just met that evening, to give her a ride home. Ms. Stemler quickly agreed. As the two

women made their way to the parking lot, however, Kritis pursued them, striking Susan Stemler on the head with a blunt object. Somehow the two women managed to climb into Susan Stemler's car and drive away, but Kritis chased them in his truck, ramming into Stemler's car and attempting to run her off the road. Witnesses called the police, who eventually pulled both vehicles over. A distraught Susan Stemler immediately told the police officers that Kritis had tried to kill her (Conni Black had by this time passed out in Stemler's car). Kritis, for his part, remained in his truck. When approached by one of the officers, Kritis told the man that Susan Stemler was a lesbian who had abducted his girlfriend. Stemler insisted then (and at the trial) that she is not a lesbian; but the officers, upon hearing that she was, arrested Stemler and charged her with driving under the influence of alcohol. They then picked up the unconscious Conni Black and put her in Kritis's truck — and this, even though Kritis himself was intoxicated. The police never asked Kritis to submit to a breathalizer or even to get out of his truck. Watching what was happening, an eyewitness to the events protested to the officers; he was told to mind his own business. Later that evening, Kritis lost control of his truck, and Conni Black was thrown from the vehicle and killed (*Susan Stemler v. City of Florence*, 126 F.3d 856 [6th Cir. 1997], *cert. denied sub nom. City of Florence v. Chipman*, 523 U.S. 1118 [1998]).

27. Consider the long-forgotten case of *Pace v. Alabama*. A black man, Tony Pace, began living with a white woman, Mary J. Cox; each was charged with interracial fornication, each was convicted, and each was imprisoned for two years at hard labor (*Pace v. Alabama*, 106 U.S. 583, 1 S.Ct. 637 [1883]). Under Alabama law in the 1880s, the crime of "living together in adultery or fornication" carried, for a first offense, a minimum fine of $100 and a discretionary prison sentence of no more than 6 months. However, in the case of an interracial couple living together, the sentence was much more severe, carrying a mandatory prison sentence of two years, up to a maximum of seven years. On appeal, Pace and Cox argued that this discrepancy in sentencing based on race violated the Equal Protection Clause. The Supreme Court disagreed, claiming that the equal application of the statute to both blacks and whites fulfilled the requirements of equality under the law. Coming as it did some thirteen years before *Plessy v. Ferguson*, the *Pace* decision was one of the first planks in the legal system that enshrined white supremacy in the South.

28. See, generally, the essays in Werner Sollors, ed., *Interracialism: Black-White Intermarriage in American History, Literature and Law* (Oxford: Oxford University Press, 2000). The word "miscegenation" was apparently coined as a hoax in 1863 to discredit abolitionists and their political supporters in the run-up to the 1864 election. It comes from the Latin *miscere*, meaning "to mix," and *genus*, meaning "species or race." The word appeared in an anonymous pamphlet entitled "Miscegenation: The Theory of the Blending of the Races, Applied to the American White Man and Negro" (New York, 1863), which purported to advocate the mixing of the races and the encouragement of whites and blacks to have children together. Similar to what we have witnessed surrounding the issue of same-sex relationships, this campaign trick obviously played on deep-seated anxieties in the imaginations of white people, anxieties that had existed

since the founding of the nation (see Elise Virginia Lemire, *"Miscegenation": Making Race in America,* New Cultural Series [Philadelphia: University of Pennsylvania Press, 2002]).

29. See Julie Novkov, "Racial Constructions: The Legal Regulation of Miscegenation in Alabama, 1890-1934," 20/2 *Law and History Review* (Summer 2002): 225-277.

30. The first court case to disallow such laws was *Perez v. Lippold,* 198 P.2d 17 (Cal. 1948), which struck down California's statute that prohibited persons of different races to marry (*Loving v. Virginia,* 388 U.S. 1 [1967]).

31. Richard Loving married Mildred Jeter in June 1958; their case was tried in 1959 and was argued before the Supreme Court on April 10, 1967.

32. *Loving v. Virginia,* 388 U.S. 1 (1967).

33. Robert Dworkin, *Taking Rights Seriously* (Cambridge, MA: Harvard University Press, 1977).

34. A classic statement of this principle is found in W. N. Hohfeld, *Fundamental Legal Conceptions as Applied in Judicial Reasoning,* ed. W. W. Cook (1919; reprint, New Haven: Yale University Press, 1964).

35. The U.S. Supreme Court upheld an Illinois law prohibiting a woman from obtaining a law license. In a concurring opinion, Justice Bradley argued: "The natural and proper timidity and delicacy which belongs to the female sex evidently unfits it for many of the occupations of civil life" (*Bradwell v. Illinois,* 83 U.S. 130 [1873]). Chief Justice Salmon P. Chase, who held radical antislavery views, dissented from the decision.

36. Eve Kosofsky Sedgwick, *Epistemology of the Closet* (Berkeley: University of California Press, 1990).

37. The remark was that of Lord Alfred Douglas in "Two Loves," *The Chameleon* 1 (1894): 28 (cited in Sedgwick, *Epistemology of the Closet,* p. 74).

38. The literature on this subject has become much too voluminous to cite in detail. The single best book-length introduction to the subject is Crompton, *Homosexuality and Civilization.* In addition, the following general introductions are must-reads: Kenneth J. Dover, *Greek Homosexuality* (Cambridge, MA: Harvard University Press, 1978; 2nd ed., 1989); John Boswell, *Christianity, Social Tolerance, and Homosexuality* (Chicago: University of Chicago Press, 1980); Lillian Faderman, *Surpassing the Love of Men: Romantic Friendship and Love from the Renaissance to the Present* (New York: Morrow, 1981); David F. Greenberg, *The Construction of Homosexuality* (Chicago and London: University of Chicago Press, 1988); Stephen O. Murray, *Homosexualities* (Chicago and London: University of Chicago Press, 2000). See, generally, Wayne R. Dynes, ed., *The Encyclopedia of Homosexuality,* 2 vols. (Chicago and London: St. James Press, 1990); Zimmerman and Haggerty, eds., *The Encyclopedia of Lesbian and Gay Histories and Cultures,* 2 vols.

39. The word was invented by a hermit named Peter Damian to address sexual infractions committed by clerics. It was then taken up by Thomas Aquinas in the 13th century to refer to any sexual acts that "violate nature" by being unreproductive in

kind. The definitive work examining the evolution of this term is Mark D. Jordan, *The Invention of Sodomy in Christian Theology* (Chicago: University of Chicago Press, 1997).

40. Michael Rocke, *Forbidden Friendships: Homosexuality and Male Culture in Renaissance Florence*, Studies in the History of Sexuality (Oxford: Oxford University Press, 1996). In Florence, which had experienced a resurgence of interest in classical antiquity, the sexual encounters mimicked the pederasty of the Greco-Roman world. That is, they were casual encounters, sometimes for money, in which adult males assumed a dominant sexual role with adolescent boys who were passive. There is also evidence of more-long-term relationships, but these were rare.

41. Examining a wealth of data, including works of literature, journal entries, letters, memoirs, and other archival evidence, Faderman traces the origins of these female same-sex friendships back to the revival of platonic notions of love in the Renaissance. Such friendships reached their height in the eighteenth century, as documented not only in archival evidence but also in the romantic literature of the day. Though it is not clear that women themselves viewed their relationships in this way, men rationalized romantic love between women as an appropriate preparation for marital love with men. Some men also considered any overtly sexual love between women to be trivial. For Europe, see Faderman, *Surpassing the Love of Men: Romantic Friendship and Love from the Renaissance to the Present* (1981); for the United States, see Faderman, *Odd Girls and Twilight Lovers: A History of Lesbian Life in Twentieth-Century America* (New York: Columbia University Press, 1991).

42. Faderman, *Surpassing the Love of Men*, pp. 120-125. Faderman points out that love between women was not threatening to men because many men assumed that sexual love between two women was physically impossible (*Surpassing the Love of Man*, p. 33).

43. In addition to Faderman, see the painstaking work of Valerie Traub on female homoeroticism in seventeenth-century arts and Martha Vicinus's portraits of intimate female friendship in the nineteenth century (Traub, *The Renaissance of Lesbianism in Early Modern England* [Cambridge, UK: Cambridge University Press, 2002]; Vicinus, *Intimate Friends: Women Who Loved Women, 1778-1928* [Chicago: University of Chicago Press, 2004]). One notable example of women whose relationship was clearly sexual was the "marriage" between Anne Lister and Ann Walker in Yorkshire in the early 1800s (see Vicinus, *Intimate Friends*, pp. 18-30).

44. Bray, *The Friend*. My perspective on this book has been informed by the excellent review by James Davidson, "Mr. and Mr. and Mrs. and Mrs.," *London Review of Books*, 27/11 (June 2, 2005).

45. The primary evidence was the liturgy of *adelphopoiēsis*, or brother-making, which Boswell saw as analogous to Eastern Orthodox ceremonies of marriage (see Boswell, *Same-Sex Unions in Premodern Europe*).

46. Of the many trenchant critiques of Boswell, including claims that he misrepresented the nature of his sources, I shall cite just a few: Claudia Rapp, "Ritual Brother-

hood in Byzantium," *Traditio* 52 (1997): 285-326; Brent D. Shaw, "Ritual Brotherhood in Roman and Post-Roman Societies, *Traditio* 52 (1997): 327-355; Shaw, "A Groom of One's Own?" *The New Republic* 211 (July 18-24, 1994): 33-41; Ralph Hexter and Brent D. Shaw, "Samesex Unions in Premodern Europe: An Exchange," *The New Republic* 211 (Oct. 3, 1994): 39-41; Robin Darling Young, "Gay Marriage: Reimagining Church History," *First Things* 47 (Nov. 1, 1994): 43-48.

47. Bray, *The Friend*, pp. 289-305.

48. *The Friend*, p. 293.

49. Bray, *Homosexuality in Renaissance England*.

50. Compton, *Homosexuality and Civilization*, pp. 213-244; Bret Hinsch, "China," in *Encyclopedia of Homosexuality*, 1:215-20.

51. Gary P. Leupp, *Male Colors: The Construction of Homosexuality in Tokugawa Japan* (Berkeley: University of California Press, 1997); see also Ihara Saikaku, *The Great Mirror of Male Love* (Palo Alto, CA: Stanford University Press, 1990).

52. See, generally, Stephen O. Murray et al., *Islamic Homosexualities: Culture, History, and Literature* (New York: New York University Press, 1997); Arno Schmitt and Jehoeda Sofer, *Sexuality and Eroticism Among Males in Moslem Societies* (Binghamton, NY: Haworth Press, 1991).

53. See, generally, José Ignacio Cabezón, *Buddhism, Sexuality, and Gender* (Albany: State University of New York Press, 1992).

54. Lingananda, "India," in Dynes, ed., *The Encyclopedia of Homosexuality*, pp. 586-593.

55. The *napumsaka* is a man "who is not a man" and who enjoys same-sex eroticism; and the *nari shandi* is an infertile woman "who has not breasts" (Sandip Roy, "Hinduism," and Michael J. Sweet, "India," in Zimmerman and Haggerty, eds., *Gay Histories and Cultures*, pp. 438, 466-467).

56. Roy, "Hinduism," p. 438.

57. "Hinduism," pp. 438-439.

58. Will Roscoe, *Changing Ones: Third and Fourth Genders in Native North America* (New York: St. Martin's Press, 1986; New York: Palgrave Macmillan, 2000); Walter L. Williams, *The Spirit and the Flesh: Sexual Diversity in American Indian Culture* (Boston: Beacon Press, 1986).

59. Stephen O. Murray and Will Roscoe, eds., *Boy-Wives and Female Husbands* (New York: Palgrave Macmillan, 1998).

60. A somewhat similar delineation is employed by Murray, *Homosexualities*, pp. 1-21. Murray is adapting a fourfold typology of age-structured, gender-defined, profession-defined, and egalitarian derived from Barry Adam, "Age, Structure, and Sexuality," *Journal of Homosexuality* 11 (1986): 19-33.

61. See Gilbert H. Herdt, *Guardians of the Flutes*, vol. 1, *Idioms of Masculinity* (Chicago: University of Chicago Press, 1994); see also Herdt, ed., *Ritualized Homosexuality in Melanesia* (Berkeley: University of California Press, 1984).

62. The classic text remains Dover, *Greek Homosexuality*.

63. James Davidson, *The Greeks and Greek Love: A Radical Reappraisal of Homosexuality in Ancient Greece* (London: Weidenfield and Nicholson, 2007).

64. Thus the *eromenos* needed to be coaxed and played "hard to get" in order not to be equated with a woman or a prostitute.

65 The classic study, originally published in 1983, is Amy Richlin, *The Garden of Priapus: Sexuality and Aggression in Roman Humor* (Oxford: Oxford University Press, 1992).

66. Marilyn B. Skinner, *Sexuality in Greek and Roman Culture* (Oxford: Blackwell, 2005), p. 197.

67. For photographs and analysis of the Warren Cup, see John R. Clarke, *Roman Sex: 100 BC–AD 250* (New York: Harry M. Abrams, 2003), pp. 77-91.

68. Richlin, *The Garden of Priapus*, p. 226.

69. The term "homosexual" was originally coined in 1869 by Károly Mária Kertbeny, a German-Hungarian writer (Manfred Herzer, "Károly Mária Kertbeny [Karl Maria Benkert; 1824-1882]," in *The Encyclopedia of Homosexuality*, 1:659-660). From the late nineteenth century forward, Western society ceased to think solely about homosexual acts and thought of the homosexual as a type of person, or as Michel Foucault put it, a "species" (Foucault, *The History of Sexuality*, vol. 1). See also David M. Halperin, *One Hundred Years of Homosexuality and Other Essays on Greek Love* (New York: Routledge, 1990).

70. For a survey of homoerotic practices in diverse civilizations, see Murray, *Homosexualities*. For a more clinical approach to the data, see Alan P. Bell and Martin S. Weinberg, *Homosexualities: A Study of Diversity Among Men and Women*, An Official Publication of The Institute for Sex Research founded by Alfred C. Kinsey (New York: Simon and Schuster, 1978).

71. Francis Mark Mondimore, *A Natural History of Homosexuality* (Baltimore and London: Johns Hopkins University Press, 1996), p. 85.

72. The scale is as follows: 0 = exclusively heterosexual; 1 = predominantly heterosexual (only incidentally homosexual); 2 = predominantly heterosexual (more than incidentally homosexual); 3 = equally heterosexual and homosexual; 4 = predominantly homosexual (more than incidentally heterosexual); 5 = predominantly homosexual (only incidently heterosexual); 6 = exclusively homosexual (Alfred Kinsey, Wardell B. Pomeroy, and Clyde E. Martin, *Sexual Behavior in the Human Male* [Philadelphia: W. B. Saunders Co., 1948], p. 638).

73. Kinsey et al., *Sexual Behavior in the Human Male;* Kinsey, Pomeroy, Martin, and Paul H. Gebhard, *Sexual Behavior in the Human Female* (Philadelphia: W. B. Saunders Co., 1953).

74. Evelyn Hooker, "The Adjustment of the Male Overt Homosexual," *Journal of Projective Techniques* 21 (1957): 18-31; also published in *Mattachine Review* (Dec. 1957):

32-39, and (Jan. 1958): 4-11; for a discussion of Hooker's work, see Mondimore, *A Natural History of Homosexuality*, pp. 89-95.

75. See Bell and Weinberg, *Homosexualities*, pp. 139-228. Bell and Weinberg found that "close-coupled" and "functional" homosexuals did not differ significantly from heterosexual counterparts and in some cases were more well adjusted (p. 218).

76. *Diagnostic and Statistical Manual of Mental Disorders II*, American Psychiatric Association (1973). The American Psychological Association followed suit in 1975.

77. The decision was, in effect, an endorsement of the approach taken by the American Law Institute in its Model Penal Code, 213.2.

78. See the discussion of sexual identity formation in Mondimore, *A Natural History of Homosexuality*, pp. 159-192.

79. Richard A. Isay, M.D., *Becoming Gay: The Journey to Self-Acceptance* (New York: Henry Holt and Company, 1996).

80. For an example of a work that seeks the lowest conceivable numbers, though it recognizes that numbers alone do not decide the moral debate, see Stanton L. Jones and Mark A. Yarhouse, *Homosexuality: The Use of Scientific Research in the Church's Moral Debate* (Downers Grove, IL: InterVarsity Press, 2000), pp. 31-46.

81. Edward O. Laumann, John H. Gagnon, Robert T. Mitchell, and Stuart Michaels, *The Social Organization of Sexuality* (Chicago: University of Chicago Press, 1994). The study came out of the National Opinion Research Center at the University of Chicago. A companion volume, written for a lay audience, is also available: Laumann, Gagnon, Michaels, and Gina Kolata, *Sex in America: A Definitive Survey* (Boston: Little, Brown and Company, 1994).

82. J. L. King, *On the Down Low: A Journey in the Lives of "Straight" Black Men Who Sleep with Men* (New York: Broadway, 2004); Keith Boykin, *Beyond the Down Low: Sex, Lies, and Denial in Black America* (Berkeley, CA: Carroll and Graf, 2005). One of the issues in the African American community is the risk of HIV infection among women living with men who are on the "down low" (see Brenda Stone Browder, *On the Up and Up: A Survival Guide for Women Living with Men on the Down Low* [New York: Dafina Books, 2005]).

83. Elisabeth Kirtsoglou, *For the Love of Women: Identity and Same-sex Relations in a Provincial Greek Town* (London: Routledge, 2004).

84. The figure of 4.3 million is based on the data from the 1994 National Opinion Research Center survey that 1.51 percent of Americans have self-identified as gay, lesbian, or bisexual.

85. Laumann et al., *Sex in America: A Definitive Survey*, p. 176.

86. William D. Mosher, Anjani Chandra, and Jo Jones, "Sexual Behavior and Selected Health Measures: Men and Women 15-44 Years of Age, United States, 2002," *Advanced Data from Vital and Health Statistics*, Center for Disease Control, No. 362, Sept. 15, 2005, p. 32. Available at: http://www.cdc.gov/nchs/data/ad/ad362.pdf. http://www.cdc.gov/nchs/products/pubs/pubd/ad/361-370/ad362.htm (accessed Oct. 2, 2005).

87. Gerulf Rieger, Meredith L. Chivers, and J. Michael Bailey, "Sexual Arousal Patterns of Bisexual Men," *Psychological Science* 16/8 (Aug. 2005): 579-584. The study was conducted jointly by Northwestern University and the Center for Addiction and Mental Health in Toronto.

88. The results of this test do not mean that men who claim to be bisexual are being dishonest. They may well experience attraction to both sexes, since romantic attraction is broader and more complex than mere physical arousal. On this point, see Benedict Carey, "Straight, Gay or Lying? Bisexuality Revisited," *New York Times, Science Times,* Tuesday, July 5, 2005, F1, F6.

89. Mosher et al., "Sexual Behavior and Selected Health Measures," p. 32.

90. Mosher et al., "Sexual Behavior and Selected Health Measures," p. 33.

91. *Report of the American Psychological Association Task Force on Appropriate Therapeutic Responses to Sexual Orientation* (Washington, DC: American Psychological Association, 2009).

92. See Stanton L. Jones and Mark A. Yarhouse, *Ex-Gay? A Longitudinal Study of Religiously Mediated Change in Sexual Orientation* (Downers Grove, IL: InterVarsity Press, 2007), p. 369. This is a study of subjects who participated in The Exodus Project, a reparative therapy ministry. In this study only 15 percent of those seeking religiously mediated sexual orientation change therapy reported a successful "conversion." But even regarding these, it is not clear that the results were enduring. Another 23 percent were able to achieve a stance of celibacy. The rest had various degrees of response ranging from lessening of same-sex attraction to outright failure. In short, change may be possible for a few, but for most the possibility of enduring change remains unlikely.

93. Investigations into the impact of postnatal hormones have been less promising.

94. The region in question is the interstitial nuclei of the anterior hypothalamus, also known as INAH. INAH3 is larger in men than in women.

95. For an account of this research, see Dean Hamer and Peter Copeland, *The Science of Desire: The Search for the Gay Gene and the Biology of Behavior* (New York: Simon and Schuster, 1994).

96. This point is made by psychologists Jones and Yarhouse in *Homosexuality: The Use of Scientific Research in the Church's Moral Debate,* p. 81.

97. Sven Bocklandt, "Extreme Skewing of X Chromosome Inactivation in Mothers of Homosexual Men," *Human Genetics* 118/6 (Feb. 2006): 691-694.

98. My reflections in this paragraph are very much influenced by Mondimore, *A Natural History of Homosexuality,* esp. pp. 147-157. For the comparison of sexual orientation to learning one's own native language, see Mondimore, *A Natural History of Homosexuality,* pp. 149-153.

99. For what follows, see the illuminating article by Janet E. Halley, "Sexual Orientation and the Politics of Biology: A Critique of the Argument from Immutability," 46/3 *Stanford Law Review* (Feb. 1994): 503-568. This article is excerpted in William N.

Eskridge Jr. and Nan Hunter, *Sexuality, Gender, and the Law* (Westbury, NY: The Foundation Press, 1997), pp. 267-71. The article relies on a typology developed by Carole S. Vance, "Social Construction Theory: Problems in the History of Sexuality," in Dennis Altman, Carole S. Vance, et al., eds., *Homosexuality, Which Homosexuality?* (Amsterdam: Schorer Boeken, 1989), pp. 13-34.

100. Judith Butler, *Gender Trouble,* 10th ann. ed. (New York: Routledge, 1999).

101. This case has been brilliantly argued by Edward Stein, *The Mismeasure of Desire: The Science, Theory, and Ethics of Sexual Orientation* (New York: Oxford University Press, 1999). Stein questions efforts to reduce sexual orientation either to nature or to nurture, arguing instead that there are multiple factors that affect a person's sexual desires.

102. See Jakobsen and Pellegrini, *Love the Sin.*

103. Gerstmann, *Same Sex Marriage and the Constitution,* p. 23.

104. These benefits were compiled by the General Accounting Office pursuant to debate over the so-called "Defense of Marriage Act" ("DOMA"). The original number of benefits (1,049) compiled in 1997 was later updated to 1,138 (see "Defense of Marriage Act: Update to Prior Report," GAO-04-353R, Feb. 24, 2004).

105. Because society has so much at stake in marriage, it must be entered into freely and without coercion or fraud. For the protection of the parties, states regulate who may enter into a marriage. Usually there is an age requirement, which is premised on the concept that, under a certain age, the consent of the person is not truly free. In most cases, persons between the ages of sixteen and eighteen must receive the consent of a parent or guardian. Close blood relatives may not marry, a rule that exists for the protection of the parties and for the prevention of birth defects.

106. Factors that figure into a divorce proceeding include such things as adultery, physical or mental cruelty, attempted murder, desertion (whether physical or sexual), habitual drunkenness or drug abuse, insanity, impotence, or venereal disease. The grounds for divorce differ from state to state. The factors I am listing here are generic in character. See, generally, Jeff Atkinson et al., *The American Bar Association Guide to Family Law* (New York: Three Rivers Press, 1996), pp. 68-69.

107. The equal rights amendment in the state of Washington provides as follows: "Equality of rights and responsibility under the law shall not be denied or abridged on account of sex." A similar provision was drafted in 1921 by Alice Paul and introduced in the U.S. Congress in 1923, and each year thereafter, until it finally was enacted in 1972. The federal Equal Rights Amendment fell three states short of the 38 states needed to ratify the amendment and make it a part of the U.S. Constitution; see Jane Manbridge, *Why We Lost the ERA* (Chicago: University of Chicago Press, 1986).

108. *Singer v. Barwick,* 11 Wash. App. 247, 522 P. 2d 1187, *review denied,* 84 Wash. 2d 1008 (1974).

109. See Joyce Murdoch and Deb Price, *Courting Justice: Gay Men and Lesbians v. the Supreme Court* (New York: Basic Books, 2002), pp. 189-193. Singer lost in the Court

of Appeals, which approved of Singer being fired for "flaunting his homosexual way of life"; but the U.S. Supreme Court vacated the decision on the grounds that the Civil Service Commission in 1975 had enacted new rules to end its ban on persons who were gay (*Singer v. United States Civil Service Commission,* 530 F.2d 247 [9th Cir. 1976], vacated 429 U.S. 1034 [1977]).

110. Eskridge, *Equality Practice,* p. 6, citing Grace Lichtenstein, "Homosexual Weddings Stir Controversy," *The New York Times,* Apr. 27, 1975.

111. Eskridge, *Equality Practice,* pp. 6-7.

112. The most often-cited article claiming that gay or lesbian parents are bad for children is by Brigham Young University law professor Lynn Wardle, "The Potential Impact of Homosexual Parenting on Children," 1997/3 *University of Illinois Law Review* (1997): 833-920. Wardle would have the law erect a rebuttable presumption that having homosexual parents is not in the best interests of the child. Among other problems with Wardle's argument is the fact that he relies uncritically on discredited findings about gays and lesbians by Paul Cameron (see Paul Cameron and Kirk Cameron, "Homosexual Parents," *Adolescence* 31 [1996]: 757-776). These "findings" have been so discredited, in fact, that Cameron has been dismissed from the American Psychological Association and censured by the American Sociological Association. For a critique of Wardle, see Carlos Ball and Janice Farrell Pea, "Warring with Wardle: Social Science, Morality, and Gay and Lesbian Parents," 1998/2 *University of Illinois Law Review* (1998): 253-339. See also Wardle's response, in which he argues that it is fair to make gays and lesbians prove they will be good parents (Lynn Wardle, "Fighting with Phantoms: A Reply to Warring with Wardle," 1998/2 *University of Illinois Law Review* [1998]: 629-641). The problem is that Wardle proceeds by way of prejudice, basically assuming that all gays and lesbians are bad parents — an assumption that the facts do not bear out and an assumption we do not make about heterosexual parents. In fact, there is some evidence that having two lesbian parents is better for a child than having a single parent (e.g., Patricia J. Falk, "Lesbian Mothers: Psychological Assumptions in Family Law," *American Psychologist* 44 [1989]: 941-947). A summary of the research findings concerning gay and lesbian parents is provided by University of Virginia professor Charlotte J. Patterson, "Lesbian and Gay Parenting," American Psychological Association (2005), http://www.apa.org/pi/parent.html (accessed Oct. 16, 2005); see her earlier survey: Patterson, "Adoption of Minor Children by Lesbian and Gay Adults: A Social Science Perspective," *Duke Journal of Law and Policy* 2/1 (1995): 195-205. Much of the literature is discussed and some of it excerpted in Eskridge and Hunter, *Sexuality, Gender, and the Law,* pp. 1182-1188.

113. For this reason, among others, the American Academy of Pediatrics, a physician organization seeking to promote the health and well-being of children, has supported adoption by gays and lesbians, including second-parent adoption (American Pediatric Association Committee on Psycho-social Aspects of Child and Family Health, "Technical Report: Co-parent or Second-parent Adoption by Same-sex Parents," *Pedi-*

atrics 109 [Feb. 2002]: 341-344). The same is true of the American Psychological Association: see *Lesbian and Gay Parenting: A Resource for Psychologists,* American Psychological Association (1996).

114. Judith Stacey and Timothy Biblarz, "(How) Does Sexual Orientation of Parents Matter?" *American Sociological Review* 66 (Apr. 2001): 159-183.

115. Fiona Tasker and Susan Golombok, *Growing Up in a Lesbian Family: Effects on Child Development* (New York: Guilford Publications, 1997). This study comprised 25 children raised by lesbians and 20 raised in heterosexual homes; of the former, 14 of 22 were open to having a homoerotic experience, compared to 3 out of 18 of the latter. The women raised by lesbians did have a higher instance (24 percent) than others of enjoying a homoerotic experience.

116. J. Michael Bailey, David Bobrow, Marilyn Wolfe, and Sarah Mikach, *Developmental Psychology* 31/1 (1995): 124-129.

117. Often the rationale used was that the gay or lesbian parent was presumptively a criminal because he or she was violating the state antisodomy law. A frequently cited case in this regard is *Bottoms v. Bottoms,* 249 Va. 410, 457 S.E.2d 102 (1995): in this case, Sharon Bottoms lost custody of her two-year-old son based in part on the fact that her sexual conduct was illegal; instead, the child was placed in the care of a grandparent. Now that antisodomy laws have been ruled unconstitutional in the case of consenting adults, this rationale no longer applies. See *Lawrence v. Texas,* 539 U.S. 558, 579 (2003), and the discussion in ch. 4 of this book.

118. Outright prohibitions are in place in Florida and Mississippi (Florida Statutes, §63.042 [2005] prohibiting "homosexuals"; Mississippi Code Annotated, §93-17-3(2) [2005] prohibiting "same-sex couples"). Utah prohibits adoption by anyone cohabiting in a relationship other than a state-recognized marriage (Utah Code 378B-6-117 [2008]). A number of states prevent second-parent adoption by a same-sex partner. For updated information on state laws, see www.lambdalegal.com.

119. See *Lofton v. Kearney,* 157 F.Supp.2d 1372 (SD Fla. 2001).

120. See *Lofton v. Sec'y of the Dep't of Children and Family Services,* 358 F.3d 804 (11th Cir. 2004). The U.S. Supreme Court refused to hear the appeal on Jan. 10, 2005: http://www.supremecourtus.gov/orders/courtorders/011005pzor.pdf.

121. *Fla. Dept. of Children & Families v. X.X.G.,* Florida Third District Court of Appeals (2010), decision obtainable at: http://www.3dca.flcourts.org/opinions/3D08-3044.pdf.

122. *Cole v. Arkansas,* The Supreme Court of Arkansas, No. 10-840, April 7, 2011.

123. *Baehr v. Lewin,* 852 P.2d 44 (Haw. 1993). The phrase "presumed to be" is important because, as I explain in more detail below, the court sent the case to trial to allow the state to prove the law constitutional by showing that it had a compelling reason for excluding gays and lesbians from marriage.

124. *Baehr v. Lewin,* 852 P.2d at 57.

125. In some ways this rationale was dictated by the laws of Hawaii themselves.

The pertinent provision of the Hawaii Constitution provides: "No person shall . . . be denied the equal protection of the laws, nor be denied the enjoyment of the person's civil rights or be discriminated against in the exercise thereof because of race, sex, or ancestry" (Hawaii Constitution, Article 1, §5).

126. In other words, the court rendered no opinion concerning the status of gay and lesbian people per se. As Evan Gerstmann has perceptively observed, "To rule in favor of the gay and lesbian plaintiffs, the *Baehr* court first had to render their homosexuality invisible" (*Same Sex Marriage and the Constitution,* p. 61).

127. Some 34 states between 1995 and 2001.

128. One of the worries was that the Full Faith and Credit Clause of the Constitution would require gay marriages from some states to be recognized in all states — even those with a majority opposed to such marriages. Regarding the definition of "marriage," the law (Defense of Marriage Act, Public Law No. 104-199, 110 Stat. 2419, 1. U.S.C. §7) provides:

> In determining the meaning of any Act of Congress, or of any ruling, regulation, or interpretation of the various administrative bureaus and agencies of the United States, the word "marriage" means only a legal union between one man and one woman as husband and wife and the word "spouse" refers only to a person of the opposite gender who is a husband and wife.

Regarding the choice-of-law, it stipulates:

> No State, territory, or possession of the United States, or Indian tribe, shall be required to give effect to any public act, record, or judicial proceeding of any other State, territory, possession, or tribe respecting a relationship between persons of the same sex that is treated as a marriage under the laws of such other State, territory, possession, or tribe, or a right or claim arising from such relationship.

A serious case can be made that DOMA's choice-of-laws section in fact violates the Full Faith and Credit Clause of the Constitution. In addition, the intent of the act would seem to run afoul of the standard in *Romer v. Evans* that a law not be enacted based solely on an animus against gay people. See the discussions in chs. 4 and 5 of this book.

129. The amendment, which passed by a 2-1 margin, provides: "The legislature shall have the power to reserve marriage to opposite-sex couples" (Hawaii Constitution, Article 1, §23).

130. Hawaii Revised Statutes, §431-10A (1997). For a more complete discussion, see Eskridge, *Equality Practice,* pp. 24-25.

131. Eskridge and Hunter, *Sexuality, Gender, and the Law,* p. 1129.

132. Martha Nussbaum, *Sex and Social Justice* (New York: Oxford University Press, 2000), p. 184.

133. *Romer v. Evans,* 517 U.S. 620 (1996).

134. I date this usage from the 1970s because, prior to that time, there were no

Slavery and Society at Rome: Key Themes in Ancient History (Cambridge, UK: Cambridge University Press, 1994).

17. John R. W. Stott, *Homosexual Partnerships? Why Same-sex Relationships Are Not a Christian Option* (Downers Grove, IL: InterVarsity Press, 1985). The continuing importance of Stott's legacy of preaching and more than forty books on the evangelical world was noted recently by David Brooks, "Who Is John Stott?" *The New York Times,* Op-Ed, Nov. 30, 2004, A23.

18. There is a massive literature on this subject. Some useful surveys of Europe include David Kertzer and Marzio Barbagli, eds., *The History of the European Family,* 3 vols. (New Haven: Yale University Press, 2001-2003); Jack Goody, *The European Family: A Historical Anthropological Essay: The Making of Europe* (Oxford: Blackwell Publishers, 2000); André Burguière et al., eds., *A History of the Family,* trans. Sarah Hanbury Tenison, 2 vols. (Cambridge, MA: Harvard University Press, 1996). For the transformation of family life in America, see Nancy Cott, *Public Vows: A History of Marriage and the Nation* (Cambridge, MA: Harvard University Press, 2000); Hendrik Hartzog, *Man and Wife in America: A History* (Cambridge, MA: Harvard University Press, 2000).

19. The work of Peter Laslett has demonstrated, for example, that in England the nuclear family appeared much earlier than had been thought, preceding the industrial revolution. Originally published in 1965, the most recent edition of his work is *The World We Have Lost: Further Explored,* 4th rev. ed. (New York: Routledge, 2004).

20. This argument is made brilliantly by Stephen Macedo, "Homosexuality and the Conservative Mind," 84 *Georgetown Law Journal* 261-300 (1995).

21. Many people make this argument. One example may be found in Stanley J. Grenz, *Welcoming but Not Affirming: An Evangelical Response to Homosexuality* (Louisville: Westminster John Knox Press, 1998), pp. 107-109.

22. People who use this argument about the inherent excellence of heterosexual union counter that rape is wrong because of an *absence* of "intent" and "commitment"; but if this is so, then the *presence* of such "intent" and "commitment" on the part of exclusively committed same-sex persons ought to qualify them for similar moral praise.

23. I am intrigued by the argument of Michel Foucault that modern culture does not strive to repress sexuality, but just the opposite: that our society is constantly drawing attention to it. Indeed, people are incited to think about it and talk about it, and none engage more in this incitement than the prohibitionists (Foucault, "Introduction," *History of Sexuality,* vol. 1, trans. Robert Hurley [New York: Random House, 1990]; see also Foucault, "Afterword: The Subject and the Power," in *Beyond Structuralism and Hermeneutics,* ed. Hubert L. Dreyfus and Paul Rabinow [Chicago: University of Chicago Press, 1982]). One theoretical question is whether fascination with sex produced the modern science of sexuality, or whether the science of sexuality made possible our current preoccupation with sex (see Arnold I. Davidson, *The Emergence of Sexuality: Histor-*

19th- or 20th-century statutes that treated sodomy as a homosexual-only crime. The best source on this is George Chauncey et al., *The Historians' Brief,* Case 01-102, *John Geddes Lawrence and Tyron Gardner v. State of Texas.*

135. A definitive 1990 study showed that over 75 percent of men, and almost 70 percent of women, had experienced oral sex in their lifetimes. For more than 25 percent of them, oral sex was their most recent sexual event. The younger the person surveyed, the higher the percentage. Thus, for example, 85 percent of men and almost 80 percent of women in the 25- to 29-year-old bracket in 1990 had experienced oral sex. The information may be found in Laumann et al., *The Social Organization of Sexuality.* In a more recent (2002) study, the figures were significantly higher: in the age group of 25- to 44-year-olds, 90 percent of men had experienced oral sex with a woman, and 88 percent of women had experienced oral sex with a man.

136. *Baker v. State of Vermont,* 170 Vt. 194, 744 A.2d 864 (1999).

137. *Goodridge v. Department of Public Health,* 440 Mass. 309, 798 NE2d 941 (2003).

Notes to Chapter One

1. Oliver O'Donovan, "Homosexuality in the Church: Can There Be a Fruitful Debate?" in Timothy Bradshaw, ed., *The Way Forward: Christian Voices on Homosexuality and the Church,* 2nd ed. (Grand Rapids: Eerdmans, 2003), p. 28.

2. Elizabeth Stuart, *Gay and Lesbian Theologies: Repetitions with Critical Difference* (Hampshire, UK: Ashgate Publishing Limited, 2003), p. 105. Stuart, who is a long-time advocate for gay and lesbian concerns in Great Britain, argues that the impasse is the result of the theological inadequacy on both sides of the debate. Her book seeks to reframe gay and lesbian theologies more directly within the traditional language of the church.

3. I first began working on this typology for a presentation in Austin, Texas, in 1993. Other typologies have been offered, but I am not aware of one that approaches the subject as this one does — that is, through the lens of creation, reconciliation, redemption. For an illuminating fourfold political typology with a constructive fifth position, see Andrew Sullivan, *Virtually Normal: An Argument about Homosexuality* (New York: Alfred A. Knopf, 1995; New York: Vintage, 1996). For a fivefold ethical typology, see Patricia Beattie Jung and Ralph F. Smith, *Heterosexism: An Ethical Challenge* (Albany: State University of New York Press, 1994), pp. 22-30. For a sixfold typology with some affinities with the present study, see L. R. Holben, *What Christians Think about Homosexuality: Six Representative Viewpoints* (North Richland Hills, TX: Bibal Press, 1999). I have been informed by all three of these typologies in refining my approach over the years.

4. Other words that point to this reconciliation include "atonement," "ransom,"

"victory," and "transformation." For a convenient summary of these various ways of conceiving the significance of Jesus Christ, see Jaroslav Pelikan, *Jesus Through the Centuries: His Place in the History of Culture* (New Haven and London: Yale University Press, 1985).

5. See, for example, 1 Thess. 5:8; Rom. 5:10, 8:23, 13:11; Phil. 1:19; Eph. 4:30; Col. 1:22; Heb. 9:28.

6. To avoid confusion, we need to remember that the work of creation, reconciliation, and redemption is the work of all three "persons" of the one God — "Father, Son, and Holy Spirit." Yet the focal point of each of the three — creation, reconciliation, and redemption — is God, Christ, and Spirit. Without intending to separate the work of God, we can say that God loves us; God saves us in Christ; and God empowers us by the Spirit to be what God would have us be. For more on creation, reconciliation, and redemption, see William Stacy Johnson, *The Mystery of God: Karl Barth and the Postmodern Foundations of Theology* (Louisville: Westminster John Knox, 1997).

7. Andrew Sullivan gives a rendition of the prohibitionist type in *Virtually Normal*, pp. 19-55.

8. Regarding gay teachers, see *Acanfora v. Board of Education of Montgomery County*, 491 F.2d 498 (4th Cir. 1973), *cert. denied* 419 U.S. (1974); *Gaylord v. Tacoma School District*, 88 Wn. 286, 559 P.2d 1340, *cert. denied* 434 U.S. 879 (1977); *National Gay Task Force v. Board of Education of Oklahoma City*, 729 F. 2d 1270, *cert. denied* 470 U.S. 903 (1985). Regarding gays in the military, see the so-called "don't ask, don't tell" policy, which is codified at 10 U.S.C. §654. Regarding the Boy Scouts, see *Boy Scouts of America v. Dale*, 530 U.S. 640 (2000).

9. They are Deut. 23:17-18, which may refer to male cult prostitution; and two parallel accounts of attempted male-on-male gang rape: first, the gentile men of Sodom (Gen. 18–19); second, the Jewish men of Gibeah (Judg. 19–21). In this cluster of texts, the biblical passage clearly condemns a certain form of conduct, but in each case there is something besides the same-sex character of the conduct that makes it bad. If Deut. 23:17-18 refers to male-on-male cult prostitution, it is wrong for the same reason that male-on-female cult prostitution would be wrong, namely, that it involves the idolatrous worship of other gods.

10. In the past decade or so, a group of Roman Catholic natural law thinkers has espoused this view vigorously. This group draws inspiration from the Catholic theologian Germain Grisez, formerly of Georgetown University and now of Mount St. Mary's College and Seminary in Emmitsburg, Maryland (see Grisez, *The Way of the Lord Jesus*, vol. 2 of *Living a Christian Life* [Quincy, IL: Franciscan Press, 1993]). Although heavily influenced by theological commitments, the arguments of these "new natural lawyers" are cast in a philosophical framework that is designed to influence public policy. Still, the emphasis on organic fellowship draws implicitly from the well of Roman Catholic sacramental theology. The sex act in marriage is a physical sign of a spiritual grace. The implication drawn from this is that sex between two men or two women does not par-

take of the intrinsic sacramental goodness of marital sex. Thus, sex outs is always wrong: by its very nature it cannot achieve such a reproductiv one engages in sex with an openness to procreation, then one is merely of another for one's own pleasure. Representative texts include John M. *Law and Natural Rights* (Oxford: Clarendon Press, 1980); Gerard V. Br ert P. George, "Marriage and the Liberal Imagination," 84 *Georgetown L* 320 (1995); Robert P. George, *The Clash of Orthodoxies: Law, Religion, Crisis* (Wilmington, DE: ISI Books, 2001). The best critique of this m phen Macedo, "Homosexuality and the Conservative Mind," 84 *George nal* 261-300 (1995).

11. Robert George's definition sums this up succinctly: "Marria one-flesh communion of persons that is consummated and actualized reproductive in type, whether or not they are reproductive in effect. union of spouses in marital acts is the biological matrix of their marri level relationship: that is, a relationship that unites persons at the bo dispositional, and spiritual levels of their being" (George, *The Clash* p. 77). For a contrary view, see ch. 3 of this book, where I present the b that the trope "one flesh" in Genesis more properly signifies "one fam

12. Thomas Aquinas, *Summa Theologiae*, vol. 43, 2a2ae, 153-154.

13. Joseph Cardinal Ratzinger, *Letter to the Bishops of the Catholi Pastoral Care of Homosexual Persons*, Documents of the Congregation fe of the Faith (San Francisco: Ignatius Press, 1987).

14. See, generally, Ezek. 16:6-48, 53-55. Similarly, in Deut. 29:22 Sodom is forgetting the covenant and idolatry. In 2 Pet. 2:6-10, the sin o to be licentiousness and lawlessness. In 3 Macc. 3:5, their sin is characte arrogance. A reference in the book of Jude (v. 7) mentions that the Sod in sexual immorality and "going after strange flesh," a reference to the sexual relations with angelic beings.

15. One does not need to argue, as do Victor Paul Furnish and that Paul was thinking here only of pederasty, i.e., sex with boys. Paul speaking more generally, but his frame of reference was the passive-act of homoerotic acts in the Roman world. Covenantal relationships betw was not something envisioned within Paul's culture. For the pederasty Furnish, *The Moral Theology of Paul* (Nashville: Abingdon, 1979), pp Scroggs, *The New Testament and Homosexuality: Contextual Background rary Debates* (Philadelphia: Fortress, 1983).

16. It is not clear whether this was for the good of the slave or property interests of the owners. For Roman legislation on castration, se *Slaves and Masters in the Roman Empire: A Study in Social Control* (New don: Oxford University Press, 1987), pp. 128-129; Alan Watson, *Roman Sl more and London: Johns Hopkins University Press, 1987), p. 123. See also

ical Epistemology and the Formation of Concepts [Cambridge, MA: Harvard University Press, 2001], p. xii).

24. See, for example, Bruce Bawer, *A Place at the Table: The Gay Individual in American Society* (New York: Simon and Schuster, 1993); Sullivan, *Virtually Normal*. From a similar vantage point, see Rauch, *Gay Marriage: Why It Is Good for Gays, Good for Straights, and Good for America*. For a critical analysis of the conservative defense of gay marriage from a liberationist perspective, see Paul Robinson, *Queer Wars: The New Gay Right and Its Critics* (Chicago: University of Chicago Press, 2005).

25. Grenz, *Welcoming but Not Affirming*.

26. These efforts have turned out to be harshly hypocritical. The pre-2011 standard of the Presbyterian Church (U.S.A.), enshrined in G-6.0106b of the *Book of Order*, is typical. It provided: "Those who are called to ordained office in the church are to lead a life in obedience to Scripture and in conformity to the historic confessional standards of the church. Among these standards is the requirement to live either in fidelity within the covenant of marriage between a man and a woman (W-4.9001), or chastity in singleness. Persons refusing to repent of any self-acknowledged practice which the confessions call sin shall not be ordained and/or installed as deacons, elders, or ministers of the Word and Sacrament." This byzantine provision reflects the contemporary politics of the closet. The language of self-acknowledgment appears to be generic in character, but it works in practice to target persons who have "come out" as gay. In fact, there is no other practice where the self-acknowledgment language is ever used in the church. Those who support this position can assuage their conscience that they have drafted a position that applies to everyone, when the only people who are caught in its snares are gays.

27. The case was *Bowers v. Hardwick* 478 U.S. 186 (1986). For a description of this case, see ch. 4 (pp. 176-178).

28. Murdoch and Price, *Courting Justice*, p. 23.

29. For this, see Paul J. Achtemeier, *Romans, Interpretation: A Commentary for Teaching and Preaching* (Atlanta: John Knox Press, 1985), pp. 35-36. My exegesis for the remainder of this paragraph is very much influenced by Achtemeier.

30. According to this now repudiated policy, gay people in the military could not be dismissed as long as they did not reveal their identity; the military itself was not allowed to ask questions about sexual identity. The policy was put forward by the Defense Department on July 19, 1993, and it was codified in law at 10 U.S.C. §654.

31. Helmut Thielicke, *The Ethics of Sex,* trans. John W. Doberstein (New York: Harper and Row, 1964). The section entitled "The Problem of Homosexuality" appears on pp. 269-292.

32. Paul K. Jewett with Marguerite Schuster, *Who We Are: Our Dignity as Human: A Neo-Evangelical Theology* (Grand Rapids: Eerdmans, 1996), p. 342.

33. See the chapter entitled "Homosexuality," in Richard B. Hays, *The Moral Vision of the New Testament: A Contemporary Introduction to New Testament Ethics* (San Francisco: HarperSanFrancisco, 1996), pp. 379-406.

34. Hays quotes favorably the judgment of Ernst Käsemann: "Moral perversion is the result of God's wrath, not the reason for it" (quoted in *Moral Vision,* p. 385).

35. *Moral Vision,* p. 396.

36. George Hunsinger presents his position in a series of five essays: Hunsinger, "There Is a Third Way: Theses for Our Crisis in the Church," *Presbyterian Outlook,* Guest Viewpoint, November 26, 2001: http://www.pres-outlook.com/HTML/ hunsinger112501.html; "Thinking Outside the Box, Part 1: Further Reflections on a Third Way for Our Church," *Presbyterian Outlook,* Guest Viewpoint, March 13, 2002: http://www.pres-outlook.com/HTML/hun031302a.html; "Thinking Outside the Box, Part 2: On the 'Plain Sense' of Scripture," *Presbyterian Outlook,* Guest Viewpoint, March 13, 2002: http://www.pres-outlook.com/HTML/hun031302b.html; "Thinking Outside the Box, Part 3: On 'Responsible Discretion' Toward Ordination Candidates," *Presbyterian Outlook,* Guest Viewpoint, March 13, 2002: http://www.pres-outlook.com/ HTML/hun031302c.html; "Thinking Outside the Box, Part 4: The Voice of 'Progressive Traditionalists,'" *Presbyterian Outlook,* Guest Viewpoint, March 13, 2002: http:// www.pres-outlook.com/HTML/hun031302d.html.

37. Hunsinger says: "Believers who form lifelong homosexual partnerships are sanctifying as best they can a condition that they did not choose. Although these partnerships cannot be placed on a direct par with marriage, they deserve the community's 'discreet toleration,' acceptance and respect. Apart from sexual disposition, sexually responsible homosexuals in the community differ from their other sexually responsible sisters and brothers in nothing. They have the same gifts, the same needs, the same foibles, the same virtues, and the same worth. It is high time for our church to stop stigmatizing them as a group. And that means, among other things, 'responsible discretion' when it comes to candidates for ordination" (Hunsinger, "Thinking Outside the Box, Part 3").

38. Hunsinger argues: "[W]hile living together is to be discouraged, it is not always completely impermissible, depending on the circumstances. We might say that living together without the intention to marry is strictly improper (and so proscribed), but that with the clear intention to marry (as soon as the way is clear), it is improper but not intolerable. . . . The question of living together, though never unambiguous, is thus to be judged, from case to case, by whether it supports or undermines the sanctity of marriage as a covenant, publicly avowed, of love and lifelong commitment. . . . From these considerations, three points are especially relevant: (i) a principle of discreet toleration for ambiguous situations that are improper but not intolerable, (ii) a principle of full and mutual commitment as a precondition for sexual intercourse, and (iii) a principle of covenantal union in fidelity that is public, exclusive and permanent. Homosexual partnerships between Christians can be accommodated within the scope of these points" (Hunsinger, "There Is a Third Way," Theses 49-52).

39. Jewett, *Who We Are,* p. 348.

Notes to Chapter Two

1. For a fuller treatment of the biblical arguments, see ch. 3.

2. Hays, *The Moral Vision,* pp. 402-403.

3. See *Westminster Larger Catechism,* Q. 137. See also the document entitled "Practices Called 'Sin' by Our Confessions," compiled by Frank B. Baldwin, III, Elder, Bryn Mawr Presbyterian Church and Legal Counsel, the Presbytery of Philadelphia: http://home.earthlink.net/~valewis/sins.html.

4. *Westminster Larger Catechism,* Q. 142.

5. *Heidelberg Catechism,* Q. 112.

6. Sullivan, *Virtually Normal,* pp. 169-187.

7. Bruce Bagemihl, *Biological Exuberance: Animal Homosexuality and Natural Diversity* (New York: St. Martin's Press, 1999).

8. James Alison, *Faith Beyond Resentment* (New York: Crossroad, 2001), p. xii.

9. Alison, *On Being Liked* (New York: Crossroad, 2003).

10. Carter Heyward, *Our Passion for Justice: Images of Power, Sexuality, and Liberation* (New York: The Pilgrim Press, 1984), p. 39.

11. See Bernadette Brooten, *Love Between Women: Early Christian Responses to Female Homoeroticism* (Chicago: University of Chicago Press, 1996), pp. 251-252 n. 103.

12. The word *atimazō* transliterates ἀτιμάζω.

13. The word *phusis* transliterates φύσις; the word *atimia* transliterates ἀγτιμία.

14. The word *aischron* transliterates αἰσχρόν.

15. Alison, *Faith Beyond Resentment.*

16. One controversial proposal was put before the Presbyterian General Assembly in 1991 by a 17-member Committee on Human Sexuality for the Presbyterian Church (U.S.A.). The paper was entitled "Keeping Body and Soul Together: Sexuality, Spirituality, and Social Justice," and it advocated an approach to sexual ethics centered in what it called "justice-love." Although the paper was not adopted by the assembly, some in the church still find that it represents their viewpoint. See Marvin M. Ellison, ed., *Body and Soul: Rethinking Sexuality as Justice-Love* (Cleveland: Pilgrim Press, 2003).

17. Just to take a typical example, the ethical statement of the More Light Presbyterians speaks of "commitment, fidelity, and integrity," but it draws short of using the words "exclusive," "permanent," "monogamous," or "not promiscuous" ("More Light on Sexual Ethics," adopted by More Light Presbyterians Board, 1999): http://www.mlp.org/resources/MLonSexEth.html (accessed Dec. 28, 2005).

18. Gustavo Gutiérrez, *A Theology of Liberation: History, Politics, and Salvation,* 15th ann. ed. (Maryknoll, NY: Orbis, 1988).

19. A significant event in the emergence of liberation theology was the 1968 Medellín Conference in Colombia, which followed on the heels of Vatican II. For an introduction to the figures and themes of liberation theology, see Paulo Freire, *Pedagogy*

of the Oppressed, trans. Myra Bergman Ramos, rev. 20th ann. ed. (New York: Continuum, 1993); Leonardo Boff and Clodovis Boff, *Introducing Liberation Theology* (Maryknoll, NY: Orbis, 1987); Philip Berryman, *Liberation Theology: The Essential Facts About the Revolutionary Movement in Latin America and Beyond* (New York: Pantheon Books, 1987); P. E. Sigmund, *Liberation Theology at the Crossroads: Democracy or Revolution?* (Oxford: Oxford University Press, 1990); Robert McAfee Brown, *Liberation Theology: An Introductory Guide* (Louisville: Westminster John Knox, 1993); Christopher Rowland, ed., *The Cambridge Companion to Liberation Theology* (Cambridge, UK: Cambridge University Press, 1999).

20. Some have dated the emergence of this movement from the Stonewall riots in New York in 1969. However, the movement had antecedents that date from the mid-20th century. One might just as easily date its emergence with the McCarthy era, when more persons with a gay or lesbian orientation were removed from government than were Communists. For a magisterial survey of the secular emergence of the gay liberation movement, see George Chauncey, *Why Marriage? The History Shaping Today's Debate over Gay Equality* (New York: Basic Books, 2004). For an excellent portrayal of the emergence of gay identity in the 20th century, see John Loughery, *The Other Side of Silence: Men's Lives and Gay Identities, A Twentieth-Century History* (New York: Henry Holt and Company, 1998).

21. Foucault gives four examples of how power has operated to regulate sexuality in modernity: conceiving women's bodies as imbued with sexuality; turning children's sexuality into a matter of sex education; placing procreative sex and the middle-class family at the center of modern society; and defining atypical sexual expression as a matter for psychiatric or medical intervention. Within this matrix of issues, Foucault observes that in the nineteenth century modern society shifted from approaching homoeroticism as a certain type of behavior to treating it as the domain of a certain type of person — the "homosexual." The perspective I am offering on Foucault is especially informed by the following: Foucault, "Introduction," *History of Sexuality,* vol. 1; Foucault, "Afterword: The Subject and the Power," in *Beyond Structuralism and Hermeneutics.*

22. See, for example, Jim Conway, *Marx and Jesus: Liberation Theology in Latin America* (New York: Carlton Press, 1973). For a critique of liberation theology on this score, see Alistair Kee, *Marx and the Failure of Liberation Theology* (Philadelphia: Trinity Press International, 1990).

23. See, for example, Erik Olin Wright, ed., *Approaches to Class Analysis* (Cambridge, UK: Cambridge University Press, 2005).

24. For a succinct statement of this position, supported by comparative analysis, see Christine Delphy and Diana Leonard, *Familiar Exploitation: A New Analysis of Marriage in Contemporary Western Societies* (Cambridge, MA: Polity Press, 1992). A major issue is the "invisible" work performed by women. This book appears in a series entitled Feminist Perspectives, edited by Michelle Stanworth; the other works in this series argue from a similar point of view.

25. For some traditionalists, bisexuality presents the hardest category of all. Traditionalists perceive bisexuals to be asking for license to have sex with both genders, thus rendering monogamy automatically out of bounds. However, the fact that a person is "bisexual" does not necessarily mean that person would claim a right or entitlement to have sex with multiple partners, both men and women. Rather, being bisexual simply means that, for some people, gender attraction is fluid. How they work that out ethically is another question.

26. See, for example, David F. Greenberg, *The Construction of Homosexuality* (Chicago and London: University of Chicago Press, 1988); David M. Halperin, *One Hundred Years of Homosexuality* (New York: Routledge, 1989); Celia Kitzinger, *The Social Construction of Lesbianism* (New York: Sage Books, 1987).

27. Although Eleanor Roosevelt developed close friendships with women, including lesbian activists, and Abraham Lincoln had intimate male friendships throughout his life (some of them incredibly intense), it is not credible to call these relationships "gay" or "lesbian." But that is precisely the point: there may be a range of intimate same-sex relationships that do not fit into our neat binary categories, and within which genital sex is not the primary focus of the relationship. See Blanche Wiesen Cook, *Eleanor Roosevelt* (New York: Penguin, 1993); C. A. Tripp, *The Intimate World of Abraham Lincoln* (New York: Free Press, 2005). It should be clear from these comments that I do not mean to endorse all of Tripp's extrapolative judgments about Lincoln's sexuality. For a contrary view, see Andrew Sullivan, "Log Cabin Republican: How Gay Was Lincoln?" *The New Republic*, Jan. 10, 2005.

28. Perhaps the best treatment of this is Sedgwick, *Epistemology of the Closet*. One of Sedgwick's main objectives is to demonstrate that the ways we talk about being gay or lesbian — and especially the binary categorizations we use — are internally incoherent. The incoherence she perceives has two dimensions. The first pertains to the process by which a person is designated as being gay or straight, homosexual or heterosexual: this process trades on two conflicting modes of discourse. One form of identification occurs through a "minoritizing" discourse, which treats being gay or lesbian as an essential identity that sets one apart from the majority population. One example of this (mine, not Sedgwick's) is the way the Centers for Disease Control in the 1980s tried to assure the public that HIV/AIDS was a condition that did not affect the general population (Randy Shilts, *And the Band Played On: Politics, People, and the AIDS Epidemic* [New York: St. Martins Press, 1987], p. 554). The subtle message was that HIV/AIDS was a problem for "them," not "us." In addition to this minoritizing discourse, Sedgwick also points to a "universalizing" discourse that treats sexual desire as though it existed for everyone along a continuum. Rather than some people being gay and others straight, the universalizing discourse assumes that everyone may experience some measure of same-sex or opposite-sex desire in relative degrees at different times.

The second incoherence Sedgwick identifies regards the way society conceives of sexual desire according to gender categories. One vocabulary adopts a separatist approach, says Sedgwick, while the other uses a transitive way of speaking. On the one hand, the separatist vocabulary deals in the classic oppositions of gay-straight or male-female; on the other hand, the transitive vocabulary treats gender identity as more fluid and harder to pin down. We speak of a man getting in touch with his feminine side. If gender identity is fluid, Sedgwick asks, then why should sexual object choice be the defining feature of one's sexuality? In Greco-Roman society, for instance, the gender of one's sexual partner was only one of many ways to categorize sexual conduct. The net result is that we act as though we know what we are talking about when we call someone gay or lesbian, while the sexuality of a given person may not fit our culturally created categories. One result is that people face a "double bind" when it comes to living out society's gender expectations. For example, a woman may feel that she has to adopt stereotypical male traits in order to succeed in a particular line of work. Yet if she does so, she may experience the backlash of those who wonder whether she is a lesbian. For more on this example within the legal context, see Eskridge and Hunter, *Sexuality, Gender, and the Law,* pp. 300-305.

29. See Deborah Rudacille, *The Riddle of Gender: Science, Activism and Transgender Rights* (New York: Pantheon, 2005).

30. Some accounts place the number much higher, perhaps as high as 4 percent (Sharon E. Preves, *Intersex and Identity: The Contested Self* [New Brunswick, NJ: Rutgers University Press, 2003], pp. 2-3).

31. See the discussion in the introductory chapter.

32. This is argued masterfully by Stein, *The Mismeasure of Desire: The Science, Theory, and Ethics of Sexual Orientation.*

33. The phrase *phusikēn chrēsin* transliterates the Greek φυσικὴν χρῆσιν.

34. We know this not only from written statements but from artistic depictions of sex acts that have been uncovered by archaeologists (see John Dominic Crossan and Jonathan L. Reed, *In Search of Paul: How Jesus' Apostle Opposed Rome's Empire with God's Kingdom: A New Vision of Paul's Words and World* [New York: HarperSanFrancisco, 2004], pp. 258-269). It is telling that Romans portrayed the nations they conquered as women whom Roman soldiers are in the act of sexually subduing.

35. The phrase transliterated *para phusin* in Greek is παρὰ φύσιν. The definitive work on female homoeroticism in antiquity interprets Romans in this way: Brooten, *Love Between Women,* p. 251.

36. Crossan and Reed, *In Search of Paul,* p. 264.

37. For information on this, see Clarke, *Roman Sex,* pp. 37-58.

38. Judith Butler, *Gender Trouble,* 10th ann. ed. (New York: Routledge, 1999); see also Sarah Salih, *The Judith Butler Reader* (New York: Blackwell, 2004).

39. Anne Fausto-Sterling, "The Five Sexes: Why Male and Female Are Not Enough," *The Sciences* 33/2 (1993): 20-25; Anne Fausto-Sterling, *Sexing the Body: Gender Politics and the Construction of Sexuality* (New York: Basic Books, 2000).

40. See, generally, Marcella Althaus-Reid, *The Queer God* (London and New York: Routledge, 2003).

41. Marcella Althaus-Reid, *Indecent Theology: Theological Perversions in Sex, Gender and Politics* (New York: Routledge, 2000).

42. Martha Nussbaum, "The Professor of Parody," *The New Republic*, February 22, 1999.

43. The publications of Rowan Williams are too numerous to list here, but they may be obtained from the following website: http://www.archbishopofcanterbury.org/pages/bibliography.html.

44. Williams, "Is There a Christian Sexual Ethic?" in Rowan Williams, *A Ray of Darkness: Sermons and Reflections* (Cambridge, MA: Cowley Publications, 1995), p. 143.

45. Williams, "The Body's Grace" (1989), reprinted in Eugene F. Rogers, Jr., ed., *Theology and Sexuality: Classic and Contemporary Readings* (Oxford: Blackwell Publishers, 2002), pp. 309-321. Available on-line: http://www.iconservatives.org.uk/bodys_grace.html.

46. Williams, "Is There a Christian Sexual Ethic?" p. 140.

47. Williams, "Is There a Christian Sexual Ethic?" p. 141.

48. Williams, "The Body's Grace."

49. Rogers, "Sanctification, Homosexuality, and God's Triune Life," in *Theology and Sexuality*, pp. 217-248; Eugene F. Rogers, Jr., *Sexuality and the Christian Body: Their Way into the Triune God*, Challenges in Contemporary Theology (New York: Blackwell Publishers, 1999).

50. Gray Temple, *Gay Unions: In the Light of Scripture, Tradition, and Reason* (New York: Church Publishing, 2004).

51. I am indebted for this insight to Rogers, *Sexuality and the Christian Body*.

52. Greek: εἰ γὰρ σὺ ἐκ τῆς **κατὰ φύσιν** ἐξεκόπης ἀγριελαίου καὶ **παρὰ φύσιν** ἐνεκεντρίσθης εἰς καλλιέλαιον, πόσῳ μᾶλλον οὗτοι οἱ **κατὰ φύσιν** ἐγκεντρισθήσονται τῇ ἰδίᾳ ἐλαίᾳ.

53. By the end of Romans, Paul cites a litany of verses from Hebrew Scripture to make clear his true concern: God's graciousness in dealing with both Jew and gentile (see Rom. 15:8-12).

54. Stanley Hauerwas, "On Gay Friendship: A Thought Experiment in Catholic Moral Theology," in Rogers, *Theology and Sexuality*, pp. 289-308.

Notes to Chapter Three

1. Quoted by Paul Ricoeur, in André LaCocque and Paul Ricoeur, *Thinking Biblically: Exegetical and Hermeneutical Studies,* trans. David Pellauer (Chicago and London: University of Chicago Press, 1998), p. 277, n. 15.

2. We must take care not to approach Scripture as though it were some kind of

statutory code. Different scriptures function in the church in different ways, according to context, genre, and a host of other factors. As Robert W. Jenson reminds us, "the very phrase 'the authority of Scripture' tempts us to suppose that Scripture has a single regulative relation to the church's discourse. It does not, as the most cursory examination of the church's actual use of Scripture must discover" (Jenson, *Systematic Theology,* vol. 1, p. 30).

3. In stating the three purposes of marriage as companionship, commitment, and community, I am framing in a positive and general way three concerns about which the tradition spoke negatively and in reverse order as procreation, a remedy for sin, and mutuality. These latter three are stated, for example, in the *Book of Common Prayer.* In my view, there is much more to the community-building function of marriage than procreation. Moreover, to speak of marriage negatively as a "remedy" for sin, lust, and incontinence derives from the predominantly prohibitionist sexual ethic that has tainted so much of Christian history. This was an ethic that usually presupposed that sex is bad, and it saw marriage as the arena in which sexual expression is grudgingly to be allowed (see ch. 1).

This negative understanding of sex and marriage derives in part from 1 Cor. 7:1-2, 8-9, where Paul observes:

> Now for the matters you wrote about: It is good for a man not to marry. But since there is so much immorality, each man should have his own wife, and each woman her own husband. . . . Now to the unmarried and the widows I say: It is good for them to stay unmarried, as I am. But if they cannot control themselves, they should marry, for it is better to marry than to burn with passion.

The tradition usually forgot to mention that Paul's recommendation not to marry was predicated on his belief that the apocalyptic end of days was imminent.

An early and slightly different version of the threefold purpose of marriage is to be found in Augustine of Hippo, the highly influential theologian of the Western church. Augustine began, quite negatively, with the idea that marriage was a compromise from the true Christian virtue of celibacy, i.e., abstaining from sexual relations altogether. Despite the superiority of celibacy as a way of life, Augustine nonetheless posited the three reasons that marriage was a permissible, though inferior, way of living: *procreation, fidelity,* and *sacrament.*

First, the primary point of marriage for Augustine is procreation, the production of offspring. According to this view of marriage, one may legitimately pursue sexual relations only in order to conceive offspring, but not for their own sake. This carries with it the implication that one's spouse is not to be desired for his or her own sake, but only for the goal of procreation. Second, marriage serves the purpose of securing the fidelity of the spouses — in two ways: by honoring the exclusivity of marriage, the parties commit themselves not to engage in adultery; and by giving themselves to one another sexually, the parties relieve each other's sexual desires. Sometimes the tradition spoke of marriage in this second sense as a "remedy for sin." The idea here is that most people are incapable of sexual continence; thus marriage becomes the lesser of the evils, an accommodation to the human propensity for sin. Third, marriage has a sacramental quality for Augustine. All marriages, whether religious or nonreligious, represent an outward and material sign of an inward and spiritual grace. Within a Christian context, marriage is also said to be a "mystery" that is rooted in the relationship between Christ as bridegroom and the church as bride (Augustine, *De bono conjugali*).

More recently, Pope John Paul II has argued that the spiritual communion that arises between a man and woman in marriage derives from the same communion that inheres within the divine life itself. And it is this same divine and human communion that is manifest in the person and work of Jesus Christ (John Paul II, *A Theology of the Body: Human Love in the Divine Plan* [New York: Pauline Books, 1997]). I am in sympathy with this view, but I see no reason why the communion in question should be limited to heterosexual couples.

4. On this point, see the brilliant essay by Paul Ricoeur, "The Nuptial Metaphor," in LaCocque and Ricoeur, *Thinking Biblically*, pp. 265-303.

5. The desire for the other has many layers of meaning in contemporary thought. There is the humanitarian meaning: caring for the concrete neighbor in need. There is the temporal meaning: hoping for a better world. And there is the philosophical meaning: being confronted with perspectives other than one's own. I shall not pursue all these meanings here. Perhaps the most influential philosopher who has written on this subject is Emmanuel Levinas, and it is significant that Levinas locates the prime example of desire for the other in the concreteness of nuptial love (see Levinas, *Totality and Infinity: An Essay on Exteriority,* trans. Alphonso Lingis [Pittsburgh: Duquesne University Press, 1969]).

6. See the literature I have referred to in ch. 1, n. 18.

7. Robert Wright, *The Moral Animal: The New Science of Evolutionary Psychology* (New York: Pantheon Books, 1994), pp. 90-91.

8. The idiom is usually a combination of the verb "to take" (*lāqaḥ;* לְקַח), and the noun "woman" (*'ishshâ;* אִשָּׁה), e.g., in Deut. 22:13.

9. The Hebrew is נָתַן; *nātan* (e.g., Gen. 38:14).

10. See, generally, John Stuart Mill, *The Subjection of Women*, ed. Susan M. Okin (Indianapolis: Hackett Publishing Company, 1988); see also Mary Lyndon Shanley, "The Subjection of Women," in *The Companion to Mill,* ed. John Skorupski (Cambridge, UK: Cambridge University Press, 1998), pp. 396-422.

11. Some, however, do not agree. See, e.g., John Witte, Jr., *From Sacrament to Contract: Marriage, Religion, and Law in the Western Tradition* (Louisville: Westminster John Knox, 1997). As a defender of "traditional" marriage, Witte seems to want it both ways: on the one hand, he applauds many of the reforms instigated by Mill and his successors; on the other, he claims that more recent reforms have reduced marriage to a terminable sexual contract between the two parties. This judgment will not hold up to

scrutiny. No marriage may be terminated without significant state involvement and the imposition of substantial legal and financial duties, including alimony and child support (something Witte downplays). Witte cites with alarm the rise in households headed by single women, but he neglects to mention that most of the divorces that resulted in this state of affairs were initiated by women themselves. What Witte favors is greater control by the state, the church, and society over the realm of marriage. But this social control is what the marriage reforms he says he favors were precisely designed to loosen.

12. The Hebrew transliterated *hā 'ādām* is הָאָדָם.

13. This is the reason the NRSV translates the Hebrew word *hā 'ādām* as though it means humankind in a generic sense. Other versions translate it more concretely as "a human being" or, more literally, as "an earth-creature."

14. Brian Racer, pastor of the Open Door Bible Church in Hanover, Maryland, recently put this view succinctly: "The male is the piercer, the female is the pierced. That is the way God designed it." Racer went on to claim (erroneously) that the Hebrew words for "male" and "female" are "actually the words for the male and female genital parts" (Russell Shorto, "What's Their Real Problem with Gay Marriage? (It's the Gay Part)" [*New York Times Magazine,* June 19, 2005, section 6, p. 39]). With greater scholarly aplomb but no further warrant in the text itself, Robert Gagnon has claimed that gay male sexuality "constitutes a conscious denial of the complementarity of male and female found not least in the fittedness (anatomical, physiological, and procreative) of the male penis and the female vaginal receptacle by attempting anal intercourse . . . with another man" (*The Bible and Homosexual Practice,* p. 139).

15. There are euphemisms: for example, the Hebrew word for "foot" or "feet" is used as a euphemism for genitalia.

16. A variation on the gender complementarity view has been put forward by the Swiss theologian Karl Barth, who construes the togetherness of "male and female" as *constituting* the divine image. It is an interpretation that has influenced many, including the Vatican, though ultimately it is one we must reject. In his reflections on what it means to be created in God's image, Barth draws attention to what he calls our "co-humanity": the irreducible fact that we need each other and are responsible for one another (Barth, *Church Dogmatics,* III/2, pp. 222-284). In our interdependence we are called to reflect the very character of God. "The being of humanity in encounter," Barth says, "is a being in correspondence to God" (*Church Dogmatics,* III/2, p. 323). Just as Jesus of Nazareth was a human being who was *for* and *with* others, so also we are called to be for and with one another. This is a compelling statement of the basic social character of human experience; and it is a statement that applies to all human beings, regardless of gender or sexual orientation. This much of Barth's approach is commendable.

Nevertheless, there are problems with what Barth then goes on to say. Building on the parallelism noted above between "image of God" and "male and female," Barth makes the questionable suggestion that sexual differentiation — or, more broadly, "gender complementarity" — is itself what constitutes the image of God (*Church Dogmatics,* III/1, pp. 183-206, 228-329). The strength of this suggestion is that it emphasizes the embodied nature of human existence. That we exist interdependently as male and female gives concrete expression to our cohumanity. Yet there are numerous problems with Barth's idea.

The first — and most obvious — weakness is that the biblical text itself contradicts what Barth is saying. For example, the animals also are created "male and female," and yet the biblical text does not say that they bear the divine image. Reducing "image of God" to sexuality smacks more of modern Romanticism than biblical theology. This leads to the second weakness: importing the notion of "gender complementarity" into this text is anachronistic. The very idea that male and female genders "complement" each other is more modern than ancient. In fact, in standard histories of sexuality, premodern societies are characterized as thinking more in terms of gender hierarchy, not gender complementarity. Moreover, the idea of gender complementarity does not emerge until the eighteenth and nineteenth centuries, and especially in European Romanticism (Thomas Laqueur, *Making Sex: The Body and Gender from the Greeks to Freud* [Cambridge, MA: Harvard University Press, 1990]). For the ancients, a female was indeed a human being, but a decidedly deficient human being. Because she was inferior to the male, she also needed to be subservient. Barth himself perpetuates this retrograde understanding of women, arguing that women are created to be subordinate to their male counterparts. This alone should give us pause in accepting Barth's line of thinking. Third, saying that human existence as male or female defines the image of God leaves us wondering how to make sense theologically of the fact that one in a thousand human births results in a person who is not clearly male or female, a fact we have already discussed in the introduction and in the preceding chapter with respect to liberation theology. Taking the biblical dichotomy here as though it exhausted all the human possibilities makes it difficult to talk about how these intersexed persons, too, are created in God's image.

Finally, and most decisively for the Christian interpreter, Barth's gloss on the "image of God" stands in serious tension with the New Testament, which (in 2 Cor. 4:4 and Col. 1:15) tells us that the place Christians should look to decipher the divine image is Jesus Christ — the true image of God. It was Barth himself, more than anyone else, who called attention to this Christocentric approach to the divine image. It is through Jesus Christ, he claims, that we know what the divine image means. And yet, as far as we know, Jesus lived life as a single man. And when he talked about family structures, as I shall discuss more fully below, he did so critically. If following the person of Jesus is the key to living into the image of God, then gender complementarity becomes a relative non-issue.

17. Robert Alter, *The Five Books of Moses: A Translation with Commentary* (New York and London: W. W. Norton, 2004), p. 19. The Hebrew is as follows:

וַיִּבְרָא אֱלֹהִים אֶת־הָאָדָם בְּצַלְמוֹ
בְּצֶלֶם אֱלֹהִים בָּרָא אֹתוֹ
זָכָר וּנְקֵבָה בָּרָא אֹתָם

18. The verse is structured in a form known as climactic parallelism. This structure is a combination of two different types of parallelism. The first is synonymous parallelism: in each of the three lines, the same thought is expressed using a different vocabulary and emphasis; the three lines together then build to a crescendo in which new information is added with each line. The gifts and responsibilities of being in the image of God rest not merely with the first human creature taken as a microcosm of the whole ("him") but with all human creatures taken inclusively, both male and female ("them"). Note that in the juxtaposition the word "him" is the third-person masculine singular (אֹתוֹ), and the "them" is the third-person masculine plural (אֹתָם). On Hebrew poetry, see Alter, *The Art of Biblical Poetry;* David L. Petersen and Kent H. Richards, *Interpreting Hebrew Poetry* (Minneapolis: Augsburg-Fortress, 1992); James Kugel, *The Idea of Biblical Poetry: Parallelism and Its History* (Baltimore: Johns Hopkins University Press, 1998).

19. On different ways of taking this verse, see Kristen Kvam, Linda S. Shearing, and Valarie H. Ziegler, eds., *Eve and Adam: Jewish, Christian, and Muslim Readings on Genesis and Gender* (Bloomington: Indiana University Press, 1999), pp. 24-25.

20. This interpretation is bolstered by the fact that throughout the Pentateuch this standard priestly phrase "male and female" is used to connote inclusivity and not sexuality per se (Gen. 1:27; 5:2; 6:19; 7:3, 9, 16; 12:16; 20:14; 24:35; 30:35, 43; 32:5, 14f.; Exod. 20:10, 17; 21:20, 26f., 32; Lev. 3:1, 6; 12:7; 15:33; 25:6, 44; 27:5ff.; Num. 5:3; Deut. 4:16; 5:14, 21; 12:12, 18; 16:11, 14; 28:68). This interpretation is supported by the fact that the third mention of human creation in Gen. 5:1-2 makes the very same point: "This is the list of the descendants of Adam. When God created humankind, he made them in the likeness of God. Male and female he created them, and he blessed them and named them 'humankind' when they were created."

In supporting an overtly sexual reading of the trope "male and female," some may wish to object that the many references to male and female slaves in the Pentateuch signal that their sexual fecundity will be beneficial to their masters. This argument, of course, raises the counter-hermeneutical question of why the Bible is so accommodating to the institution of slavery. It will not do to absolutize the cultural world of the Bible concerning sexuality when other aspects of that cultural world are so obviously questionable.

The only other place where "male and female" suggests fecundity is the admonition to Noah, prior to the Flood, to make certain that a male and female animal of every species finds its way onto the ark (Gen. 6:19; 7:3; 9:16). Here the idea is, in part, that male and female are necessary to repopulate the earth. Yet there is no explicit reflection on sexual intercourse or sexual anatomy. It is true that God's blessing of humanity includes the admonition to "be fruitful and multiply." But this is a command to the species as a whole and not to any particular individual. It is also vastly different from other ancient Near Eastern cultures that exult in the vitalities of sexual power. If anything, the Bible's relentless polemic elsewhere against the phallic symbols of the fertility cult cuts precisely in the opposite direction. To put it succinctly, a theology built from a foundation in human sexual anatomy is pagan, not biblical.

21. H. Richard Niebuhr, *Radical Monotheism and Western Culture, With Supplementary Essays* (New York: Harper and Brothers, 1960), p. 38.

22. This raises an interesting interpretive point. The contrast between the "good" of the Priestly account and the "not good" of the Yahwist account has apparently been set up not by either writer but by the community that juxtaposed them in the process of editing. This reminds us of the complex and multilayered nature of biblical meaning.

23. Alter, *The Five Books of Moses*, p. 22.

24. The Hebrew transliterated *ʿēzer kĕnegdō* is עֵזֶר כְּנֶגְדּוֹ.

25. The Hebrew transliterated *ʿēzer* is עֵזֶר.

26. Some estimate the number as much higher, perhaps 3.4 million. A massive study in 1990 showed that 3.9 percent of American men who were married or had been married had also engaged in sex with another man in the previous five years (Laumann, Gagnon, Mitchell, and Michaels, *The Social Organization of Sexuality: Sexual Practices in the United States*).

27. These movements, based on "orders," have not only been declared mistaken but actually heretical by Reformed bodies: in Germany, by *The Barmen Declaration* (1934); and in South Africa, by *The Belhar Confession* (1984). For an account of the situation in Nazi Germany, see Doris L. Bergen, *Twisted Cross: The German Christian Movement in the Third Reich* (Chapel Hill and London: University of North Carolina Press, 1996); for the situation in South Africa, see Charles Villa-Vicencio, *Trapped in Apartheid: A Socio-Theological History of the English-Speaking Churches in South Africa* (Maryknoll, NY: Orbis, 1994).

28. It is noteworthy that God is the one who presents the animals to Adam as though one of them might be the partner he needs (Gen. 2:19-20); but it soon becomes clear that a suitable companion has not yet come on the scene.

29. This is done most memorably in the book of Hosea. Hosea's wife, Gomer, is unfaithful and has left him to pursue a life of promiscuity. The prophet analogizes his own relationship with Gomer to God's relationship with Israel: just as Gomer has pursued multiple extramarital affairs, so the people of Israel have turned away from the pure worship of God. So extreme is Gomer's behavior that she ends up being sold into slavery. Nevertheless, Hosea shows steadfast love toward Gomer by entering the slave auction and buying her back to restore her as his wife (Hos. 3:1-3). In the same way, so the prophet tells us, God loves human beings with a steadfastness that is willing to pursue us even when we reject and turn away from God.

30. Anti-gay polemicists argue that gay men are frequently non-monogamous,

and they advance this as a reason that same-sex unions are lacking in integrity and should not be approved by society (see, for example, Jeffrey Satinover, M.D., *Homosexuality and the Politics of Truth* [Grand Rapids: Baker, 1996], pp. 49-70). Seldom do these polemicists consider the effect that approving and sanctioning a societal context for same-sex relationships could have in encouraging monogamy.

31. The story of the nuptials of Sir Elton John captured the headlines (Sarah Lyall, "Celebrity Trumps Sexuality at a Civil English Ceremony," *New York Times,* Thursday, Dec. 22, 2005, A4).

32. Eskridge, *Equality Practice: Civil Unions and the Future of Gay Rights,* p. 118. See, more recently, William N. Eskridge, Jr., and Darren R. Spedale, *Gay Marriage: For Better or for Worse? What We've Learned from the Evidence* (New York: Oxford University Press, 2006).

33. "Out and Into the Voting Booth: Lesbian, Gay, Bisexual, & Transgender Voters in 2000," Gill Foundation, Harris Interactive, February 16, 2001: http://www.gillfoundation.com/gotv2000/index.htm (cited in David M. Smith and Gary Gates, "Gay and Lesbian Families in the United States: Same-Sex Unmarried Partner Households," Urban Institute: http://www.urban.org/publications/1000491.html#n1 [accessed Dec. 10, 2005]). Approximately 600,000 gay couples in the United States declared themselves to be partners in the 2000 Census, and the actual number living in some form of partnership is certainly higher. The reason that it is probably higher is that (a) the Census form merely had a box to check for "unmarried partner," which gays may or may not have interpreted as applying to them; and (b) many gays may have concluded that such information was not any business of the government. Summary File 1 of the 2000 Census put the number of same-sex partnerships at 594,391; however, subsequent governmental figures suggest a somewhat higher number. One reading of the 2000 Census puts the declared figure at 601,209. Smith and Gates estimate that there are some 1,202,418 gay couples living together in the United States, but this number is probably high: it rests on the blanket assumption that 5 percent of the population is gay, but the actual number that claim a gay self-identity is lower. Suffice it to say, we do not have reliable data to form a clear conclusion.

34. Two useful discussions are John Burnaby, *Amor Dei: A Study in the Religion of St. Augustine,* 3rd ed. (London: Hodder and Stoughton, 1960); Oliver O'Donovan, *The Problem of Self-love in St. Augustine* (New Haven and London: Yale University Press, 1980).

35. See, for example, Augustine, *De doctrina Christiana,* 1.38.42 to 1.39.43; *In Epistulam Johannis ad Parthos tractatus,* 83.3.

36. This argument is often linked in Christian biblical interpretation with the mistaken belief that the witness of Leviticus has somehow been completely superseded by the teachings of the New Testament. This is not only inaccurate but it trades on a long-standing Christian neglect of the Hebrew heritage from which the church derives its life, as well as the misguided Christian claim that the church somehow supersedes

Israel. It is not that the law of Leviticus has been superseded; rather, the law has now been reinterpreted within a new context. For an excellent analysis of this problem, see Scott Bader-Saye, *Church and Israel After Christendom: The Politics of Election* (Boulder, CO: Westview Press, 1999).

37. Even a seemingly arbitrary commandment, such as the necessity of giving a Sabbath rest to the land in the seventh year (Lev. 25:4), is congruent with contemporary concerns for the environment and the replenishment of the earth. Above all, the institution of the "year of Jubilee," in which slaves are to be set free and property is to revert to its original owner (Lev. 25:8-13, 23-24; 27:23-24), resonates with contemporary demands for social and economic justice. Commands such as these underscore the pivotal place of Leviticus in the biblical canon. For a comprehensive approach to the subject of social justice in Hebrew Scripture, see Moshe Weinfeld, *Social Justice in Ancient Israel and the Ancient Near East* (Minneapolis: Augsburg-Fortress, 1995).

38. Jesus not only affirms this command from Hebrew Scripture, he intensifies it. Perhaps the best known is Jesus' response to the lawyer who asks him to define what the greatest commandment is: "He said to him, 'You shall love the Lord your God with all your heart, and with all your soul, and with all your mind.' This is the greatest and first commandment. And a second is like it: 'You shall love your neighbor as yourself'" (Matt. 22:37-39; Mark 12:28-31). Jesus gives a similar response to one who asks what must be done to inherit eternal life (Matt. 19:19; Luke 10:27). Also relevant is Jesus' intensification of the law in the Sermon on the Mount: "You have heard that it was said, 'You shall love your neighbor and hate your enemy.' But I say to you, Love your enemies and pray for those who persecute you."

39. The case can be made that Leviticus, coming after Genesis and Exodus and before Numbers and Deuteronomy, occupies the literary center of the Pentateuch (see Mary Douglas, *Leviticus as Literature* [Oxford: Oxford University Press, 2001]). And at the literary center of Leviticus itself is the love commandment of Lev. 19:18. Thus, when we view the Bible in literary terms, the command of Leviticus to love one's neighbor lies at the very heart of the Pentateuch. In Leviticus, it is through law, through ritual, and through acts of consecration that the communal identity formed through the earlier stories of Genesis and Exodus becomes a lived reality. The question for biblical interpretation is how this ancient sense of biblical identity — mediated to us from the pages of the biblical past — can become a lived reality in the new and very different context in which we live today.

40. Leviticus stands as "the foundation for the subsequent universal rejection of male same-sex intercourse within Judaism" (Hays, *The Moral Vision of the New Testament,* p. 381). To the extent that this Jewish teaching formed the horizon of Paul's own reflection in Romans, the same is true for Christianity.

41. Jacob Milgrom makes the interesting observation that, strictly speaking, these prohibitions apply only to the Jews (or those living in Israel) and not to people of other nations (Milgrom, *Leviticus 17–22* [New York: Random House, 2000], pp. 1786-

1790); cf. Robert A. J. Gagnon, "A Critique of Jacob Milgrom's Views of Leviticus 18:22 and 20:13," http://www.robgagnon.net/articles/homoMilgrom.pdf.

42. The Hebrew is as follows: וְאֶת־זָכָר לֹא תִשְׁכַּב מִשְׁכְּבֵי אִשָּׁה תּוֹעֵבָה הוּא

43. וְאִישׁ אֲשֶׁר יִשְׁכַּב אֶת־זָכָר מִשְׁכְּבֵי אִשָּׁה תּוֹעֵבָה עָשׂוּ שְׁנֵיהֶם מוֹת יוּמָתוּ דְּמֵיהֶם בָּם.

44. As one might expect, the best commentaries on Leviticus are written not by Christians but by Jews. The recent magisterial work of Rabbi Jacob Milgrom stands out: *Leviticus 1–16* (1991); *Leviticus 17–22* (2000); and *Leviticus 23–27* (2001). Other important critical commentaries are Baruch A. Levine, *Leviticus*, JPS Torah Commentary (Philadelphia: The Jewish Publication Society, 1989); Rolf Rendtorff, *Leviticus*, Biblischer Kommentar Altes Testament 3/1 (Neukirchen-Vluyn: Neukirchener, 1985); Karl Elliger, *Leviticus*, Handbuch zum Alten Testament 1/4 (Tübingen: J. C. B. Mohr Siebeck, 1966); Martin Noth, *Leviticus*, trans. J. E. Anderson (Philadelphia: Westminster Press, 1962). See also "The History of the Exposition of Leviticus" (prepared by William Yarchin) in Word Biblical Commentary, vol. 4, xliii. In his Interpretation commentary, Samuel E. Balentine ventures that Leviticus is the most neglected book in the canon (*Leviticus* [Louisville: Westminster John Knox, 2003], pp. 1-2). Milgrom indicates that it has been neglected by Christians and Jews — Christians because they read Leviticus through the lens of the New Testament, and Jews because they interpret it through rabbinic sources.

45. George Lakoff, *Women, Fire, and Dangerous Things: What Categories Reveal about the Mind* (Chicago and London: University of Chicago Press, 1987).

46. Nor is the condemnation of Onan in Gen. 38:1-10 a prohibition of masturbation; rather, Onan was told to sire children with the wife of his deceased brother so that his brother would have descendants. Onan deliberately engaged in *coitus interruptus* so that he would not impregnate her, and for this he was put to death. The act was wrong because he was refusing to fulfill the levirate obligation to give his dead brother an heir.

47. We know these commandments were given to men because of the masculine verb forms that permeate the text, as well as the subject matter of the commandments themselves. Milgrom believes that they were directed even more specifically to the head of the clan, who had authority and was responsible for deciding cases within the jurisdiction of the extended family (Milgrom, *Leviticus 17–22*, p. 1525). This does not mean that the various commandments in Leviticus had no implications for women (see Judith Romney Wegner, "Leviticus," in Carol A. Newsome and Sharon H. Ringe, eds., *The Women's Bible Commentary* [Louisville: Westminster John Knox Press, 1992], pp. 36-44). For example, Leviticus contains rules for when the natural bodily functions of women (e.g., childbirth [ch. 12]; menstruation [15:19-24]) make them ritually unclean. Still, it was the priests and male heads of households who presided over these rules.

48. This meant that within the extended clan there were numerous women whom a man might view as potential sexual partners, even though he may have been distantly related to them by blood. Another fact we need to remember is that the sexual and reproductive functioning of all the women in the clan, once they left their fathers'

protective care, belonged to the male to whom they had become attached — whether by marriage, concubinage, or, in the case of non-Hebrews, slavery. This is why Abraham — and later Isaac — could give their wives to other men sexually when it served to protect their own lives (Gen. 12:11-20; 26:1-11). Considering the power exercised by men over women, including a man's power to divorce his wife for little or no reason, a Hebrew woman's sexual life could be rather precarious. This was especially true for a woman who was a concubine, a slave, or a less-favored wife within a polygamous marriage. According to one interpretation of Deuteronomic law, a woman could be divorced simply because she displeased a man. If she then became the wife of another man and subsequently wanted to return to her first husband, the first husband was not permitted to take her back (Deut. 24:1-4; cf. Deut. 22:19-21; 22:28-29). Absent rules to the contrary, the sudden loss of her male protector could render any woman especially vulnerable to sexual exploitation.

49. A concubine's sexual availability is shown in Gen. 22:24, that of a slave in Gen. 16:1-2. A slave's availability for sex seems to be assumed in Lev. 19:20. Thus, if the slave with whom an Israelite man has had sexual relations happens to be betrothed to another man, he shall be penalized. However, the ordinary penalty of death that would apply in the case of a free woman who was betrothed does not apply here.

50. Slavery was accepted so long as the slaves were not Israelites (Lev. 25:44-46). Resident aliens who became slaves had a right eventually to be redeemed (Lev. 25:47-52). If an Israelite had to go into slavery for indebtedness, he was to serve as a hired laborer and eventually to be set free (Lev. 25:39-40).

51. The phrase transliterated as *kol-shě'ēr běsārô* in Hebrew reads כָּל־שְׁאֵר בְּשָׂרוֹ.

52. The categories of prohibited sexual partners included women who were close blood relatives of a man (Lev. 18:7-11), women who were blood relatives of a man's father or mother (18:12-14), women more distantly related by marriage (18:15-16), and women related to a current wife of a man (18:17-18). In this way of arranging the material, I follow Milgrom, *Leviticus 17–22*, p. 1526. Modern interpreters sometimes describe these as "incest rules," but this is anachronistic and misleading. Incest is prohibited universally, but what counts as incest varies from place to place, according to social rules. That is, incest rules are based less on biology and morality and more on social organization of families (see Françoise Zonabend, "An Anthropological Perspective," in André Burguière et al., eds., *A History of the Family,* vol. I of *Distant Worlds, Ancient Worlds* [Cambridge, MA: Harvard University Press, 1996], p. 25). Not surprisingly, then, the rules in Leviticus differ from the way incest is understood today. True, men were prohibited from sexual relations with near relatives, which, formally speaking, is how we think of incest. But the list in Leviticus omits any mention of sex between a father and his own daughter; the same is true of sex between a person and his full brother or sister. These are relationships that we know have special potential for both abuse and psychological harm; and they certainly would appear on any contemporary list of relationships defined as "incest." My point is not that Leviticus somehow encouraged sex-

ual relations between a father and his daughter, or between brother and sister. It did not. Instead, the question is how to account for the omission of the daughter and the full-blood sister from this list. Or, taking another example, why does the list prohibit a man from having sex with his aunt but not with his niece? Moreover, what do we make of the fact that a number of biblical characters do not keep these rules? Jacob Milgrom (*Leviticus 17–22*, p. 1528) mentions the following list: paternal half-sister (Gen. 20:2, 12; cf. Lev. 18:9; 20:17); two sisters at a time (Gen. 29:28; cf. Lev. 18:8; 20:11); daughter-in-law (Gen. 38:18; cf. Lev. 18:15; 20:12); father's wife (Gen. 35:22; cf. Lev. 18:8; 20:11); adultery (2 Sam. 11; cf. Lev. 18:20; 20:10); father's concubines (2 Sam. 16:22; cf. Lev. 18:8; 20:11); half-sister (2 Sam. 13:13, 14; cf. Lev. 18:19; 20:17). It is probably because the list was not meant to target "incest" in exactly the same way we think of it but to set limits on powerful males whose sexual appetites knew few boundaries. So much was this the case that, even though men were warned to flee prostitutes (e.g., Prov. 23:27; 29:3), it was only the priests who were specifically prohibited from having sex with them (Lev. 21:7).

Thus, when contemporary polemicists make repeated comparisons between same-gender sexuality and incest, they are telling us more about their own agendas than about the values of ancient Israel.

53. See Alter, *The Five Books of Moses*, p. 623. The key phrase is *mishkĕvê 'ishshâ*, which in Hebrew is as follows: מִשְׁכְּבֵי אִשָּׁה. This is an idiom with two parts. First, the plural noun form, *mishkĕvê*, comes from the verbal root *sh-k-v*, which means "to lie down." When used of sexual relations, it connotes the "lying down" of sexual intercourse. The companion word, *'ishshâ*, here means "of or pertaining to a woman." The net result of putting these two words together is to form a circumlocution whose most literal rendering would go something like this: "You shall not with a male . . . the lyings of a woman." Since the word *mishkĕvê* always involves situations in which one person is being sexually penetrated by another, the two texts are taken by most interpreters as a prohibition against anal sex.

This idiom has its counterpart in a similar phrase in which Scripture refers to women who engage in "lying with of a man" (*mishkav zākār*; מִשְׁכַּב זָכָר). The most striking instance is the death penalty meted out to the Midianite women who acted treacherously against the men of Israel by seducing them (see Num. 31:16-18; 25:6-18). This story is combined with a companion episode in which the Moabite women invite the men of Israel to have sexual relations with them and worship their gods (Num. 25:1-5). Moreover, the specific sentence Moses hands down against the Midianite women comes immediately after a set of ordinances about when a woman's word is and is not to be listened to (Num. 30:1-16). In each case, the status of her word is connected to her subordinate status to the man who controls her. Thus, when Moses calls for the deaths of Midianite women who have "lain with" a man (Num. 31:15), there is the suggestion that these women deserved their fate because they assumed the role of sexual aggressors, thus breaching the boundaries of Israelite sexual norms. Drawing an analogy, then, between the "lying with of a woman" and the "lying with of a man" bolsters the idea that the violation in Lev. 18:22 and 20:13 is the transgression of the proper passive and active gender roles.

54. See R. Laird Harris, Gleason L. Archer, and Bruce Waltke, eds., *Theological Wordbook of the Old Testament*, 2 vols. (Chicago: Moody Publishers, 1980), pp. 2381-2382. The same point is made by the orthodox Rabbi Milgrom, who argues "that sexual liaisons occurring with a male, falling outside the control of the paterfamilias, would be neither condemnable nor punishable" (Milgrom, *Leviticus 17–22*, p. 1569).

55. Here I take the "lying with" of v. 24 to be governed still by the illicit act of David lying with "the wife of Uriah" in v. 11. By v. 24, David has taken Bathsheba as one of his many wives, but the moral condemnation of what he did still stands. That Solomon is a child of this union does not exonerate David, but it shows that God is always at work to bring redemption out of sin.

56. In addition to these narrative contexts, the Wisdom literature warns against the seductive invitation issued by prostitutes for a man to come "lie with" them (Prov. 7:17). And, of course, the prophets speak metaphorically of Israel "lying with" other gods as a form of spiritual adultery (e.g., Ezek. 23:8, 17; Isa. 57:7, 8). Examples from legalistic material confirm this interpretation. Consider Deuteronomy and Exodus, where we are told that a person "lying with" an animal is to be cursed (Deut. 27:21) or executed (Exod. 22:19). Or again, Deut. 28:30 warns that, if one engages in illicit behavior, then one's own betrothed will end up "lying with" another man. Likewise, in Exod. 22:16, the idiom is used for the act of seducing a virgin to whom one is not betrothed. In Deut. 22:22, it is said that a man "lying with" another man's wife calls for the death penalty for both parties. Num. 5:19, 20 uses the phrase in the context of a ritual to determine whether a man has "lain with" a woman believed to be an adulterer.

This is an impressive accumulation of evidence. It might be argued that Gen. 30:15 and 2 Sam. 11:11 provide exceptions, but this is not clear. In the first case, Leah purchases from Rachel a night of "lying" with Jacob. Even though the sexual act occurs within a marital context, the bargain renders it derisive. In the second case, Uriah the Hittite refuses to "lie" with his wife (cf. 1 Sam. 21:4-5) because it is not permissible for a soldier to have sex during time of war (Deut. 23:9-11).

57. In Lev. 18:20, male Israelites, and especially heads of families, are prohibited from "lying with" near kin. As I have mentioned above, the context of these prohibitions is the need to protect the integrity of relationships in the extended household and to keep the harmony of the household itself from becoming fatally disrupted. For similar reasons, Leviticus prohibits "lying with" the female slave of another man (Lev. 19:20). The ritual commandments pertaining to sexuality in Leviticus also take context into account. Because of the sacredness of blood, Israelite men are prohibited from "lying" with any woman — even their own wives — during the time of menstruation (Lev. 15:24, 33).

There are two cases in Leviticus where an idiom employing *sh-k-v* (שׁכב) may seem to be morally neutral, but these are exceptions that prove the rule. For both involve seminal emissions irrespective of a sanctified context. The first case is in Lev. 15:16, 17, 32 and 22:4, which sets forth rules declaring that, when a man has an emission of semen (*shikĕvat zera'*; שִׁכְבַת־זֶרַע) — any seminal emission, including a nocturnal emission — he is ritually unclean. The second possible case of a morally neutral use of a *sh-k-v* derivative is Lev. 15:18. Here we are told that, if a man lies with a woman and has an emission of semen, both parties are ritually unclean. This law would seem to apply whether the couple is married or not. Alter's translation captures the open-ended context of which Leviticus speaks: "And a woman whom a man has bedded with emission of semen — they shall wash in water and be unclean until the evening" (*The Five Books of Moses*, p. 608). The fact that this rule applies even if the couple is unmarried may account for the use of "to lie with" instead of the more intimate "to know" (*yāda'*; יָדַע, e.g., Gen. 4:1).

58. Throughout his discussion of the Leviticus texts, Robert A. J. Gagnon operates as though the prohibition applies to all male same-gender sexual expression of any kind (see *The Bible and Homosexual Practice*, pp. 111-142). His reasoning is that, if one form of sexual expression is explicitly prohibited, then all forms must be prohibited (see Gagnon's discussion on pp. 142-146). He analogizes this to incest or adultery. If incestuous or adulterous sexual intercourse is prohibited, then so is incestuous kissing or fondling. On this point, Gagnon is surely right. And this is the reason that, in the prohibitions on sexual relations with near relatives, a man is forbidden even to look on a woman's nakedness (Lev. 18:6; see my discussion of Lev. 18 below). Yet no such further prohibition exists regarding same-sex relations. It is simply the one act that is condemned. The interpretive question, then, is this: What did that one act signify within the cultural world of Leviticus? And what is the carryover value of the prohibition of that act today?

59. As evidence for the intensity of the biblical pronouncement against male-to-male sexual relations, we are told by one commentator, "In the entire Holiness Code — indeed, in the entire priestly corpus of the Tetrateuch — the only forbidden act to which the designation 'abomination' is specifically attached is homosexual intercourse" (Gagnon, *The Bible and Homosexual Practice*, p. 113). This sounds impressive, but it is based on a definitional sleight of hand. By focusing his statement solely on the Holiness Code (and not the whole of Leviticus) and on the "priestly corpus of the Tetrateuch" (rather than the whole Pentateuch), Gagnon is able to limit the condemnation to one kind of act, while omitting to tell the reader of comparable instances of the term in other parts of Leviticus, in the nonpriestly portions of the Tetrateuch, or in the remainder of the Pentateuch. The word for "abomination" here is *tô'ēbâ* (תּוֹעֵבָה) (Lev. 18:29); in Leviticus it is a taboo that applies not only to male-on-male sexual intercourse but to all of the sexual prohibitions in the Holiness Code, including the prohibition against having sex with a menstruating woman (18:19). In Genesis we are told that the Egyptians consider the act of eating with Israelites (Gen. 43:32) or consorting with shepherds (Gen. 46:34) to be *tô'ēbâ*. In Exodus we learn that the various sacrifices offered up

by Israelites are considered *tôʿēbâ* to the Egyptians (Exod. 8:26; MT: 22). In Deuteronomy, not only worshiping other gods or making idols (Deut. 7:25, 26; 12:31; 13:14; 17:4; 27:15; 32:16) but eating nonkosher food is *tôʿēbâ* (14:3), as is offering a blemished sacrifice (17:1), casting spells (18:11-12), engaging in ritualized religious sex (23:18, MT: 19), using dishonest weights (25:16), or otherwise imitating gentile practices (18:9). The act of crossing gender boundaries, such as women wearing men's clothing and vice versa, is also *tôʿēbâ* (Deut. 22:5), as is remarrying one's own wife after she has lived with another man (24:4). This is by no means to trivialize actions that Scripture declares *tôʿēbâ*. The prophet Ezekiel, who uses the word more than any other writer in the canon, considers Israel's acts of *tôʿēbâ* to be responsible for their military defeat, removal from the land, and exile. Yet, when the evidence is viewed in its widest sweep, it is difficult to conclude that an act is in itself *intrinsically* evil merely by virtue of being declared *tôʿēbâ*. It is a thoroughly culturally conditioned concept.

60. Let us flesh out this conclusion in a bit more detail. We have already dispensed with the possibility that Leviticus finds male-to-male sexual intercourse objectionable merely because it constitutes a departure from the anatomical "fit" between "male and female." This notion is nowhere stated explicitly in the text, but is merely a perspective that interpreters *bring to* the text. Since Leviticus is part of the Priestly tradition in the Bible, it uses the trope "male and female" with some frequency. Yet none of these references has anything to do with sexual intercourse, let alone sexual anatomy. As is the case in Gen. 1:27, which I discussed earlier, the references have the sense of "*both* male and female" (see Lev. 3:1, 6; 12:7; 15:33; 25:6, 44; 27:5, 6, 7).

Another possibility for the prohibition, to which I have already alluded, is that for one male to lie with another male "as with a woman" would have upset the strict understanding of male gender roles in Israelite society. This is the view advanced by Martti Nissinen, *Homoeroticism in the Biblical World: A Historical Perspective*, trans. Kirsi Stjerna (Minneapolis: Fortress, 1998). In the understanding of the ancient Near Eastern world, such an act would amount to sexual humiliation. Thus, Israelite males are being admonished here not to transgress gender boundaries by sexually humiliating other males. This suggestion has much to commend it, not least that it coheres with the earlier rationale given for the rule against sex with women who are near relatives: that is, these are prohibitions that apply especially to sexual liaisons with persons over whom the male head of the clan has social control. This suggestion is further supported by reflections of the leading commentator on Leviticus (Milgrom, *Leviticus 17–22*, p. 1569). The idea that the rule is there for the protection of an Israelite's manhood, again, helps to explain why Hebrew Scripture is silent on lesbianism. It also explains why, if a man had his way sexually with another man, it was viewed just as gravely as if a man had his way sexually with another man's wife: in both cases it was an offense to the dignity of the man.

Yet another possibility is that male-to-male copulation violates the command in Genesis to "be fruitful and multiply" (Gen. 1:22, 28; 8:17; 9:1, 7). There is some textual warrant for this view, because the people are told that, as a response to their obeying the sexuality rules, God will "make you fruitful and multiply you" (Lev. 26:9). A society in which progeny meant strength and survival might well have found a nonprocreative union between two men objectionable. If this is the reason, however, it is not clear why such a view would still bind the people of God today. We certainly do not prohibit marriage between men and women who, for whatever reason, are incapable of procreating. Just as infertile married couples adopt children, so do gay and lesbian couples. Similarly, in a complex and dynamic society such as ours, people and couples have many ways of contributing to society and to the "multiplying" of its blessings — even when they happen to have no children. This is the overall position favored by Milgrom; however, he also acknowledges another possibility I have just raised, which is that sexual liaisons falling outside the control of the male head of the household are not specifically covered in the prohibition (Milgrom, *Leviticus 17–22*, pp. 1567, 1569).

A final possibility is that the prohibition here was aimed specifically at distinguishing Israel's behavior from that of the cultic worship practices of the surrounding Canaanite peoples. This view, too, has significant textual support. Regarding the entire list of banned sexual activities in Lev. 18, Israelite men are admonished not to do what the Egyptians or Canaanites do, nor to follow their statutes (Lev. 18:3). In addition, same-sex intercourse was likely associated with Canaanite practices in the story of Sodom and Gomorrah (Gen. 19). Also, the attempted same-sex intercourse by the Jewish men of Gibeah in Judges 19 suggests that they were succumbing to the ways of the surrounding peoples (see Levine, *Leviticus*, p. 123). This view would also explain why the cultically loaded word "abomination" is used of these offenses: sexual acts between men would have referred to the pagan cult. In fact, Hebrew Scripture may have such practices specifically in mind in a number of places: Gen. 38:21-22; Deut. 23:17-18; 1 Kings 14:21-24; 15:12-14; 22:46; 2 Kings 23:7; Job 36:14; Hos. 4:14 (see Nissinen, *Homoeroticism in the Biblical World,* p. 40). This would explain why male-to-male sex acts are grouped in Leviticus with the commandment against sacrificing children to Molech (Lev. 18:21; 20:2-5); against worshiping idols (19:4); against sexual relations with (cultic) animals (18:23; 20:15-16); against mediums, witches, and the calling up of spirits (19:31; 20:6, 27); against prostitutes (19:29; 21:7, 9); and against tattoos (19:28; 21:5). It is possible that the prophet Ezekiel, whose theological perspective is similar to that of Leviticus, condemns a similar set of practices precisely because they had become so widespread in Israel (Ezek. 6:9, 11; 7:20; 8:4-18; 14:6: 16:36, 43, 44-58; 18:12-13; 20:7; 22:2). Archaeological evidence certainly makes clear that some of these practices, including child sacrifice, were being carried out during portions of Israel's history. This is not only a plausible reason for the prohibition; in terms of text support, it may be the most plausible reason.

61. For example, the law of Leviticus states firmly to the men of Israel, "You shall not take a woman as a rival to her sister, uncovering her nakedness while her sister is still alive" (Lev. 18:18). This refers not to marriage per se but more generally to render-

ing sexually vulnerable ("uncovering the nakedness") or having sexual intercourse with ("you shall not take") certain women living in close proximity within one's extended family. Notwithstanding this later commandment, of course, the patriarch Jacob (who is also called "Israel") had done exactly what the commandment ostensibly forbids: he not only has sexual relations with, but he marries, both Leah and Rachel. This suggests a certain circumstantial quality to the laying down of the law. Or again, the law of Leviticus lays down a prohibition against a man "uncovering the nakedness" of a woman belonging to his brother. Yet if a man's brother dies, another part of the Old Testament obligates the surviving brother (even if he himself is already married) to have sexual relations with his deceased brother's wife in order to give his brother an heir (so-called levirate marriage [Deut. 25:5-10]).

62. The multiplicity of commandments in Leviticus has led some interpreters to make a misleading and ultimately unsustainable distinction between two types of law: the ritual — or "ceremonial" — law, which can be summarily discarded by Christians, and the "moral" law, which must still be obeyed. This distinction is not set out in the text of Leviticus itself, and it is not as helpful a distinction as interpreters think (see Jacob Milgrom, *Leviticus: A Book of Ritual and Ethics,* Continental Commentary [Minneapolis: Augsburg Fortress, 2004]). At the very least, the ritual-morality distinction is much more complex than previous delineations have recognized (see Jonathan Klawans, *Impurity and Sin in Ancient Judaism* [Oxford: Oxford University Press, 2000]). For a contrary view, see Hyam Maccoby, *Ritual and Morality: The Ritual Purity System and Its Place in Judaism* (Cambridge, UK: Cambridge University Press, 1999). Within the cultural world of Leviticus, to depart from the demands of ritual can breed immorality; and to seek to be moral, at least within the cultural world of Leviticus, *requires* that one attend to ritual. So much is at stake in keeping these commandments, in fact, that to commit an act of ritual impurity is to become ineligible to enter the temple, and therefore unable to participate in the worship life of the community.

63. The Hebrew word transliterated *tōv* is טוֹב.

64. The Hebrew word transliterated *qādôsh* is קָדוֹשׁ.

65. For discussion of other isolated verses on homoeroticism, see the discussion of the prohibition position in ch. 1.

66. Recent studies in Paul's thought have emphasized the essential Jewishness of his thinking. This so-called New Perspective in Pauline studies emphasizes that the portrait of Judaism as marked by "works righteousness" is inaccurate. Rather, as E. P. Sanders has argued, the Judaism of Paul's day was characterized by a "covenantal nomism," according to which God established a covenant with the Jewish people, who in turn were to follow the commandments of Torah, with atonement being offered when they transgressed. By contrast, Sanders argues that salvation for Paul was by participation in Christ (see Sanders, *Paul and Palestinian Judaism: A Comparison of Patterns of Religion* [Minneapolis: Fortress, 1977]). For a succinct description of the New Perspective, see James D. G. Dunn, *Jesus, Paul and the Law: Studies in Mark and*

Galatians (Louisville: Westminster John Knox, 1990), pp. 183-205. The perspective of Sanders and those in sympathy with him has not gone unchallenged. My own interpretation of Paul does not depend on following Sanders or the New Perspective in all its particulars. However, in the matter of questioning the reception of Judaism on which many older perspectives depended, I believe the perspective of Sanders has offered a needed corrective.

67. Richard B. Hays, "Three Dramatic Roles: The Law in Romans 3–4," in *The Conversion of the Imagination: Paul as Interpreter of Israel's Scripture* (Grand Rapids: Eerdmans, 2005), pp. 85-100.

68. Salvation is "coming" for Paul in the sense that it anticipates a decisive deliverance at the end of days (e.g., 1 Thess. 5:8; Phil. 1:19; Rom. 5:10; 8:23; 13:11; see also Eph. 4:30; Col. 1:22).

69. At this point in the argument it is typical for prohibitionists to respond that exclusivity of commitment is not itself a sufficient reason to make a relationship moral. An exclusive commitment to an incestuous or adulterous relationship, for example, should not be permitted. A moment's reflection will reveal the hidden sophistry in this response. Adultery and incest, by their very nature, contradict the notion of a self-giving to another that is exclusive and loving. In the case of adultery, the act itself breaks a previous commitment made to one's spouse. Similarly, incestuous relations involve the taking advantage of the vulnerabilities of a person who is a near relative.

70. This Greek neologism, ἀρσενοκοῖται, appears in no extant text prior to this one, suggesting that it was coined in Paul's day — perhaps even by Paul himself. The text of the Greek Septuagint from which the word was coined (its two component parts are in **boldface**) appears in Greek, English translation, and transliterated Greek as follows:

καὶ ὃς ἂν κοιμηθῇ μετὰ **ἄρσενος κοίτην** γυναικός. . . .

". . . and if a man sleeps with a man in the bed in a woman-like way. . . ."

*kai hos an koimēthēi meta **arsenos koitēn** gunaikos.* . . .

71. The word *malakoi* transliterates the Greek μαλακοὶ.

72. For an accessible account, see Robin Scroggs, *The New Testament and Homosexuality* (Philadelphia: Fortress, 1983), pp. 40-42.

73. For a brief account, together with clear examples from the Roman context, see Crossan and Reed, *In Search of Paul*, pp. 257-271.

74. Some have argued that, where specific New Testament ethical teachings have a countercultural thrust, they need to be given more weight. This idea is a holdover from the older biblical theology that spoke of revelation as always being at odds with culture. In fact, the relationship between gospel and culture is much more complex. Nevertheless, the fact that Paul is simply endorsing what many in his audience already believe leans against the idea that this is a uniquely Christian teaching.

75. Stoicism was founded in Athens around 300 BCE by Zeno. It is hardly surpris-

ing that an anti-imperial Jew like Paul would appeal to Stoic values, since Stoicism was, during the first century in Rome, the philosophy that provided a basis for criticism of the cult of the Roman emperor, though later Stoic philosophers themselves served as imperial advisors. Emperor Marcus Aurelius was himself a Stoic philosopher. Stoicism later had an impact on Christian theology (see, generally, Brad Inwood, ed., *The Cambridge Companion to the Stoics* [Cambridge, UK: Cambridge University Press, 2003]).

76. The Pastoral Epistles are 1 Timothy, 2 Timothy, and Titus; scholars are divided over whether Paul himself wrote these texts. Other texts where Pauline authorship is debated include the "Deutero-Pauline" texts: Ephesians, Colossians, and 2 Thessalonians.

77. The word transliterated *porneias* in Greek is πορνείας; it refers generally to sexual immorality. The word *skeuos* transliterates the Greek σκεῦος, which means "vessel" and is here translated "body." Sometimes it is used to mean "wife," but the context here suggests the broader meaning of "body." The word transliterated *epithumias* is ἐπιθυμίας, which appears again in Rom. 1:24. The word transliterated *pleonektein* is πλεονεκτεῖν. The phrase *ton adelphon* transliterates the phrase τὸν ἀδελφόν; it literally refers in the singular to "a brother," but it has been translated inclusively by the NRSV as "a brother or sister."

78. An alternative translation is: "Each one of you knows how to take a wife (or vessel) for himself." In this translation, which for our present purposes does not significantly change the point, the word σκεῦος, which literally means "vessel," is taken to mean wife. In portraying a wife as a sexual "vessel," the basic point is the same: one must order one's sexual life with a single person. However, one should not overlook the perspective of the male as dominant and hierarchical that is presupposed here.

79. See Stanley K. Stowers, "Paul and Self-Mastery," in J. Paul Sampley, ed., *Paul in the Greco-Roman World: A Handbook* (Harrisburg, PA: Trinity Press International, 2003), pp. 551-574.

80. Exod. 20:17; Deut. 5:21; 7:25; 4 Macc. 2:5.

81. This idea arose within a social world in which young women aged fourteen to sixteen were given in marriage to men who were often in their thirties or even older. In such a world, to say that the purpose of marriage was procreation was a virtual code way for saying that the purpose of *women* was procreation.

82. We need not go so far as recent Roman Catholic moral theology, however, which argues that, in order to be truly open to the other in the act of sexual intercourse, one must refrain from using artificial means of birth control.

83. One caveat needs to be added: under the doctrine of "constructive abandonment," the refusal over a long period of time to have sexual relations can constitute a grounds for divorce.

84. For a systematic account, see Francis Schüssler Fiorenza, "Marriage," in *Systematic Theology: Roman Catholic Perspectives,* vol. 2 (Minneapolis: Augsburg Fortress, 1991), pp. 305-346.

85. The classic explication of this is in Elisabeth Schüssler Fiorenza, *In Memory of Her: A Feminist Reconstruction of Christian Origins* (New York: Crossroads, 1983).

86. David L. Balch, "Paul, Families, and Households," in *Paul in the Greco-Roman World: A Handbook,* ed. J. Paul Sampley (Harrisburg, PA: Trinity Press International, 2003), p. 265.

87. The transliteration *pais* stands for the Greek παῖς. The phrase *ho pais mou,* if translated literally, does not mean "my servant" (NRSV) but "the one who is a boy to me."

88. A slave could be called by the diminutive term "boy" even after he had reached adulthood (see J. Albert Harrill, "Paul and Slavery," in Sampley, ed., *Paul in the Greco-Roman World,* p. 577). For the Greek backgound, see Kenneth J. Dover, *Greek Homosexuality* [updated with a new postscript] (Cambridge, MA: Harvard University Press, 2004).

89. Indeed, the very word *pais* is the main root of the word "pederasty," which is a term in Greco-Roman society for the practice of having sex with a young man (though not necessarily a minor); see Dover, *Greek Homosexuality,* pp. 16, 85, 165.

90. It is true that elsewhere the New Testament says that those perpetrating sexual infractions will not inherit the kingdom (e.g., Gal. 5:21; Eph. 5:5). But again, we must ask what kinds of infractions are intended. It is exploitative, hedonistic sexuality that these passages have in view.

91. Luke Timothy Johnson, *Scripture and Discernment* (Nashville: Abingdon Press, 1996), pp. 145ff.; Jeffrey Siker, "Homosexuals, the Bible, and Gentile Inclusion," *Theology Today* 51 (July 1994): 219-234 (reprinted in Jeffrey Siker, ed., *Homosexuality in the Church: Both Sides of the Debate* [Louisville: Westminster John Knox, 1994], pp. 178-194).

92. Scripture is "fulfilled" (πληρόω) in that it comes to fruition in Jesus' teaching and ministry (Matt. 1:22; 2:15, 17, 23; 4:14-16; 8:17; 12:17-21; 13:35; 21:4-5; 26:54, 56; 27:9-10). Matthew speaks in a number of places of Scripture being dynamically "accomplished" (*ginomai;* γίνομαι) in the life of Jesus (Matt. 1:22; 21:4; 26:54, 56). The coming of God's reign itself is dynamic, as shown in the parable of the mustard seed (Matt. 13:32). For other instances of a dynamic sense of "becoming" in the lives of believers, see Matt. 10:16, 25; 18:3, 19; 20:16; 21:21. There is also a dynamic devolution into destruction that occurs in the lives of unbelievers (Matt. 6:16; 9:16; 11:21, 23; 12:45; 13:21, 22; 21:19, 21; 23:15; 24:6, 21, 32, 34, 44). Most dramatic of all are the things that take place in the events of Jesus' passion (Matt. 21:42; 26:42; 27:45, 54). Although "to become" or "to reach fulfillment" is a common verb, its use is especially powerful theologically in the prologue to John's Gospel: "And the Word *became* (ἐγένετο) flesh and lived among us, and we have seen his glory, the glory as of a father's only son, full of grace and truth" (John 1:14).

93. Of the many fine commentaries available, see Katherine Doob Sakenfeld, *Ruth,* Interpretation (Louisville: Westminster John Knox, 1999).

94. According to Jewish lore, the Moabites were descended from the bastard off-

spring of the incestuous relationship between Lot and one of his daughters (Gen. 19:36-37).

95. The Hebrew is חֶסֶד.

96. For some classic texts on biblical covenant, see George E. Mendenhall, "Covenant Forms in Israelite Religion," *Biblical Archaeologist* 17 (1954): 50-76; Delbert Hillers, *Covenant: The History of an Idea* (Baltimore: Johns Hopkins Press, 1969); Jon D. Levenson, *Sinai and Zion: An Entry into the Jewish Bible* (San Francisco: HarperSanFrancisco, 1985); E. W. Nicholson, *God and His People: Covenant Theology in the Old Testament* (Oxford: Clarendon Press, 1986).

97. The Hebrew is

עַל־כֵּן יַעֲזָב־אִישׁ אֶת־אָבִיו וְאֶת־אִמּוֹ וְדָבַק בְּאִשְׁתּוֹ וְהָיוּ
לְבָשָׂר אֶחָד

98. See also Judg. 9:2; 2 Sam. 5:1; 19:12, 13; 1 Chron. 11:1.

99. Susan Ackerman has recently provided an extensive study comparing the literary pairing of David and Jonathan to that of Gilgamesh and Enkidu. Susan Ackerman, *When Heroes Love: The Ambiguity of Eros in the Stories of Gilgamesh and David* (New York: Columbia University Press, 2005). Jean-Fabrice Nardelli rejects Ackerman's strictly literary reading, arguing that David and Jonathan were a homosexual couple. Jean-Fabrice Nardelli, *Homosexuality and Liminality in the Gilgameš and Samuel* (Amsterdam : Adolf M. Hakkert, 2007). Among the many works rejecting any homoerotic pairing, see Markus Zehnder, "Exegetische Beobachtungen zu den David-Jonathan-Geschichten," *Biblica* 79 (1998): 153-179.

100. On Gal. 3:26-29 as a unit summarizing Paul's argument up to that point, see Hans Dieter Betz, *Galatians: A Commentary on Paul's Letter to the Churches in Galatia*, Hermeneia (Philadelphia: Fortress, 1979), pp. 181-185. In addition to Betz's classic commentary, see, more recently, Richard B. Hays, *The Letter to the Galatians: Introduction, Commentary, and Reflections*, vol. 11, New Interpreter's Bible, Leander Keck, ed. (Nashville: Abingdon, 2000), pp. 181-348.

101. Gal 3:28: οὐκ ἔνι Ἰουδαῖος **οὐδὲ** Ἕλλην οὐκ ἔνι δοῦλος **οὐδὲ** ἐλεύθερος οὐκ ἔνι ἄρσεν **καὶ** θῆλυ. πάντες γὰρ ὑμεῖς εἷς ἐστε ἐν Χριστῷ Ἰησοῦ. The rendering "no longer" for all three polarities in the NRSV is preferable to the "neither/nor" of the RSV, because "no longer" captures the dynamic, forward-looking "happening" — the salvation — that is breaking into the world for those who are in Christ.

102. The phrase was mistranslated in the Tyndale New Testament of 1534, in the Geneva Bible of 1559, and then again in the King James Version of the Bible of 1611. No doubt the three cadences of "neither/nor" sounded good to the bards and poets who were trying to render Scripture into English, but it does not accurately reflect the Greek text.

103. As Richard Hays has put it, "To say that this created distinction is no longer in force is to declare that the new creation has come upon us, a new creation in which

even gender roles no longer pertain" (*Galatians,* p. 273). Or, as feminist scholar Elisabeth Schüssler Fiorenza explains this passage, "Being baptized into Christ means entering the sphere of the resurrected Lord, the life-giving Spirit whose reality and power are manifested in the Christian community" (*In Memory of Her,* p. 214).

104. The point I am making would still hold true whether or not this formula derives from baptismal practice or was originally written by Paul himself. One linguistic clue to the baptismal origin is given in v. 27: "As many of you as were baptized into Christ have clothed yourselves with Christ." Another is that Paul's language shifts from the "we" of vv. 23-25 to the "you" of vv. 26-29, with the "we" resuming in 4:3, suggesting that he has shifted from his own voice to a quotation and back. Still another clue is that the "male and female" plays no part in the overall argument of Galatians, while Jew/Greek and slave/free certainly do. For a form-critical analysis of how this text matches up with other formulae for baptism, see Betz, *Galatians,* pp. 181-185. For a look at the social world surrounding the practice of baptism, see Wayne A. Meeks, *The First Urban Christians: The Social World of the Apostle Paul* (New Haven: Yale University Press, 1983), pp. 150-157.

105. Even after it was abolished, slavery left a legacy of many long years of segregation that Christians meekly tolerated, and the economic effects of all this exist to the present day. Indeed, to this day, there has been neither an apology nor any economic reparations for slavery in the United States. On this point, see Roy L. Brooks, *Atonement and Forgiveness: A New Model for Black Reparations* (Berkeley: University of California Press, 2004). In June 2005, the U.S. Senate passed a resolution apologizing for lynching, the only such official apology ever issued to African Americans for any reason (see Sharyl Gay Stolberg, "The Senate Apologizes, Mostly," *The New York Times,* Sunday, June 19, 2005, WK 3).

106. See Kevin Bales, *Disposable People: New Slavery in the Global Economy* (Berkeley: University of California Press, 2004); Kevin Bales, ed., *Understanding Global Slavery: A Reader* (Berkeley: University of California Press, 2005).

107. LXX: καὶ ἐποίησεν ὁ θεὸς τὸν ἄνθρωπον κατ᾽ εἰκόνα θεοῦ ἐποίησεν αὐτόν. ἄρσεν καὶ θῆλυ ἐποίησεν αὐτούς.

Hebrew:

וַיִּבְרָא אֱלֹהִים אֶת־הָאָדָם בְּצַלְמוֹ בְּצֶלֶם אֱלֹהִים בָּרָא אֹתוֹ
זָכָר וּנְקֵבָה בָּרָא אֹתָם

The shift in Gal. 3:28 from the nouns Jew/Greek and slave/free to the adjectives male (ἄρσεν) and female (θῆλυ) makes it clear that the formula quotes Gen. 1:27 (see Daniel Boyarin, *A Radical Jew: Paul and the Politics of Identity* [Berkeley: University of California Press, 1994], p. 186). Much has been made of the argument by Wayne Meeks ("The Image of the Androgyne: Some Uses of a Symbol in Earliest Christianity," *Journal of the History of Religions* 13/1 [1973]: 165-208) that Gal. 3:28 and early Christian baptismal formulae presuppose the myth of "Adam" as an androgynous creature who was "split" into male and female halves, which were then reunited in sexual intercourse (the argument is encapsulated in Meeks, *The First Urban Christians*, p. 155). Some contemporary commentators have invoked this myth to argue that only the "one-flesh union" of male and female is legitimated by the Genesis story. One problem with this argument is that it takes a piece of speculation that was popular in the Hellenistic world and retrojects it back on the ancient text of Genesis itself. Moreover, in the light of Gal. 3:28, the argument is really beside the point. The unity of humanity is not achieved through a particular form of sexuality but through Christ.

108. This is the principal claim of Gagnon in *The Bible and Homosexual Practice*, a book widely cited by anti-gay activists in the church but one that gives no sustained attention to the teaching of Gal. 3:28. Gagnon mentions Gal. 3:28 only three times, quoting it correctly once ("male and female," p. 443), incorrectly once ("neither male nor female," p. 368), and citing it a third time to explain why women in Corinth might have argued for the transcending of gender boundaries (p. 367, n. 27). In general, Gagnon goes out of his way to align himself with the new exegetical position, forged over the last several decades, that favors the ordination of women. This new exegetical position is just as critical of past misogynist practices in the church as the new exegetical openness to gay people that I advocate is critical of past prejudices in the church. Yet Gagnon gives us no persuasive reason why we should break with tradition and ordain women but at the same time genuflect to tradition in being anti-gay. I believe that I have refuted his claim that there is no positive warrant in Scripture for such a move with my argument in this chapter. But this is about more than marshaling arguments; it is about the lives of people. If the church takes seriously the gospel witness of Gal. 3:28, it will no longer use the abstraction "gender complementarity" as a way to denigrate gay and lesbian people. We should state it unambiguously: such a tactic does not have gospel merit.

109. Elisabeth Schüssler Fiorenza points out parallel passages from the Gospel of Thomas (Log. 22) and the Second Epistle to Clement (12:1-6). The text from Clement reads, in part: "Furthermore, 'male with the female neither male nor female' means this: that when a brother sees a sister he should not think of her sex any more than she should think of his" (12:6). Schüssler Fiorenza reads this to mean that "a Christian ought not to look at other Christians as sex objects, as males and females, but as members of the same 'family of God'" (*In Memory of Her*, p. 212).

110. A frequently cited quip from Paul's contemporary Seneca sums up the routine sexual abuse of slaves this way: "Unchastity [*impudicitia*] is a crime for the freeborn boy, a necessity for a slave, and a duty [*officium*] for the freedman" (Seneca the Elder, *Controversiae* 4, 1:431, quoted in a slightly different rendering in Crompton, *Homosexuality and Civilization*, p. 81).

111. In addition to the texts already cited, some others from the acknowledged letters of Paul in which the imagery of slavery is dominant include Rom. 1:1; 3:24; 6:6-23; 7:14; 8:12-23; 12:11; 13:4; 14:4, 18; 1 Cor. 3:5; 6:20; 9:19-23; 2 Cor. 2:14; 4:5; Gal. 1:10; 3:13-14; 4:1–5:1; 5:13; Phil. 1:1.

112. For the Romans, victory and triumph were concomitant with rape and death. The Greek verb *thriambeuo* (θριαμβεύω) in 2 Cor. 2:14 refers to a military victory parade in which the Romans led defeated generals and other leaders through the streets as conquered slaves. At the conclusion of the processional, they put some of these victims to death as a sacrifice to the gods. Building in part on accounts by Seneca, William Shakespeare included such a parade of triumph in his play *Titus Andronicus* (1594). For an exegetical treatment, see Scott J. Hafemann, *Suffering and the Spirit: An Exegetical Study of II Cor. 2:14–3:3 within the Context of the Corinthian Correspondence* (Tübingen: Mohr Siebeck, 1986). For general background, see H. S. Versnel, *Triumphus: An Inquiry into the Origin, Development, and Meaning of the Roman Triumph* (Leiden: Brill, 1970).

113. John Calvin, *The Second Epistle of Paul the Apostle to the Corinthians and the Epistles to Timothy, Titus and Philemon,* trans. T. A. Smail (Grand Rapids: Eerdmans, 1964), p. 33 (cited in Scott Hafemann, *The NIV Application Commentary: 2 Corinthians* [Grand Rapids: Zondervan, 2000], p. 108).

114. On this point, see Betz, *Galatians,* pp. 189-190. The ground-breaking philosophical analysis of "performative utterances" is J. L. Austin, *How to Do Things with Words* (Cambridge, MA: Harvard University Press, 1962). A classic example of a performative utterance is the marriage vow "I pledge thee my troth." While a "constative utterance" (e.g., "this is a chair") is true before it is uttered, in a performative utterance the saying makes it so. And yet, in another sense, both the marriage vow and the baptismal utterance must become true and be "lived into" over a span of time.

115. This point was made in paradigmatic form by H. Richard Niebuhr, *The Meaning of Revelation* (New York: Macmillan, 1941).

116. See Verna Harrison, "Male and Female in Cappadocian Theology," *Journal of Theological Studies* 41 (1990): 441-471. For a constructive reflection on Gregory's theology of gender, see Sarah Coakley, "The Eschatological Body: Gender, Transformation, and God," *Modern Theology* 16/1 (Jan. 2000): 61-73.

117. It is true that withholding sexual relations can be a grounds for divorce; but as long as both parties are comfortable not having sex, there is no requirement of sex to make a marriage valid.

Notes to Chapter Four

1. *Lawrence v. Texas,* 539 U.S. 558, 579 (2003).

2. For an accessible short biography and account of Justice Kennedy's time on the bench, see: http://www.oyez.org/justices/anthony_kennedy.

3. Groups opposing Justice Kennedy's nomination included the National Organization for Women, Americans for Democratic Action, and the Center for Constitutional Rights (see Murdoch and Price, *Courting Justice,* p. 378).

4. *Courting Justice,* p. 378. As a federal circuit court judge, Kennedy voted to up-

hold the dismissal of a federal employee for "flaunting his homosexuality" (*Singer v. U.S. Civil Service Commission,* 530 F.2d 247 [1976], *vacated and remanded,* 429 U.S. 1034 [1977]). That case was vacated after the issuance of new regulations for Civil Service employees. Kennedy also upheld a law that defined "homosexual rape" as a worse offense than "heterosexual rape" (*United States v. Smith,* 574 F.2d 988 [1978]). Kennedy was himself the author of an opinion that upheld the constitutionality of the U.S. Navy policy of dismissing gays (*Beller v. Mittendorf,* 632 F.2d 788 [1980], *cert. denied* 452 U.S. 905 [1981]). Furthermore, he authored a 2-1 affirmation of an INS ruling that the deportation of a male noncitizen partner of a male citizen (the two had been joined in a "holy union" ceremony) did not constitute extreme hardship within the meaning of the immigration law (*Sullivan v. INS,* 772 F.2d 609 [1985]).

5. This fact is not arbitrary. Over the years Justice Kennedy has obviously taken an interest in this issue, and his views have developed. His evolving view was perhaps already foreshadowed in a comment he made as a circuit court judge in the *Beller* case to the effect that, outside the military context, the decision to engage in same-gender sex acts might be a fundamental right with full constitutional protection (*Beller v. Mittendorf,* 632 F.2d at 792). This comment made Justice Kennedy suspect to certain conservatives at the time of his nomination. It is significant, then, that Justice Kennedy has authored the two most important U.S. Supreme Court cases on gay rights, *Romer v. Evans* (1996) and *Lawrence v. Texas* (2003), and was assigned to do so in both cases by the senior majority justice, Justice John Paul Stevens, who had himself dissented in the case of *Bowers v. Hardwick,* 478 U.S. 186 (1986). For an illuminating analysis of the significance of the *Lawrence* decision, see Randy E. Barnett, "Justice Kennedy's Libertarian Revolution: *Lawrence v. Texas,*" Boston Univ. School of Law Working Paper No. 03-13, http://ssrn.com/abstract=422564.

6. *Romer v. Evans,* 517 U.S. 620 (1996).

7. See Frank Rich, "Just How Gay Is the Right?" *New York Times,* Sunday, May 15, 2005, p. 14.

8. For an analysis of some of Justice Kennedy's more noteworthy opinions, see Akhil Reed Amar, "Justice Kennedy and the Ideal of Equality," *Pacific Law Journal* 28 (Spring 1997): 515-532.

9. This right applies to the federal government by virtue of the 5th Amendment and to the 50 states by virtue of the 14th Amendment. This is true because over the years the Supreme Court has applied the Bill of Rights to the states through the Due Process Clause of the 14th.

10. For a recent comprehensive treatment, see Edward Keynes, *Liberty, Property, and Privacy: Toward a Jurisprudence of Substantive Due Process* (University Park: Pennsylvania State University Press, 1996).

11. *Romer v. Evans,* 517 U.S. 620 (1996). The range of nuance in interpreting the holding of *Romer* is broad. Eskridge and Hunter summarize the possible offending features of the stricken law as follows: (a) depriving gays of the right to participate in the

democratic process; (b) a literal denial of legal protection; (c) not protecting privacy between consenting adults; (d) stigmatizing a group or turning them into a pariah; (e) prosecuting an animus against a stigmatized group; (f) a law that was overly broad (see Eskridge and Hunter, *Sexuality, Gender, and the Law,* pp. 271-272.

12. For a history and summary of equal protection jurisprudence, see Louis Michael Seidman, *Constitutional Law: Equal Protection of the Law,* Turning Point (New York: Foundation Press, 2002). For an argument about how equal protection jurisprudence has failed gay and lesbian people, see Evan Gerstmann, *The Constitutional Underclass: Gays, Lesbians, and the Failure of Class-Based Equal Protection* (Chicago: University of Chicago Press, 1999).

13. Although, by its terms, the Equal Protection Clause applies only to the states, the Supreme Court has also applied standards of equality and nondiscrimination to the federal government — on the grounds that such standards are contained implicitly in the Due Process Clause of the 5th Amendment (see *Bolling v. Sharpe,* 347 U.S. 497 [1954] [9-0]).

14. John Rawls, *A Theory of Justice* (Cambridge, MA: Belknap/Harvard University Press, 1971; rev. ed., 1999). See also the essays assembled in Rawls, *Collected Papers,* ed. Samuel Freeman (Cambridge, MA: Harvard University Press, 1999).

15. Rawls, *A Theory of Justice,* p. 303.

16. Amendment 2 provided as follows: "No Protected Status Based on Homosexual, Lesbian, or Bisexual Orientation. Neither the State of Colorado, through any of its branches or departments, nor any of its agencies, political subdivisions, municipalities or school districts shall enact, adopt or enforce any statute, regulation, ordinance, or policy whereby homosexual, lesbian, or bisexual orientation, conduct, practices, or relationships shall be the basis of or entitle any person or class of persons to have or claim any minority status, quota preferences, protected status or claim of discrimination. This Section of the Constitution shall be in all respects self-executing."

17. Martin Luther King Jr., "I Have a Dream," Aug. 28, 1963 (*Congressional Record, 88th Congress,* Washington, D.C.: U.S. Government Printing Office, 1963, vol. 109, pt. 12, pp. 16241-16242).

18. See M. V. Lee Badgett, *Money, Myths and Change: The Economic Lives of Lesbians and Gay Men* (Chicago: University of Chicago Press, 2001), esp. ch. 2; see also Dan A. Black, Hoda R. Maker, Seth G. Sanders, and Lowell J. Taylor, "The Earnings Effect of Sexual Orientation," *Industrial and Labor Relations Review* 56/3 (2003): 449-469.

19. A sample of some of this literature is collected in Eskridge and Hunter, *Sexuality, Gender, and the Law,* pp. 269-276.

20. Akhil Reed Amar, "Justice Kennedy and the Ideal of Equality," *Pacific Law Journal* 28 (Spring 1997): 529.

21. 517 U.S. at 623.

22. 517 U.S. at 626.

23. 517 U.S. at 627.

24. As we shall see, the *Romer* decision potentially has broad implications for gay rights, including spousal equality and gay marriage. However, subsequent to *Romer,* the Court refused to hear a case involving a narrower and more targeted amendment aimed against minority quotas for gays and lesbians in business. The City Charter of Cincinnati was amended to disallow gays and lesbians from receiving "minority or protected status" or "quota preference or other preferential treatment." Advocates alleged that the city might have to accept a certain quota of gay building contractors. The Sixth Circuit refused to strike down the Cincinnati provision on the grounds that no animus was present (*Equality Foundation of Greater Cincinnati v. City of Cincinnati,* 128 F.3d 289, *rehearing in banc denied,* 198 WL 101701 [1998], *cert. denied,* 525 U.S. 943 [1998]). When the U.S. Supreme Court refused to hear the case, Justices Stevens, Souter, and Ginsburg took the unusual step of issuing a memorandum indicating that their refusal to hear the case was specifically not a ruling on the merits.

25. For a history and summary of equal protection jurisprudence, see Seidman, *Constitutional Law.*

26. The idea for this "more exacting judicial scrutiny" originated in a footnote written by Chief Justice Harlan Fiske Stone, in which he opined that certain laws required a higher level of judicial review (see *United States v. Carolene Products,* 304 U.S. 144 [1938]). The *Carolene Products* case, which upheld a law regulating the transport of "filled" milk, was part of a turning point away from the so-called *Lochner* era, in which a business-oriented Supreme Court routinely struck down economic regulations passed by a reform-minded Congress (see *Lochner v. New York,* 198 U.S. 43 [1905], which struck down, on freedom-of-contract grounds, a protective law requiring that bakers work no more than 60 hours a week). For a social analysis of the issues, see Paul Kens, *Lochner v. New York: Economic Regulation on Trial, Landmark Law Cases and American Society* (Lawrence: University Press of Kansas, 1998). In the famous "footnote four" of *Carolene Products,* Chief Justice Stone indicated that laws passed by Congress are to be afforded a presumption of constitutionality and thus upheld in the absence of evidence to the contrary. However, if a federal law impinges on an enumerated constitutional right; if it restricts effective participation in the democratic process; or if it unfairly affects "discrete and insular minorities," then the law ought to undergo a more exacting degree of judicial scrutiny, which would mean that the presumption of constitutionality would fall away. The year prior to *Carolene Products,* the Court had upheld a state-imposed minimum wage law in *West Coast Hotel Co. v. Parrish,* 300 U.S. 379 (1937) and overruled a prior decision that claimed such laws violated freedom of contract, thus calling the *Lochner* era into question and signaling the Court's willingness to uphold the legislative agenda of the New Deal. Later on, in *Korematsu v. United States,* 323 U.S. 214 (1944), the Court indicated that classifications drawn up on the basis of racial minority status must be subjected to "strict scrutiny." In *Korematsu,* a law requiring Japanese citizens to relocate during World War II was upheld; but in subsequent decisions the application of "strict scrutiny" resulted in the invalidation of unfair classifica-

tions, unless the government could demonstrate a "compelling state interest" in the classification in question. Libertarian constitutional scholar Randy E. Barnett has argued that the presumption of constitutionality has inappropriately eclipsed what the Constitution actually should provide for, which is a presumption of liberty. As we shall see, he also believes that the gay-rights decision in *Lawrence v. Texas* (discussed below) marks an important shift in contemporary jurisprudence (Barnett, *Restoring the Lost Constitution: The Presumption of Liberty* [Princeton, NJ: Princeton University Press, 2004]).

27. *Palko v. Connecticut*, 302 U.S. 319 (1932) (Justice Cardozo).

28. On the right to vote, see *Harper v. Board of Elections*, 383 U.S. 663 (1966); *Kramer v. Union Free School District No. 15*, 395 U.S. 621 (1969). On access to the judicial process, see *Griffin v. Illinois*, 351 U.S. 12 (1956); *Douglas v. California*, 372 U.S. 353 (1963).

29. The Supreme Court has spoken of a right of privacy in a number of different contexts. The Court has upheld a right, for example, not to be prohibited from studying a foreign language in public school (*Meyer v. Nebraska*, 262 U.S. 390 [1923]); and a right to send one's children to a private rather than a public school (*Pierce v. Society of Sisters*, 268 U.S. 510 [1925]). In another context, the right of privacy was invoked to protect one's home from unreasonable state interference (*Mapp v. Ohio*, 367 U.S. 643 [1961]). (Fourth Amendment rules against unreasonable searches and seizures apply to the states under the Due Process Clause of the 14th Amendment.) Relevant to the discussion of same-sex relationships is the Court's embrace of a substantive right of privacy in matters of procreation and sexuality. This form of the right of privacy was first enunciated in a famous dissent by Justice John Marshall Harlan in *Poe v. Ullman*, 367 U.S. 497 (1961). The right of privacy as it pertains to sexuality was established by the Court for the first time in *Griswold v. Connecticut*, 381 U.S. 479 (1965), in which an 1879 Connecticut statute prohibiting the sale or use of contraceptives was held to be unconstitutional. The opinion, written by Justice William O. Douglas, was based on what he called the "penumbras" and "emanations" that surround the Bill of Rights. Later (in *Eisenstadt v. Baird*, 405 U.S. 438 [1972]) the Court, speaking through Justice William Brennan, extended the right of privacy in contraception usage to unmarried couples, relying on the Equal Protection Clause. Finally (in *Roe v. Wade*, 410 U.S. 113 [1973]) the Court relied on a right of privacy to support a woman's right to an abortion. In *Roe v. Wade* the Court located the privacy right in the liberty interest first articulated by Justice Harlan. For an excellent discussion of the right to sexual privacy, see the analysis and excerpted cases in the section entitled "Foundations of the Right to Sexual Privacy" in Eskridge and Hunter, *Sexuality, Gender, and the Law*, pp. 3-43.

30. *Skinner v. Oklahoma*, 316 U.S. 535 (1942).

31. Laws concerning the marital status of one's parents (i.e., illegitimacy) have also been subsumed under intermediate scrutiny; see *Levy v. Louisiana*, 391 U.S. 68 (1968) and *Stanley v. Illinois*, 405 U.S. 645 (1972); but cf. *Labine v. Vincent*, 401 U.S. 532 (1971).

32. Prior to the end of World War II, the Court upheld such discriminatory practices as the internment of persons of Japanese ancestry (*Korematsu v. United States,* 386 U.S. 213 [1944], which upheld the conviction of a Japanese American for failing to obey internment orders of the military).

33. This "substantial relationship" test was set forth in an opinion by Justice Brennan in *Craig v. Boren,* 429 U.S. 190, 197 (1976), in which the Court struck down an Oklahoma law that established a higher drinking age for men than for women. Justices Burger and Rehnquist registered dissents, arguing that this intermediate scrutiny was unwarranted. Rehnquist also objected to allowing men to claim gender discrimination. In an earlier case, Justice Brennan, along with Justices Douglas, White, and Marshall — just one shy of the necessary majority — had said they believed gender should be elevated to a suspect classification requiring strict scrutiny (*Frontiero v. Richardson,* 411 U.S. 677 [1973], which invalidated a military requirement that required women but not men to prove that they contributed more than 50 percent of their spouse's support in order to receive certain fringe benefits). Four other justices (Stewart, Blackmun, Powell, and Burger) concurred in the result of *Frontiero.* There, too, Justice Rehnquist dissented. The *Frontiero* case was argued against the government by then ACLU attorney Ruth Bader Ginsburg. Ginsburg had also argued the prior case of *Reed v. Reed,* 404 U.S. 71 (1971), in which the Court for the first time invoked the Equal Protection Clause to strike down a law on the grounds of sex discrimination. The law in question created a preference for probate courts to appoint men over women when a person died without a will. Writing for a unanimous Supreme Court, Chief Justice Warren Burger stated that gender "establishes a classification for scrutiny under the Equal Protection clause of the Fourteenth Amendment" (404 U.S. at 75). Nevertheless, the Court declined to apply "strict scrutiny" to gender cases, saying simply that laws impacting gender must have a "fair and substantial relation to the object of the legislation" (404 U.S. at 76). Ironically, it was to Chief Justice Burger's opinion in *Reed* that Justice Brennan appealed in insisting on a "heightened" level of scrutiny for gender cases. In short, the justices agree that gender cases require scrutiny, but the standard of scrutiny has been a subject of debate. In the recent 7-1 decision in *United States v. Virginia,* 518 U.S. 515 (1996), the Court applied a strengthened form of intermediate scrutiny to declare that the exclusion of women from the Virginia Military Academy was a violation of equal protection. I shall revisit the rationale of this case when we turn to the gay-marriage-versus-civil-union issue below.

34. See Robert Wintemute, "International Trends in Legal Recognition of Same-Sex Partnerships," 23 *Quinnipiac Law Review* (2004): 577-595. See also Brief of Amici Curiae International Human Rights Organizations et al. (*Goodridge v. Department of Public Health,* 440 Mass. 309, 798 NE2d 941 [2003], No. 08860), available at: http:// www.glad .org/marriage/International_Brief.pfd (accessed Mar. 26, 2005). See also Eric Heinze, *Sexual Orientation — A Human Right: An Essay on International Human Rights Law* (Leiden: Brill Academic Publishers, 1995).

35. Before he became Chief Justice, Associate Justice Rehnquist argued that there is nothing in the background of the Equal Protection Clause to indicate an intent to extend its reach beyond race. Therefore, he dissented from two decisions that treated one's status as a noncitizen as a suspect classification (*Sugarman v. Dougall*, 413 U.S. 634 [1973], which invalidated a New York law that limited certain state civil service laws to citizens only; *In re Griffiths*, 413 U.S. 717 [1973], which struck down a Connecticut law that excluded resident aliens from practicing law).

36. 517 U.S. at 631.

37. 517 U.S. at 632.

38. 517 U.S. at 633.

39. Lawrence H. Tribe, Brief in Support of Respondents (*Romer v. Evans*, 517 U.S. 620 [1996], No. 94-1039).

40. 517 U.S. at 635.

41. *U.S. Department of Agriculture v. Moreno*, 413 U.S. 528, 534 (1973).

42. Note that Justice William Rehnquist, who as Chief Justice would join Justice Scalia in his dissent from *Romer*, had previously dissented from *Moreno*. Rehnquist argued that Congress has the power to decide to support only "households" that match the traditional family structure (413 U.S. at 545-548).

43. *City of Cleburne v. Cleburne Living Center, Inc.*, 473 U.S. 432 (1985). The case is cited by Justice O'Connor in her concurring opinion to *Lawrence v. Texas*, discussed below.

44. *City of Cleburne v. Cleburne Living Center, Inc.*, 473 U.S. 432 (1985).

45. Cass R. Sunstein, *One Case at a Time: Judicial Minimalism on the Supreme Court* (Cambridge, MA: Harvard University Press, 1999), pp. 146-150.

46. Sunstein, *One Case at a Time*, p. 149.

47. 517 U.S. at 652.

48. 517 U.S. at 644.

49. Pointing out that the rules of the American Association of Law Schools prohibit discrimination against gays and lesbians, Justice Scalia levels the (ad hominem) argument that the majority opinion merely reflects the views of America's lawyer class. With his characteristic wit, Justice Scalia notes that one "may refuse to offer a job because the applicant is a Republican; because he is an adulterer; because he went to the wrong prep school or belongs to the wrong country club; because he eats snails; because he is a womanizer; because she wears real-animal fur; or even because he hates the Chicago Cubs. But if the interviewer should wish not to be an associate or partner of an applicant because he disapproves of the applicant's homosexuality, then he will have violated" the rules (517 U.S. at 652-53). This is an astonishing comment, because it completely ignores the most likely reason why lawyers as a group refuse to discriminate in this way, namely, that they have been trained in what fairness in the public realm demands. It is for this reason that many law schools have adopted policies to prevent discrimination against gays and lesbians. The Supreme Court recently upheld the power

of Congress to withhold federal funds from law schools that have protested the now re-pudiated "don't ask, don't tell" by attempting to bar government military recruiters from their campuses (see *Rumsfeld v. Forum for Academic and Institutional Rights* [2006] (Roberts, C. J.) [8-0]).

50. 517 U.S. at 651.

51. Among the many treatments of the harm of polygamy, see Andrea Moore-Emmett, *God's Brothel: The Extortion of Sex for Salvation in Contemporary Mormon and Christian Fundamentalist Polygamy and the Stories of 18 Women Who Escaped* (San Francisco: Pince-Nez Press, 2004). For a legal analysis, see Marci A. Hamilton, *God vs. the Gavel: Religion and the Rule of Law* (Cambridge, UK: Cambridge University Press, 2005), chs. 2 and 3. It could be responded, along the lines of John Stuart Mill and the dissents of Justices Blackmun and Stevens in *Bowers v. Hardwick,* that people should be at liberty to choose a polygamous lifestyle if they wish without state interference. This no doubt is true, but the state is not required to permit more than one marriage at a time.

52. Gerstmann, *Same Sex Marriage and the Constitution,* p. 104.

53. *Bowers v. Hardwick,* 478 U.S. 186 (1986).

54. The language of the statute made "any sexual act involving the sex organs of one person and the mouth or anus of another" unlawful.

55. As has been pointed out by many scholars, the opinions of Chief Justice Burger and Justice White are badly ill-informed about the history of law. Burger claims, for example, that sodomy was a crime under Roman law; however, the laws he cites were enacted after the Roman Empire had come under Christian influence. For more on this, see the discussion of *Lawrence v. Texas* below.

56. Justice Powell also filed a concurring opinion, in which he agreed that there was no fundamental right to commit sodomy but expressed his view that the law in question, which provided up to a 20-year sentence upon conviction, raised serious concerns under the 8th Amendment, which prohibits cruel and unusual punishment. In October 1990, Justice Powell publicly expressed his regret concerning his vote in *Bowers* (see "Bowers v. Hardwick," in *Oxford Companion to the Supreme Court of the United States,* 2nd ed. [New York: Oxford University Press, 2005], p. 94).

57. For a fascinating study of Justice Blackmun's evolution on the Supreme Court, see Linda Greenhouse, *Becoming Justice Blackmun: Harry Blackmun's Supreme Court Journey* (New York: Times Books, 2005).

58. 478 U.S. at 199, quoting Oliver Wendell Holmes, Jr., "The Path of the Law," 10 *Harvard Law Review* (1897): 457, 469. See Steven J. Burton, ed., *The Path of the Law and Its Influence: The Legacy of Oliver Wendell Holmes, Jr.* (Cambridge, UK: Cambridge University Press, 2000).

59. 478 U.S. at 200.

60. 478 U.S. at 205.

61. 478 U.S. a 214.

62. Texas Penal Code Ann. §21.06(a) (2003) provided: "A person commits an offense if he engages in deviate sexual intercourse with another individual of the same sex." It defined "deviate sexual intercourse" as: "(A) any contact between any part of the genitals of one person and the mouth or anus of another person; or (B) the penetration of the genitals or the anus of another person with an object" (§21.01[1]). This statute was added to the Texas Penal Code in 1973. In fact, prior to the 1970s, no post-1776 law in the United States specifically targeted homosexual sex acts. There are two reasons for this: first — and most obvious — is that such laws arose in response to the post-1969 (Stonewall) gay-rights movement; second, in 1972 the Supreme Court had made it clear in *Eisenstadt v. Baird* that consensual sexual conduct between unmarried heterosexual adults would receive constitutional protection from the criminal law. No such protection existed for homosexual acts. For a discussion of this second reason, see Eskridge and Hunter, *Sexuality, Gender, and the Law*, p. 279.

63. *Lawrence v. Texas*, 539 U.S. 558 (2003).

64. 539 U.S. at 567.

65. 539 U.S. at 571.

66. However, because there was a fear of public reaction, his notes were only published posthumously, in the twentieth century (Jeremy Bentham, "Offences Against Oneself: Paederasty, Part 1," ed. Louis Crompton, *Journal of Homosexuality* 3/4 [Summer 1978]: 389-405; "Offences Against Oneself: Paederasty, Part 2," *Journal of Homosexuality* 4/1 [Fall 1978]: 91-107). The notes are also available on-line: http://www. columbia.edu/cu/lweb/eresources/exhibitions/sw25/bentham/.

67. American Law Institute, Model Penal Code, 213.2; *The Wolfenden Report: Report of the Committee on Homosexual Offenses and Prostitution*.

68. *Lawrence v. Texas*, 539 U.S. at 562.

69. The classic statement is that of Immanuel Kant, who argued for treating people as ends in themselves and not as means (Kant, *Groundwork of the Metaphysics of Morals*, ed. Mary J. Gregor, Cambridge Texts in the History of Philosophy [Cambridge, UK: Cambridge University Press, 1998]). Thomas Aquinas argued against respect for persons on the grounds that it violates the principle of distributive justice (*Summa Theologiae*, 2.2., q. 63).

70. *Griswold v. Connecticut*, 381 U.S. 479 (1965), which invalidated prohibition against the use of contraceptives by married couples.

71. *Eisenstadt v. Baird*, 405 U.S. 438 (1972), which invalidated prohibition against the use of contraceptives by unmarried couples; *Carey v. Population Services Int'l*, 431 U.S. 678 (1977), which invalidated prohibition of sale of contraceptives to persons under 16 years of age.

72. *Planned Parenthood of Southeastern Pa. v. Casey*, 505 U.S. 833 (1992). The *Casey* decision is significant for declining to overturn the controversial abortion decision of *Roe v. Wade*, 410 U.S. 113 (1973). Instead, *Casey* was governed by a plurality opinion, coauthored by Justices Kennedy, O'Connor, and Souter, which reaffirmed the

woman's liberty interest in being able to obtain an abortion prior to the viability of the fetus, as well as the power of the state to regulate abortion after viability, and to protect both maternal and fetal health at all times. Restrictions on abortion had been approved in *Webster v. Reproductive Health Services,* 492 U.S. 490 (1989).

73. Justice Kennedy said: "Liberty gives substantial protection to adult persons in deciding how to conduct their private lives in matters pertaining to sex" (539 U.S. at 572).

74. *Planned Parenthood of Southeastern Pa. v. Casey,* 505 U.S. 833, 852 (1992).

75. Moreover, these laws were limited to only nine states: Arkansas (subsequently repealed), Kansas, Kentucky (subsequently declared unconstitutional), Missouri, Montana (subsequently declared unconstitutional on state court grounds), Nevada (subsequently repealed), Oklahoma, Tennessee (subsequently ruled unconstitutional on state court grounds), and Texas.

76. "When sexuality finds overt expression in intimate conduct with another person, the conduct can be but one element in a personal bond that is more enduring" (539 U.S. at 567).

77. 539 U.S. at 567.

78. In putting forth this rationale, Justice O'Connor also seems to be reaching out to find some common ground with Justice Scalia, who, she suggests, "apparently agrees that if [equal protection cases such as *Moreno, Eisenstadt, Cleburne, and Romer*] have *stare decisis* effect, Texas' sodomy law would not pass scrutiny under the Equal Protection Clause, regardless of the type of rational basis review that we apply [citing Justice Scalia's dissent]" (*Lawrence v. Texas,* Justice O'Connor, Slip Opinion, p. 3). Later in her opinion, she invokes the following quote from Justice Scalia's dissent in *Romer* to support her own position: "After all, there can hardly be more palpable discrimination against a class than making the conduct that defines the class criminal" (Justice O'Connor, 539 U.S. at 583, quoting *Romer v. Evans,* 517 U.S. at 641 [Scalia, dissenting]).

79. 539 U.S. at 583 (O'Connor, J., concurring).

80. Ibid.

81. *Lawrence v. Texas,* 539 U.S. at 575. Justice Kennedy goes on to point out that violations of due process and equal protection often overlap. Though Kennedy does not point it out, Justice O'Connor's own opinion demonstrates this, for she argues that laws have been most likely to be held unconstitutional under rational basis review "where they inhibit personal relationships." But is not the inhibition of personal relationships the very liberty interest that Justice Kennedy and the majority are seeking to protect?

82. 539 U.S. at 575.

83. 539 U.S. at 575.

84. 539 U.S. at 578. Note that, in her concurrence, Justice O'Connor specifically suggests that "national security" (e.g., the prohibition of gays in the military) and "pre-

serving the traditional institution of marriage" each constitutes a legitimate state interest (539 U.S. at 585).

85. To counter Justice Kennedy's opening line ("Liberty protects the person from unwarranted government intrusions into a dwelling or other private places"), Justice Scalia quotes one of Kennedy's own prior statements: "Liberty finds no refuge in a jurisprudence of doubt" (*Lawrence v. Texas*, 539 U.S. at 586 [Scalia, J., dissenting], which quoted the plurality opinion in *Planned Parenthood of Southeastern Pa. v. Casey*, 505 U.S. 833, 844 [1992] [Justices O'Connor, Kennedy, and Souter]). That statement was used in 1992 by Justice Kennedy (along with Justices O'Connor and Souter) as a reason not to overturn *Roe v. Wade*. Now Justice Scalia turns the statement around to ask why the Court should overrule *Bowers v. Hardwick*.

86. 539 U.S. at 599.

87. 539 U.S. at 591, 592.

88. Most astonishingly, even though "liberty" is specifically mentioned in the Due Process Clause, Justice Scalia asserts "there is no right to 'liberty' under the Due Process Clause" (539 U.S. at 592). He goes on to clarify that under the Supreme Court's jurisprudence it is only *fundamental* liberties that are protected. But this begs the question. If one were to adopt Justice Scalia's approach, African Americans would have no inherent right of liberty or equality but only what the 14th Amendment granted.

89. 539 U.S. at 579.

90. Justice Scalia thought the same was true of Justice O'Connor's equal protection rationale, which, he opined, "leaves on pretty shaky grounds state laws limiting marriage to opposite-sex couples" (539 U.S. at 601).

91. For the legal path toward civil unions in Vermont, see the excellent analysis of William N. Eskridge, Jr., *Equality Practice: Civil Unions and the Future of Gay Rights* (New York: Routledge, 2002), ch. 2.

92. The story of the three couples and of the legal and political path to civil unions in Vermont is told in a compelling way by David Moats, *Civil Wars: A Battle for Gay Marriage* (New York: Harcourt, 2004).

93. The "common benefits" section provides, in part, "that government is, or ought to be, instituted for the common benefit, protection, and security of the people, nation, or community, and not for the particular emolument or advantage of any single person, family, or set of persons, who are a part only of that community" (Vermont Constitution, Chapter 1, Article 7).

94. *Baker v. State of Vermont*, 170 Vt. 194, 744 A.2d 864 (1999).

95. *Baker v. State*, p. 35. This same argument was adopted by the Hawaii Supreme Court in *Baehr v. Lewin*, 852 P.2d 44 (Haw. 1993).

96. See the concurring opinion of Justice John A. Dooley and the opinion of Justice Denise R. Johnson — concurring in part and dissenting in part. Justice Dooley complains that, by failing to follow the typical three-tiered analysis, the *Baker* majority invites future courts to strike down laws in *Lochner*-like fashion.

97. 106 U.S. 583 (1883).

98. Justice Johnson concurring in part and dissenting in part, p. 18.

99. Both Justice Johnson and Justice Dooley (who filed a concurring opinion) argued for heightened scrutiny of sexual orientation.

100. In a further show of restraint, the court did not go so far as to declare sexual orientation a "suspect classification," which would have had legal implications for all discrimination affecting gay and lesbian people.

101. *Baker v. State,* p. 3.

102. The legislature also created a new institution of "reciprocal beneficiaries" for two people, not otherwise eligible for marriage or civil union, who wish to make one another their decision-makers for medical and other purposes (15 *Vermont Statutes Annotated,* §§1301-1306).

103. Howard Dean, "Vermont's Lessons on Gay Marriage," *Boston Globe,* May 17, 2004: http://www.boston.com/news/globe/editorial_opinion/oped/articles/2004/05/17/vermonts_lessons_on_gay_marriage/ (accessed Mar. 21, 2005).

104. 15 *Vermont Statutes Annotated* §1204.

105. 15 *Vermont Statutes Annotated* §§1202-1203; 5163.

106. 15 *Vermont Statutes Annotated* §§1206.

107. "Defense of Marriage Act: Update to Prior Report," February 24, 2004, GAO-04-353R, entitled United States General Accounting Office. Available at: http://www.gpoaccess.gov/gaoreports/index.html (accessed Mar. 21, 2005).

108. *Baker v. State,* p. 45.

109. 852 P.2d at 57.

110. *Same Sex Marriage and the Constitution,* p. 61.

111. See Memorandum and Order, Judge Peter A. Michalski, *Brause v. Bureau of Vital Statistics,* Superior Court, Third Judicial District, case no. 3AN-95-6562 CI, Alaska, February 27, 1998.

112. For example, Eskridge and Hunter do not mention the case in their compilation *Sexuality, Gender, and the Law;* however, Eskridge does treat the case in his *Equality Practice,* pp. 40-42.

113. At about the same time, an Alaska judge had ordered the University of Alaska at Fairbanks not to withhold spousal benefits from a gay couple; the order was subsequently affirmed by the Supreme Court of Alaska (*University of Alaska v. Tumeo,* 933 P.2d 1147 [1997]).

114. Article 1, section 22 of the Alaska Constitution provides: "The right of the people to privacy is recognized and shall not be infringed."

115. *Breese v. Smith,* 501 P.2d 159 (Alaska, 1972), which invalidated a high school regulation governing the length of a student's hair.

116. *Goodridge v. Department of Public Health,* 440 Mass. 309, 798 NE2d 941 (2003). The following cases declined to follow the approach of the Goodridge court: *Stanhardt v. Superior Court,* 206 Ariz. 276, 77 P.3d 451 (Ariz. Ct. App. 2004); *Morrison v.*

Sadler, 821 N.E.2d 941 (Ind. 2005); *Lewis v. Harris,* 378 N.J. Super 168, 875 A.2d 259 (2005); *Hernandez v. Robles,* New York Court of Appeals, July 6, 2006 [http://www.courts.state.ny.us/ctapps/decisions/jul06/86-89opn06.pdf]; *Anderson v. King County,* Nos. 75934-1, 75956-1 (Washington Supreme Court, July 26, 2006). But see the incisive and eloquent dissents by Chief Judge Judith S. Kaye in *Hernandez v. Robles,* and Justice Mary E. Fairhurst. In Anderson v. King County [http://www.courts.wa.gov/newsinfo/content/pdf/759341n03.pdf].

117. According to the court: "As of April 11, 2001, the date they filed their complaint, the plaintiffs Gloria Bailey, sixty years old, and Linda Davies, fifty-five years old, had been in a committed relationship for thirty years; the plaintiffs Maureen Brodoff, forty-nine years old, and Ellen Wade, fifty-two years old, had been in a committed relationship for twenty years and lived with their twelve-year-old daughter; the plaintiffs Hillary Goodridge, forty-four years old, and Julie Goodridge, forty-three years old, had been in a committed relationship for thirteen years and lived with their five-year-old daughter; the plaintiffs Gary Chalmers, thirty-five years old, and Richard Linnell, thirty-seven years old, had been in a committed relationship for thirteen years and lived with their eight-year-old daughter and Richard's mother; the plaintiffs Heidi Norton, thirty-six years old, and Gina Smith, thirty-six years old, had been in a committed relationship for eleven years and lived with their two sons, ages five years and one year; the plaintiffs Michael Horgan, forty-one years old, and David Balmelli, forty-one years old, had been in a committed relationship for seven years; and the plaintiffs David Wilson, fifty-seven years old, and Robert Compton, fifty-one years old, had been in a committed relationship for four years and had cared for David's mother in their home after a serious illness until she died. The plaintiffs include business executives, lawyers, an investment banker, educators, therapists, and a computer engineer. Many are active in church, community, and school groups. . . . Each plaintiff attests a desire to marry his or her partner in order to affirm publicly their commitment to each other and to secure the legal protections and benefits afforded to married couples and their children" (*Goodridge v. Department of Public Health,* p. 5).

118. *Goodridge v. Department of Public Health,* p. 11.

119. *Goodridge v. Department of Public Health,* p. 16.

120. *Goodridge v. Department of Public Health,* p. 23.

121. *Goodridge v. Department of Public Health,* p. 18.

122. *Goodridge v. Department of Public Health,* p. 35.

123. The court later clarified that the purpose of this time period was "to afford the Legislature an opportunity to conform the existing statutes to the provisions of the Goodridge decision" (Opinions of the Justices to the Senate, 440 Mass. 1201, 802 NE2d 565 [Feb. 3, 2004]).

124. A vote was taken on March 29, 2004, to ban same-sex marriage and create civil unions, and a constitutional amendment was formulated that would have, in effect, overruled the court's ruling in *Goodridge* (Rick Klein, "Vote Ties Civil Unions to

Gay-Marriage Ban: Romney to Seek Stay of SJC Order," *Boston Globe*, Mar. 30, 2004: http://www.boston.com/news/specials/gay_marriage/articles/2004/03/30/vote_ties _civil_unions_to_gay_marriage_ban/ (accessed Mar. 22, 2005).

125. Opinions of the Justices to the Senate, 440 Mass. 1201, 802 NE2d 565 (Feb. 3, 2004).

126. Sosman also offered a possible reason — i.e., a "rational basis" — for having a separate legal regime for civil unions. Since marriage and civil unions are still treated differently under federal law and by the various states, it makes sense to place them in a separate statutory category. Even if same-sex couples are "married" in Massachusetts, neither federal law nor the law of most states will recognize them as such. In other words, since there are still substantive legal differences in what it means to be united as an opposite-sex versus same-sex couple, a separate category of licensing makes a certain amount of sense. Indeed, such distinctions could actually work to the advantage of same-sex couples. For example, she argued, it might make sense to fashion remedies in Massachusetts to counteract discrimination against same-sex couples outside of Massachusetts.

127. This institution had already been anticipated in Europe, beginning in Sweden in 1987 (Eskridge and Hunter, *Sexuality, Gender, and the Law*, pp. 1122-1129).

128. *Lewis v. Harris*, 188 N.J. 415; 908 A.2d 196 (N.J. Supreme Ct. 2006).

129. In each of the spousal equality cases decided in favor of the gay and lesbian litigants above, there were counterarguments raised by the states and pressed by various interest groups. Some of these counterarguments I have already addressed in discussing Justice Scalia's dissent; I have addressed others indirectly, not only here but in other chapters. It may be useful to mention a few more that crop up with some frequency.

1. Argument from Traditional Definition of Marriage

First there is the argument from definition. As we have seen in ch. 1, this argument draws from deep wells of religious and moral tradition. Often this argument is fueled by prejudicial stereotypes about gay life. And yet, as Justice Scalia has rightly insisted, moral or religious scruples often are based on conviction and not mere prejudice. There are people who feel compassion and empathy for gay and lesbian people but who are also convinced that gay sexuality is abnormal and morally wrong.

Even though this argument has a religious base, one can advance this argument without invoking any specific moral or religious doctrines. Thus Hillary Rodham Clinton has registered her opposition to gay marriage because marriage by definition has always referred to a coupling between a man and woman. Marriage should be heterosexual, so the argument goes, because that is what marriage always has been.

The obvious answer to this first objection is that it is circular; it begs the question. It presents us with the tautology that marriage can only be between a man and a woman because it always has been between a man and a woman. On the contrary, we know that definitions of marriage have changed dramatically over the decades. Andrew Sullivan has put it memorably:

If marriage were the same today as it has been for 2,000 years, it would be possible to marry a twelve-year-old you had never met, to own a wife as property and dispose of her at will, or to imprison a person who married someone of a different race. And it would be impossible to get a divorce.

In Part One, I have presented reasons that the traditional moral and religious arguments are mistaken. They rest on an inadequate appreciation for the difference between exclusively committed relationships, on the one hand, and those that are transient and exploitative, on the other. Above all, they rest on a failure to read the biblical materials on this subject contextually.

Yet, even if the argument from tradition were thought to be sufficient from a religious point of view, it is insufficient as a matter of secular law. Exclusion from a significant legal institution in the past does not by itself justify that exclusion in the present. If it did, segregation and gender discrimination still would be the law of the land. Like discrimination on the basis of race and gender, the exclusion of gay couples from the benefits afforded by marriage violates long-standing principles of liberty and equality under the law.

2. The State's Interest in Childbearing

Opposition to gay marriage is often based on the claim that the primary purpose of marriage is procreation. Sometimes this argument is linked with the Roman Catholic natural law argument discussed in ch. 1. The claim of natural lawyers is that marriage creates a two-in-one-flesh union that is intrinsically good because of its openness to the possibility of children. Sexual expression that is not coincident with a procreative intent constitutes an instrumental use of the body that is merely animalistic.

Among the many problems with these arguments, the most obvious is one noted in ch. 3, namely, that marriage is about so much more than procreation. People marry who have no intention or no capability of bearing children. Nor do our legal statutes require procreative intent for marriage to be valid. As a society, for example, we have no qualms about permitting postmenopausal women to marry. For that matter, even death-bed marriages are not legally disallowed. In addition, in its natural law form, the opposition to same-sex unions derives from the same way of thinking that opposes artificial birth control. And yet birth control is widely available and legal.

It has been claimed that the state has an interest in encouraging marriage as a proper context for child-rearing. This is certainly true, but that is an argument *for* same-sex marriage and not against it. We have ample evidence that same-sex couples are excellent parents. The state should encourage these parents, not continue their pariah status. It should neither penalize gay couples nor stigmatize the children.

A related argument is that the state has an interest in seeing to it that children are raised by both of their biological parents. Let us assume for the sake of argument that, in some general sense, this is a legitimate goal. Even so, there is no rational relationship between that goal and the prohibition of gay marriage. If this truly were an overriding goal of the state, then the most efficacious way to achieve it would be to pro-hibit divorce, because it is divorce that is the leading cause of broken homes. In the case of gay and lesbian parents, they are raising either their own biological children or chil-dren they have adopted. When a gay couple adopts children, they are giving that adopted child the parents the child would not ordinarily have. Sometimes being raised by one's biological parents is not possible. Sometimes having both a mother and a fa-ther in the home is not a reality. Prohibiting gay marriage will do nothing to change that. Certainly there is no reason for gays and lesbians to be denied the possibility of adoption automatically. In assigning a child for adoption, the courts always seek to make decisions that are in the best interest of the child; so there is a built-in way for the state's interest in protecting the child to be served. Granting gay marriage does nothing to hurt children born of straight parents; but denying marriage to gays and lesbians does hurt their children by withholding an important status that others take for granted.

3. Against Public Morals

It is sometimes argued that legal recognition of some form of spousal rights for gays and lesbians would cause many citizens to have to endorse an activity they find morally repugnant. In other words, gays are entitled to tolerance but not acceptance. This argu-ment is based on a logic that is confused: just because an activity is legal does not mean that every citizen personally has endorsed it. This argument carried more weight when same-gender sex acts were criminalized. Now that *Lawrence v. Texas* has in effect de-criminalized consensual gay sexual activity between two adults, this argument has lost its credibility.

Notes to Chapter Five

1. These points are made eloquently by Jonathan Rauch, *Gay Marriage: Why It Is Good for Gays, Good for Straights, and Good for America* (New York: Henry Holt and Co., 2004), pp. 14-15.

2. John Witte, Jr., *From Sacrament to Contract: Marriage, Religion, and Law in Western Tradition* (Louisville: Westminster John Knox Press, 1997), pp. 42-193.

3. Nancy F. Cott, *Public Vows: A History of Marriage and the Nation* (Cambridge, MA: Harvard University Press, 2000), p. 31.

4. In addition, in Oregon same-sex marriage has been approved on the Coquille Indian reservation, provided that one party to the marriage is a member of the Coquille tribe. See Coquille Tribal Regulations, Chapter 741, "Marriage and Domestic Part-nership Regulation" (http://www.coquilletribe.org/documents/741MarriageRegulation .pdf). Since there are only between five and six hundred tribe members, this is a very narrow addition.

5. It was signed into law by Republican Governor John Lynch, who favored civil unions but was against gay marriage. The following year the New Hampshire legislature enacted a same-sex marriage law, which Lynch agreed to sign once protections were added for church groups opposing gay marriage. New Hampshire is noteworthy for passing both civil union and gay marriage laws without any pressure from the courts. Polls in New Hampshire indicated that a majority supported marriage equality. http://www.nytimes.com/2009/06/04/us/04marriage.html.

6. The pro-gay marriage bill arose in the legislature after a Maryland case held that no judicial right to gay marriage existed. *Conaway v. Deane,* 932 A. 2d 571 (Md. Ct. of Appeals 2007).

7. In 2003 New Jersey became one of the first states to enact a domestic partnership law. Then a lawsuit by gay couples claimed that the domestic partnership law did not provide full equality. In *Lewis v. Harris,* the New Jersey Supreme Court agreed and struck down the domestic partnership law. However, the court split on whether civil unions or gay marriage satisfied equal protection. The 4-3 majority opted for civil unions. *Lewis v. Harris,* 188 N.J. 415; 908 A.2d 196 (N.J. 2006). See discussion below.

8. http://www.nj.com/news/index.ssf/2008/12/goldstein.html. The Democratic governor at the time, Jon Corzine, indicated he would sign a marriage equality bill, but when a new Republican governor, Chris Christie, came into office he vowed to support a constitutional amendment to ban gay marriage. A same-sex marriage bill was introduced but on January 7, 2010, it was defeated in the State Senate.

9. *Lewis v. Harris* (Chief Justice Poritz, concurring in part, dissenting in part). (The quotation may be found on p. 7 of Chief Justice Poritz's slip opinion.)

10. *Hernandez v. Robles,* 855 N.E. 2d 1 (N.Y. Ct. of Appeals, 2006).

11. 855 N.E. 2d at 28; 7 N.Y.3d at 396.

12. New York State Bar Association, Special Committee on LGBT People and the Law, Report and Recommendation on Marriage Rights for Same-Sex Couples, May 4, 2009.

13. In the analysis that follows, I am instructed by William N. Eskridge Jr. and Nan D. Hunter, *Sexuality, Gender, and the Law,* 2nd ed., 2009 Supplement, University Casebook (New York: Tomson Reuters/Foundation Press, 2009), pp. 54-60.

14. *In re Marriage Cases,* 43 Cal.4th 757, 76 Cal.Rptr.3d 683, 183 P.3d 384 (California Supreme Ct. 2008).

15. *Perez v. Lippold,* 198 P.2d 17 (Cal. 1948) (often referred to as *Perez v. Sharp*).

16. *Kerrigan v. Commissioner of Public Health,* 289 Conn. 135, 957 A.2d 407 (2008).

17. See full analysis in *Kerrigan v. Commissioner of Public Health,* 957 A.2d at 431-61.

18. *Varnum v. Brien,* 763 N.W.2d 862 (Iowa 2009).

19. Iowa Const. art. I, §6.

20. See Marsha Ternus, "Do Americans Still Value an Independent Judiciary?" in

Book of the States, forthcoming. Marsha Ternus was the Chief Justice of the Supreme Court of Iowa before being removed on a retention vote in 2010.

21. *Strauss v. Horton,* 46 Cal.4th 364, 93 Cal.Rptr.3d 591, 207 P.3d 48 (Cal. 2009).

22. See *Perry v. Brown,* No. 10-16696 (9th Cir., Feb. 7, 2012), which affirmed *Perry v. Schwarzenegger,* 702 F.Supp. 2d 921 (N.D.Cal., 2010).

23. *Bush v. Gore,* 531 U.S. 98 (2000).

24. Transcripts of the trial are available at: http://www.afer.org/our-work/hearing-transcripts/.

25. *Perry v. Schwarzenegger,* Pre-trial hearing, October 14, 2009, 10/14 Transcript, Page 23, Line 10. See also the account by Judge Vaughn Walker at *Perry v. Schwarzenegger,* No C 09 — 2292 VRN, Pretrial Proceedings and Trial Evidence, Credibility Determinations, Findings of Fact, Conclusions of Law, Order, p. 9.

26. In fact, four proposed expert witnesses for the defense were withdrawn because their testimony in pre-trial depositions actually confirmed the case being made by the plaintiff same-sex couples. Specifically, they admitted that same-sex marriage would increase the stability of the couples' relationships and enhance the lives of their children. This deposition testimony by Canadian academics Dr. Katherine K. Young and Dr. Paul Nathanson was then submitted into evidence by attorneys for the same-sex couples. Excerpts from this testimony made be reviewed on YouTube: http://www.youtube.com/watch?v=KmactPnxYvM.

27. *Perry v. Schwarzenegger,* No C 09 — 2292 VRN, Pretrial Proceedings and Trial Evidence, Credibility Determinations, Findings of Fact, Conclusions of Law, Order, p. 113.

28. Judge Walker stayed his own ruling pending appeal to the U.S. Ninth Circuit Court of Appeals.

29. The question is who has legal "standing." In January 2011, a three-judge panel of the Ninth Circuit requested guidance from the California Supreme Court on this question.

30. *Perry v. Brown,* 52 Cal. 4th 1116 (Calif.Sup.Ct., Nov. 7, 2011).

31. *Perry v. Brown,* No. 10-16696 (9th Cir., Feb. 7, 2012).

32. See *Perry v. Schwarzenegger,* NO. C 09-02292 JW, Order Denying Defendant-Intervenors' Motion to Vacate Judgement, June 16, 2011 (Judge Ware).

33. For a similar view, see R. Claire Snyder, *Gay Marriage and Democracy: Equality for All* (Lanham, MD: Rowman and Littlefield, 2006).

34. For an illuminating discussion, see David Held, *Models of Democracy,* 2nd ed. (Palo Alto, CA: Stanford University Press, 1996).

35. Republicanism is the basic form of government in the United States, and democracy may be understood as its principal modifier. It is a republican form of government that has become more and more democratized over time. For a brilliant account of the emergence of American democratic commitment, see Sean Wilentz, *The Rise of American Democracy: Jefferson to Lincoln* (New York: W. W. Norton & Co., 2005).

36. There have been times, of course, when we have failed to live up to democracy's best lights. The withholding of democratic welcome from Native Americans, from slaves, and from women are notable examples of how American democracy has dwelled in self-contradiction for much of its history — proclaiming a democracy for all while practicing a democracy only for some. These lessons serve as a warning that true democracy is a fragile achievement, and that democratic gains are neither inevitable nor, when achieved, irreversible. We need only think of the Alien and Sedition Acts (1798), which allowed the government to violate freedom of speech; or of President Lincoln's suspension of *habeas corpus* during the Civil War, which allowed the arrest and indefinite incarceration of his political enemies; or of the action of rounding up and holding Japanese Americans in internment camps during World War II, which was justified on the grounds of national security. In hindsight, these violations of the rights of individuals have been roundly criticized and repudiated. But in their day they were applauded, and this should remind us that democratic habits of life require care, vigilance, and the ongoing exercise of wisdom.

37. For more on welcome and hospitality, see Jacques Derrida, "A Word of Welcome," in *Adieu to Emmanuel Levinas,* trans. Pascale-Anne Brault and Michael Naas (Stanford: Stanford University Press, 1999), pp. 15-123.

38. Robert A. Dahl, *On Democracy* (New Haven and London: Yale University Press, 1998), pp. 26, 10.

39. I am not arguing that democracy must be utopian; I actually favor a pragmatic approach to making democracy a reality. Yet I disagree with pragmatists who draw a sharp dichotomy between the ideal and the actual. We need both, and therefore I favor a more moral and deliberative form of democracy (cf. Richard A. Posner, *Law, Pragmatism, and Democracy* [Cambridge, MA: Harvard University Press, 2003]).

40. *West Virginia State Board of Education v. Barnette,* 319 U.S. 624, 638 (1943).

41. *Minersville School District v. Gobitis,* 310 U.S. 586 (1940). Justice Felix Frankfurter argued that it is permissible for a majority to override the free exercise of religion in certain circumstances.

42. Rehearsing the arguments against *Gobitis* is by no means merely a history lesson, since the principle it represents is apparently contested today by some members of the current U.S. Supreme Court. In the religious liberty case of *Employment Div. of Oregon v. Smith,* 494 U.S. 872 (1990), Justice Antonin Scalia quoted favorably from Justice Frankfurter's opinion in *Gobitis* as though the decision had not been overruled. The *Smith* case is notorious for substantially altering the right of religious liberty under the Free Exercise Clause. In order to pass constitutional muster prior to *Smith,* state and federal laws that substantially impinged on the exercise of religious liberty needed to be narrowly tailored and aimed at promoting a compelling state interest. However, *Smith* changed all that. At issue in *Smith* was the denial by the state of Oregon of unemployment compensation to two Native Americans who were dismissed from their jobs for the sacramental use of peyote in a religious ceremony. Writing for a 6-3 majority, Jus-

tice Scalia reasoned that generally applicable criminal laws may govern religious conduct even in the absence of a compelling state interest. In other words, *Smith* stands for the right of majorities to define what constitutes right behavior, even if that means riding roughshod over the rights and deeply held convictions of minorities. Its reasoning is of a piece with Justice Scalia's vehement dissent from *Romer v. Evans* (1996) and *Lawrence v. Texas* (2003). Over the years, Justices William J. Brennan, Thurgood Marshall, Sandra Day O'Connor, David Souter, and Stephen Breyer have raised questions about *Smith,* implying that we need to return to a case-by-case judicial analysis of the Free Exercise Clause. Congress objected, too, and by an overwhelming vote passed the Religious Freedom Restoration Act (RFRA) of 1993, and subsequently the Religious Land Use and Institutionalized Persons Act (RLUIPA) of 2000, both of which sought to restore the compelling state interest test. Again, this only reminds us that disputes over gay rights have to do with deep differences in the interpretation of the founding religious and political narratives of our society.

43. Jeffrey Stout, *Democracy and Tradition* (Princeton, NJ: Princeton University Press, 2004).

44. Even the persistently anti-gay group Focus on the Family has recently modified its stance enough to favor a mild form of domestic partnership rights for gays (reported in the *Denver Post,* Feb. 6, 2006); see http://www.denverpost.com/opinion/ci_3479371 (accessed Feb. 6, 2006). However, one reason Focus on the Family came out in support of the "reciprocal beneficiaries" kind of arrangement was to argue against a more robust effort to grant gays and lesbians civil unions.

45. Even extreme views require some measure of constitutional protection. For example, Fred Phelps, the pastor of a church in Kansas, has caused controversy by using military funerals as a venue for advocating that homoerotic activity should be punished by death. The government may legitimately regulate such protests (as, for example, requiring protesters to keep their distance from a grieving widow at a funeral), but it cannot prohibit such protests altogether or prohibit Phelps from publicly stating his opinions (see Frank Morris, "Kansas Church Uses Funerals for Anti-Gay Protest," National Public Radio, *All Things Considered,* Feb. 6, 2006).

46. This has been forcefully argued by Marci Hamilton, *God vs. the Gavel: Religion and the Rule of Law* (Cambridge, UK: Cambridge University Press, 2005).

47. *West Virginia State Board of Education v. Barnette,* 319 U.S. 624, 638 (1943). Although this decision overruled *Gobitis,* it relied not on the Free Exercise Clause (at issue in *Gobitis*) but on freedom of speech.

48. Given the American context in which the reflections of this book are situated, I have opted to focus on the work of Gutmann and Thompson. The two main works coauthored by them that are relevant in this context are *Democracy and Disagreement: Why Moral Conflict Cannot Be Avoided in Politics, and What Should Be Done about It* (Cambridge, MA: Harvard University Press, 1996) and *Why Deliberative Democracy?* (Princeton, NJ: Princeton University Press, 2004). For critical debate con-

cerning their proposals, see the following: Stephen Macedo, ed., *Deliberative Politics: Essays on Democracy and Disagreement* (New York and Oxford: Oxford University Press, 1999); Seyla Benhabib, *Democracy and Difference: Contesting the Boundaries of the Political* (Princeton, NJ: Princeton University Press, 1996). Another version of deliberative democracy that has informed my thinking — but that I see no need to discuss in detail here — is that of Jürgen Habermas, the leading philosopher in Germany today. Habermas promulgates a discourse ethics in which all perspectives and interpretations within a community of discourse are to be taken into consideration. Among his many works, see *Moral Consciousness and Communicative Action,* trans. Christian Lenhardt and Shierry Weber Nicholsen (Cambridge, MA: The MIT Press, 1992); *Between Facts and Norms: Contributions to a Discourse Theory of Law and Democracy,* trans. William Rehg, Studies in Contemporary German Social Thought (Cambridge, MA: The MIT Press, 1998); and *The Inclusion of the Other: Studies in Political Theory,* ed. Ciran Cronin and Pablo De Greiff (Cambridge, MA: The MIT Press, 1998).

49. Gutmann and Thompson, *Why Deliberative Democracy?* p. 7.

50. For a discussion of the reciprocity principle, see Gutmann and Thompson, *Democracy and Disagreement,* ch. 2.

51. Gutmann and Thompson do not understand reciprocity to function as a "foundation" that is self-evident in the way utilitarians believe the principle of utility is foundational. They say: "Reciprocity is not a principle from which justice is derived, but rather one that governs the ongoing process by which the conditions and content of justice are determined in specific cases" (*Why Deliberative Democracy?* p. 133).

52. For a discussion of publicity, see *Democracy and Disagreement,* ch. 3.

53. Benhabib, *Democracy and Difference,* pp. 100-101.

54. For a discussion of the accountability principle, see *Democracy and Disagreement,* ch. 4.

55. For a discussion of the liberty principle, see *Democracy and Disagreement,* ch. 7.

56. *Why Deliberative Democracy?* p. 137.

57. For a discussion of the basic opportunity principle, see *Democracy and Disagreement,* ch. 8.

58. For a discussion of the fair opportunity principle, see *Democracy and Disagreement,* ch. 9.

59. Iris Marion Young, "Justice, Inclusion, and Deliberative Democracy," in Macedo, ed., *Deliberative Politics,* pp. 151-158.

60. John Stuart Mill argued that individuals should be encouraged to use their liberty to achieve "human development in its richest diversity" (*On Liberty,* vol. 18, *Collected Works* [Toronto: University of Toronto Press, 1963-c1991] p. 215). This aspiration for self-improvement is sometimes called liberal perfectionism. For individuals to be able to choose their own way of life is important, according to this view, even if they happen to make mistakes or follow choices that are questionable. Free choice is conducive to growth, and growth of the individual ultimately contributes to the good of soci-

ety (Kwame Anthony Appiah, *The Ethics of Identity* [Princeton, NJ: Princeton University Press, 2004]). Thus, all other things being equal, one person or group should not be allowed to impose his, her, or their vision of the good life on others (Mill, *On Liberty,* p. 225). Liberal perfectionism also prizes the economic liberalism of Adam Smith, with his emphasis on individual choice in the context of a market economy. Indeed, the dispute between those labeled liberal and conservative today is not over whether to support liberty and equality but over which understandings of liberty and equality will prevail. Many of today's conservatives gladly espouse liberty and equality as core values, but with a strong emphasis on economic liberty and civil equality. Where they differ from liberals is that they oppose interventionist efforts by the state to enhance economic equality. See, for example, Milton Friedman, *Capitalism and Freedom,* 40th ann. ed. (Chicago: University of Chicago Press, 2002). Throughout this study I have avoided the terms "liberal" and "conservative" because the two are not always political opposites.

61. Charles Fried, *Saying What the Law Is: The Constitution in the Supreme Court* (Cambridge, MA: Harvard University Press, 2004), p. 200.

62. Patrick Devlin, *The Enforcement of Morals* (New York: Oxford University Press, 1965), pp. 178-190.

63. *Lawrence v. Texas,* 539 U.S. at 602 (Scalia, J., dissenting).

64. Andrew Sullivan, *Virtually Normal: An Argument about Homosexuality* (New York: Alfred P. Knopf, 1995), p. 158.

65. This view has been in evidence since the 1950s, when Lord Devlin objected to the recommendations of the Wolfenden Commission, which argued for the decriminalization of consensual same-gender sex acts. Lord Devlin argued that, if society is empowered to protect people from civil harm, as liberalism asserts, then it should also be entitled to protect people from moral harm (Devlin, *The Enforcement of Morals*).

66. Stanley Hauerwas, "Why Gays (as a Group) Are Morally Superior to Christians (as a Group)," in *The Hauerwas Reader,* ed. John Berkman and Michael Cartwright (Durham, NC, and London: Duke University Press, 2001), pp. 518-521; originally published as "Christian Soldiers," *Charlotte Observer,* May 31, 1993.

67. Sullivan, *Virtually Normal,* pp. 176-177.

68. Sullivan, *Virtually Normal,* p. 167.

69. The literature on this topic is too voluminous to cite. In addition to the synthetic work of Michael J. Sandel, *Liberalism and the Limits of Justice,* 2nd. ed. (Cambridge, UK: Cambridge University Press, 1998), see the suggestive essays of Michael Walzer, "The Communitarian Critique of Liberalism," *Political Theory* 18/1 (Feb. 1990): 6-23, and "The Idea of Civil Society: A Path to Social Reconstruction," *Dissent* (Spring 1991): 293-304.

70. Michael Sandel, "Moral Argument and Liberal Toleration: Abortion and Homosexuality," 77 *California Law Review* (1989): 521-538. Sandel notes that the judicial case most often cited to support gay rights is *Stanley v. Georgia,* 394 U.S. 557 (1969), a

case that upheld a person's right to own pornography. For his larger case for communitarian politics, see Sandel, *Liberalism and the Limits of Justice.*

71. Carlos Ball, *The Morality of Gay Rights: An Exploration in Political Philosophy* (New York: Routledge, 2002), p. 84.

72. Charles Taylor, *Multiculturalism and "The Politics of Recognition"* (Princeton, NJ: Princeton University Press, 1992).

73. Will Kymlicka, *Contemporary Political Philosophy: An Introduction,* 2nd ed. (Oxford: Oxford University Press, 2001), pp. 210ff.

74. One example is the judicial decisions concerning discrimination and nondiscrimination against gays in nongovernmental affinity groups. For example, in the pivotal opinion of *Hurley v. Irish-American Gay, Lesbian, Bisexual Group of Boston, Inc.,* 515 U.S. 557 (1995), the U.S. Supreme Court held that the private group sponsoring the annual St. Patrick's Day parade in Boston could exclude an organization that advocated gay rights. Justice Souter, writing for a unanimous Court, overturned the ruling of the liberal-leaning Massachusetts Supreme Judicial Court, which had held that the parade leaders had violated a state law prohibiting discrimination in a public accommodation. The Supreme Court reasoned, however, that a parade is an instance of protected free speech, not a public accommodation. Thus the liberal language of rights was bent in the direction of accommodating the traditions of a conservative community group.

Similarly, in a later, more controversial, and closely decided case, *Boy Scouts of America v. Dale,* 530 U.S. 640 (2000), the Court upheld the right of the Boy Scouts to dismiss a gay assistant scoutmaster, James Dale. Again, overruling the New Jersey Supreme Court's assessment that the discrimination violated state law, a 5-4 Supreme Court majority relied on *Hurley* to protect the Boy Scouts' right to "forbid membership to homosexuals" as a matter of their 1st Amendment freedom of expressive association. In addition to *Hurley,* the Court relied on principles from other pivotal right of association cases, including *Roberts v. United States Jaycees,* 468 U.S. 609 (1984) and *Rotary International v. Rotary Club of Duarte,* 481 U.S. 537 (1987).

The problem with this case, as was pointed out by the dissent, is that Dale was not dismissed for anything he had said or done but merely for who he was. Justices Stevens, Souter, Ginsburg, and Breyer dissented on the grounds that Dale's membership in the Boy Scouts did not, in itself, constitute speech (for Justice Stevens's opinion, see 530 U.S. at 663; Justice Souter filed a separate dissent, 530 U.S. at 700). In this sense, *Dale* was distinguishable from *Hurley,* because in the latter a parade float did arguably qualify as speech, with which the sponsors of the Boston St. Patrick's Day parade did not wish to associate. Although some considered the *Dale* case to be a defeat for gay rights, many conservative and moderate gays and lesbians themselves saw things differently. If, under the rationale of *Dale,* affinity groups are free to define their own message and mission, this protects pro-gay groups as well (see Mark V. Tushnet, *A Court Divided: The Rehnquist Court and the Future of Constitutional Law* [New York and London: W. W. Norton & Company, 2005], p. 163). However, for a critique of the decision from the standpoint of democratic theory, see Amy Gutmann, *Identity in Democracy* (Princeton, NJ, and Oxford: Princeton University Press, 2003), pp. 104-108. Gutmann acknowledges a possible legal basis for the decision, but she argues that the government itself must distance itself from the stance the Boy Scouts have taken. To this extent, *Boy Scouts v. Dale* constituted an ominous nod to prohibitionist sentiment. Leaders of progressive religious communities filed briefs in support of James Dale on the grounds that religious traditions, even when non-affirming, still strive to be welcoming. See also Andrew Koppelman, with Tobias Barrington Wolf, *A Right to Discriminate? How the Case of Boy Scouts of America v. Dale Warped the Law of Free Association* (New Haven: Yale University Press, 2009).

75. This is the thesis — with which I agree — of Beau Breslin, *The Communitarian Constitution* (Baltimore and London: Johns Hopkins University Press, 2004). If asked to choose between liberalism and communitarianism, I should quickly choose liberalism; the thesis of this chapter is that one should strive not to have to make this choice.

76. For an excellent defense of this thesis, see Stephen Macedo, *Liberal Virtues: Citizenship, Virtue, and Community in Liberal Constitutionalism* (Oxford: Oxford University Press, 1990).

77. The pertinent text of DOMA reads: "In determining the meaning of any Act of Congress, or of any ruling, regulation, or interpretation of the various administrative bureaus and agencies of the United States, the word 'marriage' means only a legal union between one man and one woman as husband and wife and the word 'spouse' refers only to a person of the opposite sex who is a husband or wife" (Pub. L. No. 104-199, 110 Stat. 2419, 1 U.S.C. §7).

78. The pertinent text of DOMA reads: "No State, territory, or possession of the United States, or Indian tribe, shall be required to give effect to any public act, record, or judicial proceeding of any other State, territory, possession, or tribe respecting a relationship between persons of the same sex that is treated as a marriage under the laws of such other State, territory, possession, or tribe, or a right or claim arising from such relationship" (Pub. L. No. 104-199, 110 Stat. 2419, 1 U.S.C. §1738C).

This is sometimes called DOMA's "choice of law" provision. It provides that a state may apply its own law when confronted with a gay or lesbian couple married in another jurisdiction and treat the marriage as null and void. Andrew Koppelman has identified the potential injustices lurking in this "choice of law" provision (Koppelman, *The Gay Rights Question in Contemporary American Law* [Chicago: University of Chicago Press, 2002], pp. 130-136). Suppose a drunken driver strikes and kills a man, A, who is married to another man, B, under the laws of the state of Massachusetts. B obtains a judgment against the driver which is enforceable in Massachusetts. B intends to use the proceeds from the judgment to cover the college education of the son that A and B had adopted together. In the meantime, the driver moves to another state, X, which does not recognize same-sex marriage. When B sues in state X to recover on his judgment, the X state court can regard the marriage as invalid, meaning that B and the boy, now bereft of the companionship and support of A, do not recover anything.

Koppelman has argued cogently that DOMA violates *Romer v. Evans* because of the way it specifically targets gays as a group. Logically speaking, he is correct. Getting the U.S. Supreme Court to agree is something else.

79. H.J. Res. 56 was first introduced in the U.S. House of Representatives on May 21, 2003. It provides in pertinent part as follows:

> Marriage in the United States shall consist only of the union of a man and a woman. Neither this Constitution or the constitution of any State, nor state or federal law, shall be construed to require that marital status or the legal incidents thereof be conferred upon unmarried couples or groups.

The phrase "or the legal incidents thereof" means that benefits conferred by means of civil unions would also be eliminated were this amendment to the U.S. Constitution to pass. This is a perfect example of how apparently innocent language can have far-reaching consequences that may not be obvious to the lay reader.

80. Cass Sunstein, *Designing Democracy: What Constitutions Do* (New York: Oxford University Press, 2001), p. 206.

81. King's first attempt (on "Bloody Sunday," Mar. 7, 1965) was met by local police, who assaulted the marchers with tear gas and billy clubs. Judge Johnson, a judge with a pro-civil-rights record, issued an order to stop the march for fear of bloodshed. On March 9, King led a symbolic march to the Edmund Pettus Bridge in Selma, but then immediately turned back in order to remain in compliance with Judge Johnson's order. Then Judge Johnson, having obtained assurances from President Lyndon Johnson that the marchers would be protected, ordered that there be no interference with the march. The march from Selma to Montgomery then went forward from March 21 to March 25.

82. William N. Eskridge Jr. and Nan D. Hunter, *Sexuality, Gender, and the Law,* 2nd ed., 2009 Supplement (New York: Tompson Reuters/Foundation Press, 2009), pp. 68-72; William N. Eskridge Jr., "The California Proposition 8: What Is a Constitution For?" 98 *California Law Review* (2010): 1236-1252.

83. Eskridge includes a discussion of the constitutional theory of John Hart Ely as an institutional approach to when courts should intervene in the political process to protect minority rights. "What's a Constitution For?" pp. 1243-1244. See also John Hart Ely, *Democracy and Distrust: A Theory of Judicial Review* (Cambridge, MA, and London: Harvard University Press, 2003).

84. California judges are subject to a retention vote in the general election held after their appointment and every twelve years thereafter.

85. *National Pride at Work v. Governor of Michigan,* 481 Mich. 56, 748 N. W.2d 524 (Mich. 2008).

86. This is documented by Justice Marilyn Kelly in her dissent to *National Pride at Work v. Governor of Michigan*.

87. For a discussion of the issues, see Matthew Mendelsohn and Andrew Parkin, eds., *Referendum Democracy: Citizens, Elites, and Deliberation in Referendum Campaigns* (New York: Palgrave Macmillan, 2001). For a comparative study of the use of referenda internationally, see Mark Clarence Walker, *The Strategic Use of Referendums: Power, Legitimacy, and Democracy* (New York: Palgrave Macmillan, 2003).

88. Ever since President Bill Clinton's first weeks in office, when he faced such a firestorm over his initial decision to lift the ban on gays in the military, most politicians have refrained from spending political capital to advance this issue. President Clinton himself had to backtrack and settle for the "don't ask, don't tell" policy (10 U.S.C. §654), which was repealed in 2011. Later he refused to veto the Defense of Marriage Act. It is no wonder, then, that politicians in the various states have been all too happy to relegate gay marriage questions to a popular vote — trumpeting democracy and the need for the people to speak (see John F. Harris, *The Survivor: Bill Clinton in the White House* [New York: Random House, 2005], pp. 13, 16-18). With a majority of Americans now favoring gay marriage, however, the political winds will change.

89. Here I am quoting Judge Joseph F. Bataillon's criticism of the Nebraska amendment in *Citizens for Equal Protection v. Bruning*, Memorandum and Order, May 12, 2005, case number 4:03-cv-03155, p. 30.

90. *Citizens for Equal Protection*, Memorandum and Order, p. 23.

91. On this point, see *Citizens for Equal Protection*, Memorandum and Order, p. 42.

Notes to the Conclusion

1. http://www.gallup.com/poll/147662/first-time-majority-americans-favor-legal-gay-marriage.aspx.

2. For example, on the eve of the gay marriage vote in New York, the specter of incest and bigamy were made repeatedly by the Roman Catholic Archbishop of New York, Timothy M. Dolan. See, e.g.: http://www.ncregister.com/daily-news/archbishop-dolan-on-same-sex-marriage-vote/.

3. See Martha C. Nussbaum, *From Disgust to Humanity: Sexual Orientation and Constitutional Law* (New York: Oxford University Press, 2010). Nussbaum shows how the politics of disgust has been used, inappropriately, to support legal restrictions affecting gay and lesbian people. In its place she advocates a politics of humanity in which people cultivate the ability to see things from the point of view of the other.

4. See David Kelsey, *Eccentric Existence: Theological Anthropology*, 2 vols. (Louisville: Westminster John Knox Press, 2009), vol. 2, pp. 792-827.

Index of Names

349

Index of Subjects

Index of Scripture References

365